D'Arcy Wentworth Thompson

A Glossary of Greek Birds

D'Arcy Wentworth Thompson

A Glossary of Greek Birds

ISBN/EAN: 9783337693978

Printed in Europe, USA, Canada, Australia, Japan

Cover: Foto ©Andreas Hilbeck / pixelio.de

More available books at **www.hansebooks.com**

A GLOSSARY OF
GREEK BIRDS

BY

D'ARCY WENTWORTH THOMPSON

PROFESSOR OF NATURAL HISTORY IN UNIVERSITY COLLEGE, DUNDEE

OXFORD

AT THE CLARENDON PRESS

M DCCC XCV

ΤΩΙ ΠΑΤΡΙ

ΧΘΟΝΟΣ ΑΡΓΕΙΑΣ ΑΡΟΤΗΡΙ

ΚΑΡΠΟΝ ΩΝ ΠΟΤΕ ΕΣΠΕΙΡΕ

ΘΑΛΥΣΙΑ ΑΤΤΑ ΘΕΡΙΣΑΣ

ΑΠΟΔΙΔΩΜΙ

RES ARDUA, VETUSTIS NOVITATEM DARE, NOVIS AUCTORI-
TATEM, OBSOLETIS NITOREM, OBSCURIS LUCEM, FASTIDITIS
GRATIAM, DUBIIS FIDEM.—PLINY.

πολλῶν τε καὶ ἄλλων τοιούτων ἐςτὶ πλῆθος ἀναγεγραμμένον ἐν τοῖς παλαιοῖς, ὕπερ εἴ τις βουληθείη ςυναγαγεῖν, εἰς ἄπειρον ἂν μῆκος ἐκτείνειε τὸν λόγον.—NEMES., *De Nat. Hom.*

PREFACE

THIS book contains materials for research in greater measure than it presents the results of it; and, accordingly, it is not my purpose to preface it with an extended summary of the many wide generalizations to which the assemblage of fact and legend here recorded may seem to lead. This book indeed includes only a small part of the notes I have gathered together since I began years ago, as an undergraduate, ignorant of the difficulties of the task, to prepare the way for a new edition of the Natural History of the Philosopher. Three points, however, in my treatment of the present subject deserve brief explanation here.

Instead of succeeding in the attempt to identify a greater number of species than other naturalist-commentators, dealing chiefly with the Aristotelian birds, have done, I have on the contrary ventured to identify a great many less. This limitation on my part is chiefly due to the circumstance that I have not ventured to use for purposes of identification a large class of statements on which others have more or less confidently relied. A single instance may serve to indicate the statements to which I allude. In the *Historia Animalium* (especially in the Ninth Book, great part of which seems to me to differ in character and probably in authorship from all but a few isolated passages of the rest of the work), in the works of such later writers as Pliny, Aelian and Phile, and scattered here and there in earlier literary allusions, we find many instances recorded of supposed hostility or friendship between different animals. When we are told, for example, that ἄνθος is hostile to ἀκανθίς and to the Horse, that πιπώ is hostile to ποικιλίς, to κορυδών, to χλωρεύς and to ἐρωδιός, that one Hawk is hostile to the Raven and another to the Dove, and one Eagle to the Goose or to the Swan, we try at first to use these statements as best we can in unravelling the probable identification of the respective species. But when we find, for instance, among the rest that the Owl is hostile to the Crow, and when we recognize in that statement the ancient Eastern fable of the War of the Owls and Crows, we are tempted to reject the whole mass of such statements and to refuse them entry into the domain of Zoological Science. While former commentators have, with greater or less caution, rejected many fables, they have often rashly accepted many others. And I fear for my part that I in turn, while rejecting a much greater number, have perhaps also erred in ascribing a fabulous or mystical meaning to too few.

For many such statements, and for others equally unintelligible in the terms of Natural History, I offer a novel and, at first sight, a somewhat startling explanation: to wit, that very many of them deserve not a zoological but an astronomical interpretation.

In the spring of 1894 I read to the Royal Society of Edinburgh a paper (which I have not yet printed) on 'Bird and Beast in Ancient Symbolism'. In that essay I sought to demonstrate the astronomic symbolism of certain ancient monuments, especially of the great bas-relief of Cybele in the Hermitage Museum[1]; secondly, of the beast and bird-emblems of classical coinage[2]; and lastly, of certain fables or myths of the philosophers and poets.

[1] This monument, a figure of which is accessible in Miss J. E. Harrison's *Mythology of Ancient Athens*, represents, according to my view, the ancient tropics of Leo and Aquarius, with Taurus and Leo in symbolic combat in the frieze below.

[2] The identical theory, in so far as it applies to numismatic emblems, was promulgated a few months afterwards by M. Jean Svoronos in a learned and scholarly paper, to be found in the *Bulletin de Correspondance Hellénique* for 1894; but the theory was not so novel as M. Svoronos and I supposed it to be. In connexion with coins or gems, it is explicitly and admirably stated by Gorius, *De*

Many illustrations of this theory of nine will be found in the pages of this Glossary[1]. Suffice it to say here, in briefest illustration, that the Eagle which attacks the Swan and is in turn defeated by it, is, according to my view, the constellation Aquila, which rises in the East immediately after Cygnus, but, setting in the West, goes down a little while before that more northern constellation; that Haliaetus and Ciris are the Sun and Moon in opposition, which rise and set alternately, like the opposite constellations of Scorpio and Orion with which the poet compares them.

Among many other opinions and testimonies to the same effect, let us listen to the words of a Father of the Church: 'The ancients believed that the legends about Osiris and Isis, and all other mythological fables [of a kindred sort], have reference either to the Stars, their configuration, their risings and their settings, or to the wax and wane of the Moon, or to the cycle of the Sun, or to the diurnal and nocti-diurnal hemispheres[2].'

The proof and the acceptance of such a theory as this are linked with considerations far-reaching in their interest. The theory has its bearing on our new knowledge of the orientation of temple-walls; it helps to explain what Quintilian meant when he said that acquaintance with Astronomy was essential to an understanding of the Poets; the wide-spread astronomic knowledge which it presupposes may account for the singular interest in and admiration of the didactic poem of Aratus, the poem translated by Germanicus and Cicero and quoted by St. Paul; and the whole hypothesis points to a broad distinction between two great orders of Myth.

Myths are spontaneous or literary, natural or artificial. Some come to us from the Childhood of Religion and the Childhood of the World; dream-pictures as it were from the half-opening eyes of awakening intelligence, archaic traces of the thoughts and ways of primitive and simple men; these

Gemmis Astriferis, 1750; and a kindred but exaggerated development, in regard to legend, of the same hypothesis forms the method of Dupuis.

[1] Cf. pp. 8, 28, 31, 63, 107, 121, 132, 192, &c.
[2] Euseb. Pr. Ev. iii. c. 4.

are the folk-lore tales and customs that are presented to us by the school of Mannhardt. But others, and these for the most part are astronomic myths, belonging to a relatively later age, were artificially invented of the wise, to adorn, preserve, or conceal their store of learning; they had their birth in cultured homes of deep religion, of treasured science, of exalted poetry. Both orders of Myth come to us with the glamour of antiquity, and each has for us a diverse but perennial interest:

ἡ σταφυλὶς σταφίς ἐστι, καὶ οὐ ῥόδον αὖον ὀλεῖται.

The distinction between these two orders of Myth was pointed out long ago by an ancient critic[1]; he drew the distinction clearly, but the tales of folk-lore, puerile in his eyes, found no echo of sympathy in the old scholar's heart. We, on the other hand, have learned nowadays to say with the poet:

'Ακλειὴς ὅδε μάντις ὃς οὐδ' ὅσα παῖδες ἴσασιν
Οἶδε.[2]

The great Signs of the Heavens are as old as our knowledge of the months and years, and about them poet-watchers of the stars wove an imperishable web of imagery. Of this kind are the Voyage in quest of the Golden Fleece[3], and the Twelve Labours of the Hero-God[4]; and I have attempted to show how into the same fabric are woven tales of Actos and Haliaetos, of Halcyon and Ciris, of Stymphalian perhaps also

---

[1] Οἱ μὲν γὰρ τῶν σοφῶν μῦθοι περὶ ἀϊδίων εἰσὶ πραγμάτων, οἱ δὲ τῶν παίδων περὶ ἐγχρόνων καὶ σμικρῶν· καὶ οἱ μὲν νοερὰν ἔχουσι τὴν ἀλήθειαν, οἱ δὲ χαμαιπετῆ καὶ οὐδὲν ὑψηλὸν ἐνδεικνυμένην: Procl. in Plat. Tim. Cf. also Porph. V. Pythag. (41) 42, Iambl. V. Pythag. 23, and other commentators on the Pythagorean Symbols.

[2] Apoll. Rh. iii. 930.

[3] 'Auf die Argonauten hatte ich immer ein Zutrauen.... Es liegen herrliche Motive darin, und gewiss liessen sich noch manche daraus entwickeln': Goethe to Schiller, Letter 496.

[4] An English scholar very recently propounded the view that the Hind with the Golden Horns was a reindeer!—

Σιγήσω κεμάδος χρύσεον κέρας· οὐ δὲ καλέσσω
Τηλίκον Ἡρακλῆα μιῆς ἐλάφοιο φονῆα·
Μὴ τρομερῇς ἐλάφου μιμνήσκεο.—Nonn. Dionys. xxv. 223.

of Diomedian and Memnonian Birds, of Pleiad-Doves and Singing Swans. All these come to us from the Land beyond the Rainbow: they are dwellers in Fairyland.

Akin to this enterprise of tracing allusions to the ancient science of the Stars in art and legend, in neglected phrases and statements, of the Greeks, is the effort I have made to ascribe to non-Aryan languages names used by Hellenic writers for many legendary as well as for many real Birds. The Master told his pupils that the gods whom men worshipped under other names were, in the childhood of religion, the Sun, the Moon, and the Stars of Heaven, to which many barbarians still bowed down [1]; and he told them also that one who should seek to explain by Greek all the words of Greek should surely go astray, for that many words in daily use were borrowed from barbaric speech [2].

The astronomic science that the ancients loved and understood, as do the wise men of China and Arabia to this day, was not the gift of Greece alone, but was the accumulated gain of ages of antecedent civilization by the River of Egypt and the Four Rivers of Chaldaea; and Eastern imagination veiled in mysterious allegory the ancient treasures of Eastern lore.

If the quest after non-Aryan words and the attempt to trace the esoteric meaning of fables to a science which had its origin on alien soil are to be justified, we must cease to believe in a gulf between the Greeks and their Eastern contemporaries and predecessors. That gulf, if gulf there was, was crossed again and again. It was crossed by the migrations of races, by the tramp of armies, by the sails of commerce; by the progress of religions, by the influence of art, by the humble footsteps of philosophers, seeking wisdom like Dervish-pilgrims of the Eastern or Wandelnde Studenten of the Western world.

[1] Plat. Cratyl., p. 397.
[2] Ibid., p. 409: Εἴ τις ζητοῖ ταῦτα κατὰ τὴν Ἑλληνικὴν φωνὴν ὡς εἰκότως κεῖται, ἀλλὰ μὴ κατ' ἐκείνην, ἐξ ἧς τὸ ὄνομα τυγχάνει ὄν, οἶσθα ὅτι ἀποροῖ ἄν. Εἰκότως γε. The doctrine of 'Loan-words' thus adumbrated in the Cratylus, is now, within certain limits, a commonplace of philology; but we do not know where the quest for such Loan-words may end.

As the White Doves came from Babylon or the Meleagrian Birds from the farther Nile, so over the sea and the islands came Eastern legends and Eastern names. And our Aryan studies must not blind us to the presence in an Aryan tongue of these immigrants from Semitic and Egyptian speech, or from the nameless and forgotten language that was spoken by the gods.

D. W. T.

A
GLOSSARY OF GREEK BIRDS

ἈΓΛΥ. ὁ κύκνος, ὑπὸ Σκυθῶν, Hesych.

ἈΓΟ'Ρ· ἀετός, Κύπριοι, Hesych.
    Bochart (Hieroz. II. c. xi, coll. 79, 80) shows good reason for supposing that ἀετός here should read γέρανος, and that ἀγόρ is merely Heb. עגור, a crane (Jerem. viii. 7; Is. xxxviii. 14). Cf. Lewysohn, Zool. d. Talmuds, p. 169.

ἈΓΡΑΚΟ'ΜΑΣ· ὄρνις τις ὑπὸ Παμφίλων, Hesych.

ἈΓΡΕΥ'Σ. An unknown bird. It is like a Blackbird, black, musical, and a mimic, Ael. viii. 24. The description is somewhat suggestive of the Indian Mynah, but it is in the main mystical. Vide s. v. **κατρεύς**.

ἈΔΩΝΗΙ'Σ, s. ἀδωνηΐς (cf. Creuzer, Symb. ii. 478). ἡ χελιδών, Hesych. Cf. ἀηδονίς, s. v. ἀηδών.

ἈΕΙ'ΣΚΩΨ, vide s. v. **σκώψ**.

ἈΕΛΛΟ'Σ, an unknown bird, Hesych.

ἈΕΡΟΚΟ'ΡΑΞ, vide s. v. **κόραξ**.

ἈΕ'ΡΟΨ, vide s. v. **μέροψ**.

ἈΕΤΟ'Σ. Ep. and Ion. αἰετός—αἰητός in Pind. P. iv, Arat. 522, 591, &c.; ἀητός, Arat. 315; αἰβετός, for αἰϝετός, Hesych. Dim. ἀετιδεύς, Ael. vii. 47, Aesop, Fab. 1. ἀετός is said to be 'the flyer,' '*the Bird*,' from root αϝ or νί, of Sk. *vi-s*, Lat. *avi-s*, and of Gk. ἄημι: the same root perhaps in οἰ-ων-ός (Curt.) and αἰ-γυπ-ιός; cf. the Greek use of οἰωνός; also the Lat. use of *ales* for Eagle, and ὄρνεον in M. Gk. for Vulture. Nevertheless, the absence of Eagle-names similar to ἀετός in other Indo-

B

ΑΕΤΟΣ (*continued*).

European languages is so striking, that I suspect for it a non-Aryan root.

An **Eagle**, the generic word; see also ἀκυλαής, ἀλιάετος, ἄνταρ, ἀργιόπους, ἄρξιφος, ἀστερίας, εὐρυμέδων, ἴβινος, ἰδέων, κυκνίας, λαγωφόνος, μελανάετος, μορφνός, νηττοφόνος, πλάγγος, πύγαργος, χρυσάετος, &c.: v. Arist. H. A. viii. 3, 592 b, ix. 32, 618 b, 619 a; on the species of Eagles cf. Cuvier ad Plin. x. 3, ed. Grandsaigne, whose identifications, however, like those of Sundevall (Thierarten des Aristoteles, Stockholm, 1863, also in Swedish, K. Akad. Wetensk. Stockholm, 1862), are in my opinion to be received with caution. Besides the Osprey, *Pandion Haliaëtus*, and the Short-toed Eagle, *Circaëtus gallicus*, the following true Eagles are regular inhabitants of Greece, *A. Chrysaetus, A. heliaca, A. naevia, A. Bonelli, A. pennata*, and *Haliaetus albicilla*. Though occasional passages may be descriptive of the habits of one rather than another of these species, there is no evidence of any of these having been recognized as distinct: such names as ἀλιάετος, μελανάετος and λαγωφόνος have a mystical or symbolic rather than a descriptive or specific meaning. On the confusion of the Eagles with the Vultures, *vide infra*. Eagles are common in Greece, though (Xen. Venat. v. 24) absent from many of the islands, for want of hills. On the Eagle in classical art and mythology cf. O. Keller, Thiere d. cl. Alterthums, pp. 236-276, 430-452.

Epithets.—Hom. ἀγκυλοχείλης (cf. Ar. Eq. 197 βυρσαίετος ἀγκυλοχείλης s. -χήλης), αἴθων, δεξιός, κάρτιστος καὶ ὤκιστος πετεηνῶν, μέλας (cf. Aesch. Ag. 115, Plut. Amat. iv. 9), ὀξύτατος δέρκεσθαι, τελειότατος (Il. viii. 247), ὑψιπέτης s. ἰψιπετήεις (cf. Soph. Oenom. fr. 423, Horap. ii. 56, &c.), Διὶ φίλτατος (Il. xxiv. 310). Hes. Th. 523 τανύπτερος (cf. Pind. P. v. 112, Il. xxiv. 317, Orphic. Lith. 124). Pind. P. i. 6, v. 48, Isthm. vi ἀρχὸς οἰωνῶν, Ol. xiii. 21 βασιλεὺς οἰωνῶν (cf. Aesch. Ag. 115; Ar. Eq. 1087; Ael. ix. 2; Nic. Ther. 448; Callim. Hymn. Jov. 68; Ovid, Met. iv. 362; the Eagle was an Egyptian symbol for the king, according to Horap. ii. 56, and was worshipped as a royal bird by the Thebans, Diod. Sic. i. 87, 9); a royal emblem also at Babylon, Philostr. Imagg. 386 K. Aesch. Pr. V. 1024 Διὸς πτηνὸς κύων, δαφοινὸς αἰετός: Soph. fr. 766 σκηπτοβάμων αἰετός, κύων Διός (cf. Ar. Av. 515, Pind. P. i. 6). Aesch. Suppl. 212, Soph. Aj. 1040, Eur. Ion 159, &c.:—Ζηνὸς ὄρνις, Ζηνὸς αἰετός, Ζηνὸς κῆρυξ. Antip. Sid. xcii in Gk. Anth. (Jac.) ii. 33 Ὄρνι, Διὸς Κρονίδαο διάκτορε. Arat. Phen. 522 Ζηνὸς μέγας ἄγγελος. Schol. Pind. I. v. 53 διόπομπος αἰετός. See also Porphyr. De Abstin. iii. 5 ὄρνιθες τοῖς ἀνθρώποις εἰσὶ κήρυκες ἄλλοι ἄλλων θεῶν, Διὸς μὲν ἀετός, κ.τ.λ. Nonn. Dionys. xxiv. 120 αἰετὸς ἡγεμόνευε δ' ἠέρος ἀντίτυπος Ζεύς. Ar. Av. 1248 (Aesch. fr. Niob.) πυρφόροισιν αἰετοῖς. Bianor in Gk. Anth. ii. 143 ἠεροδίνης αἰετός, οἰωνῶν μοῦνος ἐπουράνιος. Cf. Eurip. fr. 866 ἅπας μὲν ἀήρ

ΑΕΤΟΣ

ΑΕΤΟΣ (continued).
αἰετῷ περάσιμος. (Cf. Arist. H. A. 32, 619 b ὑψοῦ δὲ πέτεται, ὅπως ἐπὶ πλεῖστον τόπον καθορᾷ· διόπερ θεῖον οἱ ἄνθρωποί φασιν εἶναι μόνον τῶν ὀρνέων.) Opp. Venat. i. 281 αἰετὸς αἰθερίοισιν ἐπιθύων γυάλοισιν. Quint. Sm. iii. 354 οἰωνῶν προφερέστατος. Opp. Hal. ii. 539 ὦκιστον γὰρ κούφοισι μετ᾽ οἰωνοῖσιν ἄνικτες, αἰετοί. Phile, De Aq. ὑψιδρόμης, κάρτιστος ὀρνίθων, πτηνοκράτωρ. Eurip. fr. 1049 (Cram. An. Gr. Oxon. ii. 452) γύψ, κύμινδις. ἀετός, ὁ λῷστος οὗτος καὶ φιλοξενέστατος.

ἀετὸς ὁ καλ. γνήσιος. Arist. H. A. ix. 32, 619 μέγιστος τῶν ἀετῶν ἁπάντων, μείζων τε τῆς φήνης, τῶν δ᾽ ἀετῶν καὶ ἡμιόλιος, χρῶμα ξανθός, φαίνεται δὲ ὀλιγάκις ὥσπερ ἡ καλουμένη κύμινδις: cf. Plut. Amat. iv. 9; vide s. v. μορφνός. This is usually taken, as is also the χρυσάετος or ἀστερίας of Ael. H. A. ii. 39, to mean the Golden Eagle, *Aq. Chrysaetus* (L.); the former birds are however said by both authors to be very rare, whereas the Golden Eagle is the commonest eagle in Greece (Heldreich). Aristotle's statement as to its size is modified by Pliny (H. N. x. 3, media magnitudine). The passage is obscure and mythical, as shown by the allusions to κύμινδις and φήνη: Pliny's phrase *solumque incorruptae originis* is a literal but perhaps incorrect translation of γνήσιος. Many of the general references to ἀετός apply more or less closely to *Aq. Chrysaetus*, e. g. Arist. H. A. ix. 32, 619, its nesting habits; vi. 6, 563 τίκτει τρία ᾠά, ἐπῳάζει περὶ τριάκοντα ἡμέρας: ix. 32, 619 b τοὺς δασύποδας οὐκ εὐθὺς λαμβάνει, ἀλλ᾽ εἰς τὸ πεδίον ἐάσας προελθεῖν, this last statement being, however, very obscure: Ael. ii. 39, &c., &c. On the other hand accounts of the capture of snakes and stories of the combat with the Dragon (Arist. H. A. ix. 1, 609 τροφὴν γὰρ ποιεῖται τοῖς ὄφεσι ὁ ἀετός: Ael. xvii. 37; Il. xii. 200; Aesch. Choeph. 245; Soph. Antig. 110-126; Nonn. Dion. xl. 476; Nic. Theriac. 448; Aes. Fab. 120; cf. Virg. Aen. xi. 751; Hor. Carm. iv. 4; Ovid, Met. iv. 712; Flav. Vopisc. De Aurel. iv), are based on the habits of *Circaëtus gallicus*, the Short-toed Eagle, which feeds on reptiles, and partly also of the Lämmergeier. In Imhoof-Blumer and Keller's Thierbilder we have coins of Chalcis in Euboea showing an Eagle with the snake in its beak, and also (pl. v. 9) a similar coin of Cyrene in which the bird's head is evidently a Lämmergeier's.

The Vultures were frequently confused under the name ἀετός, e. g. Aesch. Ag. 138 στυγεῖ δὲ δεῖπνον αἰετῶν: as also in the story of Prometheus, e.g. Hes. Th. 523; Aesch. Pr. V. 1022; Pr. Sol. ap. Cic. Q. Tusc. ii. 10; Apoll. Rh. ii. 1254, 1263, iii. 851; Lucian, Prom. 20 (i. 203); D. Deor. i. 1 (i. 205), &c., &c.; and as in the story of the death of Aeschylus, Ael. vii. 16, Plin. x. 3, Valer. Max. ix. 12. 2, Didym. Chalc. ed. Ritter, 1845, pp. 84 &c., Hesych. Onomast. c. 16, where the ἀετός was evidently a Lämmergeier, on whose propensity to feed on tortoises v. Tristram, Fauna of Palestine, p. 94, see also Ibis, 1859, p. 177; cf. Aes.

ΑΕΤΟΣ (continued).

Fab. 419; Babr. 115. (On the mythical character of the Aeschylus legend cf. Teuffel, Rh. Mus. ix. 148, 1854; Piccolomini, Sulla morte favolosa di Eschilo, Pisa, 1883; Keller, op. c. pp. 257, 444.)

The description in Arist. H. A. ix. 32 ἐφ' ὑψηλῶν καθίζει διὰ τὸ βραδέως αἴρεσθαι ἀπὸ τῆς γῆς· ὑψοῦ δὲ πέτεται, ὅπως ἐπὶ πλεῖστον τόπον καθορᾷ, κ.τ.λ., suggests rather the habit of the Griffon Vulture (v. περκνόπτερος), which is also the 'Eagle' alluded to in like terms in Job xxxix. 28; cf. also Ael. ii. 26, Horap. i. 11, ii. 56. The Griffon Vulture is the royal bird of the East, the standard of the Assyrian and Persian armies (Xen. Cyr. vii. 1. 4, cf. Is. xlvi. 11, Habakkuk i. 8; whence probably the Roman Eagle), and the Eagle-headed God Nisroch (2 Kings xix. 37) of the Assyrians (cf. Tristram, Fauna of Palestine, p. 95; see also Hammer, Hist. Osman. i. p. 50, Creuzer's Symbolik, iii. pp. 649, 756, &c.). The crested Eagles of Assyrian sculpture (cf. Pocock's Descr. of the East, II. pl. xvi; Wood's Baalbec, pl. xxxiv), are merely a further development of the solar emblem, and it is unnecessary to suppose (as does Hogg, Ann. and Mag. N. H. (3) xiii. 1864, p. 520) that they are copied from an actual crested species.

The Persians, revering the Eagle, admired the aquiline nose and cultivated it: Olympiod. in Plat. Alcib. i. c. 16, p. 153 οἱ δοκοῦντες ἄριστοι τῶν εὐνούχων τὰ τούτου μόρια εἰς κάλλος διαπλάττουσι γρυπὴν καὶ τὴν ῥῖνα ποιοῦντες, ἐνδεικνύμενοι τὸ ἡγεμονικὸν εἶναι καὶ βασιλικὸν τὸν παῖδα· οὕτω γὰρ καὶ ὁ ἀετὸς γρυπός ἐστιν ὡς βασιλικός: cf. Hyde, Rel. vet. Pers. p. 374.

A fine description of the Eagle's flight in Apuleius, Florid. i.

Myth and legend.—The story of Prometheus, *vide supra*.

The story of Ganymede. Strato in Gk. Anth. iii. p. 82; Anon. ibid. iv. p. 118 αἰετὸς ὁ Ζεὺς ἦλθεν ἐπ' ἀντίθεον Γανυμήδην, κύκνος ἐπὶ ξανθὴν μητέρα τῆς Ἑλένης: Theocr. xv. 124; Lucian, D. Deor. iv. 1 (i. 208), Hor. Car. iv. 4. The statue of Leochares, Plin. H. N. xxxiv. 19, 29. On coins of Chalcis, Dardanos, Ilia, &c. The story referred to the constellation Aquila, Hygin. P. Astr. ii. 16, Germanic. Phen. 317, Manil. Astron. v. 486, &c.

The story of Leda: the Swan pursued by an Eagle; Eurip. Hel. 17-22. The Eagle in combat with the Swan, freq., e.g. Il. xv. 692, Arist. ap. Ael. V. H. i. 14, Phile xv. 10, Statius Theb. iii. 524, viii. 675, ix. 858, &c. On coins of Mallos in Cilicia, and Camarina (Eckhel, Doctr. Numm. i. 1. 201, Imhoof-Blumer and Keller, pl. vi. 16, 17, &c.).

The Eagle with Dolphin on coins of Sinope, and other towns, especially on the Black Sea and Hellespont, is taken by Keller as symbolic of the fish-trade (op. c. p. 262): the Dolphin here has also been referred to the Eastern emblem of Eros (cf. Weber, Hist. of Ind. Liter. 1882, p. 257), but is more probably simply the constellation

ΑΕΤΟΣ (continued).

adjacent to Aquila (cf. Manil. Astron. i. 353). See for other views, Welcker, Der Delphin und der Hymnus des Arion, Rhein. Mus. i. pp. 392-400, 1833.

The myth of Nisus and Scylla or Ciris, Virgil (?) Ciris, Hygin. Fab. 198, Ovid, Met. viii. 146, &c. (a Semitic solar myth, O. Keller, l. c. p. 259); see also E. Siecke, De Niso et Scylla in aves mutatis, Berlin, 1884, vide s. v. ἁλιάετος.

The transmigration of Agamemnon, Plato, Rep. x. p. 620; of King Periphas of Attica, Anton. Lib. Met. vi; Ov. Met. vii. 399 (cf. Th. Panofka, Zeus und Aegina, Berlin 1836); of King Merops of Cos, Anton. Lib. Met. xv. Cf. the ceremony at the consecration of a dead Emperor: ἀετὸς ἀφίεται σὺν τῷ πυρὶ ἀνελευσόμενος ἐς τὸν αἰθέρα, ὃς φέρειν ἀπὸ γῆς ἐς οὐρανὸν τὴν τοῦ βασιλέως ψυχὴν πιστεύεται ὑπὸ Ῥωμαίων, Herodian, iv. 2. 11; cf. Dio Cass. lvi. 42, lxxiv. 5.

The Eagle as a portent (ἀ. τελειότατος) in connexion with the founding of the Ptolemaic dynasty, Suid. s. v. Λάγος : of the Phrygian dynasty by Gordius, Arrian, Anab. ii. 3, Ael. xiii. 1 ; of the Persian by Achaemenes, Ael. xii. 21 ; with the birth of Alexander, Justinus xii. 16. 5.

The Eagle a portent of death : ἀετὸς ἐπικαθεσθεὶς τῇ κεφαλῇ τοῦ ἰδόντος θάνατον αὐτῷ μαντεύεται, Artemid. Oneirocrit. i. p. 112 (ed. Hercher).

On the Eagle in augury cf. Il. viii. 247, xii. 200, Od. ii. 146, xx. 242, Aesch. Ag. 115, Ar. Vesp. 15, &c.: doubtless also referred to, though unnamed, in such passages as Orph. Lith. 45, Aesch. Sept. c. T. 24, Pr. V. 486 : still more frequent in Latin, e. g. Liv. i. 24 ; Cic. De Divin. i. 47. ii. 48 ; Sueton. Octav. 94, 96, 97 ; Valer. Max. i. 4. 6, Plut. Brutus xxxvii. &c. See Hopf, Thierorakel, pp. 87 et seq.; Spanheim in Callim. Hymn. Jov. 69.

On Eagles in the Mithraic mysteries, Porphyr. De Abst. iv. 16. How the Etruscans understood the language of eagles, ibid. iii. 4.

An Eagle's nest with seven eggs (!), as a portent, Plut. Marius, xxxvi. An Eagle's nestling in symbolism and dream-prophecy, Horap. ii. 2 (cf. Leemans *in loc.*).

The mythical genealogy of the Eagle : Arist. De Mirab. 835 a, i. (60) ἐκ τοῦ ζεύγους δὲ τῶν ἀετῶν θάτερον τῶν ἐγγόνων ἁλιαίετος γίνεται παραλλάξ, ἕως ἂν σύζυγα γένηται. ἐκ δὲ ἁλιαιέτων φήνη γίνεται, ἐκ δὲ τούτων περκνοὶ κ. γῦπες, κ. τ. λ.; cf. θεόκρονος, ἁλιάετος, φήνη, &c.

How φήνη rears its young, Arist. H. A. ix. 32, 619, Antig. Hist. Mirab. 4 (52), cf. Plin. x. 3.

How the Eagle feeds and defends its young, and is affectionate towards them, Ael. ii. 40, Opp. Ven. 115, Arist. H. A. ix. 32, 619 (cf. Deut. xxxii. 11), but nevertheless casts them out, διὰ φθόνον, φύσει γὰρ ἐστι φθονερὸς καὶ ὀξύπεινος, ἔτι δὲ ὀξυλαβής, Arist. ibid. How it lays three

ΑΕΤΟΣ (*continued*).

eggs, hatches two, and rears one, Musaeus ap. Arist. vi. 6, 563, Plin. x. 4; a similar statement of ἱέραξ, Horap. ii. 99 τίκτων γὰρ τρία ᾠά, τὸ ἐν μόνον ἐπιλέγεται καὶ τρέφει, τὰ δὲ ἄλλα δύο κλᾷ· τοῦτο δὲ ποιεῖ, διὰ τὸ κατ' ἐκεῖνον τὸν χρόνον τοὺς ὄνυχας ἀποβάλλειν, καὶ ἐντεῦθεν μὴ δύνασθαι τὰ τρία βρέφη τρέφειν. How, when brooding, it goes without food, ὅπως μὴ ἁρπάζῃ τοὺς τῶν θηρίων σκύμνους (cf. Horap. i. 11). οἵ τε οὖν ὄνυχες αὐτοῦ διαστρέφονται ὀλίγας ἡμέρας, καὶ τὰ πτερὰ λευκαίνεται, ὥστε καὶ τοῖς τέκνοις τότε γίνονται χαλεποί. οὐ πάντα δὲ τὰ τῶν ἀετῶν γένη ὅμοια περὶ τὰ τέκνα, ἀλλ' ὁ πύγαργος χαλεπός, οἱ δὲ μέλανες εὔτεκνοι περὶ τὴν τροφήν εἰσιν, Arist. H. A. vi. 6, 563.

The sharp sight of the Eagle, ὀρνίθων ὀξυωπέστατος, and how its gall mingled with honey is an ointment for the eyes, Ael. i. 42; Plin. xxix. 38, &c. Cf. Il. xvii. 674, Alciphr. iii. 59 γοργὸν τὸ βλέμμα; Prov. ἀετώδες βλέπειν, Lucian Icarom. 14 (ii. 769), Hor. Sat. i. 3. 26, &c. How the Eagle's offspring look straight at the sun, and the bastards, being by this test discovered, are cast out, Ael. ii. 26, cf. Arist. H. A. ix. 34, 620, Antig. Mirab. 46 (52), Lucan ix. 902, Lucian, Pisc. 46 (i. 613), Sil. Ital. x. 107, Petron. Sat. 120, Claudian III. Cons. Hon. Praef. 12, Plin. x. (3) 4, Dion. De Avib. i. 3, Apul. Florid. i. 2, Basil. Hexaem. viii. 6. 177, Eust. Hexaem. viii. 6. 952, S. August. Mor. Manich. xvi. 50, Julian. Imp. Epp. 16 (386 C), 40 (418 d), Eunod. Ep. i. 18, id. Carm. ii. 150, Phile i. 14. Cf. Chaucer, P. of Fowles, 331 'the royal egle . . . that with his sharpe look perceth the sun.' On the Egyptian origin of this fable, see Keller, op. c. p. 268, and cf. Horap. i. 6, 11. The Solar Myth is also oriental, and in the Rig-veda the sun is frequently compared to a Vulture or Eagle hovering in the air.

The Eagle is exempt from thirst, Ael. H. A. ii. 26 οὐδέποτε ἀετὸς οὔτε πηγῆς δεῖται οὔτε γλίχεται κονίστρας, ἀλλὰ καὶ δίψους ἀμείνων ἐστί: cf. Arist. H. A. viii. 18, 601 b; but perishes of hunger (also an Egyptian fable, Keller op. c. 267), γηράσκουσι δὲ τοῖς ἀετοῖς τὸ ῥύγχος αὐξάνεται τὸ ἄνω γαμψούμενον ἀεὶ μᾶλλον, καὶ τέλος λιμῷ ἀποθνήσκουσιν. ἐπιλέγεται δέ τις καὶ μῦθος, ὡς τοῦτο πάσχει διότι ἄνθρωπός ποτ' ὢν ἠδίκησε ξένον, Arist. H. A. ix. 32, 619. Cf. Antig. 46 (52), Horap. ii. 96 (where the Eagle is said to be for that reason an Egyptian symbol for an old and starving man), Epiphan. ad Physiol. c. 6, Plin. x. 14.

It is however long-lived, μακρόβιος δ' ἐστίν· δῆλον δὲ τοῦτο ἐκ τοῦ πολὺν χρόνον τὴν νεοττιὰν τὴν αὐτὴν διαμένειν, Arist. H. A. ix. 32, 619 b.

It feeds on grass, Ael. ix. 10 (μόνος ὥσπερ καὶ Διὸς κέκληται), is poisoned by σύμφυτον, Ael. vi. 46, Phil. De An. Pr. 668, and in sickness eats tortoises as a remedy, Dion. De Av. i. 3.

Its hours of feeding: ὥρα δὲ τοῦ ἐργάζεσθαι ἀετῷ καὶ πέτεσθαι ἀπ' ἀρίστου μέχρι δείλης· τὸ γὰρ ἕωθεν κάθηται μέχρι ἀγορᾶς πληθυούσης, Arist. H. A. ix. 32, 619.

ΑΕΤΟΣ *(continued)*.

Its feathers are incorruptible, Ael. ix. 2, Plut. Q. Conv. i. 10, Plin. x. (3) 4 ; its right wing buried in the ground is an insurance against hail, Geopon. i. 14, 2.

How it walks with its toes turned in, to keep its claws sharp, Plut. De Curios. 12.

Is hostile to ἐρωδιός, σίττη, τροχίλος, Arist. H. A. ix. 1, 609 b, αἰγυπιός, ib. 610 a ; ὑβρίς, ib. 12, 615 b ; κορώνη, Ael. xv. 22 ; πιπώ, Nicand. ap. Anton. Lib. 14 ; ἐγχελυς, Aristoph. Hist. Anim. Epit. ii. 239 ; πολύπους, Ael. vii. 11, as well as to δράκων, Arist. ix. 1, 609 (cf. Ael. ii. 26, Plut. Od. et Inv. iv. p. 650), and κύκνος, ib. 12, 615 b, by which last it is conquered, Ael. xvii. 24 ; to νεβρός and ἀλώπηξ, Arist. H. A. ix. 32, 619 b), cf. Plut. Sol. Anim. xxxi. 7 ; hostile also to χήν (Od. xv. 161), δορκάς, λαγώς (Orphic. Lith. 147), ταῦρος, Phile. Cf. Plin. x. (74) 95.

It places the herb καλλίτριχον in its nest for a charm, Geopon. xv. 1, 19.

The Eagle a symbol of the Nile, Diod. Sic. i. 19. 2. Cf. Eustath. in Dionys. v. 239 ἐκλίθη [ἡ Αἴγυπτος] καὶ Ἀετία : cf. Bryant's Anc. Mythol. i. pp. 19, 378. A symbol of the year, Artemid. Oneirocr. ii. 20, as the Vulture is also said to be by Horap. i. 11 ; of elevation, Horap. i. 6 ; of the sun on the equator, Clem. Alex. Strom. v. 567. For the explanation of these hieroglyphs, into which the emblem of the Vulture enters as a phonetic element, see Lauth, Sitzungsber. Bay. Ak. 1876, p. 81.

A king who lives remote from and disdainful of his people is prefigured as an Eagle : οὗτος γὰρ ἐν τοῖς ἐρήμοις τόποις ἔχει τὴν νεοσσιάν, καὶ ὑψηλότερος πάντων τῶν πετεινῶν ἵπταται, Horap. ii. 56.

The white Eagle of Pythagoras, Iambl. V. Pyth. xxviii. 142, Ael. V. H. iv. 17, was probably a symbol for the town of Croton, on whose coins an eagle is displayed (cf. Brit. Mus. Cat. Coins, i. c. 20, also Creuzer, Symb. ii. 602, *footnote*). How Pythagoras lured an Eagle at Olympia, Iambl. V. Pyth. xiii. 62, Porph. V. Pyth. 25, Plut. Numa viii.

The constellation Aquila, Eurip. Rh. 530 μέσα δ' αἰετὸς οὐρανοῦ ποτᾶται (cf. Petavii Var. Diss., lib. v. c. 14) ; Arat. Phen. 313, Hygin. iii. 15, &c. The constellation Aquila is frequently referred to in Latin ; e.g. Ov. F. v. 732 grata Iovi fulvae rostra videbis avis ; [viii. Kal. Jun. Rostra aquilae oriuntur chronice.] Ib. vi. 194 si quaeritis astra, Tunc oritur magni praepes adunca Iovis ; [Kal. Jun. Aquila oritur chronice.] Cf. Columella xi. 2 ; Germanic. Phaen. 692 redit armiger uncis Unguibus, ante omnes gratus tibi, Iuppiter, Ales ; cf. ib. 610, &c. On the mythology of the Eagle in connexion with the constellation Aquila, see also Eratosth. c. 29, Hygin. P. Astr. ii. 16, for, *int. al.*, the stories of the metamorphosis of Ethemea, of the Eagle that brought Venus' slipper to Mercury (cf. Strabo xvii. 808, Ael. V. H. xiii. 33), the eagle that portended victory to Jove in his combat with the Titans, &c.

The complicated mythology of the Eagle baffles analysis. It is

ΑΕΤΟΣ *(continued).*

sometimes evidently a solar emblem, as is Ζηνὸς ὄρνις in Aesch. Suppl. 212. Its name χρυσάετος is in like manner probably a translation of the 'golden hawk' of Egyptian Horus. In its combat with the Hare, the Swan, the Bull, the Dragon, and so forth, these latter are probably symbolic of their stellar name-sakes, and in such cases, the hostile Eagle is, in the main, a stellar and not a solar emblem. The following are the principal facts in connexion with the constellation Aquila which seem to bear on the mythology of the Eagle. It rose nearly together with the Dolphin, and shortly after, and as it were in pursuit of, the Swan and the Serpent of Ophiuchus: it set as the Lion rose, whose leading star Regulus was also called βασιλίσκος, the Hare and the Dog-star rising simultaneously; it set together with Aquarius, known also as Ganymede the cup-bearer, and it was close beside and rose together with the Arrow of Sagittarius. It is not far distant from the constellation Lyra, which last constellation is also known as the Vulture; it and the Eagle are known respectively to later writers (and to the Arabs) as Aquila or Vultur cadens and volans or γὺψ καθήμενος and πετόμενος, nesr-el-wâki and nesr-el-tâïr, whence our modern names Vega and Altair applied to their two principal stars. (See for Arabic and other references, Ideler, Sternnamen, pp. 67, 106, &c.; also Grotius' Aratus, Notae ad Imagg. pp. 54, 60, &c., &c.) Aquila rose together with the latter stars of the Scorpion, but Lyra or the Vulture, rising a little earlier, seems to have been the true paranatellon of that sign: accordingly it is probably not the true Eagle but the Vulture or Aquila cadens, which, substituted for the unlucky Scorpion, figures with the other three cardinal signs of Leo, Taurus, and Aquarius, in the familiar imagery of Ezek. i. 10, x. 14, and Rev. iv. 7. A *solar* myth is discussed s. v. ἁλιάετος. The combat with the Hare is interesting from its representation on a famous decadrachm of Agrigentum, as well as for the equally mystical description in Aesch. Ag. 115 βοσκόμενοι λαγίναν. (The symbolism connected with the Hare seems to me to be peculiarly complicated and difficult, and all tentative hypotheses are more than commonly liable to be overthrown.) The Eagle with the Serpent or Dragon occurs not only in classical coinage (Chalcis, Agrigentum, Gortyna, Siphnos, &c.), but also on Persian and Egyptian sculptures. The Eagle with the lightning (ἀετὸς πυρφόρος) or thunderbolt (*ministrum fulminis*, cf. Plin. x. 3, Serv. in Aen. i. 398, Sil. Ital. xii. 58 adsuetis fulmina ferre Unguibus) occurs on coins of Elis, Catana, Megalopolis, &c. Philo's phrase (i. 628) φέγγος γνήσιον and φ. νόθον for *sunlight* and *moonlight* is perhaps suggestive or corroborative of a solar symbolism in ἀετὸς γνήσιος.

ἀετίτης, the eagle-stone. Ael. i. 35. Diosc. v. 161. Dion. De Avib. i. 3 οἱ μὲν αὐτὸν ἀπὸ τῶν Καυκασίων ὁρῶν, οἱ δὲ ἀπὸ τῆς τοῦ ὠκεανοῦ ὄχθης φασὶ κομίζεσθαι: Lucan vi. 676 quaeque sonant feta tepefacta sub alite saxa; Plin. x. 3, xxx. (14) 44, xxxvi. (21) 39, xxxvii. (11) 72, Horap. ii. 49,

ΑΕΤΟΣ (*continued*).

Phile 736, Geopon. xv. 1, 30, Solinus, c. 37, Philostr. V. Apollon. ii. 14, Stobaeus 98, Priscian in Periegres. p. 393. Cf. Physiol. Syrus, where the stone is called ἀντόνικον, a corruption of εὐτόκιον or ὠκυτόκιον: cf. Eustath. Hexaëm. p. 27, Epiphan. De Duodecim Gemmis, &c., ed. Romae, 1743, p. 30, Marbod. Lapidarium, 339-391 (King's Ant. Gems, p. 404). See also, for mediaeval and other references, Boch. Hieroz. ii. 312-316, and N. and Q. (8) v. 518, 1894. The Eagle with its stone, an Egyptian symbol of security, Horap. ii. 49.

Proverb and Fable.—Fable of Fox and Eagle, Archiloch. fr. 86-88 (110), Aes. Fab. 5; Ar. Av. 652. Hence according to Rutherford (Babrius p. xlvii), the proverb αἰετὸς ἐν ποτανοῖς, Pind. N. iii. 77 (138); αἰετὸς ἐν νεφέλαισι, Ar. Eq. 1013, Av. 978, 987, fr. 28, and Schol.; applied by the oracle to the Great King (cf. Ezek. xvii. 3), Schol. in Ar. Eq. 1010; cf. Zenob., Suid. ἐπὶ τῶν δυσαλώτων, παρόσον ἀετὸς ἐν νεφέλαις ὢν οὐχ ἁλίσκεται: for other explanations, see Steph. Thes.

ἀετὸν ἵπτασθαι διδάσκεις, Suid., Zenob. ii. 49; cf. Pseudo-Plutarch, Prov. 25 ἄνευ πτερῶν ζητεῖς ἵπτασθαι: hence, according to Rutherford, the fable of the Eagle and Tortoise, Babr. cxv, Aes. 419; cf. Diog. L., ii. 17, 10.

αἰετὸν κάνθαρος μαιεύσομαι, Ar. Lys. 696: ἐπὶ τῶν τιμωρουμένων τοὺς μείζονας προκατάρξαντας κακοῦ. λέγεται γὰρ τὰ ᾠὰ τοῦ ἀετοῦ ἀφανίζειν ὁ κάνθαρος, Suid.: cf. Ar. Pax, 133, and Schol., Lys. 695, Aes. Fab. 7, Keller, op. c. p. 269.

The oracle of Aëtion, Herod. v. 92.

Fable of Eagle shot with its own feathers, Aesch. Myrm. fr. 123, cf. Schol. in Ar. Av. 808, Aes. Fab. 4. The Eagle and the Archer, Bianor, Gk. Anthol. ii. p. 143.

ἀετὸς καὶ βασιλίσκος, Plut. Mor. ii. 806 E. The Fighting-cock and the Eagle, Babr. v; the Eagle and Lion in partnership, Babr. xcix; the Eagle mindful of benefits, Aes. 6, 92, 120, Ael. xvii. 37, whence the proverb αἰέτιον χάριν ἐκτίνειν, Apost. Cent. i. 78; cf. Tzetz. Chil. iv. 302.

The tame Eagle of Pyrrhus, Ael. ii. 40; the Eagle that saved Tilgamus of Babylon, Ael. xii. 21; that saved Aristomenes, Paus. iv. 18. 5: cf. Antip. Sidon. xcii in Gk. Anthol. ii. 33: see also Ael. vi. 29, Plin. x. (5) 6: cf. Marx, Gr. Märchen, 1889, pp. 29-50.

On **Hawking** with trained Eagles in India, Ctesias, fr. 11 (ed. Müller), Ael. iv. 26; in Thrace, Ael. ii. 42: cf. also Leo Africanus and Tzetzes Chiliad. iv. 134. On Eagles trained for Falconry, see (e. g.) Scully, Contr. to the Ornith. of E. Turkestan, *Stray Feathers*, vi. p. 123, 1876; also Yule's Marco Polo, Schlegel's Fauconnerie, &c.

Representations of Eagles.—On Babylonian processional sceptres, Herod. i. 195. On the sceptre of the Persian kings, Xen. Cyrop. vii.

ΑΕΤΟΣ (*continued*).

1. 4 (cf. Keller, op. c. pp. 240, 435). On the sceptre of Zeus at Olympia, Paus. v. 11. 1 (copied on a late coin of Elis); and at Megalopolis, id. viii. 31. 4 (cf. Pind. P. i. 6 εὕδει ἀνὰ σκήπτῳ Διὸς αἰετός, Soph. fr. 766 σκηπτοβάμων αἰετός, Schol. in Ar. Av. 510); on pillars before the altar of Zeus Lycaeus, in Arcadia, id. viii. 38. 5; on the Omphalos at Delphi (cf. Soph. O. T. 480), Pind. P. iv. 1 χρυσέων Διὸς αἰητῶν πάρεδρος (similarly on coins of Cyzicus). Cf. Plut. de Orac. i. 409 ἀετούς τινας, ἢ κύκνους, μυθολογοῖσιν ἀπὸ τῶν ἄκρων τῆς γῆς ἐπὶ τὸ μέσον φερομένους εἰς ταὐτὸ συμπεσεῖν Πυθοῖ περὶ τὸν κπλ. ὀμφαλόν. The great mechanical Eagle with outspread wings on the altar at Olympia, Paus. vi. 20. 12. On the shield of Aristomenes at Messene, Paus. iv. 16. 7 (cf. account of shield in Eurip. fr. Meleag. iv, and on the shield of Aeacus, Ζῆνα νόθον, σοφὸν ὄρνιν, Nonn. xiii. 214). For references to coins, v. supra, *passim*.

The gable of a temple was called ἀετός, Ar. Av. 1110, or ἄετωμα, Suid. Cf. Eur. fr. Hypsip. ἰδοὺ πρὸς αἰθέρ' ἐξαμίλλησαι κόραις, γραπτοὺς ἐν αἰετοῖσι προσβλέπων τύπους: Pind. Ol. xiii. 21 τίς γὰρ... ἢ θεῶν ναοῖσιν οἰωνῶν βασιλέα δίδυμον ἐπέθηκε; cf. Pind. fr. 53, ap. Paus. x. 5. 12, and Bergk's note; Tacit. H. iii. 71; Bekker Anecd. p. 348. 3 ἀετοῦ μιμεῖται σχῆμα ἀποτετακότος τὰ πτερά: for other references see Blaydes, in Ar. Av. 1106. Compare the Sacred Hawk or Eagle, or the winged solar disc, on Egyptian gables, &c., and on Mithraic monuments. See Brönsted, Voy. en Grèce, ii. 154; Welcker, Alte Denkmäler, i. 3. A conventional ornament on the gable even of modern buildings in the Greek style, still represents the degenerate emblem of the Eagle's wing.

See also, besides the special references to the other Eagle-names enumerated above, kindred mythological references s. vv. **γύψ, ἱέραξ, περκνόπτερος, φήνη.**

'ΑΖΕΙΝΟΙ', also ἀξέσιμοι· κύκνοι, ταῖς πτέρυξιν ἀπολαμβάνοντες ἀέρα, Hesych.

'ΑΗΔΩ'Ν, ἡ [ὁ ἀ., Anth. Pal. vii. 44, Eust. 376. 24; for grammatical forms, see Bergk. Philol. xxii. p. 10, Ahrens in Kuhn's Zeitschr. iii. p. 81, &c.] Also ἀηδονίς (Eur. Rhes. 550, Theocr. viii. 38, freq. in Gk. Anthol., &c.), ἀδονίς (Theocr., Mosch.), ἀ,δηδών = ἀξηδών, Hesych., and ἀηδώ, Soph. Aj. 628. Dim. ἀηδονιδεύς, Theocr. xv. 121. Rt. *vad*, to sing, ἀείδω, &c.

The **Nightingale**, *Motacilla luscinia*, L., *Daulias luscinia*, auctt.

Mod. Gk. ἀηδόνι, applied to various Warblers.

Od. xix. 518 Πανδαρέου κούρη χλωρηὶς ἀηδών. [German commentators, translating χλωρηίς *green*, have made many needless conjectures as to some other bird being here alluded to; cf. Groshans, p. 5: Buchholz, pp. 123-125. On the word χλωρηίς see also G. E. Marindin and W. W. Fowler, Class. Rev. 1890, pp. 50, 231, and in particular Steph.

ΑΗΔΩΝ (*continued*).

Thes. (ed. 1821), coll. 1284-5. The general significance is perhaps 'the nightingale, that clepeth forth the fresshe leves newe,' Chaucer, P. of Fowles 351, χλωραῖς ὑπὸ βάσσαις, Soph. Oed. Col. 673.]

Other Epithets.—Ἀτθίς, αἰολόδειρος (Nonn. xlvii. 33), αἰολόφωνος (Opp. Hal. i. 728), βαρύδακρυς (Phil. Thess. lxvi), δακρυόεσσα (Eur. Hel. 1110), Ἦρος ἄγγελος, ἡμερόφωνος s. ἱμερόφωνος (Sappho, p. 39, ap. Suid.), κιρκήλατος (Aesch. Suppl. 62), λίγεια (Aesch. Ag. 1146; Soph. Oed. Col. 671), λιγύφθογγος (Ar. Av. 1380), λιγύφωνος (Theocr. xii. 7), μελίγηρυς (C. I. G. 6261 ; Gk. Anthol. iv. pp. 231, 273 ; cf. Theocr. Ep. iv. 12), ὀξύφωνος (Soph. Trach. 963 Babr. xii. 3, 19), ξουθός (Aesch. Ag. 1142, Ar. Av. 676, Theocr. Ep. iv. 11 ; cf. Eur. Hel. 1111), ποικιλόδειρος (Hes. Op. et D. 201), πολυκώτιλος (Simonid. fr. 73, in Etym. M.), πυκνόπτερος (Soph. Oed. Col. 18), πανόδυρτος s. πάνδυρτος (Soph. El. 1077), τεκνολέτειρα (ib. 107), χλωραύχην (Simon. 73). [Note similarity of epithets s. v. χελιδών.]

Among innumerable poetic references, cf. Ibyc. fr. 7 τᾶμος ἄυπνος κλυτὸς ὄρθρος ἐγείρῃσιν ἀηδόνας. Simon. fr. 73 δείτ' ἀηδόνες πολυκώτιλοι, χλωραύχενες εἰαριναί. Callim. L. P. 94 μάτηρ μὲν γοερῶν οἶτον ἀηδονίδων ἄγε βαρὺ κλαίουσα. Aesch. Ag. 1116 Ἴτυν, Ἴτυν στένουσα, ἀηδών. Soph. El. 147 ἃ Ἴτυν αἰὲν Ἴτυν ὀλοφύρεται, ὄρνις ἀτυζομένα, Διὸς ἄγγελος. Eurip. Phleg. fr. 773, 23 μέλπει δὲ δένδρεσι λεπτὰν ἀηδὼν ἁρμονίαν ὀρθρευομένα γόοις Ἴτυν, Ἴτυν πολύθρηνον. Eurip. Hel. 1111 ὦ διὰ ξουθᾶν γενύων ἐλελιζομένα θρήνοις ἐμοῖς ξυνεργός. Ar. Av. 212 Ἴτυν ἐλελιζομένη (cf. Hor. Car. iv. 2. 5 Ityn flebiliter gemens, Catull. lxv. 14 Daulias absumpti fata gemens Ityli). Soph. Aj. 628 οἰκτρᾶς γόον ὄρνιθος ἀηδοῦς, cf. Aesch. fr. 412. Eur. Hec. 337 ἀηδόνος στόμα. Ar. Ran. 684 ῥύξει δ' ἐπίκλαυτον ἀηδόνιον νόμον. Mosch. iii. 37 οὐδὲ τόσον ποκ' ἄεισεν ἐνὶ σκοπέλοισιν ἀηδών: cf. v. 46. Aristaenet. Ep. i. 3 ἡδὺ καὶ ἀηδόνες, περιπετόμενοι τὰ νέμητα, μελῳδοῦσιν. Philip lxvi in Gk. Anthol. ii. p. 213 αἰεὶ δ' ἡ βαρύδακρυς, ἐπὶ στήλαις μὲν ἀηδών· μεμφομένη δὲ βυθοῖς, ἁλκυονὶς βλέπεται, &c., &c.

Description.—Arist. H. A. iv. 9, 536 ᾄδει καὶ ὁ ἄρρην καὶ ἡ θήλεια [an error, but cf. Od. xix. 518], πλὴν ἡ θήλεια παύεται ὅταν ἐπῳάζῃ καὶ τὰ νεόττια ἔχῃ. ὦπται καὶ ἀηδὼν νεοττὸν προδιδάσκουσα (cf. Ael. iii. 40, Plut. De Sol. Anim. 973, Dion. De Avib. i. 20 ἀποκτείνει δὲ τοὺς ἀφθόγγους, Porph. De Abst. iii. 5). Arist. H. A. v. 8, 542 b τίκτει τοῦ θέρους ἀρχομένου πέντε καὶ ἓξ ᾠά· φωλεύει δὲ ἀπὸ τοῦ μετοπώρου μέχρι τοῦ ἔαρος. H. A. ix. 15, 616 b οὐκ ἔχει τῆς γλώττης τὸ ὀξύ [true of the Hoopoe ; ἀηδών is an interpolation here, Aub. and Wimm., cf. Plin. x. 43 (29), but compare the version in Apollod. iii. 14]. H. A. ix. 49 B, 632 b ἡ δ' ἀηδὼν ᾄδει μὲν συνεχῶς ἡμέρας καὶ νύκτας δεκαπέντε, ὅταν τὸ ὄρος ἤδη δασύνηται· μετὰ δὲ ταῦτα ᾄδει μέν, συνεχῶς δ' οὐκέτι. τοῦ δὲ θέρους προιόντος ἄλλην ἀφίησι φωνὴν καὶ οὐκέτι παντοδαπὴν οὐδὲ τ[ρ]αχεῖαν καὶ ἐπιστρεφῆ

ΑΗΔΩΝ (*continued*).

ἀλλ' ἁπλῆν, καὶ τὸ χρῶμα μεταβάλλει· καὶ ἕν γε 'Ιταλίᾳ τὸ ὄνομα ἕτερον καλεῖται περὶ τὴν ὥραν ταύτην. φαίνεται δ' οὐ πολὺν χρόνον· φωλεῖ γάρ (cf. Ael. xii. 28; Plin. N. H. x. 29, Clem. Alex. Paedag. x): the above excerpt is very obscure and mystical; with the verb δυσύνηται cf. Etym. M. s. v. Δαυλίς, also Aesch. fr. 27 (*ibi cit.*), and Paus. x. 4, 7. Hesiod, ap. Ael. V. H. xii. 20 τὴν ἀηδόνα μόνην ὀρνίθων ἀμοιρεῖν ὕπνου καὶ διὰ τέλους ἀγρυπνεῖν. Ael. H. A. i. 43 ἀηδὼν ὀρνίθων λιγυρωτάτη, λέγουσι δὲ καὶ τὰ κρέα αὐτῆς ἐς ἀγρυπνίαν λυσιτελεῖν: cf. ib. xii. 20, Phile xviii. Ael. iii. 40 καθειργμένη ἐν οἰκίσκῳ ᾠδῆς ἀπέχεται, καὶ ἀμύνεται τὸν ὀρνιθοθήραν ὑπὲρ τῆς δουλείας τῇ σιωπῇ· οὗπερ οὖν οἱ ἄνθρωποι πεπειραμένοι, τὰς μὲν ἤδη πρεσβυτέρας μεθιᾶσι, σπουδάζουσι δὲ θηρᾶν τὰ νεόττια. Ib. v. 38 ἐν ταῖς ἐρημίαις ὅταν ᾄδη πρὸς ἑαυτήν, ἁπλοῦν τὸ μέλος· ὅταν δὲ ἁλῷ καὶ τῶν ἀκουόντων μὴ διαμαρτάνῃ, ποικίλα τε ἀναμέλπειν καὶ τυκερῶς ἑλίττειν τὸ μέλος. Its mode of capture, Dion. De Avib. iii. 13. On captive Nightingales, see also Nemesian, Ecl. ii, De Luscinia. A white or albino specimen, Plin. l. c.

The *locus classicus* for the Nightingale's song is Plin. x. (29) 43, cf. Ar. Av. 209; see also Dion. De Avib. i. 20, Phile xviii, &c.

Pausan. ix. 30. 6 λέγουσι δὲ οἱ Θρᾷκες, ὅσαι τῶν ἀηδόνων ἔχουσι νεοσσιὰς ἐπὶ τῷ τάφῳ τοῦ 'Ορφέος, ταύτας ἥδιον καὶ μεῖζόν τι ᾄδειν. Cf. Antig. Hist. Mirab. 5, Myrsili Methymn. fr. 8 (vol. iv. p. 459, Müller).

The Nightingale which sang over the infant Stesichorus, as a presage of poetry, Plin. x. 43 (29). The transmigration of Thamyras (? Thammuz), Plato, Rep. x. 620.

On talking Nightingales, Plin. N. H. x. 59 (42).

The lay of the loom, κερκίδα δ' εὐποίητον, ἀηδόνα τὰν ἐν ἐρίθοις, Antip. Sid. xxii, Gk. Anthol. ii. 11, cf. id. xxvi; cf. Ar. Ran. 1316.

The *Cricket* is called τὴν Νυμφέων παροδῖτιν ἀηδόνα, Gk. Anthol. iv. 206.

Ulysses, for his melancholy tale, is Μουσῶν ἀηδών, Eur. Palamed. viii; a poet is Μουσάων ἀηδονίς, Anthol. Pal. vii. 414 (cf. Μουσᾶν ὄρνιχες, Theocr. vii. 47); a bad poet is ἀηδόνων ἠπίαλος (enough to give a Nightingale the shivers), Phryn. Com. Inc. i.

The Sirens are called ἁρπυιόγουνοι ἀηδόνες, Lyc. 653.

Proverb and Fable.—οὐδ' ὅσον ἀηδόνες ὑπνώουσιν, Suid. ὕπνος ἀηδόνειος, Nicoch. Inc. 3 (ii. 846, Mein.), cf. Nonn. Dionys. v. 411 ὄμμασιν ἁρπάξαντες ἀηδονίου (s. ἀϊδονίου) πτερὸν ὕπνου. τοὶ σκῶπες ἀηδόσι γαρύσαιντο, Theocr. i. 136, cf. Gk. Anthol. (Jac.) iv. p. 218, also Theocr. v. 136 ποτ' ἀηδόνα κίσσας ἐρίσδεν: Luc. Pisc. 37 θᾶττον ἂν γὺψ ἀηδόνας μιμήσαιτο.

Fable of the Hawk and the Nightingale, Hes. Op. et D. 203, cf. Aes. Fab. 9, Plut. Mor. 158 B. The Nightingale and the Swallow,

ΑΗΔΩΝ (continued).

οὐ θέλω τὴν λύπην τῶν παλαιῶν μου συμφορῶν μεμνῆσθαι, Aes. Fab. 10, cf. Babr. xii. Vox et praeterea nihil, Plut. Apophth. Lacon. 123 A τίλας τις ἀηδόνα καὶ βραχεῖαν πάνυ σάρκα εὑρὼν εἶπε, φώνα τύ τίς ἐσσι καὶ οὐδὲν ἄλλο. Story of Agesilaus and one who mimicked the Nightingale's song, αὐτᾶς, εἶπεν, ἄκουκα πολλάκις, Plut. Mor. 191 B.

On the myths of Itylus, Philomela, Procne, and in general on the melancholy strain of the Nightingale, cf., *int. al.*, Theocr. xv. 121; Pherecydes, fr. p. 136 (ed. Sturtz); Ar. Av. 203, 665, and Scholia; Paus. i. 41. 8; Boios ap. Ant. Lib. xi; Hygin. Fab. 45 (209, 212); Apollod. iii. 14. 8; Virg. Georg. iv. 510, Ecl. vi. 79; Martial x. 51, xiv. 75; Ovid, Met. vi. 424, Am. ii. 6. 7; Catull. lxv. 14; Carm. de Philomela, &c., &c. See also (*int. al.*) Hartung, Relig. und Myth. d. Gr. iii. p. 33; Duntzer in Kuhn's Ztschr. xiv. p. 207; E. Oder in Rh. Mus. f. Philol. (N. S.) xliii. p. 540 et seq.; Keller op. c. pp. 304-320; Pott in Lazarus and Steinthal's Zeitschrift, xiv. p. 46, 1883; J. E. Harrison, J. Hellen. Studies, viii. 439-445, 1887, M. of Anc. Athens, p. lxxxiv.

The Nightingale's song, as Coleridge discovered, is not melancholy. It was a spirit of religious mysticism that 'First named these notes a melancholy strain, And many a poet echoes the conceit.' I believe the innumerable references to the melancholy lay of ἀδονίς or ἀηδών, and to the lament for ῎Ιτυς, to be for the most part veiled allusions to the worship of Adonis or Atys; that is to say, to the mysterious and melancholy ritual of the departing year, when women 'wept for Tammuz': Ἀδώνι ἄγομεν, καὶ τὸν Ἄδωνιν κλάιομεν! This conjecture is partially supported by the confusion between ἀηδονίς and ἀδωνηίς, by the mythical relations between the Nightingale and the Swallow, and by the known connexion of both with the rites of Adonis. Compare also Thuc. ii. 29 ὁ μὲν ἐν Δαυλίᾳ τῆς Φωκίδος νῦν καλουμένης γῆς, ὁ Τηρεὺς ᾤκει τότε ὑπὸ Ὀρηκῶν οἰκουμένης· καὶ τὸ ἔργον τὸ περὶ τὸν Ἴτυν αἱ γυναῖκες ἐν τῇ γῇ ταύτῃ ἔπριξαν· πολλοῖς δὲ καὶ τῶν ποιητῶν ἐν ἀηδόνος μνήμῃ Δαυλιὰς ἡ ὄρνις ἐπωνόμασται. (Cf. Hesych. Δαυλία κορώνη; also Etym. M. p. 250, 8 Δαυλίαν κορώνην, ἀντὶ τὸν ἀηδόνα, Ἀριστοφάνης διὰ τὸν μίθον· ἔνιοι τὴν δασεῖαν).

In the above passage from Thucydides the commentators take αἱ γυναῖκες to refer to Procne and Philomela; it seems to me to mean simply that in that spot the women-folk practised the rites of Adonis. It is noteworthy that Dodwell found an archaic village-festival, or feast of tabernacles, taking place at Daulis, when he visited the locality at the season of the vernal equinox (cf. Ezek. viii, &c.). The passage in Theocr. xv. 121 οἱοι ἀηδονιδῆες ἀεξομένων ἐπὶ δέτδρων, κ.τ.λ., with its context, is important in this connexion. As I have attempted to bring ἀηδών, Itys or Itylus, and possibly even Thamyras into relation with

ΑΗΔΩΝ (*continued*).

Adonis, Atys, and Thammuz respectively, so I am tempted to see a connexion between a fourth Adonis-name, *Duzi* or *Dazu*, and the traditional etymology (δαυσίς) of *Daulis*. Again, is it certain that ἀτθὶς ἀηδών, a late and rare epithet in Greek (Nonn. Dionys. xlvii. 32, cf. ibid. xliv. 265), means really the *Attic* nightingale; or may we not here also have an Atys-name? Lastly, a reference to a Moloch-sacrifice is indicated in Hesychius under the heading Λίβυς τε ἀηδών· αἱ γὰρ ἐν Καρχηδόνι (τῆς Λιβύης δέ εἰσι) γυναῖκες [αἱ] τὰ ἴδια τέκνα κατά τι νύμιμον ἐσφαγίαζον Κρόνῳ [et maestis late loca questibus implent!]: cf. Soph. in Andromeda, fr. 132, ap. Hesych. s. v. κουρίον.

Philomela and Procne are frequently confused, cf. Serv. ad Ecl. vi. 78. In all Greek authors, Philomel is the name of the Swallow, and Procne of the Nightingale (Ar. Av. 665). The Latins generally reverse this; but Varro De L. L. and Virg. Ecl. vi adhere to the Greek version of the story (W. H. Thompson, ad Plat. Gorg. fr. 6, p. 180). ἀηδών and ἀλκυών are also apt to be confused, e. g. Arist. H. A. viii. 3, 593 b, where MSS. have ἀηδόνων for ἀλκυόνων, and Suid. s. v. Ἡμερινὰ ζῶα, where ἀηδών occurs among the θαλάσσια ζῶα, between ἀλκυών and κῆυξ; cf. Boch. Hieroz. ii. 218. In the version of the Itylus-Myth given by Boios, ap. Anton. Lib. 11, the mother of Aëdon is transformed into the bird ἀλκυών.

See also s. vv. ἁλιάετος, ἀλκυών, χελιδών.

ΑἸ'ΒΕΤΟ'Σ (for αἰfετός). αἰβετός· ἀετός, Περγαῖοι, Hesych.

ΑἸ'ΓΙ'ΘΑΛΟΣ (also αἰγίθαλλος; cf. κορυδαλός, κορυδαλλός). A Titmouse.

Three sorts are indicated, Arist. H. A. viii. 3, 592 b ὁ μὲν σπιζίτης μέγιστος, ἔστι γὰρ ὅσον σπίζα = *Parus major*, L., the Great Tit or Ox-eye: ἕτερος δ' ὀρεινός, οὐραῖον μακρὸν ἔχων = *Acredula* (*Parus*) *caudatus*, the Long-tailed Tit (which occurs in Northern Greece, v. d. Mühle p. 49, Lindermayer p. 65): τρίτος ἐλάχιστος, including the Tom-Tit and its allies, of which, according to Heldreich (p. 39) *P. ater*, *coeruleus* and *palustris* are rare in Greece; *P. lugubris*, Nath., is commoner and now shares the same popular name κλειδωνᾶς with the Great Tit. Arist. H. A. viii. 3, 592 b ὄρνις σκωληκοφάγος: ix. 15, 616 b τίκτει ᾠὰ πλεῖστα (the Long-tailed Tit is known to lay very numerous eggs): ix. 40, 626 μάλιστα ἀδικεῖ τὰς μελίττας (cf. Ael. H. A. i. 58, Phile 650, Geopon. xv. 2, 18). According to Alex. Mynd. ap. Athen. ii. p. 65, ἐλαιός and συκαλίς are also varieties of αἰγίθαλος: vide s. v. **συκαλίς**. Mentioned also Ar. Av. 887 together with μελαγκόρυφος (into which συκαλίς is metamorphosed); Alcae. Com. ii. 825. Is hostile to ἀκανθυλλίς, Plut. De Od. et Inv. iv. 537 B. The metamorphosis of Timandra, Anton. Lib. Met. v; and of Ortygius, Met. xx. Is confused with αἰγυθίλας, Dion. De Avib. i. 15, iii. 20.

ΑΙ'ΓΙΘΟΣ (also αἴγινθος). An unknown and mythical bird, identified by the older commentators (e. g. Belon) with the Linnet.

Arist. H. A. ix. 1, 609, 610 ὄνῳ πολέμιος (cf. Antig. Hist. Mirab. 58 (63); Ael. H. A. v. 48; Dion. De Avib. i. 12 ; Phile 696 ; Plin. x. 95). πολέμιοι δὲ καὶ ἄνθος καὶ ἀκανθὶς καὶ αἴγιθος. Ib. ix. 15, 616 b εὐβίωτος καὶ πολύτεκνος, τὸν πόδα χωλός. [Many MSS. have αἰγίοθος : for χωλός some texts read ὠχρός, or χλωρός, the latter Albertus Magnus, but cf. αἴγιθος ἀμφιγνήεις, Callim. fr. ap. Antig. l. c.; Plin. x. (8) 9.] λέγεται δ' ὅτι αἰγίθου καὶ ἄνθου αἷμα οὐ συμμίγνυται ἀλλήλοις : idem, Pliny x. (74) 95 (who calls it *avis minima*), Ael. H. A. x. 32, and Phile 432, the same statement of ἀκανθὶς and αἰγίθαλος, and Antig. H. M. 106 (114) the same of αἴγιθος and ἀκανθίς. Dion. De Avib. iii. 14 θηρᾶται κλωβῷ, ἐν ᾧ πάλαι θηρωθεὶς ἕτερος ἐπὶ τὸ βοᾶν κατακλείεται. Antig. H. M. 45 (51), how αἴγιθος sucks the goats (v. αἰγοθήλας) and is χωλός. [Aegithus solo nomine huic nostrae aetati cognitus, P. Hardouin, Annott. ad Plin. x. 8.] Vide s. vv. ἀκανθίς, ἄνθος.

ΑΙ'ΓΙ'ΠΟΨ. A Macedonian name for the **Eagle**. Etymol. M.

ΑΙ'ΓΟΘΗ'ΛΑΣ. The **Goatsucker** or **Nightjar**, *Caprimulgus europaeus*, L.

The name is probably corrupt, and the mythical attribute of the bird due to a case of 'Volksetymologie.'

M. Gk. name γιδοβύστρα is a corrupt translation of αἰγοθήλας (Heldr. p. 37). Also called βυζάστρα, νυκτερίδα (i. e. the Bat, v. d. Mühle), νυκτοπάτης, and πλάνος (Erh.). (Cf. Germ. *Ziegenmelker, Kuhmelker*, Fr. *tette-chèvre*, &c.)

Arist. H. A. ix. 30, 618 b ὄρνις ὀρεινός, μικρῷ μείζων κοττύφου, κόκκυγος ἐλάττων· ᾠὰ δύο [cf. Lindermayer, p. 38, Krüper, p. 183, &c.] ἢ τρία· τὸ δὲ ἦθος βλακικός [verb. dub., cf. Aub. and Wimm. in Arist. l. c.]. θηλάζει δὲ τὰς αἶγας. οὐκ ὀξυωπὸς τῆς ἡμέρας. Ael. H. A. iii. 39 τολμηρότατος ζῴων .... ἐπιτίθεται ταῖς αἰξὶ κατὰ τὸ καρτερόν, καὶ τοῖς οὔθασιν αὐτῶν προσπετόμενος εἶτα ἐκμυζᾷ τὸ γάλα .... τυφλοῖ τὸν μαστόν, καὶ ἀποσβέννυσι τὴν ἐκεῖθεν ἐπιρροήν. Cf. Plin. x. 56 (40). Vide s. vv. αἰγίθαλος, αἴγιθος.

ΑΙ'ΓΟΚΕ'ΦΑΛΟΣ. Probably a kind of **Owl**: perhaps the Horned or Long-eared Owl, *Strix otus*, L., or its small ally *Ephialtes scops*, K. Bl. The latter is the *Asio* of Plin. x. (23), xxix. 38, which name in its Italian diminutive form is Shelley's 'Sad Aziola.'

Arist. H. A. ii. 15, 506 ὅλως οὐκ ἔχει τὸν σπλῆνα· τὴν χολὴν ἔχει πρὸς τῷ ἥπατι καὶ πρὸς τῇ κοιλίᾳ. Ib. ii. 17, 509 τὸν στόμαχον ἔχει εὐρύτερον τὸ κάτω.

Gesner (p. 62) mentions *Capriceps* as an unknown bird. Neither Sundevall nor Aubert and Wimmer pronounce an opinion on it: the

ΑΙΓΟΚΕΦΑΛΟΣ (*continued*).

former thinks it possibly identical with αἰγοθήλας. According to Scaliger p. 251, αἰγοκέφαλος = αἰγώλιος. In both passages cited above αἰγοκέφαλος is mentioned along with γλαύξ, and the name suggests a *Horned* Owl (*sic* Scaliger, Lidd. and Sc., &c.). For other suggestions, see Newton, Dict. of Birds, p. 365, s. v. *Godwit*.

ΑΙΓΥΠΙΟ'Σ. A Vulture.

Etymology very doubtful. The analogy of Lämmergeier suggests a compound of αἴξ or ὄἴς (Curt.) and γύψ, but the word is probably much more primitive and ancient. I suspect that most of the remarkably numerous bird-names beginning with *ai-* (many of which are peculiarly difficult to identify, a circumstance suggesting their generic rather than specific character), contain an element akin to *avi-s*, Sk. *vi-s* (v. ἀετός), and in this case that γύψ is the shortened or derived form. The dialectic form αἰγίπυψ is interesting in this connexion.

Hom. frequent, with ep. ἀγκυλοχείλης, γαμψῶνυξ. Not merely a carrion-eater (as in Hes. Sc. 405-412), but attacks live birds (Il. xvii. 460, Od. xx. 322, cf. Soph. Aj. 169 . . . . μέγαν αἰγυπιὸν ὑποδείσαντες). Arist. H. A. ix. 1, 609 b μάχεται ἀετῷ· πολέμιος αἰσάλωνι. A portent of αἰγυπιοί in chase of ἴρηκες in the Persian war, Herod. iii. 76; cf. Baehr's note. Is feared by τρωγλίτης, Phile 692. Sometimes distinguished from γύψ, Ael. ii. 46 ἐν μεθορίῳ γυπῶν εἰσι καὶ ἀετῶν, εἶναι καὶ ἄρρενας, καὶ τὴν χρόαν πεφυκέναι μέλανας (cf. Phil. De An. pr. 127): Nic. Ther. 406 αἰγυπιοὶ γῦπές τε. Pallad. Alex. xx, in Gk. Anthol. iii. p. 119 καὶ τὸν μὲν Τιτυὸν κατὰ γῆς δύο γῦπες ἔδουσιν, ἡμᾶς δὲ ζῶντας τέσσαρες αἰγυπιοί. Cf. Lob. Path. i. p. 87.

The metamorphosis of Aegypius and Neophron into αἰγυπιοί· χρόαν δὲ καὶ μέγεθος οὐχ ὅμοιοι, ἀλλὰ ἐλάττων ὄρνις αἰγυπιὸς ἐγένετο Νεόφρων, Boios ap. Anton. Lib. Met. v; the smaller species here alluded to is the White or Egyptian Vulture, the *Neophron percnopterus* of modern authors: vide s. vv. γύψ, περκνόπτερος.

The φιλοστοργία of αἰγυπιός, as also of φήνη, celebrated in Od. xvi. 216, Aesch. Ag. 49, Opp. Hal. i. 723, &c., is connected with the Egyptian association of the Vulture with the goddess of Maternity (cf. Horap. i. 11).

αἰγυπιός is apparently the poetic name, applied to the various species which frequent the battle-field, and on the other hand applied to an Eagle in such passages as Il. xvii. 460. That the word is an old and antiquated one seems to be meant by Suidas: αἰγυπιόν· οὕτως οἱ παλαιοί, ἀλλ' οὐ γῦπα. Cf. Bekk. An. 354. 28, Rutherford, New Phryn. p. 19.

ΑΙΓΩ'ΛΙΟΣ. Also αἰγωλιός, and αἰτώλιος (Bk., Ar. vi. 6. 3). An Owl.

Arist. H. A. viii. 3, 592 b, a nocturnal rapacious bird, mentioned with ἐλεός and σκώψ, and resembling the former (in size): θηρεύει τὰς κίττας.

ΑΙΓΩΛΙΟΣ (*continued*).

[here Camus, reading αἰτώλιος, and following Belon and Buffon, translates *Milvus niger*, the Black Kite].

Arist. H. A. ix. 17, 616 b νυκτινόμος ἐστί, καὶ ἡμέρας ὀλιγάκις φαίνεται. οἰκεῖ πέτρας καὶ σπήλυγγας· ἔστι γὰρ δίθαλλος [Gaza tr. *victus gemini*, Guil. *divaricata*, v. Aub. and Wimm. ii. p. 248], τὴν δὲ διάνοιαν βιωτικὸς καὶ εὐμήχανος. Ib. vi. 6, 562 ἐνίοτε δὲ καὶ τέτταρας ἐξάγει νεοττούς [Plin. x. 79 (60)].

The metamorphosis of Aegolius, Boios ap. Anton. Lib. Met. 19.

If δίθαλλος means particoloured, αἰγώλιος is clearly the White or Barn Owl, *Strix flammea*, L., as Littré (ad Plin.) takes it to be; it however does not catch birds, and is said to be scarce in Greece (v. d. Mühle, Lindermayer). Gesner transl. by *ulula*, and identifies it with the Tawny Owl. Sundevall librates between the Tawny and the Barn Owl; A. and W. incline to the former. See **αἰγοκέφαλος**, **ἐπόλιος**.

ΑΙΘΥΙΑ. A poetic word, of uncertain or indefinite meaning.

Probably a large Gull, e.g. *Larus marinus*, the Black-backed Gull (Sundevall), or *L. argentatus*, the Herring Gull (Krüper), the former being rare in Greece. Netolicka's hypothesis of the Merganser, and that of Groshans that it was a Diver or Grebe, do not tally with Aristotle: Schneider's identification with the Skua, *Lestris parasiticus*, fails, inasmuch as the latter does not dive (vide Buchholz, op. c. pp. 112, 113) nor does it breed in the Mediterranean. The Herring Gull is abundant during the winter and breeds about the middle of April: the Common Tern (*Sterna anglica*) lays about the same time (Krüper) but in the lagoons and not on the cliffs.

Od. v. 337, 353. Arist. H. A. v. 9, 542 b ἡ δ' αἴθυια καὶ οἱ λάροι τίκτουσι μὲν ἐν ταῖς περὶ θάλατταν πέτραις, τὸ μὲν πλῆθος δύο ἢ τρία· ἀλλ' ὁ μὲν λάρος τοῦ θέρους, ἡ δ' αἴθυια ἀρχομένου τοῦ ἔαρος [cf. *Mergus*, Plin. x. 32 (48)] εὐθὺς ἐκ τροπῶν. οὐδέτερον δὲ φωλεύει. Also i. 1, 487; viii. 3, 593 b. Arrian, Peripl., ed. Didot, 1855, i. p. 398, names it with λάροι and κορῶναι αἱ θαλάσσιοι, and Hesych. renders αἴθυιαι by εἰνάλιαι κορῶναι. Frequent in the Gk. Anthol.; e.g. Glauc. vi, vol. iii. p. 58 ὤλετο γὰρ σὺν νηΐ, τὰ δ' ὀστέα ποῦ ποτ' ἐκείνου, πίθεται, αἰθυίαις γνωστὰ μόναις ἐνέπειν, cf. Marc. Arg. xxxi, ibid. ii. p. 250; Callim. xci; Leon. Tar. xci, Gk. Anthol. i. p. 178 τὸν αἰθυίης πλείονα νηξάμενον: Anon. ibid. iv. p. 143 σήμυγγος ἀλίκτυπον ὃς τόδε ναίεις εὐστιβὲς αἰθυίαις ἰχθυβόλοισι λέπας. Phile, De Anim. Pr. 680, is hostile to πελαργός and κρέξ. Is said to be deaf and dumb, Aristoph. Hist. Anim. Epit. i. 141.

The metamorphosis of Hyperippa, daughter of Munychus, Nicander ap. Anton. Lib. Met. 14.

Arat. Phen. 918, a sign of rain; πολλάκις δ' ἀγριάδες νῆσσαι ἢ εἰναλίδιναι

ΑΙΘΥΙΑ (*continued*).

αἴθυιαι χερσαῖα τινάσσονται πτερύγεσσιν: cf. Theophr. De Sign. ii. 28, Virg. Georg. i. 362.

A long but unsatisfactory description in Dion. De Avib. ii. 5.

A title or epithet of Athene, Paus. i. 5. 3, i. 41. 6.

Said to be the name of a horse in Mnasalc. xiii. Gk. Anthol. i. p. 125.

See also **δύπτης, λάρος**.

ΑΙ͂Ξ. An unknown bird. Arist. II. A. viii. 3, 593 b: mentioned between χηναλώπηξ and πηνέλοψ as one of the ὄρνιθες στεγανόποδες βαρύτεροι (omitted in several MSS.).

According to Belon the Plover (*Vanellus cristatus*) was so called in Greece in his time: the interpretation cannot hold. Sundevall conjectures αἴξ to be one of the smaller Geese (? *Anser leucopsis*), and to be derived from the goat-like cry. Perhaps as αἰγοκέφαλος suggests the *Horned* Owl, so αἴξ here suggests the *Horned* Grebe, *Podiceps auritus*, Lath., a common bird in Greece in winter.

ΑΙΡΙΘΑΚΟ'Σ. Vide s. vv. **αἴσακος, ἐρίθακος.**

ΑΙ͂ΣΑΚΟΣ. A very doubtful word.

καλεῖται δὲ καὶ τὸ ζῷον ὁ αἰριθακὸς αἴσακος, Etym. M. Cf. Serv. in Aen. iv. 254, v. 128.

ΑΙΣΑ'ΛΩΝ (αἰσάρων, Hesych.). A sort of **Hawk**, traditionally identified with the Merlin, *Falco aesalon*, L. (Gesner, &c.).

Arist. H. A. ix. 36, 620 τῶν δὲ ἱεράκων δεύτερος [τῇ κρατίᾳ]. Ib. ix. 1, 609 b αἰγυπιῷ πολέμιος· ἀλώπεκι πολέμιος καὶ κόρακι. Ael. H. A. ii. 51 μάχεται δ' ὁ κόραξ καὶ ὄρνιθι ἰσχυρῷ τῷ καλ. αἰσάλωνι, καὶ ὅταν θεάσηται ἀλώπεκι μαχόμενον, τιμωρεῖται. Cf. Antig. H. M. 59 (64). Plin. N. H. x. (74) 95 Aesalon vocatur parva avis, ova corvi frangens, cuius pulli infestantur a vulpibus. Invicem haec catulos eius ipsamque vellit: quod ubi viderunt corvi, contra auxiliantur velut adversus communem hostem. (Some editors read *aesalona* for *epileum*, Plin. N. H. x. 9.)

ΆΚΑΛΑΝΘΙ'Σ· εἶδος ὀρνέου μικροῦ, Suid. Vide s.vv. **ἀκανθίς, ἀκανθυλλίς.**

Ar. Pax 1078 ἡ κώδων ἀκαλανθὶς (Schol. λαλὸν γὰρ τὸ ζῷον) ἐπειγομένη τυφλὰ τίκτει (cf. Paroemiogr. ed. Gaisf., p. 69). Associated with Artemis, Ar. Av. 871. One of the nine Emathidae, daughters of Pieros, was metamorphosed into the bird ἀκαλανθίς, Nicander ap. Anton. Lib. Met. ix.

ΆΚΑΝΘΙ'Σ. A small bird, usually identified with the **Linnet,** *Fringilla cannabina*, L., or the **Goldfinch,** *F. carduelis*, L., on the ground of the more than doubtful derivation from ἄκανθα. The description

ΑΚΑΝΘΙΣ (*continued*).

is in the main mythical : cf. ἄνθος. Mod. Gk. σκαθί, the Siskin, is perhaps akin (Bikélas).

Arist. H. A. viii. 3, 592 b ὄρνις ἀκανθοφάγος· ἐπὶ ἀκανθῶν νέμεται. Ib. ix. 1 ὄνῳ καὶ ἄνθῳ καὶ αἰγίθῳ πολέμιος [cf. Antig. Hist. Mirab. 106 (114), Plin. x. 74 (95)], ix. 17 κακόβιος καὶ κακόχροος, φωνὴν μέντοι λιγυρὰν ἔχουσα. Agath. xxv. 5 in Gk. Anthol. iv. p. 13 λιγυρὸν βομβεῦσιν ἀκανθίδες. Theocr. 7. 141: the Scholia in Theocr. make ἀκανθίς synonymous with ἀκανθυλλίς and ποικιλίς. Virg. Georg. iii. 338 littoraque halcyonem resonant, et acanthida [*al.* acalanthida] dumi ; cf. Serv. in Virg. alii lusciniam esse volunt, alii vero carduelem, quae spinis et carduis pascitur.

In Anton. Lib. Met. vii, the daughter of Autonous and Hippodamea is called 'Ακανθίς and 'Ακανθυλλίς indifferently ; note also that her mother was metamorphosed into κορυδός. Hesych. and Aelian have also ἄκανθος. (Cf. Anton. Lib. l. c.) Vide s. v. αἴγιθος.

ΑΚΑΝΘΥΛΛΙ'Σ (in some MSS. ἀκανθαλίς). Probably the **Goldfinch**, *Fringilla carduelis*, L.

Arist. H. A. viii. 3, 593 τὸ μέγεθος ὅσον κνιπολόγος. Ib. ix. 13, 616 τεχνικῶς δὲ καὶ ἡ τῆς ἀκανθυλλίδος ἔχει νεοττιά· πέπλεκται γὰρ ὥσπερ σφαῖρα λινῆ, ἔχουσα τὴν εἴσδυσιν μικράν : cf. Plin. x. 33 (50). Is hostile to κορυδαλός, Ael. iv. 5, Phile, De An. Pr. 683. Mentioned also Eubul. fr. iii. 268, ap. Athen. ii. p. 65, Plut. ii. 537 B, and by Hesych. as στρουθοῦ γένος.

The description in Arist. H. A. ix. 13 has suggested to scientific commentators (Sundevall, p. 116, &c.) the nest of the Long-tailed or Penduline Tits, *Aegithalus caudatus* or *pendulinus* (cf. αἰγιθαλος) or Bearded Tit, *Calamophilus biarmicus* ; but the neat round nest of the Goldfinch would suit the description well enough. The alternative form ἀκανθαλίς is evidently identical with ἀκαλανθίς, and so supports the identity of the bird with ἀκανθίς, while its identity with ποικιλίς, also asserted by the Schol. in Theocr., is strengthened by the statements of hostility to κορυδαλός in the case of both these birds. The latter statement is, of course, fabulous or mystical. In identifying ἀκανθυλλίς with the Goldfinch, I only mean that such an identification was probably adopted by Aristotle : what ἀκανθυλλίς, ἄνθος, &c. originally meant is unknown. See also αἰγίθαλος, ἄνθος.

'Α[Κ]ΚΑΛΑΝΣΙ'Ρ· ἀκανθυλλίς, παρὰ Λάκωσιν, Hesych. [On various readings cf. Valkenaer, Adon. p. 278 ; Ahr. Dor. ii. 69.]

"ΑΚΜΩΝ· γένος ἀετοῦ, Hesych. Cf. Opp. Cyneg. iii. 326, where, though ἄκμονες are cited as *wolves*, the description closely resembles that of the mystical eagles in Aesch. Ag. 111-120.

ΆΚΥΛΕΗ'Σ ἀετός, Hesych. Also **ἀκυλάς**, Eustath. ad Dionys. Perieg. 381. Perhaps akin to *aquila*; cf. Umbrian (Tab. Eugub.), angla *s.* ankla.

ΆΛΕΚΤΡΥΩ'Ν. Also ἀλέκτωρ (Batr. 191, Simon. 81, Theocr. vii. 122, Aesch. Ag. 1671, Eum. 861, &c. ἀλέκτωρ seems thus to have been an old form, retained in tragedy; cf. Rutherford, New Phryn. p. 307). Fem. ἀλεκτορίς: Com. ἀλεκτρύαινα (Ar. Nub. 666, 851, &c.) and ἡ ἀλεκτρυών (Ar. Nub. 663, Fr. 237, &c.). Cf. Hesych. ἀλεκτρυόνες· κοινῶς οἱ παλαιοὶ καὶ τὰς θηλείας ὄρνεις οὕτως ἐκάλουν: Phrynich. ccvii ἀλέκτορις εὑρίσκεται ἐν τραγῳδίᾳ που καὶ κωμῳδίᾳ, λέγε δὲ ἀλεκτρυὼν καὶ ἐπὶ θήλεος καὶ ἐπὶ ἄρρενος ὡς οἱ παλαιοί: Ar. Nub. 662 τήν τε θήλειαν καλεῖς ἀλεκτρυόνα κατὰ ταὐτὸ καὶ τὸν ἄρρενα. Dim. ἀλεκτοριδεύς, a chicken, Ael. vii. 47; also ἀλεκτορίσκος, a cockerel, Babr. v. 1, xcvii. 9, cxxiv. 12. Connected with O. P. *halak*, the sun, cf. ἀλκυών. For false etymology ἀ, λέκτρον, see below.

The **Common** or **Domestic Fowl**, *Gallus gallinaceus*, L. Often mentioned simply as ὄρνις, a 'fowl' [especially a hen, Athen. ix. 373 ἀλλὰ μὲν καὶ ὄρνιθας καὶ ὀρνίθια νῦν μόνον ἡ συνήθεια καλεῖ τὰς θηλείας], cf. ὄρνις ἐνοίκιος, Aesch. Eum. 866; ὄρνις καθοικίς, Nic. Ther. 558; κατοικάς, Id. Alex. 60, 535; κατοικίδιος, Geopon. i. 3. 8; ὤρνιθες οἱ αὔλειαι, Herondas vi. 101; ὄρνις συνέστιος, Opp. Cyneg. iii. 118; τιθὰς ὄρνις, Alpheus Mityl. in Gk. Anth., ii. p. 118, cf. Arat. Progn. 960 (228), &c., &c.

Early references.—Theogn. Scut. 861 ἑσπερίη τ' ἔξειμι, καὶ ὀρθρίη αὖτις ἔσειμι, ἅμος ἀλεκτρυόνων φθόγγος ἐγειρομένων. Simon. fr. 80 Β (Athen. ix. 374 D) ἀμερόφων' ἀλέκτωρα. Pind. Ol. xii. 20 ἐνδομάχης ἅτ' ἀλέκτωρ. Epicharm. Com. Syr. (ap. Athen. l.c.) fr. 96 (Ahr. Dial. Dor.) ὤεα χηνὸς κ' ἀλεκτορίδων πετεηνῶν. Batrachom. 191 ἕως ἐβόησεν ἀλέκτωρ. For many fragments, see Athen. l. c.

Description.—Arist. H. A. v. 13, 544, De Part. ii. 657 b, De Gen. iii. 749 b, described as γένος· ἥμερον, ἐπίγειον, κονιστικόν, βαρύ, οὐ πτητικόν, οὐκ ὀξυωπόν, σχιζόπτερον, ἀφροδισιαστικόν, &c. H. A. ii. 17, 508b, 509 πρόλοβον ἔχουσι πρὸ τῆς κοιλίας· ἀποφυάδας ἔχουσι.

Comb and **spurs.** Ar. Av. 487, 1366, Arist. H. A. ii. 12, 504 b ἔνια τῶν ὀρνέων λόφον ἔχουσι, τὰ μὲν αὐτῶν τῶν πτερῶν ἐπανεστηκότα, ὁ δ' ἀλεκτρυὼν μόνος ἴδιον· οὔτε γὰρ σάρξ ἐστιν οὔτε πόρρω σαρκὸς τὴν φύσιν. Ib. ix. 49, 50 κάλλαιον, πλῆκτρα (Hesych. has also πλακτήρ and κόπιες, the spurs). κάλλαια, distinguished from λόφος, the 'wattles,' Ael. xi. 26, Ar. Eq. 497, cf. Schol. κάλλαια δὲ τοὺς πώγωνας τῶν ἀλεκτρυόνων: in Ael. xv. 1, a fish-hook dressed with two feathers ὑπὸ τοῖς καλλέοις suggests the 'hackles.' With ep. φοινικόλοφος, Theocr. xxii. 72, Geop. xiv. 16. 2.

ΑΛΕΚΤΡΥΩΝ (*continued*).

Compared in size with φάσσα, Arist. fr. 271, 1527; with ἐλεός, Η. Α. viii. 3. 592 b; with the largest of the Woodpeckers, H. A. ix. 9, 614 b: with ἀσκαλώπας, H. A. ix. 26, 617 b.

Reproduction.—Arist. H. A. v. 2, 509 b συγκαθείσης τῆς θηλείας ἐπὶ τὴν γῆν ἐπιβαίνει τὸ ἄρρεν: cf. ib. x. 6, 637 b. Ib. vi. 9, 564 b ἄρχεις. Ib. vi. 1, 558 b ὀχεύεται καὶ τίκτει ὅλον τὸν ἐνιαυτὸν ἔξω δύο μηνῶν τῶν ἐν τῷ χειμῶνι τροπικῶν (cf. H. A. v. 13, 544, De Gen. iii. 1, 749 b, Plin. x. 74). τίκτουσι δὲ καὶ οἰκογενεῖς ἔνιαι δὶς τῆς ἡμέρας· ἤδη δέ τινες λίαν πολυτοκήσασαι ἀπέθανον διὰ ταχέων. H. A. vi. 2, 560 b αἱ νεοττίδες πρῶτον τίκτουσιν εὐθὺς ἀρχομένου τοῦ ἔαρος, καὶ πλείω τίκτουσιν ἢ αἱ πρεσβύτεραι· ἐλάττω δὲ τῷ μεγέθει τὰ ἐκ τῶν νεωτέρων. Ib. συνίσταται δὲ τὸ τῆς ἀλεκτορίδος ᾠὸν μετὰ τὴν ὀχείαν καὶ τελειοῦται ἐν δέχ' ἡμέραις. Ib. 560 a ἐν ὀκτωκαίδεκα ἡμέραις ἐν τῷ θέρει ἐκλέπουσιν, ἐν δὲ τῷ χειμῶνι ἐνίοτ' ἐν πέντε καὶ εἴκοσιν.

Plut. Q. Conv. vii. 2 (Mor. 853. 15) ἀλεκτορίδων, ὅταν τέκωσι, περικαρφισμός, cf. Plin. x. 41 (57).

The structure and development of the egg, H. A. vi. 3. ᾠὰ μαλακά, ὑπηνέμια, κυνόσουρα, οὔρια, ἢ ζεφύρια, H. A. vi. 2, 559, De Gen. iii. 1, 751: Plin. x. 60 (80); Columella, vi. 27; cf. Erasmus ad Prov. ὑπηνέμια τίκτει. ᾠὰ δίδυμα, H. A. vi. 3, 562. On crosses between fowl and partridge, De Gen. ii. 7, 749 b. How Pea-hen's eggs are put under a sitting hen, H. A. vi. 9, 564 b. How the hen takes the chicks under her wing. H. A. ix. 8, 613 b; cf. Alpheus Mityl. xii, in Gk. Anthol. ii. p. 118 χειμερίοις νιφάδεσσι παλυνομένα τιθὰς ὄρνις, τέκνοις εὐναίας ἀμφέχεε πτέρυγας: Eurip. H. Fur. 71 οὓς ὑπὸ πτεροῖς σώζω νεοσσοὺς ὄρνις ὡς ὑφειμένη: see also Plutarch. De Philost. (Mor. 599. 4); Opp. Cyneg. iii. 119. How a cock sometimes, after the hen's death, rears the brood, and ceases to crow, H. A. ix. 49, 631 b, Plin. x. (55) 76. H. A. ix. 8, 614 ἐν τοῖς ἱεροῖς, ὅπου ἄνευ θηλειῶν ἀνάκεινται [as to this day on Mount Athos], τὸν ἀνατιθέμενον πάντες εὐλόγως ὀχεύουσιν. Cf. Plut. Brut. Anim. Nat. vii (Mor. 1212. 30) ἀλεκτρυὼν δ' ἀλεκτρυόνος ἐπιβαίνων, θηλείας μὴ παρούσης, καταπίμπραται ζωός.

On eggs in medicine, Diosc. ii. 44, Galen. De Fac. Simp. Med., Plin. xxix. (3) 11, &c. The longer eggs produce male birds, and are the better to eat, Hor. Sat. ii. 4. 12, Plin. x. 74 (52).

On artificial incubation in Egypt, Arist. H. A. vi. 2, 559 b, Diod. Sic. i. 74. Geopon. xiv. 8. 1. On capons, Arist. H. A. ix. 49, 631 b; cf. Plin. x. (21) 24, &c. Varro, R. R. iii. 9, &c. On the whole management of fowls, Geopon. xiv. 7-17.

Πότερον ἡ ὄρνις πρότερον ἢ τὸ ᾠὸν ἐγένετο, Plut. Q. Conv. iii (Mor. 770. 13).

The Crowing Cock.—Among innumerable poetic and other references, cf. Theogn., Simonid., Batrachom., supra. Cratin. ap. Athen. 374 D ὥσπερ ὁ Περσικὸς [cf. Ar. Av. 277, 485, 708, &c.: v. also Suidas] ὥρων

ΑΛΕΚΤΡΥΩΝ (continued).

πᾶσαν καναχῶν ὀλόφωνος, Ἀλέκτωρ.—εἴρηται δ' οὕτως ἐπειδὴ καὶ ἐκ τοῦ λέκτρου ἡμᾶς διεγείρει. Theocr. xxiv. 63 ὄρνιθες τρίτον ἄρτι τὸν ἔσχατον ὄρθρον ἄειδον. Soph. El. 18 ὡς ἡμὶν ἤδη λαμπρὸν ἡλίου σέλας ἑῷα κινεῖ φθέγματ' ὀρνίθων σαφῆ : fr. 900 κοκκοβόας ὄρνις: cf. ep. ὀρθροβόας, Alexarch. ap. Athen. 98 E. Diph. iv. 421 (Mein.) ὀρθριοκόκκυξ [*lect. dub.*] ἀλεκτρυών. Probably alluded to also Soph. Anten. 2, fr. 141 (Ath. ix. 373 D) ὄρνιθα καὶ κήρυκα καὶ διάκονον. Plat. Symp. 223 C ἀλεκτρυόνων ᾀδόντων, at Cock-crow. Cf. Alciphr. i. 39. 20, Aristaenet. i. 24 εἰς ἀλεκτρυόνων ᾠδάς: Ar. Nub. 4, Juv. ix. 107, &c. Plut. ap. Eust. Od. p. 1479, 47 σὲ δὲ κοκκύζων ὄρθρι' ἀλέκτωρ προκαλεῖται. Antip. Thess. v, in Gk. Anthol. ii. p. 96 πάλαι δ' ἠῷος Ἀλέκτωρ, κηρύσσων φθονερὴν Ἠριγένειαν ἄγει. ὀρνίθων ἔρροις φθονερώτατος, κ.τ.λ.: cf. Ar. Vesp. 815, Anyt. xi, in Gk. Anthol. i. p. 132, Virg. Aen. viii. 456, &c. Arist. De Acoust. 800 b τοὺς τραχήλους ἔχοντες μακροὺς βιαίως φθέγγονται. Ael. N. A. iv. 29 ὁ ἀλεκτρυὼν τῆς σελήνης ἀνισχούσης ἐνθουσιᾷ φασι καὶ σκιρτᾷ. ἥλιος δὲ ἀνίσχων οὐκ ἄν ποτε αὐτὸν διαλάθοι, ᾠδικώτατος δὲ ἑαυτοῦ ἐστι τηνικάδε. Cf. Arist. H. A. iv. 9, 536. Lucian, Gallus, &c. With ep. ὠρόμαντις, Babr. cxxiv. 11.

κοκκύζειν, to crow, Cratin. ii. 186, Diph. iv. 407 (Mein.), Theocr. vii. 48, 124, &c. κακκάζειν, to cackle, Hesych., &c.

Why the Cock crows : by an affinity for the sun, or rejoicing in heat and light, Heliodor. i. 18. See also Schol. Ar. Av. 830, Cic. De Div. ii. 26. According to Theophrastus (Ael. iii. 38) in moist localities Cocks don't crow. Paus. v. 25. 9, on the shield of Idomeneus, as a descendant of Helios, ἡλίου δὲ ἱερόν φασιν εἶναι τὸν ὄρνιθα καὶ ἀγγέλλειν ἀνιέναι μέλλοντος τοῦ ἡλίου. See also Schol. Diog. L. viii. 34, Plaut. M. Gl. iii. 1. 96, Mart. xiv. 223, Isidor. De N. R. c. 3, &c., &c.

How to prevent Cocks crowing, by means of a collar of *sarmentum* wood, Plin. xxiv. 25.

On hearing a Cock crow, or an ass bray, it is a matter of common prudence to spit, Joh. Chrysost. in comm. ep. S. P. ad Ephes. iv. 12 (vol. xi. p. 93, Montef.): this reference to the ass is used to explain ὄνον ὄρνιν in Ar. Av. 721, by Haupt, Inaug. Diss., Berlin, 1864.

On **Fighting Cocks**, Aesch. Eum. 866 ; Plato, Legg. vii. 789 ; Theocr. xxii. 72 ; cf. Opp. Cyneg. ii. 189 ; cf. Schol. in Ar. Eq. 494, Ach. 165 ὅταν εἰς μάχην συμβάλλωσιν τοὺς ἀλεκτρυόνας, σκόροδα διδόασιν αὐτοῖς : Lucian, Anarch. 37 (2. 918), &c. (See also Xen. Symp. iv. 9, and cf. φυσιγγόομαι, from φύσιγξ, garlic. The annual cock-fight at Athens, instituted by Themistocles, Ael. V. H. ii. 28 ἀλεκτρυόνας ἀγωνίζεσθαι δημοσίᾳ ἐν τῷ θεάτρῳ μιᾷ ἡμέρᾳ τοῦ ἔτους: cf. J. E. Harrison, Myth. of Anc. Athens, p. 278 ; also at Pergamus, Plin. x. 21 (25). The cock-fight was depicted on the High-priest's chair in the Dionysiac theatre (Boetticher, Harrison, &c.) ; represented also in the Festival Calendar

ΑΛΕΚΤΡΥΩΝ (continued).

of Panagia Gorgopiko at Athens, as taking place in the month Poseideon, about the end of December (Boetticher, Philologus, xxii. p. 397, 1865). As an attribute of January, on a Calendar of the time of Constantius; Graevii Thes. Ant. Rom. viii. 96, Creuzer, Symb. iii. 616. Ael. N. A. iv. 29 μάχῃ δὲ ἀλεκτρυὼν καὶ τῇ πρὸς ἄλλον ἡττηθεὶς ἀγωνίᾳ οὐκ ἂν ᾄσειε· τὸ γάρ τοι φρόνημα αὐτῷ κατέσταλται, καὶ καταδύεταί γε ὑπὸ τῆς αἰδοῖς. κρατήσας δὲ γαῦρός ἐστι, καὶ ὑψαυχενεῖ, καὶ κυδρουμένῳ ἔοικε. Cf. Proverb, Galli victi silent, canunt victores, Cic. De Divin. ii. 26; cf. Ar. Av. 70 and Schol. φυσικὸν τοῦτο ἐν ταῖς συμβολαῖς τῶν ἀλεκτρυόνων τοὺς ἡττηθέντας ἕπεσθαι τοῖς νενικηκόσι: cf. Theocr. xxii. 71. On spurs for fighting-cocks, πλῆκτρα, κέντρα, cf. Ar. Av. 760, and Schol. The table with raised edges, τηλία, on which Cocks or Quails were pitted against one another (still used in the East), Aeschin. viii. 221, Alciphr. iii. 53, Poll. ix. 108; also πίναξ, Plut. Mor. 65 c. It was a matter of duty and of education to witness the cock-fights, ὡς μὴ ἀγεννέστεροι καὶ ἀτολμότεροι φαίνοιντο τῶν ἀλεκτρυόνων μηδὲ προπαγορεύοιεν ὑπὸ τραυμάτων ἢ καμάτων ἤ του ἄλλον δυσχεροῦς, Lucian, De Gymn. 37. See also s. vv. ὄρτυξ, στυφοκόμπος.

On the marks of courage, Arist. Physiogn. 2, 806 b; Plin. x. (56) 77; Geopon. xiv. 16.

The fighting-breed of Tanagra, Pausan. ix. 22. 4 (vide infra).

How the Cock fights his own father, Ar. Nub. 1427, &c., cf. Av. 758, 1364.

How a hen that has defeated the Cock in combat, crows and assumes the plumage of the male, Arist. H. A. ix. 49, 631 b, cf. Ael. v. 5; Terent. Phorm. iv. 4. 30 gallina cecinit. On wide-spread superstitions connected with the Crowing Hen, vide Hopf, Thierorakel, pp. 164, 165.

On the pugnacity of the Cock, cf. also Pind. Ol. xii. 20. Aesch. Agam. 1671 κόμπασον θυρσῶν, ἀλέκτωρ ὥστε θηλείας πέλας. Cf. Ar. Av. 835 Ἄρεως νεοττός. See also Lucian, Gallus, &c.

Placed as a symbol of battle on the head of Athene's statue in the Acropolis at Elis, Pausan. vi. 26. 23.

Varieties and Breeds.—Adrian Fowls, Arist. H. A. vi. 1, 558 b μικραὶ τὸ μέγεθος, τίκτουσι δ' ἀν' ἑκάστην ἡμέραν· εἰσὶ δὲ χαλεπαί, καὶ κτείνουσι τοὺς νεοττοὺς πολλάκις· χρώματα δὲ παντοδαπὰ ἔχουσιν. Cf. De Gen. iii. 6, Chrysipp. ap. Athen. vii. 285 E, Plin. x. 75 (53), Hecat. fr. 58, ap. Steph. Byz.

Illyrian Fowls, that lay twice or thrice a day, Arist. De Mirab. 128, 842 b; cf. H. A. vi. 1, 558 b.

At Tanagra, Paus. ix. 22. 4, were two breeds, οἵ τε μάχιμοι, καὶ οἱ κόσσυφοι καλούμενοι. Cf. Babr. Fab. 5 ἀλεκτρίσκων ἦν μάχη Ταναγραίων, οἷς φασιν εἶναι θυμὸν ὥσπερ ἀνθρώποις. See also Lucian, Gallus, on the metempsychosis of Pythagoras, ἀντὶ Σαμίου Ταναγραῖος. Cf. **κολοίφρυξ**.

ΑΛΕΚΤΡΥΩΝ (*continued*).

The Egyptian breed of Μονόσιροι, ἐξ ὧν οἱ μάχιμοι ἀλεκτρυόνες γεννῶνται, and on their exemplary patience as sitters, Geopon. xiv. 7. 30.

A silent breed at Nibas, near Thessalonica, Ael. xv. 20.

On the breeds of fowls, *galli tanagrici, medici, chalcidici*, &c., see also Varro, De R. R. iii. 9. 3; Colum. viii. 27 and 31; Plin. x. (21) 24, (56) 77.

Chrysipp. ap. Athen. ix. 373 A καθάπερ τινὲς τὰς λευκὰς ὄρνιθας τῶν μελαινῶν ἡδίους εἶναι μᾶλλον.

The fatted fowls of the Delians, and Roman laws and practices regarding the same; Plin. x. 50, cf. Columella viii. 2, Varro iii. 9, Cic. Academ. iv.

The large fowls of Ctesias, fr. 57. 3, Ael. xvi. 2, were Impeyan Pheasants; cf. Cuvier in Grandsaigne's Pliny, vii. p. 409, and Yule's Marco Polo, i. p. 242.

Myth and Legend.—Pythag. ap. Iambl. Adhort. xxi. 17 ἀλεκτρυόνα τρέφε μέν, μὴ θύε δέ· μήνῃ γὰρ καὶ ἡλίῳ καθιέρωται. Cf. Iambl. V. Pyth. xxviii. 147, 150, &c.

A white Cock sacred to the Moon, Pythag. ap. Diog. L. viii. 8. 19, Iambl. V. Pyth. xviii. 84: to the Sun, Suid. s. v. Πυθαγόρα τὰ σύμβολα.

A white or yellow Cock sacrificed to Anubis, Plut. de Is. lx.

The Cock sacred to Athene, Paus. vi. 26. To Hermes, Lucian, Gallus (cf. Montfaucon, i. pl. lxviii, lxxi, Graev. Thes. A. R. v. 718 A, &c.); cf. Plut. Conv. Disp. iii. 6. p. 666 ὁ δὲ ὄρθρος πρὸς τὴν ἐργάνην Ἀθηνᾶν καὶ τὸν ἀγοραῖον Ἑρμῆν ἐπανίστησι. To Latona, Ael. iv. 29. Sacrificed to Mars, Plut. Inst. Lacon. (Mor. 238 F.). Sacred to Demeter, and therefore not eaten at Eleusis, nor by the initiates of Mithra; Porphyr. De Abst. iv. 16. Sacrificed to Nephthys and Osiris on the 13th of Boedromion, and to Hercules and Thios on the 29th of Munychion, C. I. G. 523, Marm. Oxon. ii. 21, pp. 15, 17.

Dedicated to Aesculapius, Plat. Phaed. 118. See also Artemid. v. 9 ηὔξατό τις τῷ Ἀσκληπιῷ, εἰ διὰ τοῦ ἔτους ἄνοσος ἔλθοι, θύσειν αὐτῷ ἀλεκτρυόνα: also Porphyr. Vit. Pythag. 36, Herondas, Ascl. iv. 12. On the fowl in medicine, Nic. Ther. 557, Cels. v. 27, Diosc. Ther. 19 and 27, Galen and Pliny *passim*.

Sacrificed to the Household gods, Juv. xiii. 233 Laribus cristam promittere galli; cf. ibid. xii. 96.

The Cuthic deity Nergal (2 Kings, xvii. 30) is said to have been represented as a Cock: for which reason Rabbinical writers, according to Gesenius, connect the name with תרנגול, tharnegol, a Cock, which word old-fashioned etymologists found hid in *Tanagra*.

An image dedicated to the Twin Brethren, Callim. xxiv, in Gk. Anthol. i. p. 218; cf. Pausan. vi. 26.

How fowls were kept in the temples of Hercules and Hebe, ἐν τῇ

ΑΛΕΚΤΡΥΩΝ (*continued*).

Εὐρώπῃ, Mnaseas ap. Ael. xvii. 46 αἱ μὲν οὖν ἀλεκτορίδες ἐν τῷ τῆς "Ηβης νέμονται νεῴ, οἱ δὲ ἐν Ἡρακλέους οἱ τῶνδε γαμέται : cf. Plut. ii. 696 E, Paus. ii. 148.

Ael. N. A. ii. 30, how a new-purchased cock, if carried thrice round the table, does not seek thereafter to escape. Ib. iii. 31, how the lion fears the cock, and how the latter frightens the basilisk to death: for which reason travellers in Libya take a cock along with them. Cf. ibid. vi. 22 ἔχθιστα δὲ τῷ μὲν λέοντι πῦρ καὶ ἀλεκτρυών: Aes. Fab. 323 ; Plut. De Inv. iv (Mor. 650, 5), Sol. Anim. xxxii (Mor. 1201, 23). Hence also the use of a Cock to destroy the Lion-weed, ἡ λεόντειος πόα = ὀροβάγχη, Geopon. ii. 42. 3. A confusion is possibly indicated here with the Galli, priests of Cybele ; according to Varro, De R. R. c. 20 (Nonius, s. v. mansuetum), when the Galli saw a lion, *tympanis ... fecerunt mansuetum* : for other important references see Mayor's note to Juv. viii. 176. Note further that a mystical name for the Sun was λέων, and that those who participated in the rites of Mithra were called Lions ; Porphyr. De Abst. iv. 16. Niclas, the learned editor of the Geoponica (ed. 1781), and certain other historians quoted by him, finding that a lion in Bavaria evinced no terror at the sight of a Cock, but killed and ate the bird, still remained faithful to the old tradition, asserting that that lion's spirit must have been broken by captivity : scimus quam vim habeat consuetudo ; cum diu in galli vicinia detentus esset, quid mirum, si eum ferre didicerit, &c. !

Paus. ii. 34. 2 ; at Methana (Troezene) a Cock with white wings was torn in two by two men as a charm to protect the vines from the wind Λίψ, cf. J. G. Frazer, Folk-lore, i. 163, 1890. See on Sacrifices of the Cock, Sir J. G. Dalyell's Darker Superstitions of Scotland, 1835 ; Sir S. Baker, Nile Sources, pp. 327, 335, &c., &c.

On ἀλεκτρυομαντεία, see Lucian's Gallus, De Dea Syr. xlviii, Cic. De Div. ii, Plin. x. (21) 24 ; cf. Mém. Acad. Inscr. vii. 23, xii. 49 ; Hopf, Thierorakel, pp. 161-163.

How some cannot abide a cock or a hen, Plut. fr. viii. 10 (12. 23).

The Cock as a weather-prophet, Ael. vii. 7, Plut. Mor. 129 A, Theophr. De Sign. i. 17, Arat. Progn. 960 (228), Geopon. i. 3, 8.

How the flesh of a fowl absorbs molten gold, Plin. xxix. 25.

Is hostile to ἀτταγᾶς, Ael. vi. 45.

Proverb and Fable.

ἀλεκτρυόνος κοιλίαν ἔχειν, Ar. Vesp. 794 (i.e. the stomach of an ostrich, to swallow pebbles), cf. Suid.

ἀλέκτωρ πίνει καὶ οὐκ οὐρεῖ, Suid. q. v.

λήθουσι γάρ τοι κἀνέμων διέξοδοι θήλειαν ὄρνιν, πλὴν ὅταν τόκος παρῇ, Soph. fr. 424.

ΑΛΕΚΤΡΥΩΝ (*continued*).

κοινὸς Ἀθηναίων ἀλέκτωρ, descriptive of a bombastic talker, Demadas ap. Athen. iii. 99 D.

ἔπτηξ' ἀλέκτωρ δοῦλον ὡς κλίνας πτερόν, Phrynichus ap. Plut. Amator. xviii (Mor. 762 F); whence Ar. Vesp. 1490 πτήσσει Φρύνιχος ὥς τις ἀλέκτωρ.

With metaphorical epithet διαυλοδρόμος, διὰ γὰρ τῆς αὐλῆς τρέχει, Artemid. iv. 24; cf. Ar. Av. 291.

Fable of the Eagle which carried off the Cock crowing over his victory, Aesop, Fab. 21. The Weasel and the argumentative Cock, ib. 14. The Cock and Thieves, ib. 195. The Cock and Dog, as wayfarers, ib. 225. The two Cocks and the Partridge, ib. 22. See also Babrius and Aesop *passim*.

Fable of the Weasel and the Hen; ὡς δὴ κατ' εὔνοιαν αὐτῆς νοσούσης, ὅπως ἔχει, πυνθανομένην· Καλῶς, εἶπεν, ἂν σὺ ἀποστῇς, Plut. De Frat. Am. xix.

How the plumage of the Cock outshines the raiment of Croesus in all his glory, φυσικῷ γὰρ ἄνθει κεκόσμηται καὶ μυρίῳ καλλίονι, Solon ap. Diog. L. i. 2. 4.

Representations.—The oldest Coins with the Cock are those of Himera and Dardanus (Imhoof-Bl. and K. pl. v. 38-42) and of Carystus (B. M. C., Central Greece, p. 100, pl. xviii), all of the early fifth century. They recall the Indian *Gallus Sonneratii* (cf. J. P. Six, in Imhoof-Bl. p. 35), or rather the *Gallus ferrugineus* or *bankiva* of Northern India. Cf. also Blyth's note (Ibis, 1867, p. 157) on fowls sculptured on the Lycian marbles (c. 600 B.C.). See also Conze, Ann. de l'Inst., 1870, p. 280, on a Cock represented on an ancient relief of Dionysus and Semele (?), B.C. 580-540. In regard to Himera, it is noteworthy that Pindar's twelfth Olympian Ode, in which the Cock is mentioned, was addressed to Ergoteles, an inhabitant of Himera (cf. Buckton, N. and Q. (4) iii. 131).

The Cock with the Lion is early and frequent on coins of Asia Minor: with Athena on coins of Leucas, Corinth, Dardanus; also on coins of Ithaca, Zacynthus, Argos, &c.

On a statue of Athene, Paus. vi. 26 (v. supra); on a statue of Apollo, to indicate sunrise, Plut. De Pyth. Orac. xii. 574 (Mor. 488. 30). On the shield of Idomeneus, Paus. v. 25 (v. supra).

See also s. vv. βρητός, ἤϊκανός, κίκκος, κολοίφρυξ, κόττος, κώκαλον, ματτύης, νέβραξ, ὀρτάλιχος, σέρκος, χαλκιδικός, ψήληξ.

ΑΛΙΑΈΤΟΣ *s.* **ἁλιαίετος.** A Sea-eagle.

Arist. H. A. ix. 32, 619 ἔχουσιν αὐχένα τε μέγαν καὶ παχὺν καὶ πτερὰ καμπύλα, οὐροπύγιον δὲ πλατύ· οἰκοῦσι δὲ περὶ θάλατταν καὶ ἀκτάς, ἁρπάζοντες δὲ καὶ οὐ δυνάμενοι φέρειν πολλάκις καταφέρονται εἰς βυθόν. viii. 3, 593 b περὶ τὴν θάλατταν διατρίβει καὶ τὰ λιμναῖα κόπτει. [Here κόπτει seems

ΑΛΙΑΕΤΟΣ (*continued*).

meaningless and may be an interpolation; cf. the next reference.] ix. 34, 620 ὀξυωπέστατος μέν ἐστι, καὶ τὰ τέκνα ἀναγκάζει ἔτι ψιλὰ ὄντα πρὸς τὸν ἥλιον βλέπειν, καὶ τὸν μὴ βουλόμενον κόπτει καὶ στρέφει, καὶ ὁποτέρου ἂν ἔμπροσθεν οἱ ὀφθαλμοὶ δακρύσωσιν, τοῦτον ἀποκτείνει, τὸν δ' ἕτερον ἐκτρέφει. [The same story, s. v. ἀετός, in Ael. H. A. ii. 26, also Plin. N. H. x. 3, and in Gesner, &c.] ζῇ θηρεύων τοὺς περὶ τὴν θάλατταν ὄρνιθας, κ.τ.λ. Arist. De Mirab. 60, 835 ἐκ τοῦ ζεύγους τῶν ἀετῶν θάτερον τῶν ἐγγόνων ἁλιάετος γίνεται παραλλάξ, &c., cf. Dion. De Av. ii. 1. Mentioned also Ar. Av. 891, Eur. fr. 637 ὁρῶ δ' ἐπ' ἀκταῖς νομάδα κυματοφθόρον ἁλιάετον: Opp. Hal. i. 425 κρατεροί θ' ἁλιαίετοι ἁρπακτῆρες, &c.

See also Nonn. Dion. xlii. 531, where ἁλιάετος, associated with Poseidon, seizes a dove from the clutches of κίρκος, φειδομένοις ὀνύχεσσι μετάρσιον ὄρνιν ἀείρων. Cf. Sil. Ital. Punic. iv. 105.

A good omen to fishermen, Dion. De Avib. ii. 1.

On the fabled metamorphosis of Nisus or Pandareus see Ovid, Met. viii. 146, xii. 560; Boios ap. Anton. Lib. c. xi; Hygin. Fab. 98; Virg.(?) Ciris 536, and Keller, op. c. p. 259.

Arist. H. A. ix. 32, 619 is apparently descriptive of the Osprey, *Pandion Haliaëtus*, with which bird ἁλιάετος is commonly identified by mediaeval and modern commentators; but the description of the chase after sea-birds (ix. 620) applies rather to *Aquila naevia*, or *Hal. albicilla* (Sundevall). A Sea-eagle is very frequently alluded to under the generic name ἀετός, e.g. Pind. N. v. 21 πέραν πόντοιο πάλλοντ' αἰετοί: Soph. Oen. fr. 423, ap. Ar. Av. 1337 γενοίμαν αἰετὸς ὑψιπέτας, ὡς ἂν ποταθείην ὑπὲρ ἀτρυγέτου γλαυκᾶς ἐπ' οἶδμα λίμνας: Theocr. xiii. 24.

An Eagle with a fish is frequent on coins, e.g. Acragas (Imhoof-Bl. and K. pl. iv. 31), Sinope (ibid. v. 11, 12), and many other towns especially in the Black Sea and Hellespont (Keller, op. c. p. 262).

In all the above references, as in most passages relating to the Eagle, a mystical and symbolic meaning outweighs the zoological. The poem of Ciris is of great importance for the understanding of the myth. It is noteworthy how many birds, or names associated with birds, occur, with more or less obscure significance, in this poem; to wit, Procne, the Daulian maids, Pandion, the *Anser Ledae*, Haliaetus or Nisus, and lastly Ciris. I accept the theory that we have here to do with an elaborate Sun and Moon myth. The golden or purple lock in Nisus' hair (cui splendidus ostro Inter honoratos medio de vertice canos Crinis inhaerebat, Ov. Met. viii. 8, cf. Ciris 122, Apollod. ii. 4. 5), recalls, on the one hand, the Samson-legend (as we are expressly told by Tzetzes in Lyc. 648), and on the other, the crest of the solar ἔποψ or *picus*, both of which birds appear in the version of the legend given by Boios. The name Nisus is akin to *nesher*, *nisr*, an eagle (vide

ΑΛΙΑΕΤΟΣ (*continued*).

s. v. ἀετός), and Nisus or 'Αλιάετος plunges, like the setting Sun, into the sea. Ciris, Κεῖρις (with which I believe κείρυλος or κήρυλος to be connected), or Scylla is the Moon (cf. Porphyr. De Abst. iii. 17), which, as the watery goddess, appears in some forms of the legend as a fish. The last lines of the poem Ciris are of peculiar importance, where the mutual pursuit and flight of Haliaetus and Ciris are described, and compared with the alternate appearance and disappearance of the opposite constellations of Scorpio and Orion: Quacunque illa levem fugiens secat aethera pennis, Ecce inimicus atrox magno stridore per auras Insequitur Nisus: qua se fert Nisus ad auras, Illa levem fugiens raptim secat aethera pennis: it is the Moon in opposition, the Moon at the full, which (strictly speaking, at the sacred season of the equinox) sets and rises as the Sun rises and sets. Cf. also Cornutus, p. 72 L (teste Keller) κυνηγίᾳ δ᾽ ἔοικε καὶ τὸ μὴ διαλείπειν αὐτὴν ὁτὲ μὲν διώκουσαν τὸν ἥλιον ὁτὲ δὲ φεύγουσαν . . . οὐχ ἑτέρα δ᾽ οὖσα αὐτῆς ἡ Ἑκάτη, &c. The full understanding of the stories of ἀηδών, Procne, Philomela, and the whole Tereus-legend, depends on the further elucidation of this myth. Were it not for the comparison drawn with Scorpio and Orion, we might be rather disposed to refer the description to the Moon in the last quarter, stationed in advance of and as it were in flight before the Sun. The same four lines occur in Virg. Georg. i. 406–409, where I venture to think they are out of place and keeping.

ΆΛΙΑ´ΠΟΔΑ· τὸν κέπφον, ἢ θαλάττιον ὄρνιν . . . Hesych. (*verb. dub.*).

ΆΛΙΠΟΡΦΥΡΙ´Σ. A bird, doubtless the **Halcyon**.

Ibyc. fr. 8 (13) ap. Athen. ix. 388 D, according to Hermann and Schneidewin. Others read λαθιπορφυρίδες, v. Bergk, P. Lyric. Gr. iii. p. 239. Cf. Alcman 12 (26) ἁλιπόρφυρος εἴαρος ὄρνις (vide s. v. **κήρυλος**), whence Tennyson 'The sea-blue bird of March' (on which, see Whitley Stokes and others, Academy xxv. 1884; also Tennyson in Nature Notes, i. p. 93, ii. p. 173, where the Laureate alters the epithet). I am not inclined to admit that ἁλιπόρφυρος means *sea-blue*, nor that it is anything so simple as a mere colour-epithet; cf. **ἁλιάετος**.

ἈΛΚΥΩ´Ν s. ἀλκυών. Also ἀλκυονίς (Ap. Rhod. i. 1085, Epigr. Gr. 205 &c.), and ἀλκίων, Hesych. Cretan αὐκυών, Hesych. On the aspirate, see Förstemann, Curt. Zeitschr. iii. 48. Not from ἅλς: cf. Lat. *alc*-edo.

Probably connected with O. P. *halak* or *harac* the Sun, and so akin to ἀλεκτρυών and ἤλεκτρον, also to Ἡρακλῆς and to many other proper names, e. g. *Alc-inous*.

The **Halcyon**, a symbolic or mystical bird, early identified with the
Kingfisher, *Alcedo ispida*, L. The Kingfisher is called, in Mod.

ΑΛΚΥΩΝ (continued).

Gk., ψαροφάγος, also (Heldr.) σαρδελοφάγος, μπιρμπίλι της θαλάσσης, and (in Acarnania) βασιλοπούλι.

First mentioned in Simon. fr. 12 (ap. Arist. H. A. v. 8, 542 b, Poet. Lyr. Gr., Bergk p. 874, vide infra); Alcman 26 (12), ap. Antig. Mirab. 27; and Ibycus fr. 8 (13) ἀλκυόνες τανυσίπτεροι.

Description.—Arist. H. A. ix. 14, 616 ἡ δ' ἀλκυών ἐστι μὲν οὐ πολλῷ μείζων στρουθοῦ, τὸ δὲ χρῶμα καὶ κυανοῦν ἔχει καὶ χλωρὸν καὶ ὑποπόρφυρον· μεμιγμένως δὲ τοιοῦτον τὸ σῶμα πᾶν καὶ αἱ πτέρυγες καὶ τὰ περὶ τὸν τράχηλον, οὐ χωρὶς ἕκαστον τῶν χρωμάτων· τὸ δὲ ῥύγχος ὑπόχλωρον μέν, μακρὸν δὲ καὶ λεπτόν. viii. 3, 593 b τὸ τῶν ἀλκυόνων δὲ γένος πάρυδρόν ἐστιν· τυγχάνει δ' αὐτῶν ὄντα δύο εἴδη. καὶ ἡ μὲν φθέγγεται, καθιζάνουσα ἐπὶ τῶν δονάκων, ἡ δ' ἄφωνος· ἔστι δ' αὕτη μείζων· τὸ δὲ νῶτον ἀμφότεραι κυανοῦν ἔχουσιν. [Cf. Plin. x. 47. Two species occur in Greece, *A. (Ceryle) rudis*, L., the Spotted Kingfisher (Mod. Gk. ἄσπρον ψαροφάγον, v. d. Mühle), principally near the coast, and *A. ispida*, the Common Kingfisher. Sundevall points out that *A. rudis* has not τὸ νῶτον κυανοῦν, and suggests *A. smyrnensis*, which does not now occur in Greece (Krüper) but in Asia Minor. Neither of these birds can sing, any more than the common Kingfisher, and the attempt is hopeless to identify the second Aristotelian species with either. The whole matter is confused and mystical.]

On the 'song' of the Halcyon, cf. Tymnes ii (Gk. Anthol. i. p. 256) ὦ παρόμοιον ἀλκυόσιν τὸν σὸν φθόγγον ἰσωσάμενον: Pindar fr. 62 (34) ap. Schol. Apoll. Rhod. i. 1086 (q. v.) εὐλόγως δὲ ὅσσαν εἶπε τὴν ἀλκυόνος φωνήν: cf. Dion. De Avib. ii. 7 τῶν ἀλκυόνων δ' οὐκ ἄν εἴποι τις εἰς φωνὴν ὄρνεον ἥδιον. Its plaintive and melancholy note; Eur. I. in T. 1089 ὄρνις, ἃ παρὰ πετρίνας, πόντου δειράδας, ἀλκυών, ἔλεγον οἶτον ἀείδεις: imitated Ar. Ran. 1309 ἀλκυόνες αἳ παρ' ἀενάοις θαλάσσης κύμασι στωμύλλετε. Cf. Il. ix. 563 μήτηρ Ἀλκυόνος πολυπενθέος οἶτον ἔχουσα: Mosch. iii. 40 Ἀλκυόνος δ' οὐ τόσσον ἐπ' ἄλγεσιν ἴαχε Κῆυξ. Opp. Halieut. i. 424 στονόεντά τε φῦλα ἀλκυόνων. Epigr. in Marm. Oxon. iii. p. 111 (lxxi) μήτηρ δὲ ἡ δύστηνος ὀδύρεται οἷά τις ἄκταις Ἀλκυονίς, γοεροῖς δάκρυσι μυρομένα. See also Lucian in Alcyone, Philostr. Imagg. 362 K, Plut. Utr. Anim., Ov. Met. xi, Trist. v. 1. 60, Her. xviii. 81, &c., &c.; cf. also Eumath. De Hysm. et H. L. x. p. 448 τὴν γλῶτταν ἀλκυόνες πολυπενθέστεραι, ἀηδόνες θρηνητικώτεραι, αὐτῆς Νιόβης μιμούμεναι τὸ πολύδακρυ, πρὸς θρῆνον ἐρίζουσαι. According to the Scholia in Ar. Aves, Hom. Il. ix, Theocr. Id. vii ἐθρήνει τῶν ᾠῶν αὐτῆς ἐν τῇ θαλάσσῃ κλωμένων.

How the females carry the old males on their backs, Ael. vii. 17; cf. Plut. Utr. Anim., Antig. Hist. Mirab. 27. Cf. also Alcman (ap. Antig. l. c.) βάλε δή, βάλε κηρύλος εἴην, ὅς τ' ἐπὶ κύματος ἄνθος ἅμ' ἀλκυόνεσσι ποτῆται: imitated in Ar. Av. 251 ὧν τ' ἐπὶ πόντιον οἶδμα θαλάσσης φῦλα μετ' ἀλκυόνεσσι πυταται.

ΑΛΚΥΩΝ (*continued*).

Beloved of the Sea-nymphs, Theocr. vii. 59, cf. Virg. Georg. i. 399. Associated with Pallas, Antip. Sidon. xxvi, Gk. Anth. ii. p. 12 ἱστῶν Παλλάδος ἀλκυόνα (the shuttle, from its swift flash of colour): with Hera, Pindar fr. l. c.
With ep. ξουθός, Mnasalc. viii (Gk. Anthol. i. p. 124), [vide s. v. ἱππαλεκτρυών].

The Nest.—Arist. H. A. v. 8, 542 b τίκτει περὶ τροπὰς τὰς χειμερινάς· διὸ καὶ καλοῦνται ὅταν εὐδιειναὶ γένωνται αἱ τροπαί, ἀλκυονίδες ἡμέραι ἑπτὰ μὲν πρὸ τροπῶν, ἑπτὰ δὲ μετὰ τροπάς, καθάπερ καὶ Σιμωνίδης ἐποίησεν, "ὡς ὁπόταν χειμέριον κατὰ μῆνα πινύσκῃ Ζεὺς ἤματα τεσσαρακαίδεκα, λαθάνεμόν τέ μιν ὥραν καλέουσιν ἐπιχθόνιοι, ἱερὰν παιδοτρόφον ποικίλας ἀλκυόνος." γίνονται δ' εὐδιειναί, ὅταν συμβῇ νοτίους γίνεσθαι τὰς τροπάς, τῆς Πλειάδος βορείου γενομένης. λέγεται δ' ἐν ἑπτὰ μὲν ἡμέραις ποιεῖσθαι τὴν νεοττιάν, ἐν δὲ ταῖς λοιπαῖς ἑπτὰ ἡμέραις τίκτειν τὰ νεόττια καὶ ἐκτρέφειν. περὶ μὲν οὖν τοὺς ἐνταῦθα τόπους οὐκ ἀεὶ συμβαίνει γίνεσθαι ἀλκυονίδας ἡμέρας περὶ τὰς τροπάς, ἐν δὲ τῷ Σικελικῷ πελάγει σχεδὸν ἀεί. τίκτει δ' ἡ ἀλκυὼν περὶ πέντε ᾠά. ... πάντων δὲ σπανιώτατον ἰδεῖν ἀλκυόνα ἐστίν· σχεδὸν γὰρ περὶ Πλειάδος δύσιν καὶ τροπὰς ὁρᾶται μόνον, καὶ ἐν τοῖς ὑφόρμοις πρῶτον ὅσον περιπταμένη περὶ τὸ πλοῖον ἀφανίζεται εὐθύς, διὸ καὶ Στησίχορος τοῦτον τὸν τρόπον ἐμνήσθη περὶ αὐτῆς. (Schneider conjectures that this last refers to an Argonautic legend, cf. Apoll. Rhod. i. 1085 and Schol.) The Nest further described, ib. ix. 14, 616 παρομοία ταῖς σφαίραις ταῖς θαλαττίαις ἐστὶ καὶ ταῖς καλουμέναις ἁλοσάχναις, πλὴν τοῦ χρώματος· τὴν δὲ χρόαν ὑπόπυρρον ἔχουσιν, κ.τ.λ. καὶ κόπτοντι μὲν σιδηρίῳ ὀξεῖ οὐ ταχὺ διακόπτεται, ἅμα δὲ κόπτοντι καὶ ταῖς χερσὶ θραύοντι ταχὺ διαθρύεται, ὥσπερ ἡ ἁλοσάχνη.... δοκεῖ δὲ μάλιστα ἐκ τῶν ἀκανθῶν τῆς βελόνης. A lengthy description in Ael. H. A. ix. 17 : see also Dion. De Avib. ii. 7; Plin. x. (32) 47, (33) 49; Plut. De Sol. Anim. xxxv; Aes. Fab. 29, &c. Cf. also Callim. xxxi (Gk. Anthol. i. p. 219) ὡς πάρος τίκτηται νοτερῆς ᾠεον ἀλκυόνος. The description in Plutarch ends as follows : ἐμοὶ δὲ πολλάκις ἰδόντι καὶ θιγόντι, παρίσταται λέγειν καὶ ᾄδειν ' Δήλῳ δή ποτε τοῖον Ἀπόλλωνος παρὰ ναῷ.'

On the **ἀλκυονίδες** or **ἀλκυόνειοι ἡμέραι**, 'when birds of calm sit brooding on the charmed wave,' see also Theocr. vii. 57 κἀλκυόνες στορεσεῦντι τὰ κύματα τάν τε θάλασσαν, τόν τε νότον τόν τ' εὖρον. Apollonid. xiii (Gk. Anthol. ii. p. 121) εἰ καὶ ἐν ἀλκυόνων ἤμασι κλαυσόμεθα, ἀλκυόνων, αἷς πόντος ἀεὶ στηρίξατο κῦμα, νήνεμον. Ar. Av. 1594, Schol. in Ar. Ran. 1344, Ael. i. 36, Philoch. 180, Plut. Sol. Anim. p. 983, Quaest. Graec. pp. 1809, 1810, Apoll. Rhod. i. 1086, Plin. x. (32) 47, xviii. (26) 62, xxxii. (8) 27, Aul. Gell. iii. 10, Sil. Ital. xiv. 275, Plaut. Poen. 145, Casina, prol. 26, Diosc. iv. 136, Alciphr. i. 1, Lucian Halc. 2, Ovid Met. xi. 745, Colum. xi. 2, Dion. De Avib. ii. 7, Carm. De Philom. 383. On the number of the Halcyon days, see, in addition to the above, Suidas, according to whom Simonides made them eleven (v. supra), Dema-

ΑΛΚΥΩΝ (*continued*).

goras seven, and Philochorus nine. See also references in Bochart, Hieroz. ii. 861.

On the myth of Alcyone and Ceyx, cf. Il. ix. 563 (where the *bird* is not mentioned, but cf. Heyne, *in loc.*), Lucian, Halcyon. 2, where Alcyone and Ceyx descend from the Morning Star, Ovid, Met. xi. 410, Apollod. I. vii. 4, Serv. ad Virg. Georg. i. 399, Lutat. ad Stat. Theb. ix. 361, Tzetz. ad Lyc. p. 69, &c.

The myth of the Halcyon days is unexplained. The above statements have no zoological significance: the Kingfisher neither breeds at four months old, nor lays five eggs (but rather six or seven), nor nests in the winter season, nor on the sea. I conjecture that the story originally referred to some astronomical phenomenon, probably in connexion with the Pleiades, of which constellation Alcyone is the principal star. In what appears to have been the most vigorous period of ancient astronomy (not later than 2000 B.C., but continuing long afterwards to influence legend and nomenclature), the sun rose at the vernal equinox in conjunction with the Pleiad, in the sign Taurus: the Pleiad is in many languages associated with bird-names (cf. Engl. 'hen-and-chickens,' see also s. v. μέροψ), and I am inclined to take the bird on the bull's back in coins of Eretria, Dicaea, and Thurii for the associated constellation of the Pleiad. (Note, as a coincidence, the relation of Alcyoneus to the heavenly Bull in Pind. I. v. 47; ubi Schol. βουβόταν δὲ τὸν βουκόλον φησί, παρ' οὗ τᾶς Ἡλίου βοῖς ἀπήλασε ...) The particular bird thus associated with Taurus may vary; on some of the above-mentioned coins, where it is certainly not a Kingfisher, it is taken by Canon Tristram (Ibis, 1893, p. 215) to be a Tern; to me it seems rather to be the Swallow, figuring as the bird of spring; (on the cognate symbolism of the Dove, see s. v. πέλεια). The Halcyon is said by Canon Tristram (l. c.) to have been the sacred bird of Eretria; I cannot find a direct statement of the fact. Suidas definitely asserts that the Pleiades were called Ἀλκυόνες. At the winter solstice, in the same ancient epoch, the Pleiad culminated at night-fall in mid-heaven, a phenomenon possibly referred to in the line νὺξ μακρὴ καὶ χεῖμα μέσην δ' ἐπὶ Πλειάδα δύνει. This culmination, between three and four months after the heliacal rising of the Pleiad in Autumn, was, I conjecture, symbolized as the nesting of the Halcyon. Owing to the antiquity and corruption of the legend, it is impossible to hazard more than a very guarded conjecture; but that the phenomenon was in some form an astronomic one I have no doubt. [It might for instance refer more directly to the Sun, which anciently began its annual course at the spring equinox when in conjunction with the Pleiads, and which at the winter season, when in the lowest part of its course, might be said to brood upon the sea, only beginning its ascent a week after the actual

ΑΛΚΥΩΝ *(continued).*

tropic (cf. Ptolemy, ap. Petav. iii. 54, Kal. Jan.: Sol elevari incipit)]. The risings and settings of the Pleiads and of the Dogstar were apparently the chief landmarks of the ancient year, and in this connexion the comparison with ἀλοσάχνη is also suggestive. I take ἀλοσάχνη to be a corruption, by 'Volksetymologie,' of the Egyptian σολεχήν, the Dog-star. Cf. Chalcid. in Timaeum Plat. f. cxxiv, ed. Fabr., Cum hanc eandem stellam ἀστροκύνον quidam, Aegyptii vero σολεχήν vocant (v. Jablonsk. in Steph. Thes. and cf. Leemans in Horap. i. 3). The common Egyptian name for the Dog-star is *Sothi*, and of this we read in Plut. De Isid. p. 375 Σωθὶ Αἰγυπτιστὶ σημαίνει κύησιν ἢ τὸ κύειν.

The birds anciently associated with the season of the vernal equinox are, with the exception of the Nightingale, associated with St. Martin in modern times; viz. the House-martin or Martlet (cf. χελιδών), the Harrier (cf. κίρκος), Fr. oiseau St. Martin, and the Kingfisher, Fr. martin-pêcheur. It is precisely the same birds, with the addition of the solar Hoopoe and Woodpecker, and with the substitution of ἁλιάετος (q. v.) for κίρκος, that figure together in the story of the metamorphosis of Pandareus; Boios ap. Anton. Lib. Met. xi.

In the calendars ascribed to Geminus (?), Columella and Ptolemy (?), the Halcyon days are placed in the end of February or beginning of March. I cannot account for this discrepancy, which is clearly at variance with the older tradition; unless indeed the phrase had lost its meaning and was simply transferred to the season of the migration of birds.

See also s. vv. ἀηδών, ἀλιπορφυρίς, κηρύλος, κῆυξ.

Note.—On the mystical element in the stories of ἀλκυών and ἀηδών cf. Lucian, Halc. οὐκ ἂν ἔχοιμεν εἰπεῖν βεβαίως οὔτ' Ἀλκυόνων πέρι, οὔτ' Ἀηδόνων· κλέος δὲ μύθων, οἷον παρέδοσαν πατέρες, τοιοῦτο καὶ παισὶν ἐμοῖς, ὦ ὄρνι θρήνων μελῳδέ, παραδώσω τῶν σῶν ὕμνων πέρι, καί σου τὸν εὐσεβῆ καὶ φίλανδρον ἔρωτα πολλάκις ὑμνήσω.

ἌΜΑΛΛΟΣ· πέρδιξ, Πολυρρήνιοι, Hesych.

ἈΜΠΕΛΊΣ. An unknown bird. Ar. Av. 304. Cf. Poll. vi. 52.

ἈΜΠΕΛΊΩΝ. An unknown small bird mentioned together with ἀστήρ (q. v.), with epithet κουφότατος. Taken as identical with ἀμπελίς: ἀμπελίδες ἃς νῦν ἀμπελίωνας καλοῦσιν, J. Pollux, vi. 52; cf. Lob. Prol. p. 49. In Mod. Gk. ἀμπελουργός is the Black-headed Bunting, called also κρασοπούλι, μεθύστρα.

ἈΝΑΓΚΗΣ, s. ἀνάκης· ὀρνεόν τι Ἰνδικόν, ὅμοιον ψάρῳ, Hesych. The name is strongly suggestive of the Arabic and Syrian Anka or

ΑΝΑΓΚΗΣ (*continued*).

Onka, which is said to be identical with Simurgh, the magical bird of the Persians, and which is believed further to come into relation with Athene *Ογκα; cf. Von Hammer-Purgstall, Wien. Jahrb. d. Lit. xcvii. 126, Creuzer, Symb. iv. 397, Boch. Hieroz. ii. 812, 852. Vide s. v. ὄκνος.

ΆΝΘΟΣ. An unknown small bird. The name does not occur in Mod. Gk., and like so many of the bird-names mentioned in a non-scientific or fabulous sense, is probably an exotic.

Arist. H. A. viii. 3, 592 b ὄρνις σκωληκοφάγος, μέγεθος ὅσον σπίζα. ix. 1, 609 b ἵππῳ πολέμιος· ἐξελαύνει γὰρ ὁ ἵππος ἐκ τῆς νομῆς, πόαν γὰρ νέμεται ὁ ἄνθος. ἐπίργεμος δ' ἐστὶ καὶ οὐκ ὀξυωπός· μιμεῖται γὰρ τοῦ ἵππου τὴν φωνήν, καὶ φοβεῖ ἐπιπετόμενος καὶ ἐξελαύνει, ὅταν δὲ λάβῃ, κτείνει αὐτόν. οἰκεῖ δ' ὁ ἄνθος παρὰ ποταμὸν καὶ ἕλη, χρόαν δ' ἔχει καλὴν καὶ εὐβίοτός ἐστι. ix. 1, 610 and 12, 615 hostile to ἀκανθίς and αἴγιθος· αἰγίθου καὶ ἄνθου αἷμα οὐ συμμίγνυται ἀλλήλοις : cf. Plin. x. 74 (95). With the above fabulous account, cf. Ael. H. A. v. 48, vi. 19 ἰδιάζει δὲ ταῖς μιμήσεσι τῶν τοιούτων ὅ,τε ἄνθος καλούμενος . . . καὶ ὁ μὲν ἄνθος ὑποκρίνεται χρεμέτισμα ἵππου. Also Plin. x. (47) 52 ; see also Boios ap. Anton. Lib. c. 7, where Anthus is a son of Autonous and Hippodameia, killed by his father's horses, and metamorphosed into the bird ἄνθος. In Phile 705 it is the fish ἀνθίας that is said to be hostile to the horse.

Note.—As indicative of the mythical, fabulous, and probably exotic element in the above, compare the accounts of ἄνθος and ἀκανθίς (? ἀκ-ανθ-ίς), the former σκωληκοφάγος, εὐβίοτος, χρόαν καλός, ἵππῳ πολέμιος : the latter ἀκανθοφάγος, κακόβιος, κακόχροος, ὄνῳ πολέμιος, &c.: ἀκανθίς and αἰγι(ν)θος are perhaps two corruptions of the same word. Though the bird cannot be identified, and though it is more than doubtful whether it was ever known to the Greeks, yet Sundevall's identification of ἄνθος as the Yellow Wagtail, *Motacilla flava*, L., deserves to be recorded. This hypothetical identification is based on the brilliant colour (which according to v. d. Mühle is more brilliant in Greece even than in N. Europe) and on the localities frequented. The Yellow Wagtail frequently consorts with the cattle at pasture, feeding on flies ; it may indeed have become associated with the above fable, the origin of which, however, is doubtless more deep-seated and obscure.

ἈΝΟΠΑΓΑ. A bird associated with Athene, possibly the **Night-Heron**.

Od. i. 320 ἀπέβη γλαυκῶπις Ἀθήνη, ὄρνις δ' ὡς ἀνοπαῖα διέπτατο. For various explanations and Scholia, see Steph. Thes. (ed. 1821), Lidd. and Sc., &c. According to Rumpf, De aedibus Homericis, ii. p. 32, Giessen, 1857, Netolicka, Naturh. aus Hom. p. 11, Buchholz, Hom.

ΑΝΟΠΑΙΑ (*continued*).

Realien, p. 126, the **Swallow**, from its passing in and out through the smoke-hole, παρὰ τὸ διατρίβειν ἐν ταῖς ὀπαῖς (Herodian). Cf. Hesych. ἀνοπαῖα· ὀρνέου ὄνομα καὶ εἶδος, ἢ ἀνὰ τὴν ὀπὴν τῆς θύρας, ἢ ἀνὰ τὴν θυρίδα, ἢ ἀφανής (MS. ἄφωνος). See also Ameis in loc., Doederlein, Hom. Gloss, &c.

Bochart, Hieroz. ii. 337, suggests (not for the first time, for the statement is made in early Hebrew dictionaries) a connexion with Hebr. אֲנָפָה *anaphah*, which he supposed to be a species of eagle, partly perhaps to make it fit in with the interpretation, common in his time, of ἀνοπαῖα. But according to Lewysohn (Zool. d. Talmuds, p. 109), with whom Tristram agrees, *anaphah* is rightly translated **Heron** (Lev. xi. 19), which seems to me to lend support to the hypothesis that ἀνοπαῖα is identical with it. Cf. ἐρωδιός, Il. x. 274.

ἌΝΤΑΡ· ἀετός, ὑπὸ Τυρρηνῶν, Hesych.

ἈΝΤΙ´ΨΥΧΟΙ· οὕτως καλοῦνται οἱ Μέμνονες ὄρνιθες (q. v.), Hesych.

ἈΠΑΦΟ´Σ· ἔποψ τὸ ὄρνεον, Hesych. (Probably a Macedonian word, Schmidt in Hesych.; or more likely Egyptian, vide infra, s. v. ἔποψ).

ἌΠΟΥΣ. A bird of the swallow kind. Probably including the **Swift**, *Cypselus apus*, L., and *Hirundo rupestris*, Scop., the **Cliff Martin**; Mod. Gk. πετροχελιδόνι. Also for κύψελος, the **Sand Martin**.

Arist. H. A. i. 1, 487 b ὄρνις κακόπους (cf. Plin. xi. 47), εὔπτερος. φαίνεται ὁ μὲν ἄπους πᾶσαν ὥραν, ἡ δὲ δρεπανὶς ὅταν ὕσῃ τοῦ θέρους. Ib. ix. 30, 618 οἱ δ᾽ ἄποδες, οὓς καλοῦσί τινες κυψέλους ὅμοιοι ταῖς χελιδόσιν εἰσίν· οὐ γὰρ ῥᾴδιον διαγνῶναι πρὸς τὴν χελιδόνα, πλὴν τῷ τὴν κνήμην ἔχειν δασεῖαν. νεοττεύουσιν ἐν κυψελίσιν ἐκ πηλοῦ πεπλασμέναις μακραῖς, ὅσον εἴσδυσιν ἐχούσαις· ἐν στεγνῷ δὲ ποιεῖται τὰς νεοττιὰς ὑπὸ πέτραις καὶ σπηλαίοις, ὥστε καὶ τὰ θηρία καὶ τοὺς ἀνθρώπους διαφεύγειν. Cf. Plin. x. 39 (55) his quies nisi in nido nulla, &c.

The name is traditionally identified with the **Swift**, *Cypselus apus*, L. As regards the former passage (which is doubtfully authentic) it appears that *H. rupestris* is the only bird of the Swallow kind which is a permanent resident in Greece (Krüper p. 255, &c.), though Erhard (p. 46) says that Swifts winter in the Cyclades. The second passage is corrupt, and contains two different accounts of the nest (cf. Sundevall p. 130). *H. rupestris* builds solitarily, on the face of high cliffs (ὑπὸ πέτραις) (Krüper, l. c.). The other account (ἐν κυψελίσιν μακραῖς) seems to refer to the Sand Martin, vide s.v. κύψελος. Sundevall

ΑΝΟΠΑΙΑ—ΑΡΠΗ 35

ΑΠΟΥΣ (*continued*).

takes ἄπους to be the Swift: Aubert and Wimmer (p. 111) take it to be the House Martin (*Hirundo urbica* L.). The name πετροχελιδόνι applies in Mod. Gk. both to *H. rupestris* and to the Swift (Heldreich).

ἌΡΑΚΟΣ. An Etruscan word for a **Hawk**. ἄρακος· ἱέραξ, Τυρρηνοί, Hesych. Said to be a Lydian word, Jablonsk. in Steph. Thes. Cf. βάρβαξ.

ἌΡΑΜΟΣ. A name for a **Heron** = ἐρωδιός, Hesych.

ἈΡΓΙΌΠΟΥΣ, s. ἀργίπους. A Macedonian name for the **Eagle**, Hesych. Perhaps a corruption of αἰγίποψ, or perhaps of ἄρξιφος.

ἈΡΗΤΙΆΔΕΣ ὌΡΝΙΘΕΣ. Fabulous birds, which shot forth their feathers like arrows: doubtless an astronomical emblem. Apoll. Rhod. ii. 1035-1052. Cf. King's Ant. Gems p. 330.

ἈΡΝΕΥΤΉΡ. [Cf. Lat. *urinator*, a diver, Sk. *vári*, water (Curt.).] Supposed to mean a diving bird, diver or grebe (*Colymbus*). Perhaps only a professional diver. Cf. **δύπτης**.

Il. xvi. 742 ἀρνευτῆρι ἐοικώς. See also Il. xii. 385, Od. xii. 413.

ἌΡΞΙΦΟΣ. A Persian word for an **Eagle**, Hesych. (Pers. *karges*). Cf. ἀργιόπους.

ἌΡΠΑΣΟΣ. An unknown or fabulous bird; vide s. v. ἄρπη.

ἌΡΠΗ. (Perhaps from rt. of ἁρπ-άζω, L. *rap-io*.) An unknown or fabulous bird.

Il. xix. 350 ἄρπη εἰκυῖα τανυπτέρυγι, λιγυφώνῳ (Eustath. ζῷον θαλάσσιον, λάρῳ πολεμοῦν). Arist. H. A. ix. 1, 609-610 ἔτι οἱ ἀπὸ τῆς θαλάττης ζῶντες πολέμιοι ἀλλήλοις, υἱὸν βρένθος καὶ λάρος καὶ ἄρπη.... πίφιγξ καὶ ἄρπη καὶ ἰκτῖνος φίλοι. ix. 18, 617 πολέμιος δὲ τῇ ἄρπῃ ἡ φώυξ, καὶ γὰρ ἐκείνη ὁμοιοβίοτος. Ael. H. A. ii. 47 ἡ δὲ ὄρειος ἄρπη τῶν ὀρνίθων προσπεσοῦσα τοὺς ὀφθαλμοὺς ἀφαρπάζει. Cf. Dion. De Avib. i. 4. Plin. x. 95 (74) Dissident harpe et triorches accipiter. Harpe et milvus contra triorchem communibus inimicitiis. The wife and son of Cleinis are metamorphosed into the birds ἄρπη and ἄρπασος: Boios ap. Anton. Lib. Met. 20. According to Hesych., ἄρπη is Cretan for ἰκτῖνος.

Places ἰvý, κίσσος, in its nest for a charm, Ael. i. 35, Phile 729. Geopon. xv. 1.

The word is poetical. Dionysius (l. c.) refers to the Lämmergeier. Some mediaeval commentators (e. g. Gesner) take Harpe and Milvus (ἰκτῖνος) to be identical in Arist. and Plin. ll. cc., as does also Tzetzes, Chiliad. v. 413 ἰκτῖνος ὄρνις τίς ἐστιν, ὅνπερ καλοῦμεν ἄρπην, ἁρπάζων τὰ

D 2

ΑΡΠΗ (*continued*).

νεόττια τὰ τῶν ἀλεκτορίδων, and Sundevall makes Harpe the Black Kite, *Milvus ater*, or *M. parasiticus*. Aubert and Wimmer suspect ἅρπη to be a large Gull (*Larus*). For other hypotheses, vide Buchholz p. 137.

'ΑΣΒΗΝΟΙ'· ὄρνιθες, Hesych. Possibly akin to σπίνος.

'ΑΣΙΔΟΝ· ἐρωδιόν, Hesych. Heb. חסידה, *chasidah*, the Stork. Cf. Boch. Hieroz. ii. 321–326.

'ΑΣΚΑ'ΛΑΦΟΣ. An unknown bird, mentioned Arist. H. A. ii. 12 as possessing colic coeca (ἀποφυάδας).

Usually translated Owl, from the story of the Metamorphosis of Ascalaphus, Ovid, Met. v. 539 *Foedaque fit volucris, venturi nuncia luctus, Ignavus bubo, dirum mortalibus omen*. Cf. Apollodor. ii. p. 107 Ἀσκάλαφον οὖν Δημήτηρ ἐποίησεν ὦτον: Serv. ad Aen. iv. 462. The mystical aspect of the story is briefly indicated by Creuzer, Symbolik, iv. 378. [Quaenam sit avis, neque ex Aristotele neque ex Plinio aut ex Aeliano deprehendere potuimus. Sed Ovidius inter fabulas ostendit esse bubonis speciem: Scaliger in Arist.]

'ΑΣΚΑΛΩ'ΠΑΣ. (ἀσκόλοπας, Arist. MS. C^a). Probably identical with σκολόπαξ, q. v. **The Woodcock**, *Scolopax rusticola*.

Arist. H. A. ix. 26, 617 b ἐν τοῖς κήποις ἁλίσκεται ἕρκεσιν, τὸ μέγεθος ὅσον ἀλεκτορίς, τὸ ῥύγχος μακρόν, τὸ χρῶμα ὅμοιον ἀτταγῆνι· τρέχει δὲ ταχύ.

The Woodcock according to v. d. Mühle and Lindermayer is very abundant in Greece in November. Aubert and Wimmer rather identify ἀσκαλώπας with the Curlew.

'ΑΣΤΕΡΙ'ΑΣ.

I. An **Eagle** = χρυσάετος, Ael. ii. 39. In Arist. H. A. ix. 36, 620, mentioned as γένος ἱεράκων, and usually identified with the **Goshawk**.

Cf. Scaliger in Arist. p. 249: ἀστερίαν vertit Theodosius *stellarem*... ἀστερίαν igitur puto nostrum *asturem*: ut enim punctis quibusdam tanquam stellis totus pictus in pectore. This identification, though adopted by Sundevall, is inacceptable. ἀστερίας is said to be the largest of the eagles, and to feed on fawns, cranes, and in Crete, bulls: like χρυσάετος it seems to be used not of the actual bird but as a symbol, probably astronomical.

II. A bird of the Heron kind, supposed, for a similar and equally unsatisfactory reason, to be the **Bittern**, *Ardea stellaris*, L.

It is only mentioned in connexion with an Egyptian myth, probably relating to the Stork; and the name itself is in all probability foreign and corrupt (cf. ἄσιδον).

ΑΣΤΕΡΙΑΣ (*continued*).

Arist. H. A. ix. 1, 609 b, 18,617 τῶν ἐρωδιῶν γένος, ἐπικαλούμενος ὄκνος, μυθολογεῖται γενέσθαι ἐκ δούλων. Ael. H. A. v. 36 ὄνομά ἐστιν ὄρνιθος ἀστερίας, καὶ τιθασεύεταί γε ἐν τῇ Αἰγύπτῳ, καὶ ἀνθρώπου φωνῆς ἐπαίει. εἰ δέ τις αὐτὸν ὀνειδίζων δοῦλον εἴποι, ὁ δὲ ὀργίζεται· καὶ εἴ τις ὄκνον καλέσειεν αὐτόν, ὁ δὲ βρενθύεται καὶ ἀγανακτεῖ, ὡς καὶ ἐς τὸ ἀγεννὲς σκωπτόμενος καὶ ἐς ἀργίαν εὐθυνόμενος. Vide s. v. ἐρωδιός.

'ΑΣΤΗ'Ρ. A name for the **Goldfinch**, vide s. v. ἀκανθυλλίς.

Dion. De Avib. iii. 2 ἀστέρες οἷς ἐρυθρός τε κίκλος ἐστίν, ὥσπερ ἀστήρ, ἐπὶ ταῖς κεφαλαῖς. Arrives in spring with the North wind, and is caught with bird-lime.

'ΑΣΤΡΑΓΑΛΙ῀ΝΟΣ. An unknown small bird, mentioned along with the foregoing, with epithet ταχύς. Perhaps a synonym of ἀστήρ: Belon (cit. Bikélas) has It. *stragalino*=Goldfinch, but, according to Giglioli, the word is not known in any modern Italian dialect.

'ΑΣΤΡΑΛΟ'Σ· ὁ ψαρός, ὑπὸ Θετταλῶν, Hesych. Supposed to be akin to L. *stur-nu-s* (Curt.), L. *paru-s* (Fick), O. H. G. *sprá*, &c.

'ΑΣΦΑΛΟ'Σ. An unknown bird; Hesych. s. v. ἐνθύσκος.

'ΑΤΤΑΓΑ'Σ, *s.* ἀτταγᾶς, *s.* ἀτταγήν. Also ἀτταβυγάς, Hesych. (MSS. have ἀτταγής, ἀτταγίς, ἀταγή), and ταγηνάριον, Suid. Cf. Lob. Path. i. p. 142. Athen. 388 B notes the accent as an exception, and the plural ἀτταγαῖ, not ἀτταγῆνες; cf. Eustath. p. 854 τὸ παλαιὸν 'Ατταγαῖ μὲν 'Αττικῶς, 'Ατταγῆνες δὲ κοινῶς. Mod. Gk. ταγινάρι (Du Cange), ἀτταγινάρι (Sibthorpe ap. Walpole, Mem. rel. to Turkey, p. 262), λιβαδοπέρδιξ (Tournefort). Vide s. v. ταγήν. The word has been taken for an Egyptian one, from the phrase 'Ατταγᾶς Αἰγυπτίας, Clem. Alex. Paed. ii. 1. p. 140 ; cf. Sturzius De Dial. Aeg. p. 86, ap. Steph. Thes. p. clxxiii.

The Francolin, *Tetrao francolinus*, L. See Lilford, Ibis, 1862, p. 352.

Ar. Av. 247, 761 with ep. ποικίλος, περιποίκιλος or πτεροποίκιλος (cf. Meineke, in loc.) ; cf. Suid. ἔστι κατάστικτος ποικίλοις πτεροῖς· λέγεται δὲ ἐπὶ δούλων κατεστιγμένων. Ar. Ach. 875, common in Boeotia ; absent from Crete, praeterquam in Cydoniatarum regione, Plin. x. 58 (83). Arist. H. A. ix. 26, 617 ἀσκαλώπας τὸ χρῶμα ὅμοιον ἀτταγῆνι. ix. 49 B, 633 οὐ πτητικὸς ἀλλ' ἐπιγείος καὶ κονιστικός. Ael. H. A. iv. 42 τὸ ἴδιον ὄνομα ᾗ σθένει φωνῇ φθέγγεται καὶ ἀναμέλπει αὐτό. Ib. vi. 45 νοοῦσι δὲ ἄρα ἀτταγᾶς μὲν ἀλεκτρυόνι ἔχθιστα, ἀλεκτρυὼν δ' αὖ πάλιν ἀτταγᾷ. Socr. ap. Athen. ix. 387 f., how the ἀτταγᾶς in Egypt said in times of famine τρὶς τοῖς κακούργοις κακά (vide Casaub. in Athen. ii. p. 420, ed. 1600) : cf. Ael V. H. xv. 27. Alex. Mynd. in Athen. l. c. μικρῷ μὲν μείζων ἐστὶ πέρδικος, ὅλος

ΑΤΤΑΓΑΣ (continued).

δὲ κατάγραφος τὰ περὶ τὸ νῶτον, κεραμεοῦς τὴν χρόαν ὑποπυρρίζων μᾶλλον. θηρεύεται δὲ ὑπὸ κυνηγῶν διὰ τὸ βάρος καὶ τὴν τῶν πτερῶν βραχύτητα. (Cf. Dion. De Avib. iii. 10.) ἐστὶ δὲ κονιστικός, πολύτεκνός τε καὶ σπερμολόγος. Schol. in Ar. Av. 250 ὁ ἀτταγᾶς ὁ ἔχων τὸν λειμῶνα τοῦ Μαραθῶνος. τὰ γὰρ λιμνώδη καὶ ἕλεια χωρία καταβόσκεται ὁ ἀτταγᾶς. It is friendly with the stag, Opp. Cyneg. ii. 404.

Proverbs.—ἀτταγᾶς νουμηνίῳ [συνέρχεται], παροιμία ἐπὶ τῶν κλεπτῶν, Suid. s. v. ἀτταγᾶς, Hesych. s. v. νουμήνιος, Schol. Ar. Av. 762. Cf. Timon ap. Diog. L. ix. 16. 6, Paroem. Gr. i. p. 307, ii. pp. 16, 212 (Scaliger in Prov. metricis). Ar. Vesp. 257 τὸν πηλὸν ὥσπερ ἀτταγᾶς τυρβάσεις βαδίζων. Proverbial as a delicacy: Ar. Πελαργοῖς in Athen. 388 b ἀτταγᾶς ἥδιστον ἕψειν ἐν ἐπινικίοις κρέας. Phoenicid. 4. 509 κοὐδὲν ἦν τούτων πρὸς ἀτταγῆνα συμβαλεῖν τῶν βρωμάτων. Martial, xiii. 61 Inter sapores fertur alitum primus, Ionicarum gustus attagenarum. Cf. Ovid, F. vi. 175, Hor. Epod. ii. 54; Plin. x. 48; Apicius, De Re Coquin. vi. 3; Aul. Gell. Noct. Att. vii. 16, &c. Mentioned also, Hippon. fr. ap. Athen. l. c.

The Francolin does not now occur in Greece or Italy, though it is found in Crete, Cyprus, Sicily, Malta, and on the southern shores of the Black Sea (Lindermayer p. 125). On this account, Sundevall and others have disputed its identity with ἀτταγᾶς, and have identified the latter with various birds, especially *Perdix cinerea*, the Common (or Northern) Partridge; C. T. Newton, Cont. Rev. 1876, p. 92, taking it to be *Pterocles alchata*, a species of Sand-grouse. The descriptions, especially that of Alex. Myndius, point distinctly to the Francolin, and even Lindermayer does not doubt that the name is to be so interpreted, and that the bird was formerly abundant. The record by Sibthorpe of the modern Greek name, which I cannot find in more recent writers, suggests that the bird has only lately disappeared from Greece. According to Danford (Dresser, Birds of Europe, vii. p. 124) it is fast disappearing in Asia Minor also: likewise in Cyprus (Guillemard, The Field, Sept. 1892). The general disappearance of the Quail in recent years from England is a parallel case.

ΒΑΙ'ΒΥΚΟΣ· πελεκάνος Φιλητᾶς, Ἀμερίας [δὲ] βαύβυκος, Hesych.· For other readings, v. Steph. Thes. ii. coll. 40, 41, and Schmidt's Hesych. i. pp. 352, 366.

ΒΑΙΗ'Θ. An Egyptian name for a **Hawk**.

Horap. i. 7 ἀντὶ ψυχῆς ὁ ἱέραξ τάσσεται, ἐκ τῆς τοῦ ὀνόματος ἑρμηνείας· καλεῖται γὰρ παρ' Αἰγυπτίοις ὁ ἱέραξ, Βαϊήθ. τοῦτο δὲ τὸ ὄνομα διαιρεθέν, ψυχὴν σημαίνει καὶ καρδίαν· ἔστι γὰρ τὸ μὲν Βαϊ ψυχή, τὸ δὲ ηθ καρδία· ἡ δὲ καρδία κατ' Αἰγυπτίους ψυχῆς περίβολος, ὥστε σημαίνειν τὴν σύνθεσιν τοῦ ὀνόματος, ψυχὴν ἐγκαρδίαν· ἀφ' οὗ καὶ ὁ ἱέραξ διὰ τὸ πρὸς τὴν ψυχὴν συμ-

ΑΤΤΑΓΑΣ—ΒΕΛΛΟΥΝΗΣ

ΒΑΙΗΘ (*continued*).

παθεῖν, ὕδωρ οὐ πίνει τὸ καθόλου, ἀλλ' αἷμα, ᾧ καὶ ἡ ψυχὴ τρέφεται. Cf. Leemans in Horap. p. 151, and in particular Lauth, Sitzungsber. Bayer. Akad., 1876, p. 78; the hawk enters as a phonetic or alphabetic element into the hieroglyphic spelling of *baï* or *ba*, and in the second place becomes associated with the symbolic meaning of the word. I suspect that βαίβυκος is closely allied, especially as a bird like a pelican is figured instead of a hawk in an alternative spelling of the syllable *ba*. The Egyptian representation of the Soul as a Hawk is also mentioned by Chaeremon, ψυχή-ἥλιος-θεός=ἱέραξ; it, and the Harpy-figures which represent the disembodied soul are interesting in connexion with Plat. Phaedr. p. 246; cf. Jomard, Descr. de l'Ég. Antiq. vol. ii. pp. 366, 381, Bunsen, Egypt's Place in History, v. 135, R. Brown, jun., Dionys. Myth. i. 340, &c.

ΒΑ'Ρ[Β]ΑΞ· ἱέραξ, παρὰ Λίβυσι, Hesych. Cf. ἄρακος, βείρακες.

ΒΑΡΙ'ΤΗΣ. An unknown small bird. Dion. De Avib. iii. 2.

ΒΑΣΙΛΕΥ'Σ. A name for the **Wren**, Lat. *Regulus*.

Arist. H. A. viii. 3, 592 b, ix. 11, 615 a τροχίλος καλεῖται καὶ πρέσβυς καὶ βασιλεύς· διὸ καὶ τὸν ἀετὸν αὐτῷ, φασί, πολεμεῖν. Plin. Ep. i. 5, 14 regulus omnium bipedum nequissimus; cf. Plin. H. N. viii. 37. See also Carm. de philomela v. 42 Regulus atque merops et rubro pectore progne Consimili modulo zinzinulare sciunt. Vide s. vv. βασιλίσκος, πρέσβυς, ῥόβιλλος, τρίκκος, τροχίλος, τρωγλοδύτης, τύραννος and especially ὄρχιλος.

ΒΑΣΙΛΙ'ΣΚΟΣ. A name for the **Wren** = βασιλεύς.

Artemid. p. 234 Η τὰ δὲ μουσικὰ καὶ ἡδύφωνα φιλολόγους καὶ μουσικοῖς καὶ εὐφώνους, ὡς χελιδὼν καὶ ἀηδὼν καὶ βασιλίσκος καὶ τὰ ὅμοια. Cf. ῥόβιλλος. Fab. ἀετὸς καὶ βασιλίσκος, Plut. Mor. ii. 806 E.

ΒΑΣΚΑ'Σ. Ar. Av. 885. Vide s. v. βοσκάς.

ΒΑ'ΣΚΙΛΛΟΣ· κίσσα, Hesych. (A βάσκω, fortasse, ut loquax, Lob. Prol. p. 120.)

ΒΑΤΙ'Σ. An unknown bird.

Arist. H. A. viii. 3, 592 b ὄρνις σκωληκοφάγος. (Gaza translates *rubetra*, as if from βάτος, a name like our 'brambling,' and apparently supposed the bird to be the Stonechat, the *traquet* of Belon, to which bird, *Saxicola rubetra*, L., his name is still applied.)

ΒΑΤΥΡΡΗΓΑ'ΛΗ. A Lydian word for a **Kite**, ἰκτῖνος, Hesych.

ΒΕΙ'ΡΑΚΕΣ· ἱέρακες, Hesych. Possibly for ϝιέρακες.

ΒΕΛΛΟΥ'ΝΗΣ· τριόρχης, Λάκωνες, Hesych.

ΒΙ'ΤΤΑΚΟΣ. A Parrot. Vide s. v. ψίττακος.

ΒΟΣΚΑ'Σ, v. ll. βασκάς, φασκάς. A small Wild Duck; probably including the Teal (*Anas crecca*) and Garganey (*A. querquedula*), both common in Greece; and in Athenaeus also a larger species.

βοσκάς, Ar. Av. 885.

βοσκάς, Arist. H. A. viii. 3, 593 b mentioned among the heavier water-birds, ὅμοιος μὲν νήττῃ, τὸ δὲ μέγεθος ἐλάττων. Alex. Mynd. ap. Athen. ix. 52, 395 d ὁ μὲν ἄρρην κατάγραφος, ἔχουσι δὲ οἱ ἄρρενες σιμά τε καὶ ἐλάττονα τῇ συμμετρίᾳ τὰ ῥύγχα. ἔστι δὲ καὶ ἄλλο γένος βοσκάδων μεῖζον μὲν νήττης, ἔλαττον δὲ χηναλώπεκος.

φασκάς, Alex. Mynd. ibid. αἱ δὲ λεγόμεναι φασκάδες μικρῷ μείζονες οὖσαι τῶν μικρῶν κολυμβίδων, τὰ λοιπὰ νήτταις εἰσὶ παραπλήσιοι.

ΒΟΥΔΥ'ΤΗΣ. An unknown small bird, mentioned Dion. De Avib. iii. 2, with epithet ἀσθενής.

ΒΟΥΚΟΛΙ'ΝΗ· κίγκλος, τὸ ὄρνεον, Hesych.

ΒΟΥ'ΤΑΛΙΣ. [Said to be from βου- intens., and ταλάω (?)].
The Nightingale, in Aesop 235.

ΒΡΕ'ΝΘΟΣ. An unknown bird, or birds. ὄρνεον βρένθος, ὅπερ ἔνιοι κύσσυφον λέγουσι, Hesych.

Arist. H. A. ix. 11, 615 a βρένθος [MS. Vat. βρίνθος] ἐν τοῖς ὄρεσι καὶ τῇ ὕλῃ κατοικεῖ. εὐβίοτός ἐστι καὶ ᾠδικός [mentioned with ἔποψ]. Ibid. ix. 1, 609 a, a sea-bird, πολέμιοι δὲ οἱ ἀπὸ τῆς θαλάττης ζῶντες ἀλλήλοις, οἷον βρένθος καὶ λάρος καὶ ἅρπη. In this latter passage, βρένθος is perhaps a later interpolation; cf. *branta*, the *Brent* Goose.

ΒΡΗΤΟ'Σ· ἀλεκτρυὼν ἐνιαύσιος, Hesych.

ΒΥ'ΑΣ (v. l. βρύας), for βύfας: Mod. Gk. μποῦφος, Lat. *bubo*, It. *bufo*, Sp. *buho*, O. H. G. *ûwo*, Germ. *uhu*. [Cf. Lith. *bub-auti*, to shriek, Fick i. 685, ii. 620.]

An Owl, especially the Eagle Owl, *Strix bubo*, L., *Bubo maximus*, Bonap.

Arist. H. A. viii. 3, 592 b ἔστι δ' ὁ βύας τὴν μὲν ἰδέαν ὅμοιος γλαυκί, τὸ δὲ μέγεθος ἀετοῦ οὐδὲν ἐλάττων. A favourite word of Dion Cassius, usually as a bird of evil omen, e. g. lvi. 29 βύας ἔβυξε, also xl. 17, 47, xlii. 26, l. 8, liv. 29, lvi. 45, &c. Cf. *Bubo*, Virg. Aen. iv. 462, and Serv. in loc., Plin. x. (12) 16, Ovid, Met. v. 550, vi. 431, x. 453, xv. 791, Seneca, Herc. F. 686, &c.

The Owl, *bubo*, in medicine and magic, Plin. xxix. 26 and 38; its egg also is valuable, but difficult to obtain: quis enim, quaeso, ovum

ΒΥΑΣ (continued).

bubonis unquam videre poterit, quum ipsam avem vidisse prodigium sit?
The Eagle Owl is not rare in Greece (v. d. Mühle, Lindermayer), and is still called μπούφος or γοῦβι.

ΒΥ'ΖΑ = βύας. Nic. ap. Anton. Lib. 10, where the daughters of Minyos are metamorphosed into νυκτερίς (cf. Ov. Met. iv. 415), γλαῦξ, and βύζα· ἔφυγον δὲ αἱ τρεῖς τὴν αὐγὴν τοῦ ἡλίου. Also βύσσα = Λευκοθέας ὄρνις, Boios ap. Ant. Lib. 15. Also βυζαστρία, Herodian, 479. (Hence βυζάντιον, Curt.)

ΒΥ'ΤΘΑΝ· τὸν ψάρα, Hesych.

ΒΩ'ΚΚΑΛΙΣ, s. βάρκαλις. A small bird, mentioned with συκαλίς and others in a list of presents to the Indian king, Ael. xiii. 25.

ΒΩΜΟΛΟ'ΧΟΣ. A little Jackdaw.
Arist. H. A. ix. 24, 617 b τρίτον γένος τῶν κολοιῶν ὁ μικρός, ὁ βωμολόχος. See κολοιός.

ΓΑΥΣΑΛΙ'ΤΗΣ· ὄρνεον, παρὰ Ἰνδοῖς, Hesych.

ΓΕ'ΡΑΝΟΣ, ἡ (ὁ ap. Theophr. Sign. 1; ἐπίκοινον τῷ γένει, Suid.). Also γέρην, Hesych.; γέρην ἡ θήλεια γέρανος (?), Ael. Dion. ap. Eust. 231. 35 (175); cf. Lob. Prol. p. 49.

Etymology doubtful: according to Curtius, from rt. *gar*, to cry. Cf. Lith. *garny*, Bret. *garan*, O. H. G. *chranuh*, Germ. *Kranich*, *Kran*, Armen. *K'unk*, Eng. *crane*: without the *n* in L. *grus*, Lith. *ger-ve*, O. Sl. *geraw'*, Russ. *zurawl* (v. Edl., &c.).

The Crane. *Ardea grus*, L., *Grus cinereus*, auctt. Mod. Gk. γερανός, γεράν (Heldr.). The Crane is in Greece a bird of passage only, chiefly seen on its journey northward in the spring (cf. Strab. i. 2. 28): it breeds further north, in Macedonia (hence *grues Strymoniae*, Virgil, Seneca, Martial, Claudian, &c.; s. *Bistoniae*, Antip. Sidon. cv, Lucan, &c.) and on the Danube (Krüper, p. 267). In Hom. γέρανος doubtless includes the Stork also, the latter bird not being mentioned, though equally common in the Troad (Schliemann, Ilios, p. 113).

Description.—μακρὸν ἔχει τὸ ῥύγχος, Arist. H. A. i. 1, 486 b. τὸν τράχηλον μακρόν, id. De Acoust. 800 b; cf. Prov. φάρυγγα αἰτῷ μακρότερον γερίνου γενέσθαι ηὔξατό τις ὀψοφάγος, id. Nic. Eth. iii. 13, 118, &c. An uncomplimentary description, Athen. iv. 131 E. In colour, τεφρά (ashy, cinereous, cf. Babr. lxv. 1), μελάντερα γηράσκουσα τὰ πτερὰ ἴσχει,

ΓΕΡΑΝΟΣ (*continued*).

Arist. H.A. iii. 12, 519, cf. De Gen. v. 5, 785, Plin. x. 42 (29), Solin. c. 10. Its noisy cry, Arist. De Acoust. 800; frag. 241, p. 152 a: cf. Il. iii. 3, Antip. Sidon. xvii, Q. Smyrn. xiii. 104, Ar. Av. 710, Virg. Aen. x. 265, Mart. Ep. xxx; Lucret. iv. 182; in Carm. De Philom. grus gruit; &c. With ep. βωλοκόπος, Cratin. 2. 20.

A smaller species in the Balearic Islands, called *Vipio*, Plin. x. 49 (69).

Gregarious habits: ἀγελαῖον, H. A. i. 1, 488, iv. 12, 597 b; πολιτικὸν καὶ ὑφ' ἡγεμόνι, i. 1, 488. Pugnacity: fights with the eagle, Il. xv. 692, Q. Smyrn. xiii. 104, Ael. iii. 13; and with its own kind, H. A. ix. 12, 615 b. Its flight is lofty, οὐρανόθι πρό, Il. iii. 3; cf. Hes. Op. 446 εὖτ' ἂν γεράνου φωνὴν ἐπακούσῃς, Ὑψόθεν ἐκ νεφέων ἐνιαύσια κεκληγυίης (with which cf. Pind. Nem. vii εἴ τι πέραν ἀερθεὶς ἀνέκραγον); Aes. Fab. 397 ἄστρων ἔγγυς ἵπταμαι, Arist. H. A. ix. 10, 614 b, Avian. Fab. xv Ast ego deformi sublimis in aëra penna, Proxima sideribus numinibusque feror; Ael. iii. 14, Plin. x. 23, Isidor. Origin. xii. 7; see also Horap. ii. 98, where a watcher of the stars is said to be symbolized in Egypt as a crane, ὑψηλῶς γὰρ πάνυ ἵπταται, ἵνα θεάσηται τὰ νέφη, μὴ ἄρα χειμάζῃ, ἵνα ἐν ἡσυχίᾳ διαμένῃ: flies against the wind, Arist. H. A. viii. 13, 597. Lays two eggs, ib. ix. 12, 615 b; οὐ συγκαθείσης τῆς θηλείας ἐπιβαίνει τὸ ἄρρεν, ib. v. 2, 539 b.

Migrations.—Arist. H. A. viii. 12, 597 ἐκτοπίζουσιν ἐκ τῶν Σκυθικῶν πεδίων εἰς τὰ ἕλη τὰ ἄνω τῆς Αἰγύπτου (cf. Herod. ii. 22). A fuller account, how they alight before foul weather, how they have in front a leader, καὶ τοὺς ἐπισυρίττοντας ἐν τοῖς ἐσχάτοις: how when sleeping they stand first on one leg and then on the other: how while they rest the leader keeps watch, Arist. H.A. ix. 10, 614 b: cf. frag. 241, 1522 a, Antig. H. Mirab. 46; and how their discipline taught men the rules of government, Ael. iii. 14. . Cf. in particular Eur. Hel. 1478 Λίβυες οἰωνοὶ στολάδες ὄμβρον λιποῦσαι χειμέριον νίσσονται πρεσβυτάτᾳ σύριγγι πειθόμεναι ποιμένος, &c. How they fly aloft in the form of a triangle, with the old in front, the young in the middle, Ael. iii. 13, Plut. De Sol. Anim. Mor. 967 C, 979 A, Dion. De Av. ii. 17, iii. 11. The distance they traverse, crossing the Euxine between the promontories of Criumetopon and Carambis, Plin. x. 30: from Thrace to the river Hebrus, Ael. ii. 1; cf. Diog. Perieg. 155 αἵ τ' ἄμφω ξυνίασιν ἐναντίαι, οὐ μὲν ἐοῦσαι ἔγγυθεν, ἀλλ' ὅσον ὁλκὰς ἐπὶ τρίτον. ἦμαρ ἀνύσσῃ. The migration from Thrace takes place τοῦ Μαιμακτηριῶνος, Arist. H. A. viii. 12; φθινοπώρου ἤδη μεσοῦντος, Ael. iii. 13.

The flock was supposed to represent a Δ or other letters; cf. Philostr. Heroic. xi. 4, p. 710 αἱ γέρανοι μαρτύρονται τοῖς Ἀχαιοῖς ὅτι αὗται γράμματα εὗρον: cf. Claudian. De B. Gild. 477 ordinibus variis per nubila texitur ales Littera, pennarumque notis inscribitur aer; Lucan v. 712, Martial ix. 14, xiii. 75, &c., &c. See also Bochart, Hieroz. ii. p. 78, G. J. Voss,

ΓΕΡΑΝΟΣ (continued).
De Arte Gramm. i. 25, Mayor in Cic. Nat. Deor. ii. 49, Hemsterh. ad Lucian, i. 305, &c., &c.; cf. Cicero, De Nat. Deor. l. c., Martial xiii. 75. How each carries a stone, ὡς ἔχειν καὶ δεῖπνον καὶ πρὸς τὰς ἐμβολὰς τῶν ἀνέμων ἕρμα, Ael. ii. 1, cf. Antip. Sidon. cv, Ar. Av. 1137, 1429, Nonn. Dionys. xl. 515, Plin. x. 30 (23), also Prov. γέρανοι λίθους καταπεπτωκυῖαι, of provident men, Suid.; and how the same is a touchstone for gold, Ael. iii. 13. [In Plin. xxxvii. 72, the stone γερανῖτις is said to be so called from resembling the hue of the crane's neck.] How the oldest crane, having encircled the flock, dies and is buried, Ael. ii. 1. How they post sentinels, who hold aloft a stone for wakefulness' sake, Ael. iii. 13, Plut. Sol. Anim. x, xxix, Plin. x. 30, Phil. De An. Pr. xi. The stone still figures in heraldry as the crane and her 'vigilance.' The crane an Egyptian symbol of vigilance, Horap. ii. 94. It observes the time of its coming, 'intelligent of seasons,' Hes. Op. 448 ἧτ' ἀροτοῖό τε σῆμα φέρει, καὶ χείματος ὥρην δεικνύει ὀμβρηροῦ. Theocr. Id. x. 31 and Schol., Ar. Av. 710 σπείρειν μὲν ὅταν γέρανος κρώζουσ' ἐς τὴν Λιβύην μεταχωρῇ.

The fight with the Pigmies. Il. iii. 6 ἀνδράσι Πυγμαίοισι φόνον καὶ κῆρα φέρουσαι, and Schol.; cf. Arist. H. A. viii. 12, 597 (loc. dub.) οὐ γάρ ἐστι τοῦτο μῖθος, ἀλλ' ἔστι κατὰ τὴν ἀλήθειαν γένος μικρὸν μέν, ὥσπερ λέγεται, καὶ αὐτοὶ καὶ οἱ ἵπποι, τρωγλοδύται δ' εἰσὶ τὸν βίον. Cf. also Strab. Geogr. i. 2. 28, p. 35, xv. 1. 57, p. 711; Ctesias, Photii Biblioth. p. 68; Opp. Hal. i. 620; Philostr. Imagg. ii. p. 375, Heroic. l.c., Babrius xxvi; Apoll. Vit. iii. 50, p. 136, &c. Frequent in Latin; Plin. H. N. iv. 18, vii. 2, x. 23 (30); Ovid. Met. vi. 90; F. vi. 176 nec quae Pygmaeo sanguine gaudet avem; cf. Julian. Anticensor. Epigr. 3 αἵματι Πυγμαίων ἡδομένη γέρανος: Juv. vi. 506, xiii. 168, &c., &c. A myth of the cranes and pigmies in Boios ap. Athen. 393 C ἦν τις παρὰ τοῖς Πυγμαίοις γυνὴ διάσημος, ὄνομα Γεράνα, κ.τ.λ.: cf. Ael. xv. 29; Boios ap. Anton. Lib. 16; Eustath. in Iliad. 1444. 14; Ovid. Met. l. c. The legend of the Pigmies appears in India in the story of the hostility between the Garuda bird and the people called kirāta, i. e. dwarfs, the Σκιρῖται of Ael. xvi. 22; cf. Megasthenes ap. Plin. vii. 2. It is quite possible that this fable has an actual foundation in the pursuit of the *ostrich* by a dwarfish race. (Compare also Addison's poem Πυγμαιογερανομαχία; Tyson's Essay concerning the Pygmies, &c.

The Cranes of Ibycus: the avengers of crime. Schol. Ar. Thesmoph. 168 : Suid. s. v. Ἴβυκος· συλληφθεὶς δὲ ὑπὸ λῃστῶν ἐπ' ἐρημίας ἔφη, κἂν τὰς γεράνους, ἃς ἔτυχεν ὑπεριπτασθαι, ἐκδίκους γενέσθαι, καὶ αὐτὸς μὲν ἀνῃρέθε· μετὰ δὲ ταῦτα τῶν λῃστῶν εἰς ἐν τῇ πόλει θεασάμενος γερίνους ἔφη· ἴδε, αἱ Ἰβίκου ἔκδικοι, κ.τ.λ. Cf. Iambl. V. Pyth. xxviii. 12. 6 ὁρᾷς τοὺς μάρτυρας. Cf. also Plut. De Garrul. p. 509 F, Nemesian. De Nat. Hom. c. 42, Eudoc. p. 247, Zenob. i. 37, Apostol. ii. 14, Diogen. i. 35, H. Steph.

ΓΕΡΑΝΟΣ (*continued*).

Animadv. ad Adagia Erasmi, p. 10; Stat. Silv. v. 3. 152 volucrumque precator Ibycus. Evidently alluded to also in Ar. Av. 1427. See also Welcker's interesting article, Die Kraniche des Ibykos, Rhein. Mus. i. pp. 401-413, 1833.

A **weather-prophet**.—A sign of early winter, or of storm, ἐὰν πρωὶ πέτωνται καὶ ἀθρόοι, καὶ ἐὰν ὑποστραφῶσι πετόμενοι, Theophr. Sign. iii. 1, Geopon. i. 3. 12; cf. Hes. Op. et D. 629, and the imitation of the line in Ar. Av. 711; αἱ κλαγγαὶ καλοῦσιν ὄμβρους, Ael. i. 44; cf. Virg. Aen. x. 265, Georg. i. 351, 373, (cf. Milton, ' With clang despise the ground, under a cloud In prospect '). How mariners return to port if they see the cranes flying the contrary way, Ael. iii. 14, cf. vii. 7. A sign of fair weather, καὶ δ' ἄν που γέρανοι μαλακῆς προπάροιθε γαλήνης, ἀσφαλέως τανύσαιεν ἕνα δρόμον ἤλιθα πᾶσαι, Arat. Phen. 1010; cf. Theophr. Sign. iv οὐ γὰρ πέτονται πρὶν ἢ ἂν πετόμενοι καθαρὰ ἴδωσιν.

The crane was not molested, Lucill. 66 (Gk. Anthol. iii. p. 42) οὐδεὶς πρὸς γεράνους πόλεμος: cf. Ael. ii. 1; see however Babr. 13.

Mentioned as food, Plat. Polit. p. 114, Athen. p. 131, Plut. De Esu Carn. ii: Plin. x. 30, Hor. Sat. ii. 8, 86, Epod. ii. 35, Apic. vi. 2. Its brain used as an aphrodisiac, Ael. i. 44. How captured, by means of a beetle inside a dry gourd, Dion. De Avib. iii. 11. Grues mansuefactae, Plin. H. N. x. 23.

Their plumes carried in front of the shield by certain Eastern tribes, Herod. vii. 70; cf. iv. 175.

The Dance called γέρανος, Plut. Theseus, xxi. 1. 9 D, Luc. Salt. 34, J. Poll. iv. 20 (101). Perhaps described in Callim. Delian Hymn, 515, &c.; still danced in Greece under the name of κανδιωτής, vide Guys, Voy. littér., lettre xiii; represented in Leroy, Ruines des plus beaux monuments de la Grèce (2nd ed.), p. 22, pl. x (Ricard, Vies de Plut. i. p. 137, 1829). The dictionaries usually say that the dance mimics the *flight* of the cranes, which is incorrect: the dancing of Cranes may be seen in the opening of the year in any zoological garden.

A comic simile, ἀνυπόδητος ὄρθρου περιπατεῖν γέρανος, Aristopho 3. 361 (Mein.).

Fables.—γέρανοι καὶ γεωργός, Aesop, 93 (Babr. 26). γ. καὶ χῆνες, 421. γ. καὶ ἀλώπηξ, 34 (Plut. Mor. 614 F). γ. καὶ λύκος, 276 b. γ. καὶ ταῶς, 397 (Babr. 65).

See also **ἄγορ, σέρτης**.

ΓΙ'ΝΙΣ (*s.* γνίς). A Tuscan word for a **Crane** = γέρανος, Hesych.

ΓΛΑΥ'ΚΙΟΝ. A kind of **Duck**.

Perhaps the Golden-eye, *Anas clangula*, L., *Clangula glaucion*, Bonap., which winters in considerable numbers in all the waters of Greece

ΓΕΡΑΝΟΣ—ΓΛΑΥΞ   45

ΓΛΑΥΚΙΟΝ (*continued*).

(Lindermayer, p. 163); at least some species of duck with pale yellow eyes like those of γλαῦξ. Athen. ix. 395 C τὸ δὲ λεγόμενον γλαύκιον διὰ τὴν τῶν ὀμμάτων χρόαν μικρῷ ἔλαττόν ἐστι νήττης.

ΓΛΑΥ͂Ξ (s. γλαύξ) (γλαύσσω, γλαυκός = gleaming [cf. σκῶψ, σκέπτομαι: v. Edl. p. 37]).

The **Little Owl**, *Athene noctua*, auctt. Mod. Gk. κουκουβαία.

Description.—νυκτερώδιος, Arist. H. A. i. 1, 488, cf. Ar. Lys. 760; νυκτερινός, γαμψῶνυξ, Arist. H.A. viii. 3, 592 b; οὐκ ὀξὺ βλέπει τῆς ἡμέρας. οὐ κατὰ πᾶσαν τὴν νύκτα θηρεύει, ἀλλ' ἀκρέσπερον καὶ περὶ ὄρθρον. θηρεύει δὲ μῦς καὶ σαύρας καὶ σφονδύλας καὶ τοιαῦτ' ἄλλα ζῳδάρια, ix. 34, 619 b (cf. Ar. Av. 589). μύουσι οἱ γλαυκώδεις καὶ τῷ ἄνω βλεφάρῳ, ii. 12, 504. μικρὸν ἔχει τὸν σπλῆνα, ii. 15, 506. στόμαχον ἔχει εὐρύτερον τὸ κάτω· ἀποφυάδας ἔχει, ii. 17, 509. ὀλίγας ἡμέρας φωλεῖ, viii. 16, 600. The owl's nocturnal hootings, Ar. Lys. 760 (vide s. vv. βύας, κίκυμις).

A bird of evil omen, Men. 4. 230 ἂν γλαὺξ ἀνεκράγη δεδοίκαμεν. Dion. ix, in Gk. Anth. ii. p. 232 ἀμφὶ δὲ τύμβῳ σεῖο καὶ ἄκλαυτοι γλαῖκες ἔθεντο γόον: Ael. x. 37 (foretelling Pyrrhus' death); see also Pallad. De Re Rust. i. 35, Plin. x. 12, 16, &c. A portent of victory: Hesych. πρὸ τῆς μάχης ἐν Σαλαμῖνι γλαῖκά φασι διαπτῆναι τὴν νίκην προσημαίνουσαν. Hence Prov. γλαῦξ ἵπταται, cf. Suid., Ar. Vesp. 1086, Eq. 1091 and Schol. On the Owls released by Agathocles to encourage his soldiers, see Diod. Sic. xx. 11, 3.

A weather-prophet, ᾄσασα εὐδίαν μαντεύεται, Arist. fr. 241, 1522 a. Cf. Theophr. Sign. iv, Ael. vii. 7, Arat. 999, Geopon. i. 2. 6, Virg. Georg. i. 403.

The hostility to it of small birds, Arist. H. A. ix. 1, 609, Luc. Harm. 1 ὥσπερ ἐπὶ τὴν γλαῖκα τὰ ὄρνεα, cf. Ov. Met. xi. 24 et coeunt ut aves si quando luce vagantem Noctis avem cernunt; Plin. x. (17) 19, &c.

Capture of small birds by means of the owl, Arist. H. A. ix. 1, 609 τῆς δὲ ἡμέρας καὶ τὰ ἄλλα ὀρνίθια τὴν γλαῖκα περιπέταται, ὃ καλεῖται θαυμάζειν (cf. Timon ap. Hesych., Diog. L. iv. 42, Sillogr. Gr. p. 117, ed. Wachsmuth, οἱ δέ μιν ἠΰτε γλαῖκα πέριξ σπίζαι τερατοῖντο), καὶ προσπετόμενα τίλλουσιν· διὸ οἱ ὀρνιθοθῆραι θηρεύουσιν αὐτῇ παντοδαπὰ ὀρνίθια. Cf. Arist. H. A. ix. 22, 617 b, Ael. i. 29, Phil. De An. Pr. 468, Dio Chrys. xii. 1: an Egyptian version, Horap. ii. 51. Full account in Dion. De Avib. iii. 17 γλαυκὶ δὲ αἱ κορυδαλίδες ἀγρεύονται ἢν ὁ θηρατὴς ἐπί τινος χαλκῆς στήσας ἀψῖδος τινάσσει, σπάρτα συνεχῶς ἐπιτείνων, καὶ περιθεὶς κύκλῳ ῥαβδία περιχρισθέντα ἰξῷ· τὴν γλαῦκα τὸ νυκτερινὸν ὄρνεον σπείδουσιν αἱ κορυδαλίδες ἐλεῖν, τῷ τε ἰξῷ καὶ τοῖς ῥάβδοις ἁλίσκονται. See also Dio Prusiensis, Orat. 72 and 12, quoted in Schneider's Ecl. Phys. i. 48.

The owl itself ἀντορχούμενος ἁλίσκεται, Arist. H. A. viii. 12, 597 b, fr. 276, 1527 b.

ΓΛΑΥΞ (*continued*).

The War of the Owls and Crows : πολεμία γλαῦξ, κορώνη, ὀρχίλος. Arist. H. A. ix. 1, 609 νύκτωρ ἐπιβουλεύει τοῖς ᾠοῖς τῆς κορώνης, κ.τ.λ. Ael. iii. 9, Antig. Mirab. 57 (62), Plut. Od. et Inv. iv (Mor. 537 C). The story is oriental, and is one of the chief tales in the Mahabharata. Cf. Indian Antiq. March, 1882, p. 87; also, 'The Night of Slaughter,' by Sir Ed. Arnold. The account in Julian. Imp. Orat. iv. 149 suggests that the story is simply a parable of the Sun and Moon; vide infra. See also s. v. κορώνη. Cf. Prov. ἄλλο γλαῦξ, ἄλλο κορώνη φθέγγεται· ἐπὶ τῶν ἀλλήλοις μὴ συμφωνούντων, Suid.

Milks the ewes like a goatsucker: uses a bat's heart to keep away ants from its nestlings, Dion. De Avib. i. 15.

Sacred to Demeter, Porph. De Abst. iii. 5.

No Owls in Crete. Ael. v. 2, xvii. 10, Arist. De Mirab. 124 (130), 83 (84), Plin. x. 29 (41).

Fables of the very wise Owl, Aes. 105, 106, from Dio Chrysost. xii, lxxii. A fabled metamorphosis, Nicand. ap. Anton. Lib. 10 ; s. v. βύζα : see also Boios ap. Ant. Lib. 15.

The allusion to the Owl in Ar. Av. 358 is unexplained: it contains some obscure reference to the sacred χύτρα and probably to the feast of the χύτροι.

γλαῦξ can scarcely be said to be a generic term, except in the sense that the Little Owl, as the commonest species, is taken as typical of the rest. It is still extremely common about Athens (cf. Ar. Av. 301 γλαῦκ' εἰς 'Αθήνας, cf. Antiph. 3, 96 (Meineke), Lucian, Nigr. 1, Diog. L., Vit. Plat., Cic. ad Quint. ii. 16, &c.; Propert. ii. 20, 5 nocturna volucris funesta querela, Attica), as indeed it is, in one or other of its local forms, all round the Levant. It is the bird of Athene (cf. Ar. Av. 516, Eq. 1092, &c., &c.), doubtless in her primitive character of the Goddess of Night ; the epithet γλαυκῶπις is quite obscure, but I fancy we have it used in a very ancient sense when applied to the moon, e. g. Eur. fr. (ap. Schol. Ap. Rhod. i. 1280) γλαυκῶπίς τε στρέφεται μήνη : cf. Emped. ap. Plut. ii. 934 C; cf. also γλαυκώ, a name for the Moon, Schol. Pind. Ol. vi. 76 (cit. Fick, Beitr. Indog. Spr. xx, p. 156, 1894). On Athene as a moon-goddess, cf. Porph. ap. Euseb. P. E. iii. 11; Creuzer, Symb. iii. 380, &c. It was represented on Athenian coins (γλαῦκες Λαυριωτικαί, Ar. Av. 1106, Schol. in Ar. Eq. 1091, Plut. i. 442, Philochori fr. p. 83, Suid., Hesych.), and is still the city's badge. On a very ancient colossal Owl from the Parthenon, see Friederichs, Bausteine, p. 22 ; cf. Hesych. γλαῦξ ἐν πόλει· παροιμία, ἀνακεῖται γὰρ ὑπὸ Φαίδρου ἐν τῇ ἀκροπόλει. The owl of Athene is always a hornless, and never a horned or eared species (cf. Blumenbach, Sp. Hist. Nat. Ant. p. 20, Göttingen, 1808).

A dance called γλαῦξ, Athen. xiv. 629 f.; also σκώψ, q. v.

ΓΛΩΤΤΙ'Σ. An undetermined bird.

Arist. H. A. viii. 12, 597 b. Departs with the quails: γλῶτταν ἐξαγομένην ἔχει μέχρι πόρρω. Cf. Plin. x. 23 (33).

Supposed by Sundevall (op. c. p. 129) to be identical with ἴυγξ, the Wryneck, on account of the protrusible tongue; as also by Niphus, in Arist., v. Camus, ii. 383; the Wryneck however winters in Greece (Lindermayer p. 41). Belon identified it with the Flamingo, Gesner, followed by Linnaeus, from a confusion with Ger. or Sw. *Glutt*, with the Greenshank, in connexion with which latter bird the name survives in modern zoology. Vide s. v. ἐλαφίς.

ΓΝΑ'ΦΑΛΟΣ. An unknown bird.

Arist. H. A. ix. 16, 616 b φωνὴν ἔχει ἀγαθήν, καὶ τὸ χρῶμα καλός, καὶ βιομήχανος, καὶ τὸ εἶδος εὐπρεπής. δοκεῖ δ' εἶναι ξενικὸς ὄρνις· ὀλιγάκις γὰρ φαίνεται ἐν τοῖς μὴ οἰκείοις τόποις.

Gesner suggests the Bohemian Waxwing, *Ampelis garrulus*, L., which however has not τὴν φωνὴν ἀγαθήν, nor is there any evidence of the Waxwing reaching Greece. Probably the foreign name of a foreign bird.

ΓΟΙΝΕ'ΕΣ· κόρακες, Hesych. Perhaps for [ϝ]οἰνάς, q. v.

ΓΟ'ΛΜΙΣ· ψάρ, τὸ ὄρνεον, Hesych.

ΓΟ'ΡΤΥΞ· ὄρτυξ, Hesych. Quasi ϝόρτυξ.

ΓΡΑ'ΠΙΣ· εἶδος ὀρνέου, Hesych. Perhaps akin to θραυπίς: cf. J. G. Schneider in Arist. H. A. viii. 5. 4. p. 590.

ΓΡΑΥ'ΚΑΛΟΣ· ὄρνις τεφρός, Hesych. Cf. καυκαλίας.

ΓΡΥ'ΠΑΙ· αἱ νεοσσιαὶ τῶν γυπῶν· οἱ δὲ γύπαι, Hesych.

ΓΡΥΠΑΙ'ΕΤΟΣ. A fabulous bird. Ar. Ran. 929.

ΓΥ'ΓΗΣ. A fabulous bird: supposed to be connected with Lith. *gufa*, *guzulys*, a Stork.

Dion. De Avib. ii. 16 γίγης ὄρνις ἐστίν, ἀναβοᾶν ἀεὶ καὶ ᾄδειν τοῦτο δοκῶν, ὃς τοὺς ὄρνεις ἐν νυκτὶ κατεσθίει τοὺς ἀμφιβίους· τὴν ἐκείνου γλῶσσαν εἴ τις ἀποτέμοι χαλκῷ καὶ φαγεῖν δοίη τῷ μήπω λαλοῦντι παιδίῳ, πάντως αὐτοῦ ταχέως λύσει τὴν σιωπήν.

ΓΥ'Ψ. A Vulture. See also ἀετός, αἰγυπιός, νέρτος, περκνόπτερος, φήνη. Mod. Gk. ὄρνεον, ἀγιοῦπα (Byzantios).

Frequent in Homer, usually with the idea of feeding on carrion, Il. iv. 237, xi. 162, xvi. 836, xxii. 42; Od. xxii. 30, &c. Cf. Eur. Tr. 595 αἱματόεντα σώματα νεκρῶν γυψὶ φέρειν τέταται: Eur. Rh. 515 πετεινοῖς γυψὶ θοινατήριον. Ov. Tr. vi. 11, Lucret. iv. 680, Sil. Ital. iii. 396, &c. Used metaphorically, Eur. Andr. 75.

ΓΥΨ *(continued).*

Arist. H. A. vi. 5, 563 νεοττείει ἐπὶ πέτραις ἀπροσβάτοις (also Antig. H. Mirab. 42 (48). cf. Aesch. Suppl. 796 κρεμὰς γυπιὰς πέτρα)· διὸ σπάνιον ἰδεῖν νεοττιὰν γυπὸς καὶ νεοττούς. καὶ διὰ τοῦτο καὶ Ἡρόδωρος ὁ Βρύσωνος τοῦ σοφιστοῦ πατὴρ φησὶν εἶναι τοὺς γῦπας ἀφ' ἑτέρας γῆς, ἀδήλου ἡμῖν, τοῦτό τε λέγων τὸ σημεῖον, ὅτι οὐδεὶς ἑώρακε γυπὸς νεοττιάν, καὶ ὅτι πολλοὶ ἐξαίφνης φαίνονται ἀκολουθοῦντες τοῖς στρατεύμασιν [as the Griffon Vulture did at Sebastopol], cf. Ael. ii. 46, Basil. Hexaëm. viii ἴδοις ἂν μυρίας ἀγέλας γυπῶν τοῖς στρατοπέδοις παρεπομένας: &c. How the Vultures divine beforehand the place of battle, πρὸ ἡμερῶν ἑπτὰ ἐπ' αὐτὸν παραγινόμεναι, Horap. i. 11; cf. Ael. ii. 46; Umbricius ap. Plin. x. (6) 7; Plaut. Truc. ii. 3. 16, Martial, Ep. 62, 6.

Arist. l. c. τὸ δ' ἐστὶ χαλεπὸν μὲν ἰδεῖν, ὦπται δ' ὅμως. τίκτουσι δὲ δύο ᾠὰ οἱ γῦπες (cf. Plin. x. 7). Cf. H. A. ix. 11, 615, which latter passage has ἓν ᾠὸν ἢ δύο τὰ πλεῖστα.

On the mythical generation of vultures, how they are all females, are impregnated by the East wind, lay no eggs, and bring forth their young alive and feathered, see Ael. ii. 46, Arist. De Mirab. (6c) 835 a, 1, Horap. i. 11, Dion. De Avib. i. 5, Phile, De An. Pr. 121, Plut. Quaest. de Us. Rom. 93 (Mor. 286 A, B), Ammian. Marcell. xvii, Tzetz. Chil. xii. 439, Euseb. Pr. Ev. iii. 12, and innumerable other references in Patristic literature. On the mythical genealogy of the vultures, see also s. vv. ἀετός, ἀλιάετος, φήνη. These are Egyptian myths. *Vultur fulvus* was sacred to Maut, the Goddess of Maternity, cf. Deut. xxxii. 11, 12; cf. Horap. i. 11 μητέρα δὲ γράφοντες γύπα ζωγραφοῦσι, ἐπειδὴ ἄρρην ἐν τούτῳ τῷ γένει τῶν ζῴων οὐχ ὑπάρχει. Hence also the obstetrical value of a Vulture's feather, Plin. xxv. (14) 44. The Common Egyptian Vulture or Pharaoh's Hen, *Neophron percnopterus*, was sacred to Isis, cf. Ael. x. 22 Αἰγύπτιοι δὲ Ἥρας μὲν ἱερὸν ὄρνιν εἶναι πεπιστεύκασι τὸν γῦπα, κοσμοῦσι δὲ τὴν τῆς Ἴσιδος κεφαλὴν γυπὸς πτεροῖς. In Horapollo, γύψ is always feminine. The Vulture being sacred in Egypt, was an unclean bird among the Jews; cf. ἔποψ.

On the φιλοστοργία of the Vultures, cf. Od. xvi. 216, Aesch. Ag. 49, Plut. Q. Rom., Mor. 286 A, B, Opp. Hal. i. 723; cf. **αἰγυπιός**. The Vulture is stated to feed its young with its own flesh or blood, a myth afterwards transferred to the Pelican; Horap. i. 11, cf. Georg. Pisidas, 1064 (cit. Leemans) τὸν μηρὸν ἐκτέμοντες, ἡματωμένοις Γάλακτος ἀλκαῖς ζωπυροῦσι τὰ βρέφη. On the connexion between the Vulture and the Pelican, see s.v. **βαιήθ**. The stories of the Vulture's tenderness and affection coincide with the resemblance between the Hebrew words רַחֲמִים compassion, and רָחָם a vulture (Boch. Hieroz. ii. 803, &c.).

How a Vulture's feather, if burnt, drives serpents from their holes, Ael. i. 45, Plin. xxix. (4) 24. How the pomegranate is fatal to vultures, Ael. vi. 46. How the odour of myrrh is fatal to Vultures, Ar. De

ΓΥΨ (continued).

Mirab. (147) 845 a, 35, Ael. iii. 7, iv. 18, Geopon. xiii. 16, xiv. 26, Theophr. De C. Pl. vi. 4, Clem. Alex. Paedag. ii. 8; and why, Dion. De Avib. i. 5. Doves do not fear the Vulture, Ael. v. 50; the hawk is hostile to it, Ael. ii. 42. Most of the above mythical attributes of the Vulture are summed up by Phile, c. iii De Vulture.

The stories of Prometheus and Tityus, Od. xi. 577; Aen. vi. 595; Lucret. iii. 997; Ov. Met. iv. 456; Val. Fl. Argon. vii. 357, &c. See also s.v. ἀετός.

How the Persians exposed their dead to the Vultures, Herod. i. 140. Cf. Ael. x. 22 Βαρκαῖοι (s. Βακκαῖοι, Ἱσπανίας ἔθνος, Steph.) τοὺς ἐν πολέμῳ τὸν βίον καταστρέψαντας γυψὶ προβάλλουσιν, ἱερὸν τὸ ζῷον εἶναι πεπιστευκότες (cf. Sil. Ital. iii. 340, xiii. 470).

The augury of Romulus, Plut. Romulus ix, Quest. Rom. 93, Dio Cass. xvi. 46, Dion. Hal. i. p. 73, Ael. x. 22, Liv. Hist. i. 7, &c.; of Augustus, Sueton. Aug. c. 95. The prophecy of Vettius, drawn from the vultures of Romulus, as to the duration of Rome, Censorin. xiv.

The Vulture is sacred to Hercules, Plut. Mor. 286 A; is associated with Pallas, Eur. Tr. 594. The Vulture and Scarab together, according to their order and position, represented Neith or Phtha, Athene or Hephaestus, Horap. i. 12; cf. Creuzer, Symb. iii. 338, and Lauth op. cit.

In the system of Egyptian hieroglyphics the Vulture and the Beetle are associated or contrasted with one another. This relation bears upon certain statements made by Greek writers. The beetle, κάνθαρος, is devoid of females (Ael. x. 15) as the Vulture is of males; it is killed, as is the Vulture, by the odour of myrrh (Ael. i. 38, vi. 46, Phile 120, 1215); it shares with the 'Eagle' the gift of the renewal of youth (Arist. H. A. viii. 17, 601). For further details concerning Egyptian Vulture-myths and for many references to other sources of information, see Horap. ed. Leemans, pp. 171-191; and for the connexion between the statements of Horapollo and the phonetic value of the Vulture-symbol, see Lauth, Sitzungsber. Bayer. Akad. 1876, pp. 81-83.

A fabled metamorphosis, Boios ap. Ant. Lib. 21 Ἄγριος δὲ μετέβαλεν εἰς γῦπα, πάντων ὀρνίθων ἔχθιστον θεοῖς τε καὶ ἀνθρώποις.

A medicinal application, Dioscor. ii. cap. De stercore: γυπὸς ἄφοδος ἀποθυμιαθεῖσα ἔμβρυα ἐκτινάσσειν παραδέδοται (a statement frequently made by the Arab Doctors, Bochart). For other medicinal uses of the vulture's liver, heart, and feathers, see Plin. xxix. (4) 24, (6) 38, Galen iv. 8, Sext. Platon. ii. 2, Quint. Seren. c. 47, &c.

Proverbs.—γυπὸς σκιά· ἐπὶ τῶν μηδενὸς λόγου ἀξίων (cf. ὄνου σκιά), Suid.; the proverb may refer, on the other hand, to the shadow of coming events, in allusion to the Vulture's fabled prescience (vide supra; cf. also Erasm. in Proverbiis s.v. *vulturis umbra*). θᾶττον ἂν γὺψ ἀηδόνας μιμήσαιτο, Luc. Pisc. 37.

ΓΥΨ (*continued*).

γύψ is, like αἰγυπιός, a generic word for Vulture. In Arist. H. A. viii. 3, 592 b, two species are distinguished, ὁ μὲν μικρὸς καὶ ἐκλευκότερος, ὁ δὲ μείζων καὶ σποδοειδέστερος. Four vultures occur in Greece, *Gypaetus barbatus*, the Lämmergeier, *Vultur fulvus*, the Griffon Vulture, *V. cinereus*, the Black or Cinereous Vulture, and *Neophron percnopterus*. Sundevall and others have tried to apportion among these four the names φήνη, περκνόπτερος, and the two varieties mentioned of γύψ. But I think it certain that here the small white *Neophron* is meant as the one variety, and that the larger darker sort includes the other three. The true Vultures were usually spoken of as dark-coloured or black; e.g. Plin. x. 6 vulturum praevalent nigri, cf. Phile 130; Juv. Sat. xiii vulturis atri poena; Senec. in Thyeste, visceribus atras pascit effossis aves.

ΓΩΨ. A Macedonian name for the **Jackdaw** = κολοιός, Hesych.

ΔΑ'ΚΙΑ· τὰ ἄγρια ὀρνιθάρια, Hesych.

ΔΑΚΝΙ'Σ, Hesych. An unknown bird. Also δακνάς, Festus: Dagnades sunt avium genus, quas Aegyptii inter potandum cum coronis devincire soliti sunt, quae vellicando morsicandoque et canturiendo assidue non patiuntur dormire potantes.

ΔΑ'ΝΔΑΛΟΣ· ὁ ἐρίθακος, τὸ ὄρνεον, Hesych.

ΔΕΙ'ΡΗΣ. A name for the **Sparrow** in Elis. Nicander ap. Athen. ix. 392 a.

ΔΙ'ΓΗΡΕΣ· στρουθοί, Hesych. Cf. δρῆγες.

ΔΙ'ΚΑΙΡΟΝ, also δίκαιον (Ael. iv. 41) = Arab. *zikanon*. An Indian 'bird' as large as a Partridge's egg, whose dung causes a painless death like sleep; Ctesias p. 313, Ael. iv. 41, Phile, De Anim. Propr. 33 (32), v. 761. The 'bird' was the **Dung-beetle**, *Scarabaeus sacer*, L., Arab. *zikanon*; the 'dung' was probably confounded with *charas*, a resinous preparation of Indian hemp. Vide Valentine Ball, Indian Antiq. xiv. p. 310, 1885; also Proc. R. I. Acad. (2) ii.

ΔΙ'ΚΤΥΣ· ὁ ἰκτῖνος, ὑπὸ Λακώνων, Hesych.: cf. ἰκτίς. The word is more than doubtful as a bird-name, and is applied to a Libyan animal by Herod. iv. 192.

ΔΡΑΚΟΝΤΙ'Σ. An unknown or fabulous bird, into which one of the nine Emathidae, daughters of Pierus, was metamorphosed; Nicand. ap. Anton. Lib. Met. c. 9.

ΔΡΕΠΑΝΙ΄Σ, from δρέπανον, i. e. 'sickle-wing.' Also δραπανίς, Hesych.
Arist. H. A. i. 1, 487 b. A bird similar to ἄπους and χελιδών, εὔπτερος, κακόπους. ὁρᾶται καὶ ἁλίσκεται ὅταν ὕσῃ τοῦ θέρους· ὅλως δὲ καὶ σπάνιόν ἐστι.
Probably the larger Alpine Swift, *Cypselus melba*, L., and also perhaps the Common Swift, *C. apus*, both conspicuously 'sickle-winged.' On the other hand, Aub. and Wimm. p. 111, also Bochart ii. 62, as well as Gaza and Scaliger, say the Sand-Martin: v. κύψελος. Cf. Plin. x. (33) 49, xi. 47 (107), xxx. (4) 12. The brief account indicates that the bird is comparatively scarce, and that its period of residence in the country is short; both circumstances telling in favour of a Swift as against the Sand-Martin.

δρεπανίς is translated κεγχρίς by Hesychius.

ΔΡΗ˜[Γ]ΕΣ· στρουθοί, Μακεδόνες, Hesych. Also δίγηρες and δίρηγες. Cf. δείρης, δρικῆαι, q. v.

ΔΡΙΚΗ΄ΑΙ· ὄρνεα ποιά, Hesych. Also δρίξ. στρουθός, ap. Cyrill., Lob. Parall. p. 102. Cf. δρῆγες, &c.

ΔΡΥΟΚΟΛΑ΄ΠΤΗΣ. Also δρυηκολάπτης, δρυκολάπτης (Ar. Av. 480, 979), δρυκόλαψ (Hesych.), δρυοκόπος (Arist. De Part. iii. 1, 662 b). Cf. Sk. *dārvāghāta* (Keller).

A **Woodpecker**. Mod. Gk. ζιχλιδάρα (v. d. Mühle). See also δρύοψ, ἴπνη, κελεός, πελεκᾶν, πιπώ.
Arist. H. A. viii. 3, 593, vide s. v. πιπώ. Ib. ix. 9, 614, a full and accurate description : κόπτει δὲ τὰς δρῦς ὁ δρυοκολάπτης τῶν σκωλήκων καὶ σκνιπῶν ἔνεκεν, ἵν᾽ ἐξίωσιν. ἀναλέγεται γὰρ ἐξελθόντας αὐτοὺς τῇ γλώττῃ· πλατεῖαν δ᾽ ἔχει καὶ μεγάλην. καὶ πορεύεται ἐπὶ τοῖς δένδρεσι ταχέως πάντα τρόπον, καὶ ὕπτιος καθάπερ οἱ ἀσκαλαβῶται. ἔχει δὲ καὶ τοὺς ὄνυχας βελτίους τῶν κολοιῶν πεφυκότας πρὸς τὴν ἀσφάλειαν τῆς ἐπὶ τοῖς δένδρεσιν ἐφεδρείας· τούτους γὰρ ἐμπηγνὺς πορεύεται. ἔστι δὲ τῶν δρυοκολάπτων ἐν μὲν γένος ἔλαττον τοῦ κοττύφου, ἔχει δ᾽ ὑπέρυθρα μικρά, ἕτερον δὲ γένος μεῖζον ἢ κόττυφος· τὸ δὲ τρίτον γένος αὐτῶν οὐ πολλῷ ἔλαττόν ἐστιν ἀλεκτορίδος θηλείας. νεοττεύει δ᾽ ἐπὶ τῶν δένδρων, ἐν ἄλλοις τε τῶν δένδρων καὶ ἐν ἐλαίαις ... καὶ τιθασσευόμενος δέ τις ἤδη ἀμύγδαλον εἰς ῥωγμὴν ξύλου ἐνθείς, ὅπως ἐναρμοσθὲν ὑπομείνειεν αὐτοῦ τὴν πληγήν, ἐν τῇ τρίτῃ πληγῇ διέκοψε καὶ κατήσθιε τὸ μαλακόν. Cf. Arist. De Mirab. 13, 831 b : the hard bill of the woodpecker, Arist. De Part. iii. 1, 662 b.

Four well-defined species occur in Greece. (*a*) the Great Black Woodpecker, *Picus Martius*, which evidently answers to the last and largest variety mentioned above ; (*b*) the Green Woodpecker, *P. viridis*,

ΔΡΥΟΚΟΛΑΠΤΗΣ (continued).

with its close ally, *P. canus*; (*c, d*) the Greater and Lesser Spotted Woodpeckers, *P. major* and *minor*. The Green Woodpecker is described under the name κελεός, and accordingly Sundevall and others make the remaining two of the three Aristotelian varieties to be the Greater and Lesser Spotted Woodpeckers respectively. But as *P. viridis*, whether it had another name or not, would certainly be still classed as δρυοκολάπτης, it is better to take it as the middle-sized sort, uniting the Greater and Lesser Spotted Woodpeckers as the last and least variety.

The Woodpecker is not in Greek, as it is in Latin (e.g. Ov. Met. xiv. 321, F. iii. 37, 54, Virg. Aen. vii. 191, Plin. x. 18 (20), Plut. Q. Rom. xxi. 268 F, Romulus iv; Aug. Civ. Dei, xiii. 15), a bird of great mythological importance, though the Dryopes were probably, like the descendants of Picus, a Woodpecker-tribe. It figures in the oriental Samir-legend (vide s.v. ἔποψ) in Ael. i. 45 as making its nest in a tree, and, by virtue of a certain herb, removing a stone with which one shall have blocked up the entrance; cf. Plin. x. (18) 20, xxv. 5; Plut. p. 269; Dion. De Avib. i. 14; and is accordingly spoken of as a rival power to ἔποψ in Ar. Av. 480. Cf. Alb. Magnus, De Mirab. 1601, p. 225. See also Baring-Gould, Myths of the Middle Ages, p. 397. The Woodpecker and the Hoopoe come into relation also in the version of the Tereus-myth given by Boios ap. Anton. Lib. Met. 11, where the brother of Aëdon is transformed into the bird ἔποψ, and her husband into πελεκᾶν.

ΔΡΥΟ'Ψ. A Woodpecker = δρυοκολάπτης, Ar. Av. 304.

ΔΥ'ΠΤΗΣ. A diving bird, identical with αἴθυια (q.v.), ἔνιοι καύηκες. Etym. M.

Callim. 167, ap. Etym. M. δύπται τ' ἐξ ἁλὸς ἐρχόμενοι; with which cf. Arat. 914, s.v. ἐρωδιός. Lyc. 73 στένω σε, πάτρα, καὶ τάφους Ἀτλαντίδος, δίπτου κέλωρος. Applied to a professional diver or sponge-fisher in Opp. Hal. ii. 436, and possibly also, therefore, in the preceding reference. Cf. ἀρνευτήρ.

ΔΥΤΙ^ΝΟΣ. An unknown water-bird. Dion. De Avib. ii. 13, iii. 24.

ΕΙ'ΔΑΛΙ'Σ, also ἰδαλίς. ὄρνις ποιός, Hesych.

ΕΛΑΙΟΣ s. ἐλαιός. According to Alex. Mynd. ap. Athen. ii. 65 B a kind of αἰγιθαλός or titmouse, called by some πυρρίας (MS. πιρίας), συκαλὶς δ' [ὅτι ἁλίσκεται] ὅταν ἀκμάζῃ τὰ σῦκα. Conj. in Anth. Pal. vii. 199 ed. Mackail xi. 13 φίλ' ἔλαιε. Probably one of the many **Warblers** which frequent the olive-gardens, e.g. *Salicaria olivetorum*, Strickl., and *S. elaeica*, Linderm. (v. Lindermayer, pp. 88–92).

ΔΡΥΟΚΟΛΑΠΤΗΣ—ΕΛΩΡΙΟΣ 53

ἜΛΑΝΟΣ = ἰκτῖνος, Hesych.

ἘΛΑΣΑ͂Σ. An unknown bird, Ar. Av. 886.

ἘΛΑΦΊΣ. An unknown water-bird.

Dion. De Avib. ii. 11 ἐλαφὶς δ' ὄρνεόν ἐστι τὰ πτερὰ πάντα ἐπὶ τοῖς νώτοις ἐλάφων ἔχον ἐοικότα θριξί, καὶ τρέφεται κατὰ τοὺς χερσαίους ἴυγγας, τὴν γλῶσσαν μηκίστην οὖσαν ὥσπερ ὁρμιὰν εἰς τὸ ὕδωρ ἐπὶ πολὺ καθιεῖσα, κ.τ.λ. The hair-like feathers on the back suggest, if anything, a Heron or Egret. A gem in the British Museum represents a Heron or Stork, with the antlers of a Stag; v. Torr, Rhodes, pl. I, Imhoof-Bl. and K., pl. xxvi. 59.

ἘΛΕΆ. MSS. have also ἐλαία, (qy. = ἔλεια Sundev.), ἔλεια Callim. s. ἐλεᾶς Ar. Av. 302, s. ἐλέας, Hesych. Cf. ἔλαιος.

A small bird, probably the **Reed-Warbler**, *Salicaria arundinacea*, Selby, and allied species.

Arist. H. A. ix. 16, 616 b ὄρνις εὐβίοτος, καθίζει θέρους μὲν ἐν προσηνέμῳ καὶ σκιᾷ, χειμῶνος δ' ἐν εἰηλίῳ, καὶ ἐπισκεπεῖ ἐπὶ τῶν δονάκων περὶ τὰ ἕλη· ἔστι δὲ τὸ μὲν μέγεθος βραχύς, φωνὴν δ' ἔχει ἀγαθήν. In Ar. Av. 302 ἐλεᾶς may or may not be the same bird. Callim. ap. Schol. Ar. Av. 302 ἔλεια μικρόν, φωνῇ ἀγαθόν.

The Reed-Warbler is a permanent resident in Greece, and is very common in all marshy places (Krüper, &c.).

ἘΛΕΙΌΣ· εἶδος ἱέρακος, Hesych.

Sch. conjectures ἔλειος *palustris* in Arist. H. A. ix. 36, 1, and for the common reading λεῖοι writes ἔτι δ' ἔλειοι οἱ καὶ φρυνολόγοι. Cf. A. and W. ii. p. 264. Vide s. v. ἐπιλείος.

ἘΛΕΌΣ. A kind of **Owl**.

Arist. H. A. viii. 3, 592 b; mentioned with, and said to resemble, αἰγώλιος and σκώψ: μείζων ἀλεκτρυόνος, θηρεύει τὰς κίττας. ix. 1, 609 b κρέξ ἐλεῷ πολέμιος (alternative readings, κολεῷ, γολεῷ).

The size accords with that of the Tawny Owl, *Syrnium Aluco*, L., which is common in Greece and is not definitely ascribed to any other classical name. Scaliger so identifies it, taking ἐλεός from the owl's cry, cf. ἐλελεῦ, &c., also Lat. *ulula*. Sundevall reads ἐλεός s. ἔλειος = *palustris*, supporting this view by the mention of *Crex* in the context, and identifies the bird with *Strix brachyotus*, L., the Short-eared or Marsh Owl. But both etymological suggestions are more than doubtful, and neither Tawny nor Short-eared Owl θηρεύει τὰς κίττας. Artemidor. iii. 65, Zonar. c. 684.

ἘΛΏΡΙΟΣ. A water-bird, similar to κρέξ (*verb. dub.*).

Clearch. ap. Athen. viii. 332 E (Casaubon), where later editors read ἐρωδιός: numbered among τοὺς ὄρνιθας τοὺς παρενδιαστὰς καλουμένους.

ἘΝΘΥ'ΣΚΟΣ· ὁ ἀσφαλός, τὸ ὄρνεον, Hesych.

ἘΠΙΖΑ· ὄρνεα, Κύπριοι, Hesych. (σπίζια, conj. Salmas.)

ἘΠΙΛΑΙ˚Σ. An unknown small bird.

Arist. H. A. viii. 3, 592 b ὄρνις σκωληκοφάγος. Sylburge, Schneider, Piccolos and others read ἰπολαῖς, q. v.

ἘΠΙΛΕΓΟΣ, s. ἐπίλεος. A bird of prey, perhaps the Buzzard, *Buteo vulgaris*, Bechst.

Plin. H. N. x. 9 epileum Graeci vocant qui solus omni tempore apparet, caeteri hieme abeunt (vide s. v. αἰσάλων). This passage, following on a reference to *Buteo*, and stating a fact recorded by Aristotle of τριόρχης (q. v.), suggests that all three are identical. Perhaps connected with, or a mere variant of, ἐλειός or λεῖος, q. v.

ἘΠΟ'ΛΙΟΣ. εἶδος ὀρνέου νυκτερινοῦ, Suid. Ambiguum an illud, quod ab Aristotele αἰγωλιός, H. St. Thesaur. App. p. 942 E.

Note.—We have above (ἔλαιος, ἐλέα — ἐλεός, ἐπιλαῖς, ἐπιλεῖος) a succession of bird-names all very similar, whose meaning and derivation are alike obscure.

ἜΠΟΨ. The Hoopoe, *Upupa epops*, L. Hesych. has also ἔποπος, ὄρνεον: ἔπωπα, ἀλεκτρυόνα ἄγριον: and also ἀπαφός.

Mod. Gk. τζαλοπετεινός or τσαλοπετεινός (Erhard, Heldreich), ἀγριοκόκορος (Boch., Jonston; still on Mt. Taygetus, Heldr.), ἀγριοκόκοραξ (v. d. Mühle). ἔποψ is, in form, onomatopoeic, like *upupa*, but is very probably based on an Egyptian solar name, Ἄποπις, Ἡλίου ἀδελφός, Plut. De Is. xxxvi; with which cf. Ἔπαφος—Herod. ii. 153, &c., &c.; also Ἔπιφι, Plut. Is. et Os. lii. p. 372 B : the form ἀπαφός preserved in Hesychius is identical with the name used by the Syriac Physiologist. For fanciful derivation see Aesch. fr. 305 ἔποψ ἐπόπτης τῶν αὐτοῦ κακῶν: cf. Hesych. s. v. See also s. vv. **κουκούφα, πούπος.**

First mentioned by Epicharm. ap. Athen. ix. 391 D (fr. 116, Ahrens) σκῶπας ἔποπας γλαῖκας.

Description.—Arist. H. A. i. 488 b ὄρνις ὄρειος, cf. ix. 11. 615 a (vide Boch. Hier. ii. p. 343 for similar interpretation of Heb. or Arab. dukiphat, duk kepha, *gallus montanus*). H. A. ix. 15, 616 b οὐκ ἔχει τῆς γλώττης τὸ ὀξύ, vide s. vv. **ἀηδών, μελαγκόρυφος**: cf. Giebel, Z. f. ges. Naturw. x. 236. Pausan. x. 4 ὁ δὲ ἔποψ ἐς ὃν ἔχει λόγος τὸν Τηρέα ἀλλαγῆναι, μέγεθος μὲν ὀλίγον ἐστὶν ὑπὲρ ὄρτυγα, ἐπὶ τῇ κεφαλῇ δὲ οἱ τὰ πτερὰ ἐς λόφου σχῆμα ἐξῆρται. Cf. Ar. Av. 94, 99, 279; Ovid, Metam. vi. 671 cui stant in vertice cristae, Prominet immodicum pro longo cuspide rostrum, Plin. x. (65) 36 cum fetum eduxere abeunt. Is destructive to bees, Phil. De An. 712.

ΕΝΘΥΣΚΟΣ—ΕΠΟΨ 55

ΕΠΟΨ (*continued*).

The cry represented, ἐποποποποποποποποῖ, Ar. Av. 227, &c. Vv. 237, 243, 260 τιὼ τιώ &c., though incorporated in the same speech, are evidently from the nightingale and other birds behind the scenes: κικκαβαῦ, v. 261, is the owl's hoot.

Nest.—Arist. H. A. vi. 1, 559 a μόνος οὐ ποιεῖται νεοττιὰν τῶν καθ' ἑαυτὰ νεοττευόντων, ἀλλ' εἰσδυόμενος εἰς τὰ στελέχη ἐν τοῖς κοίλοις αὐτῶν τίκτει, οὐδὲν συμφοροίμενος. Ib. ix. 15, 616 b νεοττιὰν ποιεῖται ἐκ τῆς ἀνθρωπίνης κόπρου. According to Heldreich (p. 38) the Hoopoe is a spring and autumn migrant through Greece, but does not now breed there: it however seems to breed in Macedonia and perhaps in Epirus (Krüper). The story of the nest ἐκ κόπρου ἀνθρωπίνης (also in Ael. H. A. iii. 26) arises (1) from the Hoopoe's habit of seeking its insect food among dung (avis obscoeno pastu, Plin. H. N. x. 29; cf. Fr. coq puant, Germ. Kothhahn, Stinkhahn, Mistvogel, &c.), and (2) from the nest having an evil smell from the accumulation within of excrement, and perhaps also from a peculiar secretion of the birds (see for scientific references, Aub. and Wimm. i. p. 91).

Myth and Legend.—The Tereus-myth (see also s. v. ἀηδών, ἁλιάετος, χελιδών) Aesch. fr. 297, in Arist. H. A. ix. 49 B, 633 a (more probably from the lost *Sophoclean* tragedy of Tereus, cf. Schol. Ar. Av. 284, Welcker, Gr. Trag. i. 384) τοῦτον δ' ἐπόπτην ἔποπα τῶν αὑτοῦ κακῶν | πεποικίλωκε κἀποδηλώσας ἔχει | θρασὺν πετραῖον ὄρνιν ἐν παντευχίᾳ· | ὃς ἦρι μὲν φανέντι διαπάλλει πτερὸν | κίρκου λεπάργου· κ.τ.λ. Cf. Arist. H. A. ix. 15, 617 a, and 49 B, 633 a τὴν ἰδέαν μεταβάλλει τοῦ θέρους καὶ τοῦ χειμῶνος, Plin. x. (30) 44. With the phrase ἐπόπτην τῶν αὑτοῦ κακῶν, cf. Plat. Phaedo p. 86 A φασὶ διὰ λύπην ᾄδειν: also Ach. Tat. v. 5 ὁ Τηρεὺς ὄρνις γίνεται· καὶ τηροῦσι ἔτι τοῦ πάθους τὴν εἰκόνα. In the use of the word ἐπόπτης, we have not merely a fanciful derivation of ἔποψ, but also an allusion to the mysteries.

In this very obscure story we have frequent indications of confusion between Hoopoe and Cuckoo, and the 'metamorphosis' is in part connected with the resemblance between the Cuckoo and the Hawk; cf. Arist. vi. 7, Theophr. H. Pl. ii. 6, Geopon. xv. 1, 22, Plin. H. N. x. 8, 11. See also Lenz, Zool. d. Gr. u. R. p. 318. For the relations between Hoopoe and Cuckoo, der Kuckuk und sein Küster, v. Grimm, D. M. p. 646, Grohmann, Aberglaube aus Böhmen, Leipzig, 1864, p. 68, &c. On the metamorphosis of the Cuckoo into a Hawk in English and German Folk-lore, see Swainson, Provincial Names of British Birds, p. 113.

How the Hoopoe first appeared at Tereus' tomb in Megara, Paus. i. 41, 9. The Tereus-myth also in Aesch. Suppl. 60, Apollod. iii. 14, Ach. Tat. v. 5, Ovid, Metam. vi, &c.

ΕΠΟΨ *(continued)*.

On the Tereus-myth, and the mythology of the Hoopoe in general, see in particular E. Oder, Der Wiedehopf in d. gr. Sage, Rhein. Mus. (N. F.), xliii. pp. 541–556, 1888.

A weather-prophet, Horap. ii. 92 ἐὰν πρὸ τοῦ καίρου τῶν ἀμπέλων πολλὰ κράζῃ, εὐοινίαν σημαίνει. The same of the Cuckoo, Plin. H. N. xviii. 249, Hor. Sat. i. 7, 30. With ep. αἴσιος, Anton. Lib. xi.

Phil. De An. Pr. 667 φθίσις δὲ τοῖς ἔποψι δορκάδων στέαρ (also Ael. H. A. vi. 46). Ib. 724, uses ἄγρωστις as a remedy (cf. κορυδός). Ael. i. 35 places ἀδίαντον or καλλίτριχον (cf. ἀετός) as an amulet in its nest or heals itself when injured, Horap. ii. 93; also written ἀμίαντον, Geopon. xv. 1, 19.

How the Hoopoe by means of a certain herb (the same ἀδίαντον) liberates its imprisoned young, Ael. iii. 26, cf. Ar. Av. 654, 655. The same story of Picus, Plin. H. N. x. 18 (20), vide s. v. δρυοκολάπτης. This is a version of the well-known Samir-legend (the 'open Sesame' of the Forty Thieves), and is told also of the Hoopoe in connexion with Solomon (Boch. Hieroz. ii. 347). See also Buxdorf, Lex. Talmud. col. 2455: on similar German superstitions see Meier, Schwab. Sagen, Nr. 265. On Indian versions of the story of the Hoopoe which sheltered Solomon from the sun, see W. F. Sinclair, Ind. Antiquary, 1874. also ib. 1873, p. 229, Curzon's Monast. of the Levant, c. xii, &c. The story of the Indian Hoopoe, Ael. xvi. 5, which buried its father in its head (vide s. v. κορυδός) is probably connected with the same legend; see Lassen, Ind. Alterth. 2nd ed. i. p. 304. The statement (Ael. l. c.) that the ἔποψ Ἰνδικός is διπλάσιον τοῦ παρ' ἡμῖν, καὶ ὡραιότερον ἰδεῖν, is purely fabulous.

Filial affection of the Hoopoe, Ael. x. 16, vide s. v. κουκούφα, πελαργός. The Hoopoe on coins of Antoninus as a symbol of filial love. Eckhel, Doctr. numm. vi. 531, Creuzer, Symbolik, ii. p. 64, Zoega, Numm. Eg. Imp. pl. x. 1, Seguin. Scl. Numism. p. 152.

The evil smell of the Hoopoe suggests a connexion with Pitumnus in the story of Pilumnus and Pitumnus or Sterculinius; Serv. Aen. ix. 4 fratres fuerunt dii; horum Pitumnus usum stercorandorum invenit agrorum, Oder, op. c. p. 556: cf. Jordan-Preller, Röm. Myth. i. 375.

The Hoopoe was a sacred bird in Egypt, as it still is among the Arabs (cf. Creuzer, l. c., Denon pl. 119, 8, &c., &c.). From its rayed crest it was a solar emblem, and it is in part as such that it comes into relation with κίρκος, the sacred hawk of the solar Apollo. The woodpecker, with its red or golden crest (cf. Ov. Met. xiv. 394) becomes in like manner a solar emblem, and there is a curious parallel in the connexion between *Circe* and the metamorphosis of Picus. As a solar emblem also, the Hoopoe figures in the version of the Phoenix-myth

ΕΠΟΨ (*continued*).

in Ael. xvi. 5. To a like source is traceable the Samir-legend, and possibly also the obscure origin of the Tereus-myth. From its sanctity in Egypt it became an unclean bird among the Jews, Lev. xi. 19, Deut. xiv. 18, where its name דוּכִיפַת *dukiphat* (cf. κουκούφα) is rendered *Lapwing*, as being the crested bird with which the translators were most familiar (cf. Newton, Dict. of Birds, p. 505).

In the Birds of Aristophanes we have many veiled allusions to the mythology of the Hoopoe. The confusion with κόκκυξ (vide s. v. κουκούφα) is indicated throughout; the fables of Tereus and Procne are frequently referred to, e.g. ἡ γὰρ ἄνθρωπος, v. 98 τὴν ἐμὴν ἀηδόνα, vv. 203, 367, &c.: the Hoopoe's first cry, ἄνοιγε τὴν ὕλην, v. 93, is a reference to the Samir-legend; the kindred fable of κορυδός appears in vv. 472–476; the mysterious root in v. 654 is the magical ἀδίαντον: the mention of ἡλιαστής, v. 109, is a pun on ἥλιος: the allied solar symbolism of δρυοκολάπτης is suggested in v. 480; and the nauseous reputation of the nest is probably hinted at in the Hoopoe's pressing invitation to Peisthetairus, v. 641, that he should enter in.

ἘΡΙ'ΘΑΚΟΣ, *s.* ἐριθακός (Arist., Ael.), ἐριθεύς (Arat., Theophr.), ἐρίθυλος (Schol. ad Ar. Vesp.). The Robin, *Erithacus rubecula*, L.

Arist. H. A. viii. 3, 592 b ὄρνις σκωληκοφάγος. ix. 49 B, 632 b μεταβάλλουσιν οἱ ἐρίθακοι καὶ οἱ καλούμενοι φοινίκουροι ἐξ ἀλλήλων· ἔστι δ' ὁ μὲν ἐρίθακος χειμερινόν, οἱ δὲ φοινίκουροι θερινοί, διαφέρουσι δ' ἀλλήλων οὐθὲν ὡς εἰπεῖν ἀλλ' ἢ τῇ χρόᾳ μόνον: Geopon. xv. 1. 22.

A weather-prophet, Arat. Phen. 1025, Theophr. fr. vi. 3, 2 χειμῶνος μέγα σῆμα καὶ ὄρχιλος καὶ ἐριθεύς, δύνων ἐς κοίλας ὀχεάς. Arist. fr. 241, 1522 b ἐρίθακος ἐς τὰ αὔλια καὶ τὰ οἰκούμενα παριὼν δηλός ἐστι χειμῶνος ἐπιδημίαν ἀποδιδράσκων. Cf. Ael. vii. 7.

A mimetic bird, μιμοῦνται καὶ μέμνηνται ὧν ἂν ἀκούσωσιν, Porphyr. De Abst. iii. 4 (ἐρίθακος here is either an interpolation, or is used of some other bird).

Proverb, Schol. in Ar. Vesp. 922 (927) μία λόχμη δύο ἐριθάκους οὐ τρέφει. ἔστι δὲ ὄρνεον ὑπὸ μέν τινων καλούμενον ἐριθεύς, ὑπὸ δὲ ἑτέρων ἐρίθυλος, ὑπὸ τῶν πλειόνων ἐρίθακος: cf. Photius. Also ἐριθεύς· ὁ ἐριθακός, τὸ ὄρνεον, Hesych. ἐρίθακος· ὄρνεον μονῆρες καὶ μονότροπον, Suid.

Sundevall derives ἐρίθακος from ἐρυθρός, θᾶκος (cf. Eng. *redstart*, Germ. Rothsteiss), and identifies the bird in Arist. with the Redstart, *Lusciola phoenicurus*, L., in winter plumage: vide s. v. φοινίκουρος. The derivation is far-fetched, and the identification is discountenanced by the fact that the Redstart does not, at least in Attica, remain through the winter (Krüper p. 245), during which season the Robin is as common there as with us. See also αἴσακος, δάνδαλος.

ἝΡΜΑΚΟΝ· ὄρνεον, Hesych. Probably by error for ἐρίθακον.

ἜΡΟΨ· ὄρνις ποιός, Hesych. Probably for ἔποψ, or else μέροψ.

ἘΡΥΘΡΟ'ΠΟΥΣ. In Ar. Av. 303, usually translated **Redshank**, which bird, *Totanus calidris*, L., is common in Greece in winter. Used as an epithet of πέλεια, Arist. H. A. v. 13, 544 b.

ἘΡΩΓΑ'Σ· ἐρωδιός, Hesych. A very doubtful word.

ἘΡΩΔΙΟ'Σ (ῥωδιός, Hippon. 59, ap. Etym. M. Also ἐδωλιός, Hesych.)
A **Heron**, L. *ardea*; etym. dub.

Various species are mentioned: ὁ πέλλος, the common Heron, *Ardea cinerea*, L.; ὁ λευκός, the Egret, *A. alba* and *A. gazetta*; ὁ ἀστερίας καλ., *A. (Botaurus) stellaris*, L., the Bittern; Arist. H. A. ix. 1, 609 b; cf. Dion. De Avib. ii. 8 ἔστιν αὐτῶν γένη μυρία· οἱ μὲν γὰρ βραχεῖς τ' εἰσὶ καὶ λευκοί, ἄλλοι δὲ ποικίλοι καὶ μείζονες, μέσοι δ' ἕτεροι, καὶ τοῖς μὲν οὐκ ἔστιν ἐπὶ τῆς κεφαλῆς πλόκαμος, ἄλλοις δ' ὥσπερ τις βόστρυχος ἀπῃώρηται. Plin. x. 60 (79).

The above identifications of πέλλος and ἀστερίας (q. v.) are doubtful: the same words occur in relation to one another as proper names in Apoll. Rh. i. 176; cf. Pott in Lazarus and Steinthal's Zeitschrift, xiv. p. 43.

Arist. H. A. viii. 3, 593 b περὶ τὰς λίμνας καὶ τοὺς ποταμοὺς βιοτεύει. Ael. H. N. v. 35, x. 5 ὄστρεα ἐσθίειν δεινός ἐστι (?); cf. Plut. Sol. Anim. x. (Mor. 967 D). Its flight described, Arist. De Inc. 10, 710 a, fr. 241, 1522 a.

Mentioned also Ar. Av. 886, 1142. With ep. μακροκαμπυλαύχενες, Epich. 49, ap. Athen. ix. 398 D.

Myth and Legend.—Sent by Athene, to Odysseus and Diomede, as a favourable augury, Il. x. 274. Here from the nocturnal appearance of the bird and its loud cry, Netolicka (Naturh. a. Homer p. 10) and others suggest the Night-Heron, *Ardea Nycticorax*, L., which is abundant in the Troad; cf. Hippon. l. c. κνεφαῖος ἐλθὼν ῥωδιῷ κατηυλίσθην. In Il. x. 275 there is an alternative reading πέλλον Ἀθηναίη (Zopyrus, De Mileto Cond. iv (Schol. Venet.), cf. Groshans, Prodr. Faun. pp. 15, 16, Buchholz p. 119; for a discussion of important Scholia on this passage, and for notes on ἐρωδιός in general, see J. G. Schneider, in Arist. vol. iv. pp. 45-47; vide s. v. πέλλος). See also s. v. ἀνοπαῖα.

The Heron as a symbol of Athene on coins of Ambracia and Corinth (Imh.-Bl. and K. p. 38, pl. vi). Said also to be sacred to Aphrodite, Etym. M. A bird of good omen, Ael. x. 37, Plut. Mor. 405 D, especially the White Heron, Plin. xi. 37. A weather-prophet, Arat. Phaen. 913, 972, Athen. viii. 332 E (where Casaub. reads ἐλώριος), Ael. vii. 7, Theophr. De Sign. i. 18, ii. 28, Virg. Georg. i. 363, Lucan, v. 553, Cic. Div. i. 8, Callim. s. v. **δύπτης**; hence beloved of men, Dion. De Avib. ii. 8.

ΕΡΩΔΙΟΣ (continued).

Hostile to πίπω, τὰ γὰρ ᾠὰ κατεσθίει καὶ τοὺς νεοττοὺς τοῦ ἐρωδιοῦ, Arist. H. A. ix. 1, 609, cf. Nicand. ap. Ant. Lib. Met. 14 ; ἀετῷ πολέμιος, ἁρπάζει γὰρ αὐτόν, καὶ ἀλώπεκι, φθείρει γὰρ αὐτὸν τῆς νυκτός, καὶ κορύδῳ, τὰ γὰρ ᾠὰ αὐτοῦ κλέπτει, Arist. H. A. 609 b ; hostile also to ὁ λευκὸς λαρός, Ael. iv. 5, Phile, De An. 682, and to *sorex*, Plin. x. (74) 95. Friendly with κορώνη, Arist. H. A. ix. 1, 610, Ael. v. 48.

Erodius, who tended the horses of his father Autonous, was turned into the bird ἐρωδιός, his father being metamorphosed into ὄκνος, and the groom into ἐρωδιός. ἀλλ' οὐχ ὅμοιον· ἧσσον γάρ ἐστιν ἱκανῶς τοῦ πελλοῦ: Boios ap. Ant. Lib. Met. 7.

Swallows a crab, κάρκινον, as a remedy, Phile 724, or places one in its nest as a charm, Ael. i. 35, Geopon. xv. 1. Noted, like the stork, for filial and parental affection, Ael. iii. 23.

On the painful generation of the Heron cf. Arist. H. A. ix. 1, 609 b, Plin. x. (60) 79 ; hence a fanciful derivation of ἐρωδιός in Etym. M. and Eust. ad Il. x. 274. Vide infra, s. v. πέλλος.

Fable of λύκος καὶ ἐρωδιός (*s. γέρανος*): ἀρκεῖ σοι καὶ τὸ μόνον σώαν ἐξελεῖν τὴν κεφαλήν, Aes. Fab. 276, Babr. 94. A fragment : ἐρωδιὸς γὰρ ἔγχελυν Μαιανδρίην τρίορχον εὑρὼν ἐσθίοντ' ἀφείλετο, Simonid. ap. Athen. vii. 299 C.

Deprived by Neptune of the power of swimming, and why, Dion. De Avib. ii. 8. The Island of Diomedea, Ael. H. A. i. 1 καλεῖταί τις Διομήδεια νῆσος, καὶ ἐρωδιοὺς ἔχει πολλούς, and how these ἐρωδιοί, once the comrades of Diomede, give welcome to Greek visitors ; also Lycus ap. Antig. Mirab. 172 (188), Anton. Lib. Met. 37, Phile, De Anim. Pr. 152. Cf. Ovid, Metam. xiv. 498, Aen. xi. 271 et Serv. in loc., Plin. x. 44 (61). Cf. also S. Augustin, De Civ. Dei, xviii. 16, Lachmund, De Ave Diomedea diss., Amstelod. (1672) 1686. There is evident but obscure connexion between the story of the birds of Diomede, and the metamorphosis above alluded to : where the son of Autonous and Hippodameia is killed by his father's horses, and his father and his servant are turned into ἐρωδιοί. A story similar to that of the birds of Diomede is wide-spread, and usually told of the Stork, cf. Alex. Mynd. ap. Ael. iii. 23 ; for Modern Greek references, see Marx, Gr. Märchen, 1876, pp. 52, 55.

See also ἄσιδον, ἀστερίας, ἑλώριος, λευκερωδιός, ὄκνος, πέλλος.

ΕΥ'ΡΥΜΕ'ΔΩΝ· ἀετός, Hesych. (*verb. dub.*; for ἀετός, Kuster cj. Αἰήτης).

ΖΑ'ΡΙΚΕΣ· ἐπίθετον πελα[ρ];ῶν, Hesych. (*verb. dub.*).

'ΗΔΥ'ΤΕΡΑΙ· αἱ τρυγόνες, Hesych. (*verb. dub.*).

'ΗΕ'ΡΟΠΟΣ· A bird doubtless identical with ἀέροψ ; vide s. v. μέροψ.

According to Boios ap. Ant. Lib. Met. 18, the boy Botres was

ΗΕΡΟΠΟΣ (*continued*).

transformed into the bird ἤεροπος, ὅς ἔτι νῦν τίκτει μὲν ὑπὸ γῆς, αἰεὶ δὲ μελετᾷ πέτεσθαι.

ἩΓΚΑΝΟ'Σ· ὁ ἀλεκτρυών, Hesych. Cf. κίκκος : forte κίκκαν, Schmidt.

ἩΜΙΟ'ΝΙΟΝ· ὄρνις ποιός, Hesych.

ἩΡΙΣΑ'ΛΠΙΓΞ· ὀρνέου τι εἶδος, Hesych. Also ἐρισάλπιγξ, Callim. Schol. ad Ar. Av. 884.

ΘΕΟ'ΚΡΟΝΟΣ. A fabulous bird.

Dion. De Av. ii. 15 εἷς τῶν ἀμφιβίων ὀρνίθων ἐστὶ καὶ ὁ θεύκρονος, ὃς ἐξ ἀετῶν εἶναι νόθος καὶ ἱεράκων πιστεύεται, κ.τ.λ.

ΘΡΑ'Ξ. A water-bird, mentioned with δυτῖνος and κόλυμβος, Dion. De Avib. ii. 13, iii. 24, q. v.

ΘΡΑΥΠΙ'Σ. (θλυπίς in Cod. Med. Cᵃ. θραπίς, θλιπίς also occur. Perhaps identical with γλάπις, γράπις, Hesych.) An unknown species of Finch. Cf. J. G. Schneider in Arist. l. c.

Arist. H. A. viii. 3, 592 b ὄρνις ἀκανθοφάγος, mentioned with ἀκανθίς and χρυσομήτρις.

ΘΩΟ'Σ· ὄρνις ποιός, Hesych.

Ἴ ΒΙΝΟΣ· ἀετός, Hesych.

Ἴ ΒΙΣ, *s.* ἴβις ; also ἴβυξ, Hesych., Suid. The **Ibis**.

An Egyptian word, *bahu*: cf. *hib* or *hip* in copt. vers. Lev. xi. 17 for יַנְשׁוּף A. V. *great owl*; cf. Is. xxxiv. 11; tr. *ibis* in LXX and Vulg.); vide Scholtzii Lex. Aegypt., Oxon. 1775, p. 155. Another Egyptian name *leheras* still survives as Arab. *el hareiz*, and is preserved in the following fragment: Albert. Magn. vi. p. 255 Avis autem, quae ab incolis Aegypti secundum Aristotelem ieheras (*s.* leheras) vocatur, et habet duos modos, et unus illorum est albus et alius est niger. Cf. Gesner, iii. p. 546 Avis (inquit Albertus, de ibide sentiens) quae ab Aegyptiis secundum Aristotelem leheras (*s.* icheras) dicitur. secundum Avicennam Caseuz vocatur. Cf. Belletête, Annot. ad op. Savigny (infra cit.), p. 39.

Of the two species of Ibis, the **White** or **Sacred Ibis**, which was first recognized by Bruce (Travels in Abyss. v. p. 173, 1790) is *Tantalus aethiopicus*, Latham, *Numenius Ibis*, Savigny, or *Ibis religiosa*, Cuv.: the Abou Hannes or Father John of the Abyssinians (Bruce), and Abou Mengel or Father Sickle-bill of the fellaheen. The Sacred Ibis still regularly visits Lower Egypt at the time of the inundation, coming from Nubia (cf. Newton, Dict. of Birds, s.v.). Before the time of Bruce's discovery, the name had been variously assigned to several

ΗΕΡΟΠΟΣ—ΙΒΙΣ

ΙΒΙΣ (*continued*).

birds: having been likened to a Stork by Strabo, it was identified with that bird by Belon, by Prosp. Alpin., Hist. Eg. Nat. p. 199, and by Caylus, Antiq. Eg. vii. p. 54, though such an identification was expressly rejected by (e.g.) Albertus Magnus (vi. p. 640 non est ciconia: quia rostrum longum quidem sed aduncum habet), and Vincent. Burgund., Bibl. Mund. i. p. 1212; it was supposed to be a Curlew (*falcinellus*) by Gesner (H. A. iii. 546) and Aldrovandi (Orn. iii. p. 312) and an Egret or White Heron by Hasselquist (Iter Palest. (2) cl. 2, no. 25), an identification adopted by Linnaeus (Syst. Nat. ed. x. p. 114); by Perrault (Acad. des Sc. Paris, iii. p. 58, pt. xiii) it was taken to be a much larger bird, the *Tantalus ibis* of Linnaeus (Syst. Nat. ed. xii); and yet others, e.g. Maillet (Descr. de l'Égypte, 4to ii. p. 22) confounded it with the Egyptian Vulture or 'Pharaoh's Hen.' The White Ibis is figured on the Mosaic of Palestrina (cf. the coloured figures in the Pitture ant. di Petr. S. Bartholi) and in the Pitture ant. d' Erculaneo (ii. pll. 59, 60).

The **Black Ibis** of Herodotus, the Glossy Ibis of ornithologists, is *Ibis falcinellus*, Temm., *Falcinellus igneus* or *Plegades falcinellus* of more recent writers. It is confounded by L. & Sc. with the Scarlet Ibis, an American bird. To it the Arab name *el hareiz* is said especially to apply.

On both species, see Cuvier, Ann. du Mus. iv. pp. 103-135, 1804; and especially the learned memoir of J. C. Savigny, Hist. nat. et mythol. de l'Ibis, 8vo Paris, 1805. On Ibis mummies, cf. T. Shaw, Levant, 1738, pp. 422, 428, G. Edwards, Nat. Hist. 1743-1764, Blumenbach, Phil. Trans. 1794, and later writers.

The Sacred Ibis is said to nest in palm-trees, Ael. x. 29 τοὺς αἰλούρους ἀποδιδράσκουσα, cf. Phile xvi; according to Vierthaler, ap. Lenz, Z. d Gr. u. R. p. 379, it breeds in Sennaar, nesting on mimosa-trees, and building twenty to thirty nests on a tree: see also Heuglin, Ornith. Nord. Afrikas, p. 1138.

Herod. ii. 75, 76 ἔστι δὲ χῶρος τῆς Ἀραβίης κατὰ Βουτοῦν πόλιν μάλιστά κη κείμενος· καὶ ἐς τοῦτο τὸ χωρίον ἦλθον, πυνθανόμενος περὶ τῶν πτερωτῶν ὀφίων... λόγος δέ ἐστι, ἅμα τῷ ἔαρι πτερωτοὺς ὄφις ἐκ τῆς Ἀραβίης πέτεσθαι ἐπ' Αἴγυπτον· τὰς δὲ ἴβις τὰς ὄρνιθας ἀπαντώσας ἐς τὴν ἐσβολὴν ταύτης τῆς χώρης οὐ παριέναι τοὺς ὄφις, ἀλλὰ κατακτείνειν· καὶ τὴν ἶβιν διὰ τοῦτο τὸ ἔργον τετιμῆσθαι λέγουσι Ἀράβιοι μεγάλως πρὸς Αἰγυπτίων. ὁμολογέουσι δὲ καὶ Αἰγύπτιοι διὰ ταῦτα τιμᾶν τὰς ὄρνιθας ταύτας. εἶδος δὲ τῆς μὲν ἴβιος τόδε· μέλαινα δεινῶς πᾶσα, σκέλεα δὲ φορέει γεράνου, πρόσωπον δὲ ἐς τὰ μάλιστα ἐπίγρυπον, μέγαθος ὅσον κρέξ. τῶν μὲν δὴ μελαινέων, τῶν μαχομένων πρὸς τοὺς ὄφις, ἥδε ἰδέη. τῶν δ' ἐν ποσὶ μᾶλλον εἰλευμένων τοῖσι ἀνθρώποισι (διξαὶ γὰρ δή εἰσι αἱ ἴβιες) ψιλὴ τὴν κεφαλήν, καὶ τὴν δειρὴν πᾶσαν· λευκὴ πτεροῖσι, πλὴν κεφαλῆς καὶ τοῦ αὐχένος καὶ ἄκρων

ΙΒΙΣ (*continued*).

τῶν πτερύγων καὶ τοῦ πυγαίου ἄκρου· ταῦτα δὲ τὰ εἶπον πάντα, μέλαινά ἐστι δεινῶς· σκέλεα δὲ καὶ πρόσωπον, ἐμφερὴς τῇ ἑτέρῃ. Cf. Arist. H. A. ix. 27, 617 b ἐν μὲν οὖν τῇ ἄλλῃ Αἰγύπτῳ αἱ λευκαί εἰσιν, πλὴν ἐν Πηλουσίῳ οὐ γίνονται· αἱ δὲ μέλαιναι ἐν τῇ ἄλλῃ Αἰγύπτῳ οὐκ εἰσίν, ἐν Πηλουσίῳ δ' εἰσίν. Cf. Plin. x. (30) 45, Solin. xxxv. p. 95. On the geographical confusion implied in these accounts, vide J. G. Schneid. in Arist. vol. iv. pp. 493-496.

The annual fight between the Ibis and the flying serpents is also alluded to: Cic. Nat. D. i. 101, Ael. ii. 38, Philo, De An. xvi, Solin. xxxv, Pomp. Mela iii. 9, Amm. Marcell. xx. 15, Isidor. i. p. 306, Albert. M. vi. p. 640, &c.

The Ibis in conflict with a winged serpent on coins of Jubah II, and Cleopatra of Mauretania (Imhoof-Bl. and K. p. 37). The 'Winged Serpents' were probably the hot winds and sandstorms (cf. Diod. Sic. i. 128) of spring, which disappeared as the Etesian winds (ὀρνιθίαι ἄνεμοι) supervened, and the Ibis returned in the month of Thoth from its migration, with the season of the inundations which freed Egypt from all her pests: cf. Savigny, op. cit. pp. 91, 134, Pluche, Hist. du Ciel, i. 1, p. 77; an interpretation of the Winged Serpents, more subtle than this, is however possible: cf. the ὄφις ἱερακόμορφος, Philo ap. Euseb. Praep. Evang. i. p. 41, Lydus De Menss. pp. 53, 137, Creuzer Symb. ii. 246, &c. On the other hand the *Indian* ὄφεις πτερωτοί of Megasthenes (ap. Ael. xvi. 41) seem to have been real, not mythical, and were very probably 'Vampire' Bats, *Pteropus medius*, Temm. (Val. Ball). On the Ibis as a useful destroyer of ordinary serpents, see Cic. Nat. D. i. 36, ii. 50, Diod. Sic. i. 97, Strabo, Geogr. xvii. p. 823, Plin. N. H. x. 28 (40), &c. How Moses brought it in cages of papyrus to destroy the serpents of the Ethiopian desert, Joseph. ii. 10. p. 127. How serpents are terrified by an Ibis' feather, Ael. i. 38, Phile, De An. v. 715, or even paralyzed by it, Zoroast. in Geopon. xv. 1, cf. ib. xiii. 8, Theoph. Simoc. Quest. Phys. xiv. p. 19, &c.; likewise the crocodile: an indolent and rapacious man symbolized by a crocodile crowned with a plume of Ibis' feathers, τούτου γὰρ ἐὰν ἴβεως πτερῷ θίγῃς, ἀκίνητον εὑρήσεις, Horap. ii. 81, Pier. Valer. xvii. 22. The Ibis was also hostile to the scorpion, Ael. x. 29, including 'winged scorpions,' Phile, De Ibi: and is associated [obscurely] with the Scorpion on the small zodiac of Dendera, Savigny, op. cit. p. 131, Denon, Voy. pl. 130; cf. Kircher, Oedip. ii. pp. 207, 213. The Ibis also destroyed locusts and caterpillars, Diod. Sic.; it fed on fish, avoiding strong currents, Physiol. Syr. c. xviii, Procop. Comm. in Levit. p. 344, Vincent. Burg. Specul. i. p. 1212; and on the refuse of the markets of Alexandria, Strabo, l. c. Its flesh was poisonous and fatal, Vinc. B. i. 1212, ii. 1489 ejus ova si quis comediturbed, moritur; cf. Albert. M. xxiii. 24, Gesner,

ΙΒΙΣ (continued).

cap. De Ibi. How the basilisk springs from an egg, the product of poison eaten by the Ibis: ex aliquo quod illa peperit, ut putredinoso, magnum aliquid malum enascitur basiliscus, &c., Theoph. Simoc. l. c.; cf. Pier. Valer. p. 175.

It was foul-feeding and insatiable of poison, Ael. x. 29, Phile xvi; cf. Gesner v. 547 apud Graecos lexicorum conditores ibin ὀφιοφάγον ab esu serpentium, et ῥυπαροφάγον ab impuritate victus cognominare invenit. Nevertheless. it was in other respects cleanly (Ael. x. 29), and the Egyptian priests washed in water from which the Ibis had drunk (Ael. vii. 45), οὐ πίνει γὰρ ἢ νοσῶδες ἢ πεφαρυγμένον, Plut. De Is. p. 381. It is killed by hyaena's gall, Ael. vi. 46, Phile 666.

Mentioned with name Λυκοῦργος, Ar. Av. 1296. Compared with the Stymphalian birds, Paus. viii. 22, 5. Its tameness noted, Strabo, l. c., Joseph. Antiq. Jud. p. 127, Amm. Marcell. p. 337.

Its name a term of reproach, Ovid, Ibis, v. 62 Ibidis interea tu quoque nomen habe: cf. Callim. Alciati embl. 87, in sordidos.

The Ibis was sacred to Isis, the Moon-Goddess : Ael. ii. 38 ἱερὰ τῆς σελήνης ἡ ὄρνις ἐστί, τοσούτων γοῦν ἡμερῶν τὰ ᾠὰ ἐκγλύφει, ὅσων ἡ θεὸς αὔξει τε καὶ λήγει (cf. ib. ii. 35). τῆς δὲ Αἰγύπτου οὔποτε ἀποδημεῖ, τὸ δὲ αἴτιον, νοτιωτάτη χωρῶν ἁπασῶν Αἴγυπτός ἐστι, καὶ ἡ σελήνη δὲ νοτιωτάτη τῶν πλανωμένων ἄστρων πεπίστευεται, cf. Plin. x. 48. Hence an emblem of Egypt, Pier. Valer. xvii. 18, Kircher, Oedip. iv. p. 324, and as such on coins and medals of Hadrian and Q. Marius. See also Phile xvi καὶ τῆς σελήνης οὐ παρῆλθε τοὺς δρόμους μειουμένης . . . καὶ πληρουμένης. Plut. De Is. p. 381 ἔτι δὲ ἡ τῶν μελάνων πτερῶν περὶ τὰ λευκὰ ποικιλία καὶ μίξις ἐμφαίνει σελήνην ἀμφίκυρτον, also Symp. 4, 5. Cf. Pignor. Mens. Isiac. Expl. p. 76; Wilkinson, Anc. Egyptians, (2) ii. pp. 217-224; Renouf, Hibbert Lectures 1879, pp. 116, 237. It is figured together with the new moon on the southern Temple of Jupiter Ammon at Karnak (Descr. de l'Égypte, Thèbes, ii. 261, pl. 52; Creuzer, ii. p 208, &c.). On the connexion between Thoth and the Moon, discussed in explanation of the Ibis' relation to the latter, see Leemans in Horap. p. 247.

It represented the moon (as a hawk symbolized the solar Osiris) at Egyptian banquets of the gods, Clem. Alex. Stromat. v. 7. Its mode of generation was probably related to lunar superstitions : Ael. x. 29 μίγνυνται δὲ τοῖς στόμασι καὶ παιδοποιοῦνται τὸν τρόπον τοῦτον: cf. Anaxagoras ap. Arist. De Gen. iii. 6, 756 B, Schol. in Pl. Phaedr., Solin. xxxv, &c. Its ashes prevent abortion, Plin. xxx. (15) 49.

The Ibis was sacred also to Thoth or Hermes : cf. Socr. ap. Pl. Phaedr. p. 274; Ael. x. 29; Plut. Symp. ix. 3 ; Diod. Sic. i. 8 ; Horap. i. capp. 10, 36 ; Pier. Valer. xvii. 19 ; Kircher, Obel. Pamph. iv. 325, Oedip. i. 15, ii. 213, &c. Thoth was the patron or emblem of Sirius, which star on the small zodiac of Dendera is represented close to a double-

ΙΒΙΣ *(continued).*

headed snake with ibis-heads; cf. Savigny, op. cit. p. 159, Kircher, Oedip. iii. p. 96, &c.: on the same zodiac an ibis-headed man rides on Capricornus, under which sign Sirius rose anti-heliacally (Dupuis, Orig. de tous les cultes, v. 1); in this connexion, cf. Timoch. 3. 590 πῶς ἂν σώσειεν ἶβις ἢ κίων. Thoth is figured as an Ibis, or with an ibis-head, Plut. Symp. ix, cf. Pherecydes, Hymn. Merc. Ὦ Ἑρμῆς ἰβίμορφε, ἀρχηγὸς ὑδνόοιο, συγγραμμάτων γεννητώρ, μεξήσεώς τε πάσης: Hermes, pursued by Typhon, changed himself into an Ibis, Hygin. Astr. P. ii. c. 28, Ant. Lib. Met. c. 28, Ovid, Met. v. 331. Many of the bird's peculiarities, real or fabulous, are mystically associated with the same god: e.g. its dainty walk (Ael. ii. 38) with the inventor of the dance; its numerical constants (e.g. its intestine 96 cubits long, and its pace of one cubit, Ael. x. 29) with the inventor of arithmetic; the equilateral triangle or Δ that its beak and legs made (Plut. Is. et Osir. 381; or its legs alone, Pier. Valer. xvii. 18, xlvii) with the inventor of letters (cf. also Kircher, Obel. Pamphil. pp. 125-131), its knowledge of physic with the founder of the medical art. On the Ibis as the inventor of clysters, cf. Cic. N. D. ii. 50, 126, Plut. De Sol. Anim. p. 974 C τῆς ἴβεως τὸν ὑποκλυσμὸν ἄλμῃ καθαιρομένης Αἰγύπτιοι συνιδεῖν καὶ μιμήσασθαι λέγουσιν: id. De Is. et Osir. p. 381, Ael. ii. 35, x. 29, Phile xvi, Plin. viii. (27) 41, x. 30, Galen, De Ven. Sect. i, &c.; the same story of the Stork, Don Quixote, ii. p. 63 (edit. Lond. 1749): cf. N. and Q. (4) ix. p. 216: see also Bacon, De Augm. v. 2. The opposed black and white of the Ibis' plumage, as sometimes of Mercury's raiment, suggested various symbolic parallels. the opposition of male and female, of light and darkness, of order and disorder, of speech and silence. of truth and falsehood: cf. Ael. x. 29, Schol. in Pl. Phaedr., Plut. De Is. 381 D, Clem. Alex. Str. v. 7. The Ibis is a symbol of the heart (περὶ οὗ λόγος ἐστὶ πλεῖστος παρ' Αἰγυπτίοις φερόμενος, Horap. i. 36), an organ under the protection of Hermes; and the bird has a heart-shaped outline (Ael. x. 29 καρδίας σχῆμα, ὅταν ὑποκρύψηται τὴν δέρην καὶ τὴν κεφαλὴν τοῖς ὑπὸ τῷ στέρνῳ πτεροῖς) as indeed its mummies have still; a weight as it issues from the egg equal to the heart of a new-born child (Plut. Symp. 670), or a heart of its own of exceptional size (Gaudent. Merula, Memorab. iii. c. 50); in this connexion we may compare the Eg. *bahu* with *ba* or *bai* the soul (Lauth, op. cit.); cf. supra s. v. **βαιήθ**. The Ibis was emblematic of the ecliptic or zodiacal ring: ἀριθμοῦ γὰρ ἐπινοίαις καὶ μέτρου μάλιστα τῶν ζῴων ἡ ἶβις ἀρχὴν παρέχεσθαι τοῖς Αἰγυπτίοις δοκεῖ, ὡς τῶν κύκλων λοξός, Clem. Alex. Stromat. p. 671. It enjoyed freedom from sickness, longevity, or even immortality (Apion ap. Ael. x. 29); it was buried at Hermopolis (Herod. ii. 67, Ael. l. c.).

ἼΒΥΞ. Hesych., Suid.; vide s. v. **ἶβις**.

ἸΔΑΛΙ'Σ, also εἰδαλίς· ὄρνις ποιός, Hesych.

'ΙΔΕ'ΩΝ· είδος [ίδος, cf. Schmidt] άετοῦ, Hesych.

'ΙΕ'ΡΑΞ (Ep. and Ion. ἴρηξ, s. ἴρηξ: ἵ). Not connected with ἱερός (ἵ); perhaps from root Fῖ swift (cf. Maass, Indo-Germ. Forsch. i. p. 159), but the etymology is quite obscure.

A Hawk. The generic term especially for the smaller hawks and falcons. Mod. Gk. ἱεράκι or γεράκι, applied to the Sparrow-hawk, Kestrel, Hobby, &c., and also to the Kite (Erhard). Dimin. ἱερακιδεύς, Eust. 753, 56; ἱερακίσκος, Ar. Av. 1112.

In Hom. with epithets ὠκύς Il. xvi. 582, ὠκίπτερος xiii. 62, ὤκιστος πετεηνῶν xv. 237, ἐλαφρότατος πετεηνῶν xiii. 86: also Od. v. 66. In Hes. Op. et D. 210 ὠκυπέτης ἴρηξ, τανυσίπτερος ὄρνις: cf. Ar. Av. 1453. In Arist. with ep. γαμψώνυχος, σαρκοφάγος, ὠμοφάγος, &c. Alcman 16 ap. Athen. 373 λῦσαν δ' ἄπρακτα νεανίδες, "Ὥστ' ὄρνεις ἱέρακος ὑπερπταμένω: Eur. Andr. 1141 οἱ δ' ὅπως πελειάδες ἱέρακ' ἰδοῦσαι πρὸς φυγὴν ἐνώτισαν.

Varieties.—Arist. H. A. ix. 36, 620 τῶν δ' ἱεράκων κράτιστος μὲν ὁ τριόρχης, δεύτερος δ' ὁ αἰσάλων, τρίτος ὁ κίρκος· ὁ δ' ἀστερίας καὶ ὁ φασσοφόνος καὶ ὁ πτέρνις ἀλλοῖοι· οἱ δὲ πλατύτεροι ἱέρακες ὑποτριόρχαι καλοῦνται, ἄλλοι δὲ πέρκοι καὶ σπιζίαι, οἱ δὲ λεῖοι καὶ οἱ φρυνολόγοι· γένη δὲ τῶν ἱεράκων φασί τινες εἶναι οὐκ ἐλάττω τῶν δέκα, διαφέρουσι δ' ἀλλήλων, κ. τ. λ. Cf. ib. viii. 3, 592 b. That there were ten species of hawks is asserted by Callimachus, Etym. M. Vide Callim. fr. p. 468, ibique Bentleii; cf. Schol. ad Ap. Rhod. i. 1049. For lists of the species, cf. Ar. Av. 1178, Ael. xii. 4, Dion. De Avib. i. 6, Plin. x. 8, 9, 10. The Egyptian hawks were smaller, Arist. H. A. xii. 4. The various hawks migrate during winter (cf. Job xxxix. 26) except τριόρχης, Arist. H. A. viii. 3, or *epileus*, Plin. x. (8) 9.

Anatomical particulars.—χολὴν ἅμα πρὸς τῷ ἥπατι καὶ τοῖς ἐντέροις ἔχουσι, θερμὴν τὴν κοιλίαν, μικρὸν τὸν σπλῆνα, Arist. H. A. ii. 15, 506 a, 16, 506 b; De Part. iii. 7, 670 a.

Breeding habits.—Arist. H. A. vi. 6, 563, incubates twenty days; ix. 11, 615 ἐν ἀποτόμοις νεοττεύει. De Gen. ii. 7, 746 b δοκοῦσιν οἱ διαφέροντες τῷ εἴδει μίγνυσθαι πρὸς ἀλλήλους (an error naturally arising from the sexual difference in size and plumage in many species). H. A. vi. 7, 564 γίνονται οἱ νεοττοὶ ἡδύκρεῳ σφόδρα καὶ πίονες. Ael. H. N. ii. 43 δεινῶς φιλόθηλυς, cf. Horap. i. 8. Antig. Mirab. 99 (107) τρία μὲν τίκτειν, αὐξανομένων δὲ τῶν νεοττῶν ἐκλέγειν τὸν ἕνα, κ. τ. λ. See also supra s. v. ἀετός, and cf. Horap. ii. 99.

On Hawking.—Arist. H. A. ix. 36, 620 ἐν Θράκῃ τῇ καλουμένῃ ποτὲ Κεδρειπόλει ἐν τῷ ἕλει θηρεύουσιν οἱ ἄνθρωποι τὰ ὀρνίθια κοινῇ μετὰ τῶν ἱεράκων. Cf. De Mirab. vi. 118, 841 b, Ctesias in Phot. Excerpt. and ap. Ael. iv. 26, Ael. ii. 42, Antig. Hist. Mirab. [Amphipolis], 28 (34), Plin. H. N. x. 8 (10), &c. The account in Dion. De Avib. i. 6, iii. 5, and

ΙΕΡΑΞ (continued).

probably also in Martial, Ep. xiv. 216, refers to bird-catching with a *captive* hawk, as with the owl. See also for much curious information, 'Ιερακοσόφιον, s. rei accipitrariae scriptores, ed. Paris, 1612, and Leipzig, 1866, also Schlegel's Fauconnerie, &c.

Metamorphosis with the Cuckoo.—Arist. H. A. vi. 7, 562 b, Plut. Arat. cap. xxx, Tzetz. ad Lyc. 395; Geopon. xv. 1. Theophr. De Pl. ii. 4, 4. Vide s. vv. ἔποψ, κόκκυξ.

Myth and Legend.—Worship of Hawks in Egypt, Herod. ii. 65, 67; Ael. x. 14 Αἰγύπτιοι τὸν ἱέρακα Ἀπόλλωνι τιμᾶν ἐοίκασι (cf. Il. xv. 237, Od. xv. 526 and Eust. in loc., Ar. Av. 516, Eq. 1052), καὶ τὸν μὲν θεὸν 'Ωρὸν καλοῦσι τῇ φωνῇ τῇ σφετέρᾳ ... οἱ γὰρ ἱέρακες ὀρνίθων μόνοι ταῖς ἀκτῖσι τοῦ ἡλίου ῥᾳδίως καὶ ἀβασανιστῶς ἀντιβλέποντες, κ. τ. λ.: cf. ib. xi. 39 and vii. 9, where the priests are called ἱερακοβοσκοί; cf. also Plut. Is. et Os. li. p. 371. Ael. xii. 4 ὁ μὲν περδικοθήρας καὶ ὠκύπτερος Ἀπόλλωνός ἐστι θεράπων φασί, φήνην δὲ καὶ ἅρπην Ἀθηνᾷ προσνέμουσιν, Ἑρμοῦ δὲ τὸν φασσοφόντην ἄθυρμα εἶναί φασιν, Ἥρας δὲ τὸν τανυσίπτερον, καὶ τὸν τριόρχην οὕτω καλούμενον Ἀρτέμιδος. μητρὶ δὲ θεῶν τὸν μέρμνον. See also Strabo, Geogr. xvii. 1. 47, Horap. i. 8, Pier. Valer. Hierogl. xxi, &c. τίνες δέ φασιν ἐν τοῖς ἀρχαίοις χρόνοις, ἱέρακα βιβλίον ἐνεγκεῖν εἰς Θήβας τοῖς ἱερεῦσι φοινικῷ ῥάμματι περιειλημμένον, ἔχον γεγραμμένας τὰς τῶν θεραπείας τε καὶ τιμάς· διόπερ καὶ τοὺς ἱερογραμματεῖς φορεῖν φοινικοῦν ῥάμμα καὶ πτερὸν ἱέρακος ἐπὶ τῆς κεφαλῆς, Diod. Sic. i. 87, 8. The Egyptian Sun-god Phra with a hawk's head, ἱερακόμορφος, ἱερακοπρόσωπος, Philo ap. Eus. P. E. 41 D, 116 D (i. 10, iii. 12), Horap. i. 6. In the Rig-Veda the sun is frequently compared to a hawk, hovering in the air. The hawk associated with fire-worship, Ael. x. 24. A three-legged hawk sometimes seen in Egypt, Ael. xi. 39. Moult before the inundation, ib. xii. 4; live seventy years, ib. x. 14; the leg-bone has an attraction for gold, ib.; throw earth on an unburied corpse, ib. ii. 42. Salve their eyes with θριδακίνη or wild lettuce, ib. ii. 43 (also Dion. De Avib. i. 6); hence, as well as by reason of their sharp sight, the Hawk or Eagle in medicine constitute a remedy for diseases of the eye, Plin. xxix. (6) 38, &c.; as does the herb ἱεράκιον, Horap. i. 6, Plin. xx. (7) 26, xxxiv. (11) 27: it is seldom possible to trace any meaning in the mystical herbs associated with particular animals, and it is therefore worth noting in this instance that θριδακίνη is the sacred herb of Adonis. Are supposed by some to be bastard eagles, Ael. ii. 43; how a hawk caused the apprehension of a sacrilegious thief at Delphi, ib.; how the hawks in Egypt repair to certain Libyan islands to breed, having sent two messengers in front, ib. (cf. Plin. H. N. x. 8, Diod. Sic. i. 87); do not eat the heart, ib. ii. 42; hostile to the fox, the eagle, and the vulture, ib. Are exempt from thirst, Damasc. V. Isid. 97 (cf. s. v. ἀετός), but drink blood instead of water, Horap. i. 7. Their

ΙΕΡΑΞ (*continued*).

heart is eaten, to obtain prophetic powers, Porph. De Abst. ii. 48. A Hawk sitting on a tree a sign of rain, Theophr. Sign. fr. vi. 2, 17.

The Fable of the Hawk and the Nightingale, Hes. Op. et D. 201, Aes. fab. 9.

A metaphor of the Hawk and the Crows, Ar. Eq. 1052.

The metamorphosis of Hierax, Boios ap. Anton. Lib. iii; cf. that of Deucalion, Ov. Met. xi. 340.

The Hawk entered in Egypt into innumerable hieroglyphics, in which its image is, in the main, a phonetic element, the symbolic ideas being, for the most part, secondary (cf. supra, s. v. βαιήθ). According to Horap. i. 8 "Αρεα γράφοντες καὶ 'Αφροδίτην, δύο ἱέρακας ζωγραφοῦσιν; these are the symbols 🦅 and 🦅, Horus and Hat-Hor, the latter being the οἶκος "Ωρου of Plutarch. According to Chaeremon, fr. 8 Ψυχή-ἥλιος-θεός = ἱέραξ. On the sanctity of hawks in Egypt, and the solar symbolism associated with them there, see also (besides the references quoted above), Porph. De Abst. iii. 4; the Sun called ἱέραξ, ibid. iv. 16, Plut. De Is. et Osir. c. 51, Eus. P. E. iii. 10, Clem. Alex. Strom. v. 7.

For other words and phrases in which the hieroglyph of the Hawk had part, see Horap. i. 6 θεὸν βουλόμενοι σημῆναι, ἢ ὕψος, ἢ ταπείνωσιν, ἢ ὑπεροχήν, ἢ αἷμα, ἢ νίκην, ἱέρακα ζωγραφοῦσι: id. ii. 15 ἱέραξ διατεταμένος τὰς πτέρυγας ἐν ἀέρι, οἷον πτέρυγας ἔχοντα ἄνεμον σημῆναι: id. ii. 99 ἄνθρωπον ἀποταξάμενον τὰ ἴδια τέκνα δι' ἀπορίαν βουλόμενοι σημῆναι, ἱέρακα ἐγκύμονα ζωγραφοῦσιν: Diod. Sic. iii. 4. 2 ἱέραξ αὐτοῖς σημαίνει πάντα τὰ ὀξέως γενόμενα. Cf. Klaproth ad Goulianoff De Inv. Hierogl. Acrolog., cit. Leemans in Horap. p. 150, and especially Lauth, Sitzungsber. Bayer. Akad., 1876, pp. 77-79.

See also **αἰσάλων, ἄρακος, βαιήθ, βάρβαξ, βελλούνης, ἐλειός, ἐπιλεῖος, κίρκος, πέρκος, πτέρνις, σπιζίας, τριόρχης, ὑποτριόρχης, φασσοφόνος, φρυνολόγος,** &c.

'**ΙΖΙ'ΝΕΣ**· οἰωνοί, ὄρνιθες, Hesych. Cf. ἀζεινοί.

"**ΙΚΤΕΡΟΣ**. A bird with fabulous attributes; according to Pliny, identical with *galgulus*, the **Golden Oriole**.

Plin. xxx. 11 (28) Avis icterus vocatur a colore, quae si spectetur, sanari id malum [ἴκτερον, *malum regium*, the jaundice] tradunt, et avem mori. Hanc puto Latine vocari galgulum (*galbula*, Mart. xiii. 68). Cf. Dion. De Avib. i. 27; Coel. Aurel. Chron. iii. 5 passio vocabulum sumpsit secundum Graecos ab animalis nomine, quod sit coloris fellei. Cf. Schneider, in Arist. H. A. ix. 12; and Suid., who derives the word from ἰκτῖνος. Vide infra s.v. **χαραδριός**.

ἸΚΤΙ͂ΝΟΣ, or ἴκτινος (Aristoph., cf. Suid.): also ἰκτίς (Περγαῖοι, Hesych.). In plur. ἴκτινες (Ael. i. 35, ii. 47) or ἰκτῖνες (Paus.). For other grammatical forms, see L. & Sc., &c. Derivation unknown; sometimes said to be connected with Sk. çyēna.

A **Kite**: including the Common Kite, *Milvus regalis*, Briss., *M. ictinus*, Sav., and the Black Kite, *M. ater*, Gm. The Black Kite is still called ἰκτίνος in the Cyclades, where it is the commoner species of the two (Erh.). The Common Kite is also called τσίφτης in Attica (Heldreich).

In minor references frequent, usually as a robber, e. g. Theogn. 1261, 1302; Soph. Fr. 890 ἴκτινος ὡς ἔκλαγξε παρασύρας κρέας; Plat. Phaed. 82; Men. 4, 329 (493); Plat. Com. 2, 695 (69): Aristoph. fr. 2, 1192 (71), Ar. fr. 525, Etym. M. p. 470. 34 ἰκτινα παντόφθαλμον ἅρπαγα: Simon. Iambl. 11, Automed. viii, in Gk. Anth. ii. 192 οὗτος ἔχει γὰρ ἅρπαγος ἰκτίνου χεῖρα κραταιοτέρην.

Description.—Arist. De Part. 670, 34 μικρὸς ὁ σπλήν· τὴν χολὴν ἔχει πρὸς τῷ ἥπατι καὶ πρὸς τῇ κοιλίᾳ: H. A. vi. 6, 563 δύο ᾠά· ἐνίοτε δὲ καὶ τρία· ἐπῳάζει περὶ εἴκοσιν ἡμέρας: ib. viii. 3, 592 μέγεθος ὅσον τριόρχης: ib. 594 ὀλιγάκις πίνει, ὦπται δὲ πίνων. Very destructive to poultry; οὐδὲν ἄν τις ἀναιδέστερον εἴποι, Dion. De Avib. i. 7; cf. Theogn. 1302 ἰκτίνου σχέτλιον ἦθος.

A migratory bird: it arrives before the swallow, at the spring shearing-time, Ar. Av. 714; in Egypt it does not migrate, Herod. ii. 22; it sometimes hibernates, Arist. H. A. viii. 16, 600 οἱ μὲν πλησίον ὄντες τοιούτων τόπων, ἐν οἷς ἀεὶ διαμένουσι, καὶ ἰκτῖνοι καὶ χελιδόνες, ἀποχωροῦσιν ἐνταῦθα, οἱ δὲ πορρωτέρω ὄντες οὐκ ἐκτοπίζουσιν ἀλλὰ κρύπτουσιν ἑαυτούς· ἤδη γὰρ ὠμμέναι πολλαὶ χελιδόνες εἰσὶν ἐν ἀγγείοις ἐψιλωμέναι πάμπαν, καὶ ἰκτῖνοι ἐκ τοιούτων ἐκπετόμενοι χωρίων, ὅταν φαίνωνται τὸ πρῶτον. The common Kite is merely a bird of passage in Greece, a very few remaining to winter there (Krüper); the Black Kite is a rare visitor to the mainland of Greece. Both species are common, and breed, in Macedonia (Krüper, Elwes, &c.).

The statement Ἰκτῖνος φαίνεται appears in various Calendars, e. g. Geminus, Isag. in Arat. Phaen. c. xvi, who dates its advent, according to Eudoxus thirteen days, to Euctemon eight, and to Callippus one day, before the vernal equinox. According to Grotius, Arat. Phaen. notae ad imagg. p. 55, Milvus, in Latin, refers to the constellation Cygnus: cf. Ov. F. iii. 793 Stella Lycaoniam vergit declivis ad Arcton Milvus. Haec illa nocte [xvi. Kal. April.] videnda venit; see also Plin. xviii. 6; but according to Ideler, Sternnamen, p. 77, the dates given do not tally with this hypothesis, the heliacal rising of Cygnus being three months earlier; and he prefers to assume that the statements in the older Calendars referred to the bird of passage, and were mistakenly

ΙΚΤΙΝΟΣ (continued).

attributed to a constellation by Ovid and Pliny. I am for myself inclined to think that Ovid did allude to the constellation, but that he did not mean (nor say) that on the date in question it rose *with the sun*; as a matter of fact it then rose at midnight, and was on the meridian when it disappeared at sunrise. Ἰκτῖνος is also the name of one of the mystical λύκοι or ἄκμονες (q. v.) in Opp. Cyneg. iii. 331.

Myth and Legend.—Hostile to κόραξ, Arist. H. A. ix. 1, 609, Ael. iv. 5, Phile, De An. 688, Cic. De Nat. Deor. ii. 49; friendly to πίφιγξ and ἄρπη, Arist. l. c., Ael. v. 48. Use θρῖος as a remedy, Phile 725; place ῥάμνον in the nest as a charm, Ael. i. 55; how a stick from a Kite's nest is a remedy for headache, Plin. xxix. (6) 36, xxx. (4) 12; detest the pomegranate, ῥοία, so that they never even alight on that tree, and why, Dion. De Avib. i. 7. Suffer at certain seasons from sore feet, Dion. l. c., namely, at the time of the Solstice, Plin. x. (10) 12; and from sore eyes, Suid. s. v. ἴκτερος. See also Albert. M. De Animal. xxiii. 24, p. 641. Cf. supra, s. v. ἱέραξ. How the Kites in Elis rob men in the market-place (cf. Ar. Av. 1624), but never molest the ἱερόθυτοι, Ael. ii. 47, Arist. De Mirab. 123, 842 a, Theopomp. ap. Apollon. Hist. Mirab. x, Pausan. v. 14, Plin. l. c.; on the Kite as dangerous to sacrifices, cf. Ar. Pax 1099, Av. 892; cf. τῷ ἰκτίνῳ τῷ ἑστιούχῳ, Ar. Av. 865. How the Kite was once a King, Ar. Av. 499. The story in Plin. l. c., milvos artem gubernandi docuisse caudae flexibus, does not seem to occur in Greek. In Latin, Milvus is proverbial for its powers of flight and of vision; cf. Pers. Sat. iv. 26, Juv. ix. 25, Martial ix. Ep. 55.

Fable of ἰκτῖνος that lost its voice trying to neigh, Aes. Fab. ed. Halm, 170, Babr. 73; Suid.; cf. Julian in Misopogone, p. 366 (cit. Schneider in Arist. H. A. vi. 6) τὸν ἴκτινα ἐπιθέσθαι τῷ χρεμετίζειν, ὥσπερ οἱ γενναῖοι τῶν ἵππων, εἶτα τοῦ μὲν ἐπιλαθόμενον, τὸ δὲ μὴ δυνηθέντα ἐλεῖν ἱκανῶς, ἀμφοῖν στέρεσθαι καὶ φαυλότερον τῶν ἄλλων ὀρνίθων εἶναι τὴν φωνήν : cf. ἄνθος. Fable of λάρος καὶ ἰκτίνος, Aes. 239. Proverb, προκυλινδεῖσθαι ἰκτίνοις, Ar. Av. 501; cf. Suid. ἔαρος γὰρ ἀρχομένου ἴκτινος φαίνεται. οἱ πένητες οὖν ἀπαλλαγέντες χειμῶνος προεκυλινδοῦντο καὶ προσεκύνουν αὐτούς.

See also ἄρπη, βατυρρηγάλη, δίκτυς, ἔλανος.

ΙΛΙΑΣ.

Also ἰλλάς, Athen. ii. 65 a, Eust. 947, 8. In some MSS. of Athen. also τυλάς. Perhaps akin to ἴχλα, i. e. κίχλα.

A kind of **Thrush**: for references, see κίχλη.

Gesner, Belon, and others identify ἰλιάς as the Redwing, *Turdus iliacus*, L., on account of its small size (Arist. H. A. ix. 20, 617). Sundevall points out that the expression ἧττον ποικίλη (l. c.) is inapplicable. In Athen. ii. 65 a (c. 68) these words are omitted from a corresponding passage; and the account of the nesting habits of κίχλη (H. A. vi. 1)

ΙΛΙΑΣ (continued).

are transferred to ἰλλάς. Both the Redwing and the Fieldfare are now winter-migrants in Greece, and not very common (Krüper, Lindermayer, &c.). The word was probably an old or dialectic form, meaning simply *thrush*, to which it was sought to apply a specific meaning in Aristotle.

ΙΜΑΝΤΟ'ΠΟΥΣ. A wading-bird; the name is now allotted to the Stilt.

Dion. De Avib. ii. 9 αἱ δ' ἱμαντόποδες λεπτοῖς μὲν σκέλεσι χρῶνται, καὶ ἔχουσι τὴν προσηγορίαν ἐκ τούτου. καινὸν δ' ἐπ' αὐτῶν ἐστιν, ὅτι τὴν κάτωθεν γένυν ἔχοντες πεπηγυῖαν, μόνον κινοῦσι τὴν ἄνωθεν. Cf. Plin. x. 47 (64).

ΙΝΔΙΚΟ'Σ 'ΟΡΝΙΣ. *The Phoenix* (q. v.), Aristid. ii. p. 107; cf. Creuzer, Symbolik, ii. p. 167.

ΙΝΥΞ· ὄρνεόν τι, ᾧ χρῶνται αἱ φαρμακίδες, Hesych. Vide s. v. ἴυγξ.

ΙΞΟΒΟ'ΡΟΣ, or ἰξοφάγος, Athen. 65 a (ἴξος = *viscum*, mistletoe, cf. Ital. *viscada*, the *Missel*-thrush).

The **Missel-thrush**, *Turdus viscivorus*, L. Mod. Gr. κιριαρίνα (v. d. Mühle), δενδροτσίχλα on Parnassus, κυρὰ Εἰρήνη in Eurytania, βουνοτσίχλα in Laconia (Heldreich). The only one of the true thrushes resident in Greece throughout the year (Krüper).

Arist. H. A. ix. 20, 617. Vide s. v. κίχλη.

ΙΠΠΑΛΕΚΤΡΥΩ'Ν· τὸν μέγαν ἀλεκτρυόνα, ἢ τὸν γραφόμενον ἐν τοῖς Περσικοῖς περιστρώμασι. γράφονται δὲ οἷον γρύπες. ἔνιοι γύπα, Hesych.

Cf. Ar. Ran. 932 (959), Pax 1177, Av. 800 τὸν ξουθὸν ἱππαλεκτρυόνα: cf. Aesch. Myrm. fr. 130, &c., &c.

Note.—The epithet ξουθός is applied to various creatures, e. g. ἀηδών, ἀλκυών, χελιδών, μέλισσα, τέττιξ, all of which agree in being closely linked with religious symbolism. The meaning of the adjective is quite unknown. With the various conjectures of modern commentators cf. Photius: ξουθόν· λεπτόν, ἁπαλόν, ἐλαφρόν, χλωρόν, ὑγρόν, ξανθόν, καλόν, πυκνόν, ὀξύ, ταχύ. οἱ δὲ ποικιλόν, εὐειδές, διαυγές.

ΙΠΠΑ'ΡΙΟΝ· ὄρνεον ποιόν, παραπλήσιον χηναλώπεκι, Hesych.

ΙΠΠΗ, (s. ἵππα, s. ἵπτα, s. ἵττα). ὁ δρυοκώλαψ, ἐθνικῶς, Hesych. The root is supposed to be ιπ, Lat. *ic-o* (Vaniček 82), cf. ἶπος; and the word is taken to be identical with πίπω (q. v.); but the ἴττα suggests identity with σίττη.

Doubtless identical also with ἴπνη, Boios ap. Anton. Lib. 21 καὶ ἔστιν ἀγαθὸς οὗτος ὁ ὄρνις ἐπὶ θήραν ἰόντι.

ΙΛΙΑΣ—ΙΥΓΞ 71

ΙΠΠΟ'ΚΑΜΠΤΟΣ· στρουθίον τι, Hesych. (*verb. dub.*).

ΊΣΚΛΑ, v. ἴχλα.

ΊΣΤΡΑΞ· ὄρνις ποιός, Hesych. Perhaps for τέτραξ (q. v.).

ΊΤΥΞ. ὄρνεον, Suid., Phot., Lex. Seg. Cf. ἴυγξ.

ΊΥΓΞ. Perhaps from the hissing cry, cf. ἰυγή, a snake's hiss, Nic. Th. 400; but more probably a word of foreign and unknown origin.

The **Wryneck,** *Yunx torquilla,* L. Mod. Gk. σφενδόλι, μυρμηκολόγος (Heldreich). See also ἴνυξ, ἴτυξ, κιναίδιον, σεισοπυγίς.

Arist. H. A. ii. 12, 504 a (a full and accurate description) ὀλίγοι δέ τινες δύο μὲν [δακτύλους] ἔμπροσθεν δύο δ' ὄπισθεν, οἷον ἡ καλουμένη ἴυγξ [cf. De Part. iv. 12, 695]. αὕτη δ' ἐστὶ μικρῷ μὲν μείζων σπίζης, τὸ δ' εἶδος ποικίλον, ἰδίᾳ δ' ἔχει τά τε περὶ [τοὺς δακτύλους καὶ] τὴν γλῶτταν ὁμοίαν τοῖς ὄφεσιν· ἔχει γὰρ ἐπὶ μῆκος ἔκτασιν καὶ ἐπὶ τέτταρας δακτύλους, καὶ πάλιν συστέλλεται εἰς ἑαυτήν. ἔτι δὲ περιστρέφει τὸν τράχηλον εἰς τοὐπίσω τοῦ λοιποῦ σώματος ἠρεμοῦντος, καθάπερ οἱ ὄφεις. ὄνυχας δ' ἔχει μεγάλους μὲν ὁμοίους μέντοι πεφυκότας τοῖς τῶν κολοιῶν· τῇ δὲ φωνῇ τρίζει (cf. Plin. xi. (47) 107). Ael. H. A. ix. 13 ἴυγγας, ἐρωτικὰς ἄνθρωποί φασιν εἶναί τινες: cf. ibid. xv. 19. Mentioned among mimetic birds, Ael. H. A. vi. 19 ὑποκρίνεται τὸν πλάγιον ἡ ἴυγξ αὐλόν.

Superstition, interwoven with a phallic symbolism (cf. Dion. De Avib. i. 23), used the ἴυγξ as a charm to bring back a strayed lover. Pind. P. iv. 214 (in connexion with Jason and Medea) πότνια δ' ὀξυτάτων βελέων ποικίλαν ἴυγγα τετράκναμον Οὐλυμπόθεν ἐν ἀλύτῳ ζεύξαισα κύκλῳ μαινάδ' ὄρνιν Κυπρογένεια φέρεν πρῶτον ἀνθρώποισι. Theocr. Id. ii "Ἴυγξ ἕλκε τὸ τῆνον ἐμὸν ποτὶ δῶμα τὸν ἄνδρα. Gk. Anth. (Jac. iv. 140, Anth. Pal. v. 205) "Ἴυγξ ἡ Νικοῦς ἡ καὶ διαπόντιον ἕλκειν | ἄνδρα καὶ ἐκ θαλάμων παῖδας ἐπισταμένη. Cf. Soph. Oenom. iii. 1 ἴυγγα θηρητηρίαν ἔρωτος. The bird was bound upon a wheel and spun round, cf. Theocr. ii. 30; Schol. Pindar, l. c. ap. Suid. ed. Gaisford λαμβάνουσαι γὰρ αὐτὸ δεσμεύουσιν ἐκ τροχοῦ τινος, ὃν περιρρομβοῦσιν ἅμα ἐπάδουσαι. οἱ δέ φασιν ὅτι τὰ ἔντερα αὐτοῦ ἐξελκύσασαι καθάπτουσι τῷ τροχῷ. Cf. Hesych., Suidas, Tzetzes in Lycophr. 310, Ael. H. A. ix. 13, &c. In Pind. P. iv. 214 ἴυγγα τετράκναμον is supposed to be the bird thus bound, and cross-fixed or spread-eagled; cf. Pind. P. ii. 40 τετράκναμον δεσμόν. See also King, Ant. Gems, i. 381.

In Xen. Mem. iii. 12, 17 ἕλκειν ἴυγγα ἐπί τινι is to work the bird against some one (Schn.), and perhaps the word is here used for the wheel itself or for a charm in a more general sense; cf. Aristaenet. ii. 18 τὸν φιλτροποιὸν ἱκέτευε πάλιν κατ' ἐκείνης ἀνακινῆσαι τὰς ἴυγγας: cf. also Pind. Nem. iv. 35 ἴυγγι δ' ἕλκομαι ἦτορ νεομηνίᾳ θιγέμεν: Luc. Dom. 13 ὥσπερ ἀπὸ ἴυγγος τῷ κάλλει ἑλκόμενος: Ar. Lys. 1110, Diog. L. vi. 2, 76;

ΙΥΓΞ (*continued*).

Ael. xv. 19, Opp. Hal. iv. 132; still more loosely used in Ael. ii. 9, v. 40, xii. 46, xiv. 15, &c. Compare also Virgil's translation of Theocritus, Ducite ab urbe domum *mea carmina*, ducite Daphnin. The magic wheel was properly called ῥόμβος, Theocr. ii. 30, Orphic. fr. xvii (Hermann) ap. Clem. Alex. Strom. p. 15. 8, Luc. D. Meretr. iv. 5, &c.; στρόφαλος, Schol. ad Synes. 361 D, Psell. in Schol. ad Orac. Chald., τροχίσκος, Tzetz. Chil. xi. 380 (trochiscilus, Apul. De Mag. xxx), cf. Clem. Alex. Strom. v. 8, or ῥικώς, Suid., and in Lat. *rhombus*, Mart. ix. 30, Propert. iii. 6, 26, *rota*, Plaut. Cistell. ii. 1. 4, or *turbo*, Hor. Epod. xvii. 7. It was probably similar to, though not identical with, the ῥόπτρον, or tambourine of the Corybantes, and the bird was, like that instrument, associated with the worship of Rhea, Dion. De Avib. i. 23. According to Marcellus in Nonn. Dionys. ix. 116, the ῥόμβος was (and under the same name still is, in Italy) an instrument twirled round at the end of a thong, which means to say, I suppose, that it was a 'bull-roarer'; if this be so, the ἴυγξ τετράκναμος was not rotated round on its own axis, but spun at the end of a string, as we spin cockchafers. Concerning the magic wheel, see also Selden, De Diis Syr. i. 1, 33.

The bird is represented on a vase in connexion with Dionysus, Brit. Mus. Vase Cat. No. 1293; and the Pindaric epithet ποικίλη has been interpreted as a link in its Dionysiac character (cf. R. Brown, jun., Dionys. Myth, i. 339). In this connexion the name Ἰύγγυι for Dionysus (Hesych.), is very interesting. Another vase (No. 1356) represents Adonis holding out the bird to Aphrodite.

ἴυγξ was also used metaphorically for *love* or desire, cf. Aesch. Pers. 989, Lyc. 310 and Schol. Heliodor. iv. 15, &c.

The ἴυγξ in Anth. Pal. v. 205 was engraved on an amethyst, χρύσῳ ποικιλθεῖσα, διαυγέος ἐξ ἀμεθύστου | γλυπτή: it is represented on a gem, associated with Jason and the Golden Fleece (Imh.-Bl. and K. pl. xxi. 21, p. 131) probably in illustration of Pind. Pyth. iv.

According to Nicander, ap. Anton. Lib. Met. 9, one of the nine Emathidae, daughters of Pierus, was metamorphosed into the bird ἴυγξ.

The ἴυγξ was equally sacred among the ancient Persians and Babylonians, Marini Proclus, xxviii, cf. Hopf, Thierorakel, p. 144. See also the remarkable description of the Royal Judgement-seat at Babylon, Philostr. V. Apollon. i. 25, where however the precise meaning of ἴυγξ is not clear: δικάζει μὲν δὴ ὁ βασιλεὺς ἐνταῦθα· χρυσαῖ δὲ ἴυγγες ἀποκρέμανται τοῦ ὀρόφου τέτταρες, τὴν Ἀδράστειαν αὐτῷ παρεγγυῶσαι, καὶ τὸ μὴ ὑπὲρ τοὺς ἀνθρώπους αἴρεσθαι· ταύτας οἱ μάγοι αὐτοί φασιν ἁρμόττεσθαι, φοιτῶντες ἐς τὰ βασίλεια· καλοῦσι δὲ αὐτὰς θεῶν γλώσσας; cf. Creuzer, Symb. ii. 221. See also Pseudo-Zoroaster, fr. 54, ed. Cory.

ΙΥΓΞ (continued).

Bury (J. of Hellen. St. vii. pp. 157-160) supposes, chiefly from Theocritus Id. ii, and Pindar Nem. iv, that the ἴυγξ was originally a *moon-charm* or invocation to the Moon-Goddess Ἰώ, a theory supported by Mart. ix. 30, where *rhombus* is in like manner a *moon-charm*, as also by such parallel passages as Virg. Ecl. viii. 69, and Tibull. i. 8. 21. The ἴυγξ was undoubtedly thus used in lunar rites, but the bird does not cry Ἰώ, Ἰώ, and the suggested derivation of its name and sanctity from such a cry cannot hold. It is interesting, however, to find that Io and ἴυγξ do come into relation with one another, the witch who by her spells had made Zeus enamoured of Io, being transformed by Juno into the bird ἴυγξ, Niceph. in Schol. ad Synesium, p. 360, Creuzer, Symb. iii. 249; see also Schol. Pind. l. c. It is thus quite possible that Ἰώ and ἴυγξ are after all cognate, though the bird's cry had nothing to do with their etymology.

ἴυγξ and ἶβις come into relation with one another, as both connected with moon-worship; and the dialectic form of the latter, ἴβυξ (Hesych., ? ἴϝυξ) suggests perhaps an ancient confusion between the two names.

ἼΧΛΑ. A form of κίχλα, Hesych. Cf. Lob. Path. p. 107. Also ἴσκλα, ἰχάλη, Hesych.: cf. Mod. Gk. τσίχλα.

ἸΧΝΕΎΜΩΝ. An unknown or fabulous small bird; mentioned by Nicander ap. Anton. Lib. c. 14.

ἸΩΝΑ͂Σ· περιστερά, Hesych. Vide s. v. οἰνάς.

ἸΩΝΊΣ. An unknown bird; mentioned among the ὄρνιθας ποταμίους ἅμα καὶ λιμναίους, Aristoph. Hist. Anim. Epit. i. 24 (Supplem. Aristot. i. 1. p. 5, Berolini, 1885).

ΚΑΚΚΆΒΗ, s. **κακκαβίς.** κακκάβα, Hesych. (Cf. Sk. *kukkubha*.) A name for the **Partridge.**

Athen. ix. 390 a καλοῦνται δ' οἱ πέρδικες ὑπ' ἐνίων κακκάβαι, ὡς καὶ ὑπ' Ἀλκμᾶνος· ἔπη τάδε καὶ μέλος Ἀλκμάν | εὗρε, γεγλωσσαμένον | κακκαβίδων στόμα [ὄνομα, Casaub.] συνθέμενος (Alcman, fr. 25 Bergk). Hence κακκαβίζειν, Arist. H. A. iv. 9, 536 b; Athen. l. c.; cf. Anthol. Lat. 733 (ed. Riese) Interea perdix cacabat nidumque revisit. Cf. Stat. Sylv. ii. 4. 20 quaeque refert iungens iterata vocabula perdix. Vide s. v. **πέρδιξ.**

ΚΑΛΑΜΟΔΎΤΗΣ. An unknown bird.

Ael. vi. 46 κέδρου τὸν καλαμοδύτην ἀπόλλυσι φύλλα. Cf. Phile, 664.

ΚΑ΄ΛΑΝΔΡΟΣ. The **Calandra Lark,** *Alauda Calandra*, L., *Melancorypha calandra*, auctt. The Chelaundre or Calendre of Chaucer, who distinguishes it from the lark or *laverokke*, Rom. of the Rose, 662, cf. v. 655. Skeat (in loc.) derives the word,

ΚΑΛΑΝΔΡΟΣ (continued).

through O. F. calandre, caladre, from L. caradrius, Gk. χαραδριός (cf. Babr. lxxxii; and vide infra s. v. χαραδριός). Said by others to be connected with L. *caliendrum*, a tufted head-dress, a top-knot.

Dion. De Avib. iii. 15 κάλανδρον δὲ οὐκ ἄν τις ἕλοι ῥᾳδίως, εἰ μὴ πλησίον ὕδατος θείη τὸ λίνον· ὁ μὲν γὰρ τοῦ ποτοῦ χρῄζων προσίπταται, ὁ δὲ ἀγρευτὴς τέως ἐν καλύβῃ λανθάνων καὶ ἐπιτείνων τὸ δίκτυον, πίνοντα καλύψει τὸν κάλανδρον. The same device is still used for the capture of small birds in Italy; cf. Frederick II, De Venat. p. 32; J. G. Schneider, Anm. z. d. Ecl. Phys. p. 41; see also Bechstein's 'Cage Birds,' &c.

ΚΑ΄ΛΑΡΙΣ. (In MS. D^a κόλαρις). An unknown bird.

Arist. H. A. ix. 1, 609 τὸν δὲ κάλαριν ὁ αἰγωλιὸς καὶ οἱ ἄλλοι γαμψώνυχες κατεσθίουσιν· ὅθεν ὁ πόλεμος αὐτοῖς. Gesner suggested κολλυρίωνα, Billerbeck κίλλυρον s. κίλλουρον : cf. J. G. Schneider *in loc*. The whole chapter is replete with difficulties, and, in my opinion, with signs of foreign influence or even of spurious origin.

ΚΑ΄ΛΑΦΟΣ· ἀσκάλαφος, Hesych.

ΚΑΛΙ΄ΔΡΙΣ. Vide s. v. σκαλίδρις.

ΚΑ΄ΛΛΩΝ. A name for the Cock.

Κάλλαια, τὰ ὑπὸ τὰ γένεια τῶν ἀλεκτρυόνων, οὓς κάλλωνας οἱ Ἀττικοὶ λέγουσιν, Moeris. Cf. χειλῶνες.

ΚΑΛΟΤΥ΄ΠΟΣ· ὁ δρυοκολάπτης, Hesych. Cf. ξυλοκόπος.

ΚΑ΄ΡΥΔΟΣ, ΚΑΡΥ΄ΔΑΛΟΣ, Hesych. Vide s. v. κόρυδος.

ΚΑ΄ΡΦΥΡΟΙ· οἱ νεοσσοί, Hesych.

ΚΑΣΑΝΔΗ΄ΡΙΟΝ· ἰκτῖνος, Hesych. A very doubtful word; an emended reading is κάσυν· θηρίον (Schmidt).

ΚΑ΄ΣΠΙΟΣ ΌΡΝΙΣ. A remarkable bird, of three varieties, of which one croaks like a frog, one bleats like a goat, and the third barks like a dog. Full description in Ael. xvii. 33, 38. It is not identified by Gesner.

ΚΑΤΑΡΡΑ΄ΚΤΗΣ, s. καταράκτης (Arist., Codd. Med. Vatic., &c.). An unknown bird; the references to which are so discordant as to suggest that the meaning was early lost, if indeed the name was ever applied to an actual species. It is the 'Cormorant,' שלך, of the LXX.

Mentioned in Ar. Av. 886. In Soph. frr. 344, 641, applied to the Eagle and to the Harpies (cf. Hesych.), as καταρρακτήρ is to κίρκος, Lyc.

ΚΑΛΑΝΔΡΟΣ—ΚΑΤΡΕΥΣ 75

ΚΑΤΑΡΡΑΚΤΗΣ (*continued*).

169. In Aristotle, said to be a sea-bird, but not web-footed: mentioned as ὄρνις ποτάμιος, Aristoph. H. A. Epit. i. 24, and θαλάσσιος, ib. i. 23.

Arist. H. A. ii. 17, 509 τὸν στόμαχον ἔχει εὐρὺν καὶ πλατὺν ὅλον. Ib. ix. 12, 615 ὄρνις σχιζόπους· ζῇ μὲν περὶ θάλατταν, ὅταν δὲ καθῇ αὐτὸν εἰς τὸ βαθύ, μένει χρόνον οὐκ ἐλάττονα ἢ ὅσον πλέθρον διελθοι τις· ἔστι δ' ἔλαττον ἱέρακος. From this account and from its mention in ii. 17, between τὰ σχιζόποδα (ὠτίς) and τὰ στεγανόποδα (λάρος), Aubert and Wimmer identify καταρράκτης with *Podiceps auritus*, the Eared Grebe, Mod. Gk. καραπαταίκιον (Erh. p. 48); Sundevall, on the other hand, with the Little Cormorant, *Phalacrocorax* or *Graculus pygmaeus* (vide κολοιός, β). Neither of these birds, however, suggests by its habits the name καταρράκτης : and neither is white in colour, so that they at least conflict with the following excerpt from Dion. De Avib. ii. 2 ὡς οἱ τῶν λάρων ἐλάσσονες, ἰσχυρὸς δὲ καὶ τὴν χρόαν λευκός, καὶ τοῖς τὰς φάσσας ἀναιροῦσιν ἱέραξι προσόμοιος . . . εἰς τὸν πόντον οἷα πίπτων οἴσεται . . . τοῖς σκοπέλοις καὶ τοῖς αἰγιαλοῖς ἐφιζάνει. Further, a fabulous account of the breeding-habits. According to the same author (iii. 22) σανίσιν εἰκόνας ἐπιγράψαντες ἰχθίων θηρῶσι τοὺς καταρράκτας· σὺν ὁρμῇ γὰρ ὡς ἐπί τινα καταπτάντες ἰχθὺν περιρρήγνυνται ταῖς σανίσι καὶ διαφθείρονται. These accounts are usually applied to the Gannet or Solan Goose, *Sula bassana* (cf. Oedmann, Act. Acad. Stockh., vii. 1786, Schneid. in Arist. vol. ii. p. 88); but the size is incompatible with such an identification, and the bird is not a native of Greece. The account in Plin. x. (44) 51 is wholly fabulous, and includes the story of the Birds of Diomede, οἱ καταράσσουσιν εἰς τὰς τῶν βαρβάρων κεφαλάς, Arist. De Mirab. 79, 836 a; cf. Ael. i. 1, and vide s. v. ἐρωδιός.

Gesner, who is followed in modern ornithological nomenclature and by the lexicographers, identified καταρράκτης with the Skua, *Lestris catarrhactes*, L., a bird which does not occur in the Mediterranean.

ΚΑΤΡΕΥ'Σ. An unknown or mystical bird.

Cleitarch. fr. 18, ap. Ael. xvii. 23 μέγεθος πρὸς τὸν ταών· τὰ δὲ ἄκρα τῶν πτέρων ἔοικε σμαράγδῳ καὶ ὁρῶν μὲν ἄλλως, οἷκ οἶδας οἷους ὀφθαλμοὺς ἔχει· εἰ δὲ εἰς σὲ ἀπίδοι, ἐρεῖς κιννάβαριν τὸ ὄμμα, κ.τ.λ. Cf. Strabo, xv. i. 69. Nonn. Dion. xxvi. 206 κατρεὺς δ' ἐσσομένοιο προθεσπίζει χύσιν ὄμβρου | ξανθοφυὴς λιγύφωνος· ἀπὸ βλεφάρων δὲ οἱ αἴγλη | πέμπεται, ὀρθρινῇσι βολαῖς ἀντίρροπος ἠοῦς. | πολλάκι δ' ἠνεμόεντος ὑπὲρ δένδροιο λιγαίνων, | σύνθρονος ὠρίωνος ἀνέπλεκε γείτονα μολπὴν | φοινικέαις πτερύγεσσι κεκασμένος· ἢ τάχα φαίης, | μελπομένου κατρῆος ἑῷον ὕμνον ἀκούων, | ὄρθριον αἰολόδειρον ἀηδόνα κῶμον ὑφαίνειν.

The description of the plumage in Aelian has suggested to some commentators the Manâl or Impeyan Pheasant, *Lophopus impeyanus* (cf. Val. Ball, Ind. Antiq., xiv. 305, 1885), which bird is very possibly

ΚΑΤΡΕΥΣ (*continued*).

meant by the partridge larger than a vulture, Strabo, xv. 1, 73, and by the ἀλεκτρυόνες μέγισται of Ael. xvi. 2: but the identification of κατρεύς with that bird is precluded by the comparison of its voice with the Nightingale's, a statement which suggests comparison with Sk. *kalára*, melodious. The various accounts are all fabulous or mystical, and the bird is always coupled with the equally mystical ὠρίων. The ἀγρεύς of Ael. viii. 24, though described as τὸ γένος κοσσύφων φρήτωρ καὶ συγγενής, is probably akin.

ΚΑΥ'ΑΞ (=κάϝαξ), s. καύηξ. Apparently a Doric form of κῆϋξ: also καύης, Hippon. 5. Root unknown: a comparison with such words as Lith. *kovas*, Dutch *kanuw*, Eng. *chough*, is tempting, but unwarranted: cf. Fick, ii. 63. A diving sea-bird. κανάξ· λάρος, Hesych.

Antim. fr. 2 (57), ap. Schol. in Apoll. Rhod. i. 1008 ἠΰτε τις καύηξ δύπτησιν ἐς ἁλμυρὸν ὕδωρ. Cf. Lyc. 425 "Ἀλεντος οὐκ ἄπωθε καύηκας ποτῶν: Euphor. 87; Leon. Tar. 74; Anth. P. vii. 652. Vide s. vv. κῆϋξ, κήξ.

ΚΑΥΚΑΛΙ'ΑΣ, s. **καυκίαλος**, s. **καυκιάλης**. ὄρνις ποιός, Hesych.

ΚΕ'ΑΡΟΣ· ὄρτυξ, Hesych. A very doubtful word.

ΚΕΒΛΗ'ΠΥΡΙΣ. In Ar. Av. 303 usually translated Redpoll (from κεβλή = κεφαλή), which bird, *Fringilla linaria*, L., only occurs in Greece rarely, during severe winters. The meaning is unknown.

ΚΕΓΧΡΗΙ'Σ (Arist. H. A. ii. 17, Ael. ii. 43), κεγχρίς (Arist., Ael. xiii. 25), κερχνηίς or κερχνήις (Aristoph., Ael. xii. 3, Eubul. fr. ap. Athen. ii. 65 e, Photius), κέγχρη (Aristoph. H. A. Epit. i. 22, i. 28), κέρχνη, Hesych. Cf. also κέρκαξ, κέρκνος.

A **Kestrel-Hawk**. Mod. Gk. ἱεράκι, κιρκινέζι ἀνεμογάμος (Heldr.). The Common Kestrel, *Falco tinnunculus*, L., is a permanent resident in Greece, and not rare; but the Lesser Kestrel, *F. cenchris*, Naum. or *F. tinnunculoides*, Natt., a summer migrant, is in its season the commonest of Greek hawks; cf. G. St. Hilaire ap. Bory de St. Vincent, *Morée*, Oiseaux, p. 29, pl. ii, iii: Aub. u. Wimm., Arist. De Gen., Introd. p. 28; Krüper, op. cit., p. 161; and Lindermayer, p. 14, who says 'Ich habe im Jahre 1848 von 5-7 Uhr Morgens an dem Thore der Akropolis 14 Stücke erlegt, ohne mich von der Stelle zu bewegen.'

Derivation unknown. L. and S. compare κέγχρος, κεγχρηίς with Lat. *milium, miluus*; but derive the name from κέρχνος, 'hoarse': cf. Fr. cresserelle, O. F. quercerelle. Scalig. in Arist. p. 251

ΚΕΓΧΡΗΣ (*continued*).

Quercerellam vocant Franci, non corrupta voce, quasi Cenchrellellam, ut ait Ruellius, sed quasi Querquerellam; nam Querquerum, lamentabile, dixerunt veteres; semper enim stridet et queri videtur. The derivation from κέγχρος is also old, cf. Camus ii. p. 257 'parce qu'elle a le plumage couvert de petites taches comme de petites graines.'

Arist. H. A. ii. 17, 509 τῆς κοιλίας αὐτῆς τι ἔχει ὅμοιον προλόβῳ. (Cf. Gesner, p. 284 Dieses Vogels Magen ist dem Kropf gleich und gar nicht fleischigt). Ib. vi. 1, 558 b πλεῖστα τίκτει τῶν γαμψωνύχων. ὦπται μὲν οὖν καὶ τέτταρα ἤδη, τίκτει δὲ καὶ πλείω. Ib. vi. 2, 559 ᾠὰ ἐρυθρά ἐστιν ὥσπερ μίλτος. Aristoph. H. A. Epit. i. 28 μόνη τίκτει ᾠὰ φοινικᾶ. De Gen. iii. 750 μάλιστα δὲ ἡ κεγχρὶς πολύγονον· μόνον γὰρ σχεδὸν τοῦτο καὶ πίνει τῶν γαμψωνύχων, ἡ δ' ὑγρότης καὶ ἡ σύμφυτος καὶ ἡ ἐπακτὸς σπερματικὸν μετὰ τῆς ὑπαρχούσης αὐτῇ θερμότητος. τίκτει δ' οὐδ' αὐτὴ πολλὰ λίαν ἀλλὰ τέτταρα τὸ πλεῖστον. Cf. H. A. viii. 3, 594; Plin. x. (37) 52. On the other hand, according to Ael. ii. 43 ἐστὶ φῦλον ἱεράκων ὃ καλεῖται κεγχρηίς, καὶ πότου δέεται οὐδέν.

Mentioned also in Ar. Av. 304, 589, 1181: Ael. xii. 4. One of the daughters of Pieros was transformed by the Muses into the bird κεγχρίς, Nicand. ap. Anton. Lib. c. 9.

In Ael. xiii. 25, κεγχρίς seems to refer to a different bird, being mentioned as a dainty with συκαλίς, and κερχνής is mentioned in a similar way by Eubul. ap. Athen. ii. 65 e.

ΚΕΓΧΡΙΤΗΣ. Apparently a sort of wild **duck** or **goose**, Dion. De Avib. iii. 23.

ΚΕΙ͂ΡΙΣ· ὄρνεον· ἱέραξ, οἱ δὲ ἀλκυόνα, Hesych.

On the fabled metamorphosis of Ciris, Nisus, Pandion, &c., vide supra, s.v. **ἁλιάετος**; cf. also **κηρύλος, κίρις**.

ΚΕΙ͂ΣΣΑ· κίσσα, Λάκωνες, Hesych.

ΚΕΛΕΟ͂Σ (MSS. have κηλιός, καλιός, κολιός). The **Green Woodpecker**, *Picus viridis*, L. (a scarce bird in Greece, Lindermayer). Mod. Gk. πελεκάνος, τσικλιδάρα, δενδροφάγος, Heldr.

Arist. H. A. ii. 4, 504: has feet like ἴυγξ. Ib. viii. 3, 593 τὸ μέγεθος ὅσον τρυγών, τὸ δὲ χρῶμα χλωρὸς ὅλος· ἔστι δὲ ξυλοκόπος σφόδρα, καὶ νέμεται ἐπὶ τῶν ξύλων τὰ πολλά, φωνήν τε μεγάλην ἔχει· γίνεται δὲ μάλιστα περὶ Πελοπόννησον. The preceding reference is as accurate as the following is unmeaning or mystical: Ib. ix. 1, 609, 610 φίλοι λαεδὸς καὶ κελεός· ὁ μὲν γὰρ κελεὸς παρὰ ποταμὸν οἰκεῖ καὶ λόχμας· πολέμιοι κελεὸς καὶ λιβυός. Suid. ὄρνεον ταχύτατον. The identification of κελεός with

ΚΕΛΕΟΣ (*continued*).

the Green Woodpecker is said to have been first given by Gesner, cf. Schn. in Arist., vol. iii. p. 592.

The bird κελεός figures, together with λαιός and others, in a very mystical story of Boios, ap. Anton. Lib. c. xix. Celeus is also the name of a mystical king of Attica, in connexion with the story of Ceres and Triptolemus; this circumstance may be correlated with other Woodpecker-myths in Greek and Latin referred to s. v. **δρυοκολάπτης**: cf. Mythogr. Vatic. i. 7. 8, iii. 7. 2; Schol. ad Greg. Nazianz. p. 48, ed. Gaisf., &c. On other relations between Celeus and the Ceres-myth, cf. Hom. Hymn. Cer. 475; Ar. Ach. 48; Pausan. i. 14, 38, 39, ii. 14; Anton. Lib. c. xix; vide also Creuzer's Symbolik (ed. 1836) i. 152, iv. 368, 384.

ΚΕ'ΠΦΟΣ. MSS. have also κέμφος, κίπφος, γείφος. An unknown water-bird; usually, but without warrant, identified (after Schneider in Arist., and Promt. Lips. 1786, p. 501) with the Stormy Petrel, *Thalassidroma pelagica*, L. According to Hesych., identical with **κήξ**. The accounts are fabulous, and the name is very probably foreign.

Arist. H. A. viii. 3, 593 b, a sea-bird, mentioned with λάρος and αἴθυια. Ib. ix. 35, 620 ἁλίσκονται τῷ ἀφρῷ· κάπτουσι γὰρ αὐτόν, διὸ προσραίνοντες θηρεύουσιν. ἔχει δὲ τὴν μὲν ἄλλην σάρκα εὐώδη, τὸ δὲ πυγαῖον μόνον θινὸς ὄζει. γίνονται δὲ πίονες. Cf. Nic. Alexiph. 165-169 ἀφρὸν ἐπεγκεράσαιο θυοῦ δορπήϊα κέπφου, κ.τ.λ. See also Lyc. 76, 836, and Tzetz. ad Lyc. 76 θαλάσσιον ὄρνεον λαροειδές, ὅπερ ἀμφῷ (sc. ἀφρῷ) θηρῶσιν οἱ παῖδες τῶν ἁλιέων. Cf. also Suidas, s. v. According to the Schol. in Ar. Pax 1067 εἶναι πολὺν μὲν ἐν τοῖς πτεροῖς, ὀλίγον δὲ ἐν τοῖς κρέασι.

Dion. De Avib. ii. 10 ἐκ τῆς κουφότητος οἱ ἁλιεῖς ὀνομάζουσιν· τὸ γὰρ ὕδωρ ἄκρον τοῖς ποσὶν ἐπιτρέχει καὶ σημαίνει τοῖς ἁλιεῦσιν ἐπιτυχίαν. Feeds on small fish killed by tunnies and dolphins; sleeps seldom; afraid of thunder. Arat. Prognost. 916 καί ποτε καὶ κέπφοι ὁπότ' εὔδιοι ποτέωνται | ἀντία μελλόντων ἀνέμων εἰληδὰ φέρονται: cf. Schol.; see also Theophr. Fr. vi. 28; Symmach. (Schol. Ar. Pax 1067) p. 217. See also Hesych.: εἶδος ὀρνέου κουφοτάτου περὶ τὴν θάλασσαν διατρίβοντος, ὁ εὐχερῶς ὑπὸ ἀνέμου μετάγεται· ἔνθεν λέγεται ὀξὺς καὶ κοῦφος ἄνθρωπος κέπφος (i.e. a *booby*); cf. Ar. Pax 1067 κέπφοι τρήρωνες: Id. Plut. 912 ὦ κέπφε (Schol. καλεῖται δὲ κοινῶς λάρος, a *gull*). Hence κεπφωθείς, Prov. vii. 22 (ed. LXX); cf. Cic. Att. 13. 40.

ΚΕΡΑΪ'Σ· κορώνη, Hesych. Cf. Lyc. 1317. αὐτόκλητον κεραΐδα applied to Medea.

ΚΕ'ΡΒΕΡΟΣ. Mentioned as a bird-name in Anton. Lib., Met. c. xix; cf. s. v. **λαεδός**.

ΚΕΛΕΟΣ—ΚΗΞ 79

ΚΕ'ΡΘΙΟΣ. Perhaps the **Tree Creeper,** *Certhia familiaris,* L. Vide s. v. κνιπολόγος.

Arist. H. A. ix. 17,616 b ὀρνίθιον μικρόν· τὸ μὲν ἦθος θρασύς, καὶ οἰκεῖ περὶ δένδρα, καὶ ἔστι θριποφάγος, τὴν δὲ διάνοιαν εὐβίοτος, καὶ τὴν φωνὴν ἔχει λαμπράν. The passage contains several birds difficult to identify. The description of κέρθιος suggests the Tree Creeper, with which it is usually identified (Belon, Sundevall, &c.), but κνιπολόγος is certainly the Creeper, and the above description is not enough to reveal an indubitable synonym.

ΚΕ'ΡΚΑΞ· ἱέραξ, Hesych.

ΚΕΡΚΑ'Σ· κρὲξ τὸ ὄρνεον, Hesych.

ΚΕΡΚΙΘΑΛΙ'Σ, s. **κερκιθαλλίς·** ἐρωδιός, Hesych.

ΚΕΡΚΙ'Σ· εἶδος ὀρνέου, Hesych.

ΚΕΡΚΙ'ΩΝ. (For a discussion of possible Sk. roots, see Temple, infra cit.). An Indian talking bird.

Ael. xvi. 3; is the size of a starling, particoloured, docile, and learns to speak; it is impatient of captivity, and gets its name ἐπειδὴ καὶ αὐτὸς διασείεται τὸν ὄρρον, ὡς ποιοῦνται οἱ κίγκλοι. In spite of these two discrepant statements, it is possible that Aelian refers to the Common Mynah, *Acridotheres tristis,* the Talking Mynah, *Gracula religiosa,* or allied species, Hind. *sarak* or *shârak* ; Temple, Ind. Antiq. 1882, p. 291 ; Val. Ball, ib. 1885, p. 305 ; cf. Lassen, Ind. Alterth. iii. p. 321 (1858).

ΚΕ'ΡΚΝΟΣ· ἱέραξ, ἡ ἀλεκτρυών, Hesych.

ΚΕΡΚΟΡΩ͡ΝΟΣ. An Indian bird, probably identical with **κερκίων,** Ael. xv. 14.

ΚΕ'ΡΚΟΣ· ἀλεκτρυών, Hesych.

ΚΕΡΧΝΗ͂Σ. Vide s.v. **κεγχρηίς.**

ΚΗ'ΛΑΣ. Cf. Hind. *Hargēla.* An Indian bird; the **Adjutant,** *Leptoptilus argala,* L. See Val. Ball, Ind. Antiq. xiv. p. 305, 1885.

Ael. xvi. 4 τὸ μέγεθος τριπλάσιον ὠτίδος, καὶ τὸ στόμα γενναῖον δεινῶς, καὶ μακρὰ τὰ σκέλη. φέρει δὲ τὸν πρηγορεῶνα καὶ ἐκεῖνον μέγιστον, προσεμφερῆ κωρύκῳ, φθέγμα δὲ ἔχει καὶ μάλα ἀπηχές, καὶ τὴν μὲν ἄλλην πτίλωσίν ἐστι τεφρός, τὰς δὲ πτέρυγας ἄκρας ὠχρός ἐστι.

ΚΗ'Ξ. An unknown sea-bird. Probably the same word as **καύαξ,** κῆϋξ. In Hesych. **κάκα,** probably for κᾶκα, κῆκα. Od. xv. 479 ἄντλῳ δ' ἐνδούπησε πεσοῦσ' ὡς εἰναλίη κήξ. Cf. Schol. ὄρνεον

ΚΗΞ (*continued*).

θαλάσσιον παραπλήσιον χελιδόνι· ἔνιοι δὲ λάρον αὐτὸν λέγουσιν, οἱ δὲ αἴθυιαν. Cf. Hesych. κήξ· ὁ λάρος κατὰ Ἀπίωνα. λέγεται δὲ καὶ καύηξ, τινὲς καὶ αἴθυιαν ἀποδιδόασιν· οἱ δὲ κέπφον· οἱ δὲ διαφέροιτα ἀλλήλων. Usually identified with the Gannet, *Sula bassana*, L. (vide s. v. **καταρράκτης**), which does not occur, save by the rarest chance, in Greece. Among other more than dubious hypotheses, Netolicka (Naturh. aus Homer, p. 14), with whom Buchholz, Körner, and others agree, suggests the Great Crested Grebe, *Podiceps cristatus*, L., whose cry is *keck, keck*. (Cf. s. v. **κῆϋξ**.)

ΚΗΡΎΛΟΣ, *s.* κήρυλος, *s.* κειρύλος (Ar. Av. 300), *s.* κήρυλλος (Eustath. ad Hom.), *s.* κίρυλος (Hesych.). A doubtful, perhaps foreign, word, sometimes applied to the Halcyon, sometimes compared with it. Sundevall's identification of κηρύλος with a second species which occurs in Greece, *Alcedo* (*Ceryle*) *rudis*, the Smyrna Kingfisher, is quite untenable, the poetical and mythical use of both κηρύλος and ἀλκυών being opposed to so concrete an interpretation. The suggested connexion with Lat. *coeruleus* (O. Keller, Lat. Etym., 1893, p. 15) is in equal degree improbable.

Alcman, 12 (20) βάλε δή, βάλε κηρύλος εἴην, | ὅς τ' ἐπὶ κύματος ἄνθος ἅμ' ἀλκυόνεσσι ποτῆται | νηλεὲς ἦτορ ἔχων ἁλιπόρφυρος εἴαρος ὄρνις. Cf. s. v. **ἁλιπορφυρίς**.

Mosch. iii. 41 οὐδὲ τόσον γλαυκοῖς ἐνὶ κύμασι κηρύλος ᾆδεν. Arist. H. A. viii. 3, 593 b περὶ τὴν θάλατταν καὶ ἀλκυὼν καὶ κηρύλος. Ael. v. 48 ἀλκυόνα καὶ κήρυλον ποθοῦντας ἀλλήλων πάλαι ἴσμεν. Ib. vii. 17 κήρυλος καὶ ἀλκυὼν ὁμώνυμοι καὶ σύμβιοι, καὶ γήρᾳ γε παρειμένους αὐτοὺς ἐπιτιθέμεναι αἱ ἀλκυόνες περιάγουσιν ἐπὶ τῶν καλουμένων μεσοπτερυγίων. Cf. Antig. H. Mirab. 23 (27), where κηρύλος is said to be the male kingfisher; cf. also Hesych. κηρύλος· ἄρσην ὄρνις συνουσιαστικός, τινὲς δὲ ἀλκυόνα: also Tzetzes ad Lyc. 387; Schol. Ar. Av., Schol. Theocr. vii. 57; Eustath. ad Hom. Il. i. 558. In Clearch. ap. Athen. x. 332 E, numbered among τοὺς ὄρνιθας τοὺς παρενδιαστὰς καλουμένους, with τρόχιλος and ὁ τῇ κρέκι προσεμφερὴς ἐρῳδιός. Mentioned also by Archilochus, fr. 121 ap. Ael. xii. 9 κίγκλος—κινεῖ δὲ καὶ τὰ οὐραῖα πτερά, ὡσπεροῦν ὁ παρὰ τῷ Ἀρχιλόχῳ κήρυλος.

In Ar. Av. 299, usually written κείρυλος, as if from κείρω. Cf. infra s. v. **σποργίλος**.

The names and attributes of κηρύλος are undoubtedly akin to those of κεῖρις or Ciris; and it is interesting to note that, according to Hesychius, the name κεῖρις applies either to a hawk or to the Halcyon. I would place the legend of ἀλκυών and κηρύλος side by side with the astronomic parable of Haliaetus and Ciris. Vide s. vv. **ἁλιάετος, κίρις**.

ΚΗΞ—ΚΙΓΚΛΟΣ 81

ΚΗ͂ΥΞ. (See also s. vv. **καύαξ, κήξ.**) A sea-bird.

Babr. cxv. 2 λάροις τε ταὶ κήυξιν εἶπεν ἀγρώσταις. Apollod. 28, ad Lucian. i. 178; said by Schol. to be the male ἀλκυών, and identical with κηρύλος. In Dion. De Avib. ii. 7, applied rather to the female ἀλκυών· εἰ τὸν ἄρρενα τελευτῆσαι συμβαίη, βορᾶς ἀπεχόμεναι καὶ ποτοῦ παντὸς ἐπὶ πολὺ θρηνοῦσι καὶ διαφθείρονται, καὶ τὰς ᾠδὰς δ᾽ εἰ καταπαύειν μέλλοιεν, κήυξ κήυξ συνεχῶς ἐπειπούσαι σιγῶσιν. Κήυκος δὲ φωνῆς μήτ᾽ ἐγώ, μήτ᾽ ἄλλος ἀκούσαι τις· φροντίδας γὰρ καὶ τελευτὰς σημαίνει καὶ δυστυχήματα. Suidas, s. v. Ἡμερινὰ ζῷα (whatever that may mean) mentions κήυκες as sea-birds, together with ἀλκυόνες and ἀηδόνες. On the fable of Ceyx, Alcyone, &c., see Ovid. Met. xi. 269, &c., &c.; Ceyx comes into relation with Hercules and the Argonautic legends in Anton. Lib. c. xxvi; and the Hesiodic myth of Ceyx and Cycnus is of the same order. We may, I think, rest assured that κῆυξ was not originally a concrete and specific bird-name, but a mystical term associated with the Halcyon-myth (cf. s. v. **κηρύλος**).

ΚΙ΄ΓΚΛΟΣ. (MSS. of Arist. have κίγχλος, κίχλος, κόχλος. Other forms are κέγκλος, κίγκαλος Suid., κιγκλίς, Etym. Mag.) Cf. Sk. *ćan-ćala*, mobile (Burnouf, Dict. 237).

A **Wagtail**, *Motacilla* sp. According to Hesychius, Photius, and Suidas, also called **κίλλουρος** and **σεισοπυγίς** (q. v.).

Arist. H. A. viii. 3, 593 b mentioned among the smaller aquatic birds with σχοινίλος and πύγαργος; is less than the latter, which is as large as a thrush. πάντες δ᾽ οὗτοι τὸ οὐραῖον κινοῦσιν. Ib. ix. 12, 615 περὶ τὴν θάλατταν βιοῖ. τὸ ἦθος πανοῦργος καὶ δυσθήρατος, ὅταν δὲ ληφθῇ, τιθασσότατος. τυγχάνει δ᾽ ὢν καὶ ἀνάπηρος· ἀκρατὴς [cf. De Gen. ii. 99] γὰρ τῶν ὄπισθέν ἐστιν.

Ael. xii. 9 πτηνόν ἐστι ἀσθενὲς τὰ κατόπιν, καὶ διὰ τοῦτό φασι μὴ ἰδίᾳ μηδὲ καθ᾽ ἑαυτὸν δυνάμενον αὐτὸν νεοττιὰν συμπλέξαι, ἐν ταῖς ἄλλων δὲ τίκτειν· ἔνθεν τοι καὶ τοὺς πτωχοὺς κίγκλους ἐκάλουν αἱ τῶν ἀγροίκων παροιμίαι (cf. Menand. Thais 4, ap. Suid. and Phot. (4.132, Meineke) κίγκλου πτωχότερος). κινεῖ δὲ τὰ οὐραῖα πτερά. Cf. Aristoph. in Antiar. (2. 955) ap. Ael. l. c. ὀσφὺν δ᾽ ἐξ ἄκρων, διακίγκλισον ἠΰτε κίγκλου. Autocr. in Tympan. (2. 891) ap. Ael. l. c. οἷα παίζουσι παρθένοι ... οἷα κίγκλος ἅλλεται. Cf. also Theogn. 1257 κίγκλος πολυπλάγκτος: also verb κιγκλίζω, Theogn. 303, προσκιγκλίζομαι, Theocr. v. 117; also κιγκλοβάταν ῥυθμόν Aristoph. fr. 6 (2. 997) ap. Ael. l. c. Vide Hesych. κίγκλος, ὄρνεον πυκνῶς τὴν οὐρὰν κινοῦν· ἀφ᾽ οὗ καὶ τὸ κιγκλίζειν, ὅ ἐστι διασείεσθαι· τινὲς δὲ σ[ε]ισοπυγίδα.

Sundevall takes κίγκλος to be a Sandpiper, *Tringa* sp., chiefly, as it seems, because σχοινίλος is doubtless a name for the Wagtail, *Motacilla*. But I prefer to believe that κίγκλος is also a Wagtail, firstly because the movement is much more characteristic and noticeable in that bird than in the Sandpiper, secondly because of the statement as to its size, and

G

ΚΙΓΚΛΟΣ (*continued*).

thirdly because of its asserted tameness in captivity. The statement in Aelian, about the nest (also ap. Phile, 492), may perhaps be explained by the fact that, according to Krüper, the Wagtails in Greece all leave the plains in summer to breed, resorting to the hills, or in the case of *M. melanocephala* to the salt-marshes and lagoons. At the same time it is evident that allusions to κίγκλος, &c., are much influenced by notions and superstitions connected with the bird ἴυγξ.

ΚΙΓΚΡΑ'ΜΑΣ· ὄρνεον, Hesych. Cf. κύχραμος.

ΚΙ'ΚΙΡΡΟΣ, *s.* **κίκκος**, and **κίκκη**. Cock and Hen, Hesych. Cf. Mod. Gk. κόκκορας.

ΚΙΚΚΑ'ΒΗ. Also **κίκυβος, κικυβῆϊς, κίκυμος, κίτυμις**, Hesych. **κικυμίς**. Call. fr. 318. Perhaps connected also with κύμινδις, *s.* κύβινδις. An **Owl**. Lat. *cicuma* (Festus).

Schol. ad Ar. Av. 262; sub voce κικκαβαῦ. Τὰς γλαῦκας οὕτω φωνεῖν λέγουσιν· ὅθεν καὶ κικκάβας αὐτὰς λέγουσιν, οἱ δὲ κικυμίδας, ὡς Καλλίμαχος, "κάρτ' ἀγαθὴ κικυμίς," καὶ Ὅμηρος δὲ "χάλκιδα κικλήσκουσι θεοί," κ.τ.λ.

Cf. κουκουβαγία, and κοῦκκος, the modern Athenian popular names for γλαῦξ. Vide s.v. κοκκοβάρη.

ΚΙΚΥΜΗ^ΓΣ· γλαῦξ, Hesych. Also ib. κιτύμινα· γλαῦκα; qy. κικυμίδα. Cf. κικκάβη.

ΚΙΛΙ'ΑΣ· στρουθὸς ἄρσην, Hesych.

ΚΙ'ΛΛΟΥΡΟΣ. A **Wagtail**. With κιλλ-ουρος, cf. L. *mota-cilla*, and perhaps κίγ-κλ-ος. On the root, cf. Benfey's Zeitschr. viii. 1892. Fick, i. 527. Vide s. vv. **κίγκλος, σεισοπυγίς, σείσουρα**.

ΚΙΝΑΙ'ΔΙΟΝ. A name for ἴυγξ, Hesych., Phot. Cf. Dion. De Avib. i. 23, Schol. in Theocr. ii. 17.

ΚΙΝΔΑΨΟΙ· ὄρνεα, Hesych.

ΚΙΝΝΑ'ΜΩΜΟΝ ΟΡΝΕΟΝ. Also κινναμολόγος, Plin. x. (33) 50; cf. Solin. (33) 46. The fabled **Cinnamon Bird**.

Herod. iii. 111; how the Arab merchants left pieces of flesh which might break down by their weight the nests to which the birds carried them, and in which the cinnamon was found. In Arist. H. A. ix. 13, 616, a variation of the same story, the nests being brought down with weighted arrows. Cf. Ael. ii. 34, xvii. 21; Antig. H. Mirab. c. 49; Phile De Pr. An. 28 (27); Plin. xii. (19) 42; Sindbad the Sailor, &c. Sometimes confused with the Phoenix; cf. Claud. Epist. ii. 15 Venit et extremo Phoenix longaevus ab Euro, Apportans unco cinnama rara pede; Ovid, Met. xv. 399; Stat. Silv. ii. 6. 87.

ΚΙΓΚΛΟΣ—ΚΙΡΚΟΣ

ΚΙΝΝΥΡΙ'ΔΕΣ· τὰ μικρὰ ὀρνιθάρια, Hesych. (Perhaps akin to κινύρομαι.)

ΚΙΝΥ'ΤΙΔΟΣ· χαραδριός, Hesych. A very doubtful word.

ΚΙ'ΡΙΣ· λύχνος, ὄρνεον, ἢ "Αδωνις Λάκωνες, Hesych. Also κίρρις· εἶδος ἱέρακος. ὁμοίως δὲ λέγεται παρὰ Κυπρίοις Κίρρις ὁ "Αδωνις, παρὰ Λάκωσι δέ, ὁ λύχνος, Et. M. Cf. Κύρις, ὁ "Αδωνις, Hesych. These references are important in connexion with the solar symbolism underlying the stories of Ciris, κηρύλος, &c.; cf. the version of the Ciris-myth, s. v. κίρρις (s. κιρρίς), Dion. De Avib. ii. 14.

ΚΙ'ΡΚΗ. A poetic or mystical bird-name; different from, and hostile to, κίρκος.

Ael. iv. 5 σειρήν, μελίσσης ὄνομα, πρὸς κίρκην ἐχθρός. κίρκη δὲ πρὸς κίρκον, οὐ τῷ γένει μόνον, ἀλλὰ καὶ τῇ φύσει διαφέροντα πεφώρασθον. Cf. ib. iv. 58.

ΚΙ'ΡΚΟΣ. A poetic and mystical name for a **Hawk**: the sacred Hawk of Apollo; in the main an astronomical, perhaps solar, emblem. In Mod. Gk. κιρκινέζι is said to be a name for the Kestrel (Heldr.), vide s. v. κεγχρηίς.

In Homer, the bird of Apollo, δεξιὸς ὄρνις, Ἀπόλλωνος ταχὺς ἄγγελος, Od. xv. 525; an emblem of swiftness, ἐλαφρότατος πετεηνῶν, Il. xxii. 139, Od. xiii. 87; cf. Apoll. Rh. ii. 935, Opp. Cyn. i. 282 ἢ κίρκος ταναῇσι τινασσόμενος πτερύγεσσιν: usually as an enemy of the Dove, Il. xxii. 140 (cf. ἴρηξ, xxi. 493), Od. xv. 526, cf. Apoll. Rh. i. 1049 ἠΰτε κίρκους | ὠκυπέτας ἀγεληδὸν ἀποτρέσσωσι πέλειαι: ib. iii. 543, 561, iv. 486; hostile to ψάρ, κολοιός, and other small birds, Il. xvii. 757. Frequent in Aesch., usually, as in Homer, an enemy of the Dove; Suppl. 223 ἐσμὸς ὡς πελειάδων | ἵζεσθε, κίρκων τῶν ὁμοπτέρων φόβῳ, Pr. V. 857 κίρκοι πελειῶν οὐ μακρὰν λελειμμένοι (note in this passage the association with Egyptian Ἔπαφος); mentioned in connexion with the Tereus-myth, as metamorphosing with ἔποψ, fr. 32, ap. Arist. H. A. ix. 49 b ἔποψ ... ὃς ἦρι μὲν φαίνονται διαπάλλει πτερόν | κίρκου λεπάργου: as a portent, pursuing an eagle, πρὸς ἐσχάραν Φοίβου, Pers. 205; cf. Suppl. 60 ὄπα τᾶς Τηρείας μήτιδος οἰκτρᾶς ἀλόχου, κιρκηλάτου τ' ἀηδόνος.

Arist. H. A. ix. 36, 620 τρίτος τῶν ἱεράκων [τῷ κράτει]; ib. ix. 1. 609 b ἀλώπεκι πολέμιος, cf. Ael. v. 48, Phile, 704, Wotton, De Diff. Anim. vii. 143, &c. In Plin. x. 8 *circos* occurs as an alternative reading for *aegithus*; cf. *circus* as the name of a gem, similis accipitri, Plin. xxxvii. 10.

Mentioned as hostile to the Dove also in Ael. iii. 46, v. 50 αἱ δὲ περιστεραὶ πρὸς ἀετῶν μὲν κλαγγὴν καὶ γυπῶν θαρροῦσι, κίρκων δὲ καὶ ἁλιαέτων οὐκέτι: to τρυγών and to κορώνη, ib. vi. 45; to κίρκη, ib. iv. 5, 58; and to mice, Batrach. 49. How it places chicory (πικρίς) in its nest as a charm, Ael. i. 35, Phile, 722, or wild lettuce, ἄγρια θριδακίνη, Geopon.

ΚΙΡΚΟΣ *(continued).*

xv. 1. 19, with which it salves its eyes, Anatol. p. 297 (cf. ἱέραξ); and is killed by pomegranate-seed (ῥοιᾶς σίδην κοπεῖσαν), Ael. vi. 46, Phile, 637. Used by fowlers, Opp. Cyn. i. 64 αὐτοῖς ἐπὶ δρυμὰ συνέμπορος ἕσπετο κίρκος.

The bird is not identifiable as a separate species, and is so recognized by Scaliger and others. Neither the brief note as to its size in a corrupt passage of the ninth book of the History of Animals, nor the mystical references to its alleged hostilities and attributes in Aristotle, Aelian, and Phile, are sufficient to prove that the name indicated at any time a certain particular species. The word is poetical, and is chiefly used in relation to πέλεια, or with reference to Apollo. The attempts on the part of commentators to assign κίρκος to a particular species are all based on the epithet λέπαργος. Thus Sundevall suggests the Hen Harrier or Ringtail, *Circus cyaneus*, of which the male is blueish-grey: while Belon and others of the older naturalists, followed by Camus, assigned the name to the Moor Buzzard or Marsh Harrier, *C. aeruginosus*, which is only white beneath the tail. But the meaning of λέπαργος is in reality unknown; it will not bear using, nor is it likely to have been used, as a specific or diagnostic epithet. Cf. s.v. **πύγαργος**.

The chief allusions to κίρκος are obviously mystical, though the underlying symbolism, involving also the symbolic meanings of the Hoopoe, the Dove, the Crow, the Fox, the Pomegranate, &c., is not decipherable. In this connexion, the passage in Opp. Cyn. iii. 293-339 is important and suggestive, but I refrain from putting forward a tentative hypothesis as to its meaning; we have here enumerated five kinds of λύκοι, of which the first is τοξευτήρ or ξουθός, the next three are **κίρκος**, χρύσεος, ἰκτῖνος, and the last θηρεύει ἐπὶ πτώκεσσιν ὁμοίων, i.e. is λαγωφόνος (the last two are called **ἄκμονες**, q.v.); of these five names the last four are all also names or epithets of hawks.

ΚΙ'ΡΥΛΟΣ, Hesych., for **κείρυλος**, **κηρύλος**.

ΚΙ'ΣΣΑ, *s.* **κίττα**, also **κεῖσσα** (Hesych.). The **Jay**, *Garrulus glandarius*, L. Mod. Gk. κίσσα (Heldr.); cf. Ital. *Gazza*, in its many dialectic forms. Perhaps one of the many bird-names connected with rt. *kak*, to cry, quasi *kik-ja* (v. Edl., p. 52); cf. Sk. *kiki*, a Jackdaw, with which Von Edlinger connects O. H. G. *heh-aro*, Germ. *Häher*, the Nutcracker. See also s.v. **βάσκιλλος**.

Ar. Av. 302, 1297; with ed. Συρακούσιος. Arist. H. A. viii. 3, 592 b persecuted by ἐλεός and αἰγώλιος. (Cf. De Gen. iv. 6, 774 b; Plin. x. 79 [60].) Arist. H. A. ix. 13, 615 b, 616 φωνὰς μεταβάλλει πλείστας (καθ' ἑκάστην γὰρ ὡς εἰπεῖν ἡμέραν ἄλλην ἀφίησι)· τίκτει δὲ περὶ ἐννέα ᾠά, ποιεῖται

ΚΙΣΣΑ (*continued*).

δὲ τὴν νεοττιὰν ἐπὶ τῶν δένδρων ἐκ τριχῶν καὶ ἐρίων: makes a store of acorns, ὅταν δ' ὑπολίπωσιν αἱ βάλανοι, ἀποκρύπτουσα ταμιεύεται. Ib. ix. 20, 617 a, is the size of ἰξοβόρος, the Missel-Thrush.
Its garrulity: Alexid. Thras. 1 (3, 420 Mein.) λαλιστέραν οὐ κίτταν, οὔτ' ἀηδών' οὔτε τρυγόνα; Lyc. 1319 τὴν λάληθρον κίσσαν: and imitative faculty, Ael. vi. 19, Plut. De Sol. Anim. p. 973 C, Dion. De Avib. i. 18, Plin. x. 42 (59), Porph. De Abst. iii. 4; hence κισσαβίζω, Poll. v. 90. How it is caught with a springe and bait of olive, Dion. De Avib. iii. 18. Mentioned also in frr. Antiph. 3. 145, Anaxand. 3. 185, Mnesim. 3. 570 (Meineke). According to Nicand. ap. Anton. Lib. c. 9, one of the Emathides, daughters of Pierus, was metamorphosed into the bird κίσσα; cf. Ovid, Met. v. 294, 663; Mart. Ep. xiv. 76; Pers. Prol.; Plin. x. 33.

Sundevall supposes the Magpie (which is very much rarer in Greece than the Jay) to have been meant, but the description tallies much better with the Jay, which still retains the name. The Magpie is now called καρακάξα (Heldr.). In Italian, *gazza*, *chéca*, *cecca*, *pica*, &c., apply both to the Magpie and to the Jay, as very possibly κίσσα also did in Greek. Pliny (x. 29) gives an accurate account of the Magpie, describing it as a variety of *pica* of recent advent to the neighbourhood of Rome.

ΚΙ'ΣΣΙΡΙΣ, Suid., κίσιρνις, Hesych. An unknown bird.

ΚΙ'ΧΛΗ. Dor. κιχήλη (Ar. Nub. 339, Epicharm. in Athen. ii. 64 f (68)). A **Thrush**: the generic term including ἰλιάς *s*. ἰλλάς, ἰξοβόρος, τριχάς, q. v. The root appears in Russ. *kwickzol*, a thrush, with which *ouzel* is perhaps cognate. Mod. Gk. τζήχλα. Cf. also ἴχλα, ἴσχλα.

Mentioned in Od. xxii. 468 κίχλαι τανυσίπτεροι. Homer is said to have received a present of κίχλαι for reciting a certain poem, hence called 'Επικιχλίδες: Menaech. ap. Athen. ii. 65 b.

Description.—Arist. H. A. viii. 3, 593 b, ix. 22, 617 b, is as large as πύγαργος, and a little larger than μαλακοκρανεύς. Ib. ix. 49 B. 632 b μεταβάλλει δὲ καὶ ἡ κίχλη τὸ χρῶμα· τοῦ μὲν γὰρ χειμῶνος ψαρά, τοῦ δὲ θέρους ποικίλα τὰ περὶ τὸν αὐχένα ἴσχει· τὴν μέντοι φωνὴν οὐδὲν μεταβάλλει. Cf. Ael. xii. 28. This would suggest a confusion of species: the more variegated birds being Fieldfares and Redwings; the latter are said to occur in large flocks in Spring (v. d. Mühle), though all alike have departed by Summer. Its song alluded to, Ar. Ach. 1116 πύτερον ἀκρίδες ἡδιόν ἐστιν, ἢ κίχλαι; Ar. Pax 531, &c.

Nesting.—Builds in a spray of myrtle, θάλλον μυρρίνης, or places one in the nest for a charm, Ael. i. 35, Phile, De An. 723, Geopon. xv. 1. 19, Anatol. p. 298: cf. Fab. Aes. 194. A different account, Arist. H. A. vi. 1, 559 αἱ δὲ κίχλαι νεοττιὰν μὲν ποιοῦνται ὥσπερ αἱ χελιδόνες ἐκ πηλοῦ

ΚΙΧΛΗ (*continued*).

ἐπὶ ταῖς ὑψηλοῖς τῶν δένδρων, ἐφεξῆς δὲ ποιοῦσιν ἀλλήλαις καὶ ἐχομένας, ὥστ' εἶναι διὰ τὴν συνέχειαν ὥσπερ ὁρμαθὸν νεοττιῶν. A similar account, restricted to the variety ἰλλάς, Alex. Mynd. ap. Athen. ii. 65 a ἦν καὶ συναγελαστικὴν εἶναι καὶ νεοττεύειν ὡς καὶ τὰς χελιδόνας. *Note.*—The Fieldfare, *T. pilaris*, L., which breeds only in Northern Europe, is the only Thrush which nests in colonies. Sundevall takes the above passage (Arist. II. A. vi. 1) to indicate that the Fieldfare formerly nested in Greece or at least in Macedonia. In Anth. Pal. ix. 373, Mackail (p. 358) takes κίχλη to be either the Thrush or the Fieldfare, which latter however is a winter-migrant in Greece. (For other references to the Anthology, vide s. v. **κόσσυφος**.) The Missel-Thrush is, now at least, the only species, except the Blackbird, which remains to breed in Greece or Asia Minor.

Migration.—Arist. II. Λ. viii. 16, 600 φωλεῖ, i. e. hibernates. Cf. Plin. x. 24 (35) Abeunt et merulae turdique. Sed plumam non amittunt nec occultantur; visi saepe ibi quò hibernum pabulum petunt: itaque in Germaniâ hyeme maxime turdi cernuntur.

Varieties.—Arist. H. A. ix. 20, 617 κιχλῶν δ' εἴδη τρία· ἡ μὲν ἰξοβόρος [ἰξοφάγος Athen.]· αὕτη δ' οὐκ ἐσθίει ἀλλ' ἢ ἰξὸν καὶ ῥητίνην, τὸ δὲ μέγεθος ὅσον κίττα ἐστίν. ἑτέρα τριχάς· αὕτη δ' ὀξὺ φθέγγεται, τὸ δὲ μέγεθος ὅσον κόττυφος. ἄλλη δ' ἦν καλοῦσί τινες ἰλιάδα [ἰλλάδα, s. τυλάδα, Athen.], ἐλαχίστη τε τούτων καὶ ἧττον ποικίλη. Cf. Athen. ii. 65 a.

The Thrush as Food: frequent in Com. Poets, ὀπταὶ κίχλαι, Pher. 2, 300 (1, 23), Telecl. 2, 362 (1, 12); ἀνάβραστοι κίχλαι, Pher. 2, 316 (1, 10); κρέα τ' ὀρνίθεια κιχηλᾶν, Ar. Nub. 339, and elsewhere frequent; κίχλαι μέλιτι μεμιγμέναι, Plat. Com. 2, 674 (2, 8); ἐλαιοφιλοφάγους κιχήλας, Epicharm. 281 L. ap. Athen. l. c., &c. &c. Cf. Athen. ii. pp. 64, 65, Geopon. xiv. 24, Colum. De R. R. viii. 10, Varro, De R. R. iii. 5, Pallad. i. 26, Martial, Ep. xiii. 51, 92, Hor. Epist. i. 15, 41, Plin. x. 23 (30), &c. &c. Prescribed as a remedy for Pompey, and obtained from the aviaries of Lucullus; hence the saying Εἰ μὴ Λούκουλλος ἐτρύφα, Πομπήϊος οὐκ ἂν ἔζησε, Plut. i. 518 F, 620 B, ii. 204 B, 786 A. Capture by traps and nets, παγίδας καὶ νεφέλας, Athen. ii. 64: cf. Dion. De Avib. iii. 13, Pallad. xiii. 6, &c.

A talking thrush, Plin. x. (42) 59.

Proverb and Fable.—κωφότερος κίχλης, Eubul. iii. 220 (5). κίχλη ἐν μυρσινῶνι, Aes. Fab. 194.

ΚΛΑ'ΓΓΟΣ. An alternative reading for **πλάγγος**, q. v. Cf. κλαγγάζειν, Lat. clangunt aquilae, Carm. De Philom., &c.

ΚΛΑΔΑΡΟ'ΡΥΓΧΟΣ, i. e. clapper-bill. A name for **τρόχιλος**, Ael. xii. 15.

ΚΛΟΙΩ͂Ν. εἶδος ὀρνέου, Hesych. Perhaps for κολοιῶν.

ΚΝΙΠΟΛΟ'ΓΟΣ. (MSS. have also κνίδολος, κνιδολόγος, κνιπολόχος.)
The **Tree Creeper**, *Certhia familiaris*, L. Vide s. v. **κέρθιος**.

Arist. H. A. viii. 3, 593 τὸ μέγεθος μικρὸς ὅσον ἀκανθυλλίς, τὴν δὲ χρόαν σποδοειδὴς καὶ κατάστικτος· φωνεῖ δὲ μικρόν. ἔστι δὲ καὶ τοῦτο ξυλοκόπον. (Mentioned at the end of the list of Woodpeckers.) Gloger, Sundevall, Aubert u. Wimmer, and others, agree in the above identification. The word is used by Nicander, ap. Anton. Lib. c. 14, as an epithet or synonym of **πιπώ**, q. v.

ΚΟΚΚΟ'ΑΞ· κορώνη, Hesych.

ΚΟΚΚΟΒΆ'ΡΗ. An Owl = γλαῦξ, Hesych. Cf. κικκάβη, also Mod. Gk. and Calabr. κουκουβαγία, Neap. *cucuveggia*, Alban. *kukuvaïke*, all meaning the Little Owl, γλαῦξ: also Mod. Gk. χουχουριστής, the Tawny Owl, Sp. *chucha*; vide O. Keller, Lat. Etym. 1893, p. 111. Bikélas cites, from Wagner's Carm. Gr. Med. Aevi, the form **κουκουβᾶς**. Coray would read for **κοκκοβάρη, κοκκοβόη**, and for **κικκάβη** (q. v.), **κικαβόη**.

ΚΟΚΚΟΒΟ'ΑΣ ΌΡΝΙΣ. ὁ ἀλεκτρυών, παρὰ Σοφοκλεῖ. Eust. 1479, 44 (Soph. fr. 900).

ΚΟΚΚΟΘΡΑΥ'ΣΤΗΣ· ὄρνις ποιός, Hesych.

ΚΟ'ΚΚΥΞ. Cf. Sk. *kokilas*, Lith. *kukuti*, O. H. G. *gauh*, Scot. *gowk*, &c. The **Cuckoo**, *Cuculus canorus*, L. Mod. Gk. κούκκος.

Full Description and comparison with ἱέραξ, Arist. H. A. vi. 7, 563, 564.

Its Cry, freq.; e. g. Hes. Op. et D. 484 ἦμος κόκκυξ κοκκύζει δρυὸς ἐν πετάλοισι | τοπρῶτον τέρπει τε βροτοὺς ἐπ᾽ ἀπείρονα γαῖαν: Ar. Av. 507, Ran. 1379, 1384. Cf. Lyc. 395 κόκκυγα κομπάζοντα μαψαύρας στόβους.

Note.—κοκκίζειν is still more frequently used of the Crowing Cock; vide s. v. **ἀλεκτρυών.** On Ar. Ach. 598 ἐχειροτόνησάν με κόκκυγές γε τρεῖς, cf. Dind. Thes. iv. c. 1737 B, also L. and S., s. v. **κόκκυξ**.

Nesting and Breeding.—Arist. l. c. νεοττοὺς δὲ κόκκυγος λέγουσιν ὡς οὐδεὶς ἑώρακεν· ὁ δὲ τίκτει μέν, ἀλλ᾽ οὐ ποιησάμενος νεοττιάν. ἀλλ᾽ ἐνίοτε μὲν ἐν τῇ τῶν ἐλαττόνων ὀρνίθων ἐντίκτει καταφαγὼν τὰ ᾠὰ τὰ ἐκείνων, μάλιστα δ᾽ ἐν ταῖς τῶν φαβῶν νεοττιαῖς ... τίκτει δ᾽ ὀλιγάκις μὲν δύο, τὰ δὲ πλεῖστα ἕν. ἐντίκτει δὲ καὶ τῇ τῆς ὑπολαΐδος νεοττιᾷ· ἡ δ᾽ ἐκπέττει καὶ ἐκτρέφει. Id. H. A. ix. 29, 618 a τίκτει μάλιστα μὲν ἐν ταῖς τῶν φαβῶν καὶ ἐν ὑπολαΐδος καὶ κορύδου χαμαί, ἐπὶ δένδρου δ᾽ ἐν τῇ τῆς χλωρίδος καλουμένης νεοττιᾷ. τίκτει ἐν ᾠόν. ὅταν αὐξάνηται ὁ τοῦ κύκκυγος νεοττός, ἐκβάλλει τὰ αὐτῆς [ἡ τρέφουσα] καὶ ἀπόλλυνται οὕτως. οἱ δὲ λέγουσιν ὡς καὶ ἀποκτείνασα ἡ τρέφουσα δίδωσι καταφαγεῖν· διὰ γὰρ τὸ καλὸν εἶναι τὸν τοῦ κόκκυγος νεοττὸν ἀποδοκιμάζειν τὰ αὐτῆς. Id. De Mirab. 3. 830 b τοὺς κύκκυγας τοὺς ἐν τῇ Ἑλίκῃ (?), ἐν ταῖς νεοττιαῖς τῶν φάττων ἢ τῶν τρυγόνων

ΚΟΚΚΥΞ (*continued*).

ἐντίκτειν. See also Arist. De Gen. iii. 1, 750, Ael. iii. 30, Theophr. Caus. Pl. ii. 18, 9, Dion. De Avib. i. 13, Plin. x. (9) 26, Phile, De An. Pr. xxiv.

A species that builds its own nest: Arist. H. A. vi. 7, 564 νεοττεύει γένος τι αὐτῶν πόρρω καὶ ἐν ἀποτόμοις πέτραις. [Ib. vi. 1, 559, κόκκυξ probably for κόττυφος].

The Cuckoo is said by Krüper (p. 184) to lay in Greece chiefly in the nest of *Sylvia orphea*, and also of the species of Saxicola. *Coccystes glandarius*, the Great Spotted Cuckoo, which also occurs in Greece, (Mod. Gk. κρᾶνος), lays in the nests of the Jackdaw, Magpie and Crow. The repeated statement that κόκκυξ lays in the nest of φάττα or φάψ is inexplicable, unless such a statement be of foreign origin and refer originally to some Oriental species; a little light is perhaps thrown upon the point by the circumstance that in certain Chinese legends the Dove and the Cuckoo are confounded together: vide infra s. v. περιστερά. This discrepancy deprives of all value the attempted identifications of ὑπολαΐς, wihch are based on its being some bird in whose nest the Common Cuckoo habitually lays its egg; see also s. v. πάππος.

Migration.—Arist. H. A. vi. 7, 563 b φαίνεται ἐπ' ὀλίγον χρόνον τοῦ θέρους, τὸν δὲ χειμῶνα ἀφανίζεται. Ib. ix. 49 B, 633 μεταβάλλει τὸ χρῶμα καὶ τῇ φωνῇ [οὐ] σαφηνίζει, ὅταν μέλλῃ ἀφανίζεσθαι· ἀφανίζεται δ' ὑπὸ κύνα, φανερὸς δὲ γίνεται ἀπὸ τοῦ ἔαρος ἀρξάμενος μέχρι κυνὸς ἐπιτολῆς. Cf. Ael. iii. 30 ὁρᾶται ὁ κόκκυξ ἦρος ὑπαρχομένου εἰς ἀνατολὰς Σειρίου: Dion. De Avib. i. 13 πρῶτος τῶν λοιπῶν πτηνῶν ἡμῖν τὸ ἔαρ ἀγγέλλων.

Metamorphosis with the Hawk, Arist. H. A. vi. 7, 563 b, ix. 49 B, 633. Cf. Plut. Arat. xxx (i. 1041 C) καὶ καθάπερ τῷ κόκκυγί φησιν Αἴσωπος ἐρωτῶντι τοὺς λεπτοὺς ὄρνιθας, ὅτι φεύγοιεν αὐτόν, εἰπεῖν ἐκείνους ὡς ἔσται ποτὲ ἱέραξ (Aes. Fab. 198, ed. Halm). Cf. also Tzetz. ad Lyc. 395. See also supra, s. vv. ἔποψ, κίρκος.

Other Myths and Legends.—How Jupiter, in the shape of a Cuckoo, sought Hera on Mount Thornax; and how for this reason the cuckoo figures on Hera's sceptre, Pausan. ii. 17, 4: cf. Schol. ad Theocr. xv. 64; hence the mountain was called ὄρος Κοκκύγιον, Pausan. ii. 36, 1; cf. Creuzer, Symb. iii. 248; cf. also the Teutonic *Gauchsberg*, Grimm, D. Myth. p. 646, &c.

From its propinquity to Sparta, and from the circumstance of the Cuckoo having come in a cloud, Creuzer (l. c.) conjectures an allusion to the same story in Ar. Av. 814; cf. also the weather prophecy in Hesiod, l. c.

How the Cuckoo was king over Egypt and Phoenicia, Ar. Av. 504. In these latter statements we have evidence of a confusion with the

ΚΟΚΚΥΞ (*continued*).

Hoopoe, vide s. vv. ἔποψ, κουκούφα; for the relations between the Cuckoo and the Hoopoe, Der Kuckuk und sein Küster, v. Grimm, l. c.

On the mythology of the Cuckoo, see also (*int. al.*) Von Mannhardt, Zeitsch. f. d. Myth. iii. pp. 209-298; Hardy, Pop. Hist. of the Cuckoo, Folk-lore Record, pt. ii ; Hopf, Orakelthiere, p. 152.

How the Amphisbaena, alone among serpents, appears before the Cuckoo is heard, i. e. in early spring, Plin. xxx. (10) 25 ; a magic remedy for fleas, Plin. l. c.; a Cuckoo in a hare-skin, a remedy for sleeplessness, Plin. xxx. (15) 48 ; the Cuckoo as food, Plin. x. 9; cf. Arist. H. A. vi. 7, 564 (spurious passage).

ΚΟ'ΛΑΡΙΣ. Vide s. v. κάλαρις.

ΚΟΛΛΥΡΙ'ΩΝ, *s.* κορυλλίων, Hesych. An undetermined bird.

Arist. H. A. ix. 23, 617 b τὰ αὐτὰ ἐσθίει τῷ κοττύφῳ . . . ἁλίσκεται δὲ κατὰ χειμῶνα μάλιστα. Is of a size with κόττυφος, πάρδαλος, μαλακοκρανεύς, χλωρίων.

Belon's unsupported hypothesis of the *Shrike* (Observ. ii. 98) is handed down in the modern scientific name of *Lanius collurio*. Buffon, quoted by Camus, ii. p. 238, says (Hist. Des Ois. ii. p. 70) that in Mod. Gk. the Shrike is called κολλυρίων; there is no recent evidence of this. Gloger suggests with more probability, *Turdus pilaris*, L., the Fieldfare.

ΚΟΛΟΙΟ'Σ, α. The **Jackdaw**. *Corvus monedula*, L. Root very doubtful.

Mod. Gk. κολοιός, καλοιακοῦδα. Hesych. κολοιός· [ὄρνεον] ὃ οὐ τάχα ὁρᾶται ἐν 'Αλεξανδρείᾳ : also, κολοιοί· σκῶπες, μικραὶ κορῶναι.

Il. xvi. 583 ; xvii. 755 ψαρῶν νέφος ἔρχεται ἠὲ κολοιῶν, | οὖλον κεκλήγοντες. In regard to the Jackdaw's cry, cf. Pind. N. 3, 143 (78) κολοιοὶ κραγέται : Antip. Sid. 47 κολοιῶν κρωγμός : J. Poll. vi. 13 κολοιοὺς κλώζειν : hence the verb κολοιάω, Poll. v. 89.

Frequent in Aristophanes; Av. passim, Ach. 875, Vesp. 129, Eq. 1020, &c.

Arist. H. A. ix. 24, 617 b εἴδη τρία· **κορακίας, λύκος, βωμολόχος**, q. v. Ib. ii. 17, 509 τὸ πρὸς τὴν κοιλίαν τεῖνον ἔχει εὐρὺ καὶ πλατύ. Its claws are weaker than those of δρυοκολάπτης, ib. ix. 9, 614 (here Schneider, followed by Sundevall, would read for κολοιῶν, κολιῶν *s.* κελεῶν). De Gen. iii. 6, 756 b ἡ τοῖς ῥύγχεσι εἰς ἄλληλα κοινωνία δῆλον ἐπὶ τῶν τιθασευομένων κολοιῶν.

How the Jackdaw, a victim to sociality, is caught with a dish of oil, into which, looking at his own reflection, he falls; Ael. iv. 30, Athen. ix. 393 b, Dion. De Avib. iii. 19. Caught also with springes baited with an olive, Dion. ib. iii. 18.

A weather-prophet. οἱ κολοιοὶ ἐκ τῶν νήσων πετόμενοι τοῖς γεωργοῖς

ΚΟΛΟΙΟΣ (*continued*).

σημεῖον αὐχμοῦ καὶ ἀφορίας εἰσίν, Arist. fr. 240, 1522. A sign of rain, φαινόμενοι ἀγεληδὰ καὶ ἰρήκεσσιν ὁμοῖον | φθεγξάμενοι, Arat. Ph. 965; cf. ib. 970. κόραξ δὲ αὖ κορώνη καὶ κολοιὸς δείλης ὀψίας εἰ φθέγγοιντο χειμῶνος ἔσεσθαί τινα ἐπιδημίαν διδάσκουσι· κολοιοὶ δὲ ἱερακίζοντες, καὶ πετόμενοι πῆ μὲν ἀνωτέρω πῆ δὲ κατωτέρω, κρυμὸν καὶ ὑετὸν δηλοῦσι, Arist. ap. Ael. vii. 7; cf. Theophr. De Sign. vi. 1; Arat. 1023, 1026; Ovid, Amor. ii. 6, 34 pluviae graculus auctor aquae; Lucret. v. 1082.

In augury, frequent. Ar. Av. 50 χὠ κολοιὸς οὑτοσὶ ἄνω κέχηνεν: cf. W. H. Thompson's note on Plat. Phaed. 249 D.

How the Jackdaws, destroying the grasshoppers' eggs, are cherished by the Thessalians, Illyrians, and Lemnians, Ael. iii. 12, Plin. xi. 29. How the Veneti bribe the Jackdaws to spare their crops, and how the Daws respect the compact, Ael. xvii. 16, Antig. Hist. Mir. 173 (189), Arist. De Mirab. ii. 9, 841 b. On the construction of scare-crows, cf. Geopon. xiv. 25.

Story of a Jackdaw enamoured of a certain youth, Ael. i. 6, xii. 37. The Jackdaw in medicine, Plin. xxix. (6) 36, xxx. (11) 30, &c. Uses laurel as a remedy, Plin. viii. 27.

Fables.—The Daws and the Husbandman, Babr. xxxiii. The Daw in borrowed plumes, ib. lxxii : also κολοιὸς καὶ γλαῦξ, in Fab. Aes. ed. Halm, 200; Phaedr. i. 3; cf. Luc. Apol. 4 κολοιὸς ἀλλοτρίοις πτεροῖς ἀγάλλεται: Hor. Ep. i. 3. 19, 20 moveat cornicula risum, Furtivis nudata coloribus. See also Aes. Fab. 201, 202, 398.

Proverb.—κολοιὸς παρὰ κολοιὸν ἱζάνει, Arist. Rhet. i. 11, 1371 b; cf. Nic. Eth. viii. 2, 1155, &c. κακῶν πανάριστε κολοιῶν, Lucian, Fugit. 30 (3, 382). Of chatterers, πολλοὶ γὰρ μίσει σφε κατακρώζουσι κολοιοί, Ar. Eq. 1020.

ΚΟΛΟΙΟ΄Σ, β. The **Little Cormorant.** *Phalacrocorax pygmaeus*, Bonap.; vide s. v. **καταρράκτης**.

Arist. H. A. ix. 24, 617 b ἔστι δὲ καὶ ἄλλο γένος κολοιῶν περὶ τὴν Λυδίαν καὶ Φρυγίαν, ὃ στεγανόπουν ἐστίν. Is friendly with λάρος (ὁ καλ. κολοιός), Ael. v. 48.

Sundevall ingeniously suggests the above interpretation, the large or Common Cormorant, 'corvo marino,' being known as κόραξ (Arist. H. A. viii. 3, 593 b). Ar. Ach. 875 (883) νάσσας, κολοιούς, ἀτταγᾶς, φαλαρίδας, &c., is quoted by Athen. ix. 395 E as a list of *water-birds*. Cf. s. v. κορώνη ἡ θαλάσσιος.

ΚΟΛΟΙ΄ΦΡΥΞ· Ταναγραῖος ἀλεκτρυών, Hesych.

ΚΟΛΟΚΤΡΥΩ΄Ν. In Hesych., supposed to be based on an ancient error in MS. Ravenn. of Ar. Ran. 935, for κἀλεκτρυόνα.

ΚΟΛΥΜΒΙ΄Σ, *s.* κόλυμβος (Ar. Ach.), κολυμβάς (Athen. 395 e, Anton. Lib.). A water-bird; especially a **Grebe.**

ΚΟΛΟΙΟΣ—ΚΟΡΑΞ 91

ΚΟΛΥΜΒΙΣ (*continued*).

Ar. Av. 304, Ach. 875, brought to market from Boeotia. Mentioned among the water-birds in Arist. H. A. i. 1, 487, viii. 3, 593 b; Alex. Mynd. in Athen. ix. 395 d ἡ μικρὰ κολυμβὶς πάντων ἐλαχίστη τῶν ἐνύδρων, ῥυπαρομέλαινα τὴν χροιὰν καὶ τὸ ῥύγχος ὀξὺ ἔχει, σκέπτον τε (lect. dub.) τὰ ὄμματα, τὰ δὲ πολλὰ καταδύεται. Dion. De Avib. ii. 12 τοῖς κολύμβαις ἐστὶν ἀεὶ τὸ νήχεσθαι φίλον, καὶ οὐδ' ἂν ὕπνου χάριν ἢ τροφῆς ἐπὶ τὴν γῆν ἔλθοιεν, κ.τ.λ.: ib. iii. 24, capture of κολυμβίς at night, with net and lantern. The above passage from Alex. Mynd., so far as it is intelligible, is a good description of the Little Grebe or Dabchick, *Podiceps minor*, L., which is a common resident in Greece (Mod. Gk. βουτηκτάρα). In Arist. De Part. iv. 12 we find a minute account of the Grebe's foot, but without a name.

According to Nicand. ap. Anton. Lib. c. ix, one of the Emathides, daughters of Pierus, was metamorphosed into the bird κολυμβίς.

ΚΟ'ΜΒΑ· κορώνη, Πολυρρήνιοι, Hesych.

ΚΟΝΤΙ'ΛΟΣ· εἶδος ὀρνέου, ἢ ὄρτυξ, Hesych. It is possible that the word may be connected with κόντος, and that it may relate to the game of ὀρτυγοκοπία, or quail-tapping.

ΚΟΡΑΚΙ'ΑΣ. Also κορακῖνος (synonymous according to Hesych.).

A **Chough**. *Pyrrhocorax alpinus*, the Alpine Chough, and *Fregilus graculus*, the Cornish Chough; both found in Greece, the latter more rarely. Mod. Gk. καλιακοῦδα in Attica, κορωνοποῦλι in Laconia (Heldr.).

Arist. H. A. ix. 24, 617 b. A sort of κολοιός· ὅσον κορώνη, φοινικόρυγχος. Hesych. ὁ μέλας κολοιός, καὶ κορακῖνος ὁμοίως.

ΚΟ'ΡΑΞ, a. The **Raven**. *Corvus corax*, L. Cf. Sk. *kar-âvas*, L. *cor-vus*, Sw. *krå-ka*, O. N. *hrö-kr*, A. S. *hro-c*, Eng. *crow*, *rook*, O. N. *hra-fn*, Eng. *raven*: the same root in κράζω, *crepare*, *raucus*, O. H. G. *hruofan*, Ger. *rufen*, Eng. *croak*. Mod. Gk. κάραξ, κόρακας, κύρκοραξ (Erh.). Dim. κορακῖνος, Ar. Eq. 1053; κορακίσκος, Gloss.

Not in Homer. Poet., frequent, with the idea of ravenous, carrion-feeding, e. g. Aesch. Suppl. 751, Ag. 1473; Gk. Anthol. (Jac.) iv. 179 ἄγκειμαι μέγα δεῖπνον ἀμετροβίοις κοράκεσσι. Hence Prov. εἰς κόρακας, Ar. Vesp. 51, 852, Nub. 123, 133, 789, Pax 500, 1221, Thesmoph. 1226, &c., Arist. fr. 454, 1552 b, Plut. ix. 415, Lucian, Alex. 46 (2, 552); frequent also in the comic fragments. See also the long note of Photius; cf. also Antisthenes ap. D. L. vi. 1, 4 κρεῖττον ἔλεγε καθά φησιν Ἑκάτων ἐν ταῖς Χρείαις, εἰς κόρακας ἢ εἰς κόλακας ἐκπεσεῖν· οἱ μὲν γὰρ νεκρούς, οἱ δὲ ζῶντας ἐσθίουσιν: cf. Pallad. 32, Gk. Anthol. iii. 121 ρ καὶ λ μόνον κόρακας

ΚΟΡΑΞ (continued).

κολοίκων διορίζει, | λοιπόν τ' αὐτὸ κόραξ βωμολόχος τε κόλαξ. With epithet κυανόπτερος, Eur. Andr. 862.

Anatomical particulars.—Arist. De Part. iv. 1, 626 b τὸ ῥύγχος ἔχει ἰσχυρὸν καὶ σκληρόν, τοῦ στομάχου τὸ πρὸς τὴν κοιλίαν τεῖνον εὐρὺ καὶ πλατύ, χόλην πρὸς τοῖς ἐντέροις.

Breeding.—Arist. De Gen. iii. 6, 756 b ἡ μὲν ὀχεία ὀλιγάκις ὁρᾶται, ἡ δὲ τοῖς ῥύγχεσι πρὸς ἄλληλα κοινωνία πολλάκις, εἰσὶ γάρ τινες οἱ λέγουσι κατὰ τὸ στόμα μίγνυσθαι τοὺς κόρακας, cf. Plin. x. (12) 15; Dion. De Avib. i. 9 οὐ μίγνυνται πρίν τινα ταῖς θηλείαις ᾠδὴν ὥσπερ γαμήλιον περικράξαι. Pair for life, Athen. ix. 506. Lays four to five eggs, Arist. H. A. ix. 31, 618 b. Incubates twenty days and expels the fledglings, ib. vi. 6, 563 b.; cf. Plin. l. c. Ael. iii. 43 ὁ κόραξ ὁ ἤδη γέρων ὅταν μὴ δύνηται τρέφειν τοὺς νεοττούς, ἑαυτὸν αὐτοῖς προτείνει τροφήν, | οἱ δὲ ἐσθίουσι τὸν πατέρα; cf. Phile, De Anim. Pr. vi.

Habits.—Mentioned among τὰ κατὰ πόλεις εἰωθότα μάλιστα ζῆν, Arist. H. A. ix. 23, 617 b. Is a mimic, Ael. ii. 51. βούλεται δὲ τῶν ὄμβρων μιμεῖσθαι τὰς σταγόνας, ib. vi. 19. οὐ μεταβάλλει τοὺς τόπους οὐδὲ φωλεύει, Arist. H. A. ix. 23, 617 b. How the Ravens pick out sheeps' eyes, Ar. Av. 582.

Myth and Legend.—How there are never more than two Ravens περὶ τὴν καλουμένην Κόπτον in Egypt, Ael. vii. 18; at Krannon in Thessaly, Arist. De Mirab. 126, 842 b, Plin. x. (12) 15; in Pedasia in Caria, Arist. De Mirab. 137, 844 b. In this last instance they inhabit the temple, and one has a white throat. Perhaps the κόρακες here were priests or priestesses, cf. πέλεια. See also Arist. H. A. ix. 31.

On the κόρακες or κοράκια, as a grade in the Mithraic hierarchy, cf. Porphyr. De Abst. iv. 16, Hieronym. ad Laet. 7, Diodor. i. 62, Inscr. Grüter. p. 1087. 4, &c.; cf. Montfaucon, ii. p. 377, Creuzer's Symbolik i. p. 253, Münter ad Jul. Firmic. v. p. 20, &c. Creuzer (i. p. 431) correlates the Indian myth of Brahma appearing in one of his incarnations as a Raven, and compares in turn this latter story (ii. p. 655) with that in Herod. iv. 15. The Raven of Odin is, perhaps, also cognate.

The Raven as a messenger of Apollo. Hesiod, fr. 125 (142) ap. Schol. Pind. P. 48 (28) τῷ μὲν ἄρ' ἄγγελος ἦλθε κόραξ ἱερῆς ἀπὸ δαιτός | Πυθῶ ἐς ἠγαθέην καὶ ῥ' ἔφρασεν ἔργ' ἀίδηλα Φοίβῳ ἀκερσεκόμῃ: cf. Ael. i. 47 Ἀπόλλωνος θεράπων, with which cf. *famulum* in Cat. lxvi. 57, and Ellis's note; see also Bianor iv in Gk. Anthol. ii. 142 Φοίβου λάτρις: Ael. i. 47, 48, vii. 18, Porph. De Abst. iii. 5, Stat. Silv. ii. 4 Phoebeius ales, &c.

Hence with the laurel-emblem, on coins of Delphi. Hence also Stat. Theb. iii. 506 comes _obscurus tripodum; Petron. Sat. c. 122 delphicus ales.

ΚΟΡΑΞ

ΚΟΡΑΞ (*continued*).

The legend of Coronis (Paus. ii. 26, 6), mother of Aesculapius : the raven sent for water by Apollo, and punished for dallying by the way; hence the raven, alone of birds, does not bring water to its young: Dion. De Avib. i. 9, Phil. De An. Pr. vi : cf. Callim. fr. nuper edit., Gompertz, Mitth. a. d. Rainersammlung, 1893, Kenyon, Class. Rev. 1893, p. 430. See further, Ael. i. 47; also Ovid, F. ii. 249, where *Corvus* in the same story appears as a constellation ; according to Hyginus, Poet. Astron. c. xl, the raven waited to devour some ripening figs, and the punishment of everlasting thirst is correlated with the juxtaposition of the constellations Corvus and Crater, which latter the Hydra guards (Ovid, F. ii. 243 Continuata loco tria sidera Corvus et Anguis, Et medius Crater inter utrumque iacet). Hence Prov. κόραξ ὑδρεύει, Hesych., Suid. In the version of the same story in Ovid, Met. ii, the raven was originally white (v. 536) Nam fuit haec quondam niveis argentea pennis Ales, ut aequaret totas sine labe columbas ; a worldwide legend : cf. Hygin. Fab. 202, Gower, Conf. Amant. iii, &c.

On the name Coronis in connexion with Moon-symbolism, cf. Pott in Lazarus and Steintheil's Zeitschr., xiv. p. 18, 1883.

It is skilled in augury, Ael. i. 48; cf. Aes. Fab. 212, Plin. x. (12), 15, Cic. Divin. i. 39, Ovid, Met. ii. 534, Plaut. Aulul. iv. 3, 1, Id. Asin. ii. 1, 12, Hor. Car. iii. 17, Stat. Theb. iii. 506, Petron. Sat. 122, Valer. Max. i. c. 4, Festus, 197, &c.

How ravens conducted Alexander to the Temple of Jupiter Ammon, and subsequently gave warning of his death, Plut. V. Alex. c. 27.

How the ravens flocked to Delphi, and despoiled the gifts of the Athenians, before the Sicilian disaster, Pausan. x. 15, 5.

How ravens guided the Boeotians to the site of a new city, Photius, s. v. ἐς κόρακας.

How all the ravens departed from Athens and the Peloponnese on the defeat of Medius at Pharsalus, Arist. ix. 31, 618 b : cf. Plin. x. 15 ; see Schneider in loc., and ad Xen. Hellen. ii. 3, 4, further Diodor. xiv. 82, and Strab. xi. p. 591. Some similar incident seems to be alluded to in Ar. Eq. 1052 ἀλλ' ἱέρακα φίλει, μεμνημένος ἐν φρεσίν, ὅς σοι | ἤγαγε συνδήσας Λακεδαιμονίων κορακίνους.

How in Egypt the ravens beg of those sailing by in boats, and if denied, cut the cordage, Ael. ii. 48. Places ἄγνον in its nest as a charm, Ael. i. 35 : cf. Phile, 727. Detests τὴν εὔζωμον πόαν, Phile, De An. 670, or εὐζώμου σπέρμα, Ael. vi. 46. Is hostile to ἰκτῖνος, αἰσάλων, ταῦρος, ὄνος, Arist. H. A. ix. 1, 609 b, Ael. v. 48, Phile, 388, 705, and to χλωρεύς, Phile, 690. A raven and an ass together on a coin of Mindaon, Imh. Bl., and Kell., p. 32, pl. 24 (the constellation Corvus set shortly after Cancer, with which latter the Ass is associated). The hare detests the voice of the raven, Ael. xiii. 11 (and the constellation Lepus sets soon

ΚΟΡΑΞ (*continued*).

after the rising of Corvus, as does also Taurus). The raven is friendly to the fox, Arist. H. A. ix. 1, 609 b. The raven's eggs dye the hair and the teeth black, Ael. i. 48, Phile, De An. vi, Plin. xxix. (6) 34. The raven in medicine, Plin. xxix. (4) 13, &c. After killing a chameleon, the raven uses a leaf of laurel as an antidote to the reptile's venom, Plin. viii. (27) 41.

For an account of the various Raven-myths discussed in connexion with the astronomic symbolism of the constellation Corvus, see Hygin. Poet. Astron. xl, Fab. ccii, German. c. xl, Eratosthen. c. xli, Theon. p. 151, Vitruv. ix. 7, Ovid. l. c., Dupuis, Orig. de tous les cultes, vi. p. 457, &c.

A **Weather-prophet**.—A prophet of storm: Arat. 963–969 δή ποτε καὶ γενεαὶ κοράκων καὶ φῦλα κολοιῶν | ὕδατος ἐρχομένοιο Διὸς πάρα σῆμ' ἐγένοντο, | φαινόμενοι ἀγεληδὰ καὶ ἰρήκεσσιν ὁμοῖα | φθεγξάμενοι ... ἤ ποτε καὶ κρώξαντε βαρείῃ δισσάκι φωνῇ | μακρὸν ἐπιρροιζεῦσι τινασσόμενοι πτερὰ πυκνά: cf. Theophr. De Sign. vi. 1, 16 κόραξ πολλὰς μεταβάλλειν εἰωθὼς φωνάς, τούτων ἐὰν ταχὺ δὶς φθέγξηται καὶ ἐπιρροιζήσῃ καὶ τινάξῃ τὰ πτερὰ ὕδωρ σημαίνει· καὶ ἐὰν ὑετῶν ὄντων πολλὰς μεταβάλλῃ φωνὰς καὶ ἐὰν φθειρίζηται ἐπ' ἐλαίας· καὶ ἐάν τε εὐδίας ἐάν τε ὕδατος ὄντος μιμῆται τῇ φωνῇ οἷον σταλαγμοὺς ὕδωρ σημαίνει (vide Aratus, l. c.), cf. ib. c. 3; Arist. ap. Ael. vii. 7 ταχέως καὶ ἐπιτρόχως φθεγγόμενος καὶ κρούων τὰς πτέρυγας καὶ κροτῶν αὐτάς, ὅτι χειμὼν ἔσται κατέγνω πρῶτος. κόραξ δὲ αὖ καὶ κορώνη καὶ κολοιὸς δείλης ὀψίας εἰ φθέγγοιντο, χειμῶνος ἔσεσθαί τινα ἐπιδημίαν διδάσκουσι: Plut. Sol. Anim. ii. 129 A, Nic. Ther. 406 and Schol., &c. A sign of fair weather: Arat. 1003 καὶ κόρακες μουνούμεν' ἐρημαῖοι βοόωντες | δισσάκις, αὐτὰρ ἔπειτα μέγ' ἀθρόα κεκληγῶτες | πλειότεροι, ἀγεληδὸν ἐπὴν κοίτοιο μέδωνται | φωνῆς ἔμπλειοι: cf. Theophr. op. cit. vi. 4, 13, Q. Smyrn. xii. 513, Geopon. i. 2, 6; i. 3, 8, Plin. xviii. 87, Virg. G. i. 382, 410. In the Georgics, the allusion is evidently to *rooks*, as is perhaps also the case, though more doubtfully, in Aratus; cf. W. W. Fowler, 'A Year with the Birds' (3rd ed.), p. 234.

Varieties.—White ravens, Arist. H. A. iii. 12, 519: cf. De Color. 6, 799 b; Cod. Rhod. Lect. Antiq. xvii. 11; though λευκὸς κόραξ = *cygnus niger*, an unheard-of thing, Anth. Pal. xi. 417 (Jac. iv. 130) τί πειράζεις λευκὸν ἰδεῖν κόρακα; see also Photius, s.v. ἐς κόρακας; Athen. 359 E; Lucian, Epigr. 9 (3, 689) θᾶττον ἔην λευκοὺς κόρακας, πτηνάς τε χελῶνας | εὑρεῖν ἢ δοκιμὸν ῥήτορα Καππαδόκην: cf. Schol. in Ar. Nub. 133; Juv. Sat. vii. 202. Cf. fable of κόραξ καὶ κύκνος, Aes. 206. According to Boios and Simmias, ap. Anton. Lib. c. xx, Lycias, son of Cleinis, was metamorphosed into a white Raven. The ravens in Egypt are smaller than in Greece, Arist. H. A. viii. 28, 606.

ἀεροκόραξ, a fabulous variety, Lucian, Ver. Hist. i. 16. **κόραξ**

ΚΟΡΑΞ—ΚΟΡΥΔΑΛΟΣ   95

ΚΟΡΑΞ (*continued*).

in Athen. 353 a, and κόραξ νυκτερινός in Lucian Asin. 12 (ii. 581), for νυκτικόραξ, q.v.

On talking Ravens, Porph. De Abst. iii. 4, Plin. x. (43) 60, &c.

Fables.—Fable of the pitcher and the stones, Bianor iv, in Gk. Anthol. ii. 142; Ael. ii. 48, vii. 7. Fox and Crow, Babr. 77, Aes. (ed. Halm), 204: cf. Hor. Sat. ii. 5, 56. The Sick Raven, Babr. 78, Aes. 208 τίς τῶν θεῶν, τέκνον, σώσει, | τίνος γὰρ ὑπὸ σοῦ βωμὸς οὐχ ἐσυλήθη; Daw and Raven, Aes. 201. Raven and Serpent, Aes. 207: cf. Gk. Anthol. ii. 97. Raven (ὑπὸ παγίδος κρατηθείς) and Hermes, Aes. 205. Prov. κακοῦ κόρακος κακὸν ᾠόν, Ael. iii. 43; Paroem. Gr. ii. p. 466, ed. Leutsch: cf. W. H. Thompson's Phaedrus, p. 132.

ΚΟ'ΡΑΞ. β. A Cormorant, *Phalacrocorax carbo*, L., and *P. graculus*, L. Mod. Gk. καλιτζακοῦ.

Arist. H. A. viii. 3, 593 b ὁ καλούμενος κόραξ ἐστὶ τὸ μὲν μέγεθος οἷον πελαργός, πλὴν τὰ σκέλη ἔχει ἐλάττω, στεγανόπους δὲ καὶ νευστικός, τὸ δὲ χρῶμα μέλας. καθίζει δὲ οὗτος ἐπὶ τῶν δένδρων καὶ νεοττεύει ἐνταῦθα μόνος τῶν τοιούτων.

The Cormorant appears in various Italian dialects as *cormoran*, *corvo marin*, *corvastro*, &c., the Little Cormorant (vide s. v. **κολοιός**) as *corvo marin piccolo*, and in Venetia, *corvéto marin*, i. e. Sea-Jackdaw (Giglioli).

The *corvus aquaticus* of Plin. xi. (37) 47, mentioned as *bald* (quibus apud Graecos nomen est inde), and therefore presumably identical with the *phalacrocorax*, ib. x. (48) 68, must have been a different bird.

ΚΟ'ΡΑΦΟΣ. An unknown bird, Hesych. According to Schn., for κόρυφος, whence **μελαγκόρυφος**.

ΚΟ'ΡΘΙΛΟΣ· ὄρνις ὃν τινες βασιλίσκον, Hesych. Cf. **τρόχιλος**.

ΚΟ'ΡΚΟΡΑ· ὄρνις, Περγαῖοι, Hesych.

ΚΟΡΥ'ΔΑΛΟΣ. κόρυδος, *s.* κορυδός, Plato, Euthyd., Ar. Av. 302, 472, &c., Anaxandrides ap. Athen. iv. 131, Arist. H. A. &c., Theocr. vii. 141, Plut. De Is., &c., Galen, &c.; **κορυδαλλή**, Epich. 25 Ahr.; **κορυδαλλίς**, Simon. 68; **κορῡδαλίς**, Phile, De An. Pr. 683; κορυδαλλός, *s.* κορύδαλος, Theocr. x. 50, Babr. 88, Eubul. fr. ap. Phryn., Arist. H. A. ix. 15; **κορυδών**, Arist. H. A. ix. 1, 609, cf. Schol. ad Ar. Av. 303; **κόρυθος**, Hesych. (a doubtful word, defined as εἷς τῶν τροχίλων : cf. **κορυθών**), &c.: cf. Lob. Phryn. 338; Rutherford, New Phryn. p. 426. On the gender, cf. Schol. ad Ar. Av. 472 θηλυκῶς εἴρηκε τὴν κορυδόν, ὁ δὲ Πλάτων (Euthyd. 291 D) τοὺς κορυδούς.

ΚΟΡΥΔΑΛΟΣ (continued).

A **Lark** (from κόρυς). Mod. Gk. κορυδαλός, σκορδαλός, χαμοκελάδι (Belon), and in Santorini σκουριανλός (Bikélas) qy. σ-κουρι[δ]αυλός.

Description.—Arist. H. A. ix. 13, 615 b ἡ χλωρίς ἐστιν ἡλίκον κόρυδος: ix. 49 B, 633 b ἐπίγειος, κονιστικός (i. e. bathes in the sand, like a hen): viii. 16, 600 a φωλεῖ: vi. 1, 559 τίκτει ἐν τῇ γῇ, like the quail and the partridge : ix. 8, 614 a ἐπὶ δένδρου οὐ καθίζει ἀλλ' ἐπὶ τῆς γῆς: ix. 29, 618 a the cuckoo lays in its nest, which is placed on the ground, cf. Ael. iii. 30. Is caught with bird-lime, Dion. De Avib. iii. 2, or by help of the owl, ib. iii. 17. The crest referred to proverbially, Simon. fr. 68 (Plut. ii. 91 E, 809 A, V. Timol. xxxvii, 253 E) πάσαισιν κορυδαλλίσιν χρὴ λόφον ἐγγίνεσθαι. Arist. mentions neither the singing nor the soaring of the lark; but Theocr. vii. 141 has ἄειδον κόρυδοι καὶ ἀκανθίδες, and x. 50 ἐγειρομένῳ κορυδαλλῷ, *surgente corydalo*. The lark's song was apparently not appreciated : cf. Alciphr. Epist. 48 ὃν ἐγὼ τῆς ἀχαρίστου φωνῆς ἕνεκα ὀρθῶς κορυδὸν [s. ὀρθοκόρυδον] καλεῖσθαι πρὸς ἡμῶν ἔκρινα : Epigr. εἰ κύκνῳ δύναται κορυδὸς παραπλήσιον ᾄδειν : and proverbs cited by Schneider in Arist. vol. iv. p. 128.

Varieties.—Arist. H. A. ix. 25, 617 b δύο γένη, ἡ μὲν ἑτέρα ἐπίγειος καὶ λόφον ἔχουσα, ἡ δ' ἑτέρα ἀγελαία καὶ οὐ σποράς ὥσπερ ἐκείνη, τὸ μέντοι χρῶμα ὅμοιον τῇ ἑτέρᾳ ἔχουσα, τὸ δὲ μέγεθος ἔλαττον· καὶ λόφον οὐκ ἔχει, ἐσθίεται δέ. The first species is the Crested Lark, *Alauda cristata*, L., a permanent resident in Greece ; the other is the Common Lark, *Alauda arvensis*, L., a winter migrant (v. d. Mühle, p. 36, Lindermayer, p. 49). Both species receive the name κορυδαλός in Mod. Gk. (Erhard).

Myth and Legend.—Arist. H. A. ix. 1, 610 φίλαι σχοινίων καὶ κόρυδος καὶ λίβυος καὶ κελεός. ix. 1, 609 b ὁ πέλλος πολεμεῖ κορύδῳ, τὰ γὰρ ᾠὰ αὐτοῦ κλέπτει. Ib. 609 πολέμια ποικιλίδες καὶ κορυδῶνες καὶ πίπρα καὶ χλωρεύς. Hostile also to ἀκανθυλλίς, Phile, 683, Ael. iv. 5. Uses the grass ἄγρωστις as an amulet or protection, Ael. i. 35, as does the Hoopoe, Phile, 724; whence the proverb ἐν κορυδοῦ κοίτῃ σκολιὴ κέκρυπται ἄγρωστις, Geopon. xv. 1, 19. Uses, in like manner, oak-leaves, Phile, 725. Is killed by mustard-seed, νάπυος σπέρματι, Phile, 662, Ael. vi. 46; cf. Galen, Theriac. i. 9, 943, &c., Diosc. ii. 59, 796. How the lark led an Attic colony to Corone in Messenia, and how Apollo, under the name Κόρυδος, had a temple and cured diseases there, Paus. iv. 34, 8. How the Lemnians honoured the larks, τὰ τῶν ἀττελάβων εὑρίσκοντας ᾠὰ καὶ κύπτοντας, Plut. ii. 380 F. The story of the Lark and his Father, Aesop ap. Ar. Av. 471 κορυδὸν πάντων πρώτην ὄρνιθα γενέσθαι, προτέραν τῆς γῆς, κἄπειτα νόσῳ τὸν πατέρ' αὐτῆς ἀποθνῄσκειν· γῆν δ' οὐκ εἶναι, τὸν δὲ προκεῖσθαι πεμπταῖον· τὴν δ' ἀπορροῦσαν ὑπ' ἀμηχανίας τὸν πατέρ' αὐτῆς ἐν τῇ κεφαλῇ κατορύξαι. The same story told in great detail of the Hoopoe, ἔποψ Ἰνδικός (Ael. N. A. xvi. 5)

ΚΟΡΥΔΑΛΟΣ—ΚΟΡΩΝΗ

ΚΟΡΥΔΑΛΟΣ (*continued*).

with the statement that the Greeks probably transferred the legend to the lark; vide s.v. ἔποψ. The legend, which probably includes a solar myth, is very obscure. Connected with it is probably the epithet ἐπιτυμβίδιοι κορυδαλλίδες, Theocr. vii. 27, but the line in Babrius lxxii. 20 κορυδαλλὸς οὖν τάφοις παίζων is spurious and unreliable (W. G. R.). The κορυδός and ἔποψ (both crested birds) are frequently confused: the very word *Alauda* is possibly an Eastern word for the Hoopoe, Arab. *al hudhud*. Cf. Plin. xi. 37 galerita appellata quondam, postea gallico (?) vocabulo alauda.

Associated with the name Philoclees, Ar. Av. 1295.

The superficial resemblance between κορύδαλος and the name of Ἄρτεμις Κορυθαλία (Athen. iv. 139) may help to explain Ἄρτεμις Ἀκαλανθίς and the other similar epithets in Ar. Av. 870-877.

A fabled metamorphosis, Boios ap. Anton. Lib. c. 7, where Hippodameia is transformed into a lark, ὅτι ἐκορύσσετο πρὸς τὰς ἵππους.

Fables.—κορύδαλος εἰς πάγην ἁλούς, Aes. 209 (c. 55, F. 228). κορύδαλος καὶ γεωργός, Ib. 210 (F. 379, C. 421, B. 88).

ΚΟΡΥΘΩΝ, also **κορυνθεύς**· ἀλεκτρυών, Hesych. Very probably identical with **κορυδών**, s. v. **κορύδαλος**.

ΚΟΡΥΛΛΙΩΝ· ὄρνιθος εἶδος, Hesych. Vide s. v. **κολλυρίων**.

ΚΟΡΩΝΗ. The Crow, *Corvus corone*, L., including also the Hooded Crow, *C. cornix*, L. Mod. Gk. κορῶνα (Erh.), κουροῦνα (v. d. M.). Sometimes the Rook, which only appears in Greece during the winter, and appears to have received no special name: vide s.v. **σπερμολόγος**. On the confusion in Latin between *cornix*, *corvus*, &c., v. Wedgwood, Tr. Philol. Soc., 1854, p. 107; also W. W. Fowler, 'A Year with the Birds,' c. vii. Dim. **κορωνιδεύς**, Cratin. Πυλ. 10.

First in Hes. Op. 747 μή τοι ἐφεζομένη κρώζῃ λακέρυζα κορώνη: cf. Ar. Av. 609; Apoll. Rhod. iii. 928; Arat. 950.

Described as frequenting cities, Arist. H. A. ix. 23, 617 b, not a migrant, ib. (cf. Fab. Aes. 415). No bigger in Egypt than in Greece, ib. viii. 28, 606; alimentary canal as in the Raven, ib. ii. 17, 504; frequent the seashore, to feed on jettisoned carcases, being omnivorous, ib. viii. 3, 593 b; Archil. 44, ap. Athen. 594 συκῆ πετραίη πολλὰς βόσκουσα κορώνας (? rooks).

Breeding habits.—Arist. De Gen. iv. 6, 774 b τίκτουσιν ἀτελῆ καὶ τυφλά. H. A. vi. 8, 564 ἐπῳάζουσι δὲ αἱ θήλειαι μόναι, καὶ διατελοῦσιν ἐπ' αὐτῶν οὖσαι διὰ παντός· τρέφουσι δ' αὐτὰς οἱ ἄρρενες κομίζοντες τὴν τροφὴν αὐταῖς καὶ σιτίζοντες: ib. 6, 563 b ἐπί τινα χρόνον ἐπιμελεῖται· καὶ γὰρ ἤδη πετομένων σιτίζει παραπετομένη. On their monogamous habits, mutual affec-

H

ΚΟΡΩΝΗ (continued).

tion and constancy, whence their invocation at weddings, vide Ael. iii. 9 (*infra cit.*).

Myth and Legend.—Its proverbial longevity. Hes. in Plut. De Orac. Def. ii. p. 415 C ἐννέα τοι ζώει γενεὰς λακέρυζα κορώνη, | ἀνδρῶν ἡβώντων : cf. Ar. Av. 609, Arat. 1023 ἐννεάνειρα κορώνη : Opp. Cyn. iii. 117 αἰετόεντά τε φῦλα πολύζωοί (? πολύκρωζοί) τε κορῶνοι. Cf. also Ar. Av. 967 πολιαὶ κορῶναι : Babr. Fab. 46, 9 κορώνην δευτέραν ἀναπλήσας, lived two crows' lives ; Automed. ix (Gk. Anthol. ii. 193) βίον ζώοιτε κορώνης : Lucill. xcvii (ib. iii. 49) εἰ μὲν ζῆς ταναὸν ἐλάφου χρόνον ἠὲ κορώνης : Com. Anon. 4, 680 (Meineke) ὑπὲρ τὰς κορώνας βεβιωκώς, &c. See also Plin. vii. 48, Horat. Car. iii. 17, 16 annosa cornix; Martial, x. 67 cornicibus omnibus superstes, &c.; Lucret. v. 1083, Juv. x. 247, Ovid, Amor. ii. 6, 36. Auson. Id. xviii.

Is hostile to γαλῆ, γλαῦξ, ὄρχιλος, πρέσβυς, τύπανος, Arist. H. A. ix. 1, 609, 610: to ἀκανθυλλίς, Ael. iv. 5 : to ἀετός and κίρκος, Ael. xv. 22 ; friendly to ἐρωδιός, Arist. l. c., Ael. v. 48. The War of the Owls and Crows, Ael. iii. 9, v. 48 ἐπεὶ δὲ ἡ γλαῦξ ἐστιν αὐτῇ πολέμιον, καὶ νύκτωρ ἐπιβουλεύει τοῖς ᾠοῖς τῆς κορώνης, ἡ δὲ μεθ' ἡμέραν ἐκείνην ταὐτὸ δρᾷ τοῦτο, εἰδυῖα ἔχειν τὴν ὄψιν τὴν γλαῦκα τηνικαῦτα ἀσθενῆ. Cf. Jataka, p. 270 ; Ind. Antiq., 1882, p. 87; De Gubern. Zool. Myth., &c. Vide s. v. **γλαῦξ** for a discussion of the moon-symbolism of the latter bird, and compare the Chinese expression of the Golden Crow and the Jewelled Hare to signify the Sun and Moon. The same legend may account for Athene's supposed enmity to the Crow, cf. Ovid, Amor. ii. 6, 35 cornix invisa Minervae.

Uses ἀριστερῶν as a charm, Ael. i. 35 ; also ῥάμνον, Phile, De Am. Pr. 725; and περιστερεῶνα τὸν ὕπτιον, Geopon. xv. 1, 19.

A weather-prophet : of storm, Theophr. Sign. vi. 3, 39 ἐὰν ταχὺ δὶς κρώζῃ καὶ τρίτον χειμέρια σημαίνει . . . καὶ ὀψὲ ᾄδουσα : Arat. 1002 καὶ ἥσυχα ποικίλλουσα [s. κωτίλλουσα, Lob.] | ὥρη ἐν ἑσπερίῃ κρωγμὸν πολύφωνα κορώνη : ib. 1022 καὶ ἐννεάνειρα κορώνη | νύκτερον ἀείδουσα : cf. Arist. fr. 241, 1522 b, ap. Ael. vii. 7, Plut. ii. 674 B, Virg. G. i. 388, Hor. C. iii. 17, 13, Lucan v. 556; a sign of fair weather, Theophr. vi. 4, 53 καὶ κορώνη ἕωθεν εὐθὺς ἐὰν κράξῃ τρίς, εὐδίαν σημαίνει, καὶ ἑσπέρας χειμῶνος ἡσυχαίαν ᾄδουσα : cf. Ael. l. c., Virg. G. i. 410, Geopon. i. 2, 6, &c. A bad summer is portended when the fig-leaves are shaped like a crow's foot, Plut. ii. 410 E.

The Crow in augury, seldom mentioned in Greek, save in Ar. Aves; see also Ael. iii. 9, where a solitary crow is mentioned as an evil omen ; according to Porph. De Abst. iii. 4, the Arabs understood the language of crows. A crow on the left-hand is unlucky, Virg. Ecl. ix. 15, Cic. De Div. i. 39, Plaut. Asin. ii. 1, 12, &c. ; cf. Hopf, Orakelthiere, p. 115.

According to Bent, Cyclades, 1885, p. 394, the inhabitants of Anti-

ΚΟΡΩΝΗ

ΚΟΡΩΝΗ (*continued*).

paros are called κουροῦναι by their neighbours in Paros, the reason assigned being that if the former see a crow on the south side of a tree, they are in terror. How a crow never enters the Acropolis at Athens, Arist. fr. 324, 1532 b, Ael. v. 8, Apollon. viii, Plin. x. (12) 14. (This statement is believed by some modern travellers, cf. Dr. Chandler, Trav. in Greece, c. xi. p. 54 ; and may have a foundation in fact, due simply to the height of the hill.) How a crow in Egypt used to carry messages for King Marres, and was honoured with a sepulchre, Ael. vi. 7. How a crow dies if it falls in with the leavings of a wolf's dinner (!), Ael. vi. 46, Phile, 671. How a brazen crow was found in the foundation of Coronea, Paus. iv. 34, 5. How the crows showed the grave of Hesiod, Paus. ix. 38, 3. How the young crow leaves the egg feet first, Dion. De Avib. i. 10. The heart eaten, to secure prophetic powers, Porph. De Abst. ii. 48 (cf. ἱέραξ).

It was invoked at weddings, Ael. iii. 9 ἀκούω δὲ τοὺς πάλαι καὶ ἐν τοῖς γάμοις μετὰ τὸ ὑμέναιον τὴν κορώνην καλεῖν, σύνθημα ὁμονοίας τοῦτο τοῖς συνιοῦσιν ἐπὶ παιδοποιίᾳ διδόντες. Cf. Horap. i. 9 γάμον δὲ δηλοῦντες, δύο κορώνας ζωγραφοῦσι [οἱ Αἰγύπτιοι] : regarding which statement, see Lauth, Sitzungsber. Bayer. Akad. 1876, p. 79. Cf. also Horap. i. 8 τὸν Ἄρεα καὶ τὴν Ἀφροδίτην γράφοντες, δύο κορώνας ζωγραφοῦσιν, ὡς ἄνδρα καὶ γυναῖκα, ἐπεὶ τοῦτο τὸ ζῷον δύο ᾠὰ γεννᾷ, ἀφ' ὧν ἄρρεν καὶ θῆλυ γεννᾶσθαι δεῖ. ἐπειδὰν δὲ γεννήσῃ, ὅπερ σπανίως γίνεται, δύο ἀρσενικά, ἢ δύο θηλυκά, τὰ ἀρσενικὰ τὰς θηλείας γαμήσαντα οὐ μίσγεται ἑτέρᾳ κορώνῃ, οὐδὲ μὴν ἡ θήλεια ἑτέρᾳ κορώνῃ μέχρι θανάτου, ἀλλὰ μόνα τὰ ἀποζυγέντα διατελεῖ. διὸ καὶ μιᾷ κορώνῃ συναντήσαντες οἰωνίζονται οἱ ἄνθρωποι, ὡς χηρεύοντι συνηντηκότες ζῴῳ· τῆς δὲ τοιαύτης αὐτῶν ὁμονοίας χάριν μέχρι νῦν οἱ Ἕλληνες ἐν τοῖς γάμοις· ἐκκορί, κορί, κορώνη' λέγουσιν ἀγνοοῦντες. Cf. the Delphic oracle ap. Pausan. ix. 37, 4 ὄψ' ἦλθες γενεὴν διζήμενος, ἀλλ' ἔτι καὶ νῦν | ἰστοβοῆι γέροντι νέην ποτίβαλλε κορώνην.

The much-discussed words ἐκκορί, κορί, κορώνη, or (Prov.) κόρε, ἐκκόρει κορώνην are quite obscure (cf. Herm. Opusc. ii. 227, Leemans in Horap. p. 156, various commentators on Pind. P. iii. 19, &c.). They are probably part of a 'Crow-song,' and very likely involve a corruption of foreign words : ΠΙΚΟΡΙ (which word includes the article) is said to be Coptic for a Crow or Daw. Various uses of ἐκκορέω, ὑποκορίζομαι, &c., are perhaps involved in the same corruption ; cf. also the word-play on κόρη, κοῦρος, &c., in the Crow-song next referred to.

On the Crow-song, κορώνισμα, and its singers, κορωνισταί, see Athen. viii. 359 οἶδα δὲ Φοίνικα τὸν Κολοφώνιον ἰαμβοποιὸν μνημονεύοντα τινῶν ἀνδρῶν ὡς ἀγειρόντων τῇ Κορώνῃ (cf. Hesych. s. v. κορωνισταί), καὶ λεγόντων ταῦτα· Ἐσθλοὶ Κορώνῃ χεῖρα πρόσδοτε κριθῶν, Τῇ παιδὶ τοῦ Ἀπόλλωιος, ἢ λέχος πυρῶν, κ.τ.λ. Ilgen, Poet. Gr. Mendicorum Spec., in Opusc.

ΚΟΡΩΝΗ (*continued*).

Var. Phil., i. p. 169; Fauriel, Chants de la Gr. Mod., i. p. cix. See also s. v. χελιδών.

Frequent in Fable, e.g. κορώνη καὶ κόραξ (the Crow that could not prophesy), Fab. Aes. 202; κορώνη Ἀθηνᾷ θύουσα, ib. 213. χελιδὼν καὶ κορώνη, ib. 416.

Proverb κορώνη σκορπίον [ἥρπασε]. Anth. Pal. xii. 92, Hesych., Suid., cf. Ael. vii. 7, Zenob. iv. 60, p. 101.

ΚΟΡΩ΄ΝΗ Ἡ ΔΑΥΛΙ΄ΑΣ. The **Nightingale**; vide s. v. ἀηδών.

ΚΟΡΩ΄ΝΗ Ἡ ΘΑΛΑ΄ΣΣΙΟΣ. An undetermined sea-bird.

Od. v. 66 τανύγλωσσοί τε κορῶναι | εἰνάλιαι, τῇσίν τε θαλάσσια ἔργα μέμηλεν. Ib. xii. 418, xiv. 308 οἱ δὲ κορώνῃσιν ἴκελοι περὶ νῆα μέλαιναν | κύμασιν ἐμφορέοντο.

Arrian. Peripl. c. 21 λάροι καὶ αἴθυιαι καὶ κορῶναι αἱ θαλάσσιαι τὸ πλῆθος οὐ σταθμητοί· οὗτοι οἱ ὄρνιθες θεραπεύουσιν τοῦ Ἀχιλλέως τὸν νεών. ἕωθεν ὁσημέραι καταπέτονται ἐς τὴν θάλασσαν· ἔπειτα ἀπὸ τῆς θαλάσσης βεβρεγμένοι τὰ πτερὰ σπουδῇ αὖ ἐσπέτονται ἐς τὸν νεών, καὶ ῥαίνουσι τὸν νεών.

Arat. Progn. 950 ἢ που καὶ λακέρυζα παρ' ἠϊόνι προυχούσῃ | χείματος ἐρχομένου χέρσῳ ὑπέτυψε κορώνη, | ἢ που καὶ ποταμοῖο ἐβάψατο μέχρι παρ' ἄκρους | ὤμους ἐκ κεφαλῆς, ἢ καὶ μάλα πᾶσα κολυμβᾷ, | ἢ πολλὴ στρέφεται παρ' ὕδωρ παχέα κρώζουσα: cf. Geopon. i. 3, 7 καὶ κορώνη ἐπ' αἰγιαλοῦ τὴν κεφαλὴν διαβρέχουσα, ἢ πᾶσα νηχομένη, καὶ νυκτὸς σφοδρότερον κρώζουσα, ὄμβρους προμηνύει: Theophr. Sign. vi. 1, 16 κορώνη ἐπὶ πέτρας κορυσσομένη ἣν κῖμα κατακλύζει ὕδωρ σημαίνει· καὶ κολυμβῶσα πολλάκις καὶ περιπετομένη ὕδωρ σημαίνει.

These passages, with which compare Arist. H. A. viii. 3, 593 b, and Ael. xv. 22, denote a different bird altogether from κορώνη, evidently a swimming and diving bird, and not merely one frequenting the sea-shore as the Carrion Crow and Hooded Crow do. It is neither a λάρος nor an αἴθυια (Arrian, l. c.) though identified with them by the Scholiast in Od. v. 66, with whom cf. Hesych. κορῶναι· ἅλιαι αἴθυιαι, κολυμβίδες. It may be another name for the **Cormorant** (vide s. v. κόραξ, β): but it is not safely identifiable.

It is apparently such passages which are imitated in Virg. G. i. 388 Tum cornix plena pluviam vocat improba voce, Et sola in sicca secum spatiatur arena; cf. Claud. De Bell. Gild. 492 Heu nimium segnes, cauta qui mente notatis, Si revolant mergi, graditur si littore cornix. Cf. however the weather-prophecies s. v. κολοιός. It is at least pretty clear that in such passages the Latin poets were thinking more of what they had read than of what they had seen.

ΚΟ΄ΣΚΙΚΟΣ, κοτίκας, κοττός, κόττυλος. The **Common Fowl**. Hesych.

κόσκικοι· οἱ κατοικίδιαι ὄρνιθες. κοτίκας· ἀλέκτωρ. κοττός· ὄρνις. κύττυλοι· κατοικίδιαι ὄρνεις.

ΚΟΣΚΙΚΟΣ (*continued*).

These obscure words do not occur elsewhere. κοττός is said to be connected with κοττίς, for a crest or top-knot, cf. Hesych. s. v. προκόττα: καὶ οἱ ἀλεκτρυόνες κοττοὶ διὰ τὸν ἐπὶ τῇ κεφαλῇ λόφον (cf. supra, s. v. κάλλων). For κόσκικος, κόττυλος, cf. κύσσιχος, κόσσυφος, κόττυφος : κοτίκας, on the other hand, suggests a corruption of κατοικάς. Cf. Lob. Proll. 327; Schmidt ad Hesych. 3758, 3790.

ΚΟ΄ΣΣΥΦΟΣ, α. Also κόψικος, Ar. Av. 306, 806, 1081; Nicostr. ap. Athen. ii. 65 D, &c.; κόψυκος, Suid.

The **Blackbird**, *Turdus merula*, L. Mod. Gk. κόσσυφος, κότσυφος, κοτσύφι, κότζιφος.

Description.—Its size compared with the Woodpecker, Arist. H. A. ix. 9, 614 b; with λαϊός, ib. 19, 617; with τριχάς, ib. 20, 617; with κύανος, ib. 21, 617; with ψάρος, ib. 26, 617 b. φοινικοῦν ἔχει τὸ ῥύγχος, ib. 29, 617. Dion. De Avib. i. 27 δύο δ' ἐστὶ γένη κοσσύφων· καὶ οἱ μὲν πάντη μέλανες, οἱ δὲ κηρῷ τὰ χείλη προσεοικότες, καὶ τῶν ἑτέρων μᾶλλον πρὸς τὰς ᾠδὰς ἐπιτήδειοι: this is plainly the sexual difference.

Migration, Arist. H. A. viii. 16, 600, φωλεῖ. Change of plumage, ib. ix. 49 B, 632 b τῶν δ' ὀρνέων πολλὰ μεταβάλλουσι κατὰ τὰς ὥρας καὶ τὸ χρῶμα καὶ τὴν φωνήν, οἷον ὁ κόττυφος ἀντὶ μέλανος ξανθός· καὶ τὴν φωνὴν δ' ἴσχει ἀλλοίαν· ἐν μὲν γὰρ τῷ θέρει ᾄδει, τοῦ δὲ χειμῶνος παταγεῖ καὶ φθέγγεται θορυβῶδες. Cf. Arist. fr. 273, 1527 b; Ael. xii. 28. Eustath. Hexaem. p. 30 ἐξ ᾠδικοῦ κρακτικός : cf. also Clem. Alex. Paedag. x, Plin. x. 28 Merula ex nigrâ rufescit, canit aestate, hyeme balbutit, circa solstitium mutat. Song referred to also, Ael. vi. 19; Theocr. Ep. iv. 10 εἰαρινοὶ δὲ λιγυφθόγγοισιν ἀοιδαῖς | κόσσυφοι ἀχεῦσιν ποικιλότρυυλα μέλη.

Nesting.—Arist. H. A. v. 13, 554 δὶς τίκτει ὁ κόσσυφος· τὰ μὲν οὖν πρῶτα τοῦ κοσσύφου ὑπὸ χειμῶνος ἀπόλλυται, πρωϊαίτατα γὰρ τίκτει τῶν ὀρνέων ἁπάντων, τὸν δ' ὕστερον τόκον εἰς τέλος ἐκτρέφει : cf. Dion. De Avib. i. 27. Arist. H. A. ix. 13, 616, builds a nest lined with hair and wool like χλωρίς.

White Blackbirds on Cyllene.—Arist. H. A. ix. 19, 617, De Mirab. 15, 831 b, Pausan. viii. 17, 3, Sostrat. ap. Ael. v. 27, Plin. x. 30, Steph. Byz. s. v. κυλλήνη, &c.; according to Lindermayer (p. 30) white or albino blackbirds are still remarkably common on Cyllene, but in Aristotle the fact is mixed with fable.

Mode of capture.— Dion. De Avib. iii. 13. Frequently mentioned, together with κίχλη, in the Anthology; Rhian. vi (Gk. Anth. Jac. i. 231) ἔξω Δεξιόνικος ὑπὸ χλωρῇ πλατανίστῳ | κόσσυφον ἀγρεύσας, εἷλε κατὰ πτερύγων· | χὠ μὲν ἀναστενάχων ἐπεκώκυεν ἱερὸς ὄρνις : Archias xxiii (ib. ii. 85) δίσσαις σὺν κίχλαισιν ὑπὲρ φραγμοῖο διωχθείς | κόσσυφος ἠερίης κόλπον ἔδυ νεφέλης : Antip. Sid. lxii (ib. ii. 23) δισσᾶν ἐκ βροχίδων ἁ μὲν μία πίονα κίχλαν | ἁ μία δ' ἱππείᾳ κόσσυφον εἷλε πάγᾳ : Paul. Sil. lxxii (ib. iv. 63) ὄρθριος εὐπλέκτοιο λίνου νεφοειδέϊ κόλπῳ | ἔμπεσε σὺν κίχλῃ κόσσυφος

ΚΟΣΣΥΦΟΣ (*continued*).

ἡδυβόας. Mentioned as a destructive bird, Anon. 416 (ib. iv. 206) ἤνιδε καὶ κίχλην καὶ κόσσυφον, ἤνιδε τόσσους | ψᾶρας, ἀρουραίης ἅρπαγας εὐπορίης.

Myth and Legend.—Arist. H. A. ix. 1, 608 b, hostile to κρέξ, friendly with τρυγών: cf. Ael. vi. 46. Is killed by pomegranate, cf. Phile, De An. Pr. 657.

ΚΟ'ΣΣΥΦΟΣ, β. A breed of fowls at Tanagra.

Pausan. ix. 22, 4 τούτων τῶν κοσσύφων μέγεθος μὲν κατὰ τοὺς Λυδοὺς ἐστιν ὄρνιθας, χρόα δὲ ἐμφερὴς κόρακι, κάλλαια δὲ καὶ ὁ λόφος κατὰ ἀνεμώνην μάλιστα. λευκὰ δὲ σημεῖα οὐ μεγάλα ἐπί τε ἄκρῳ τῷ ῥάμφει καὶ ἐπὶ ἄκρας ἔχουσι τῆς οὐρᾶς: cf. ib. viii. 17, 3.

ΚΟΤΤΟ'Σ. ὄρνις [i. e. ἀλεκτρυών] Hesych. Hence κοττοβολεῖν, τὸ παρατηρεῖν τινα ὄρνιν, ib.; cf. κορωνοβολεῖν, Anth. Pal. vii. 546; also κοττάναρθρον, ἔνθα αἱ ὄρνιθες κοιμῶνται, Hesych. Among the Mod. Gk. names for a Fowl are κόττα and κυτταπούλι.

ΚΟΥΚΟΥ'ΦΑ, *s.* **κουκούφας,** *s.* **κούκουφος.** The Egyptian name for the Hoopoe. Vide s. v. ἔποψ. Cf. Lib. MS. Anon. De Avibus (cit. Ducange in Gloss. Med. et Inf. Gr., s. v. κούκουφος, Leemans ad Horap. p. 280) ἔποψ ὄρνεον ἐν ἀέρι πετόμενον· οὗτος καλεῖται κούκουφος, καὶ ποῦπος.

Horapollo, i. 55 Αἰγύπτιοι εὐχαριστίαν γράφοντες κουκούφαν ζωγραφοῦσι, διότι τοῦτο μόνον τῶν ἀλόγων ζῴων ἐπειδὰν ὑπὸ τῶν γονέων ἐκτραφῇ, γηράσασιν αἰτοῖς τὴν αὐτὴν ἀνταποδίδωσι χάριν (cf. Ael. x. 16): ὅθεν καὶ ἐπὶ τῶν θείων σκήπτρων κουκούφα προτίμησίς ἐστι. Cf. the Cuckoo on Hera's sceptre at Mycenae, s. v. κόκκυξ. On the Hoopoe on Egyptian sceptres or staves, see Creuzer's Symbolik, ii. 64, 280, pl. iv. 17; Denon, Pl. cxix. 8, &c., &c. For an account of the hieroglyphic symbol of the Hoopoe, and an explanation of the statements of Horapollo, vide Lauth, in Sitzungsb. d. Bayer. Akad. 1876, p. 106. To the Egyptian references given above, s.v. ἔποψ, add the following : ἐσοφίζετο [Φαῖνος] παρὰ τοῖς Αἰγυπτίοις, οἰωνῶν τε λόγους καὶ ἐπόπων προσαγγελίας καὶ ἵππων χρεμετισμοὺς μαθών, Exc. Gr. Barbari, Chron. Min., ed. Fick, 1893, p. 239.

ΚΟΥΡΕΥ'Σ· ὄρνις ποιός, ἀπὸ τοῦ φθέγγεσθαι ἐμφερὲς ἤχῳ γναφικοῦ μαχαιρίου, Hesych.

ΚΟΥΤΙ'ΔΕΣ· συκαλλίδες, Hesych. Cf. κουτίδια· δίκτυα τὰ πρὸς τὰς συκαλλίδας, Hesych.

ΚΡΑ'ΒΟΣ· ὁ λάρος, Hesych.

ΚΡΑΓΓΩ'Ν· κίσσα, Hesych.

ΚΡΑ'ΜΒΩΤΟΝ· ἰκτῖνος τὸ ζῷον, Hesych.

ΚΡΑΥΓΟ'Σ. A **Woodpecker**. δρυοκολάπτου εἶδος, Hesych.: who has also κρυυγόν· ποιὸς ὄρνις. Von Edlinger cites Lith. *kraki*: cf. κράζω.

ΚΡΕ'Ξ, also **κερκάς** (Hesych.). A very doubtful bird, usually identified, by Sundevall and others, with the **Corn-crake** or **Land-rail**, *Rallus crex*, L., *Crex pratensis*, auctt. = ὀρτυγομήτρα = κύχραμος. The name is lost in Mod. Gk.

Herod. ii. 76, compared in size with the Ibis.

Ar. Av. 1138 τούτους δ᾽ ἐτύκιζον αἱ κρέκες τοῖς ῥύγχεσιν. Schol. in Ar. (Suid.) ὄρνεον δυσοιώνιστον τοῖς γαμοῦσιν, ὀξὺ πάνυ τὸ ῥύγχος καὶ πριονῶδες ἔχον: cf. Hesych. ὄρνεόν τι, ὃ τοῖς γαμοῦσιν οἰωνίζεται· τάσσεται δὲ καὶ ἐπὶ τρόχου [cf. ἴυγξ]. As a bird of evil omen to the newly married, cf. Euphor. 4 (quoted by Tzetzes) ὃν δ᾽ ἤεισε γάμον κακὸν ἐχθόμενος κρέξ, and Lycophr. 513, where Helen is δυσάρπαγος κρέξ. A messenger of Athene, Porph. De Abst. iii. 5.

Arist. H. A. ix. 1, 609 b κρὲξ πολέμιος ἐλεῷ καὶ κοττύφῳ καὶ χλωρίωνι ... καὶ γὰρ αὐτοὺς βλάπτει καὶ τὰ τέκνα αὐτῶν. In Ael. iv. 5 (*loc dub.*) κρέξ is hostile to αἴθυια: also Phile, De An. Pr. 681, with epithet βραδύπτερος. Arist. H. A. ix. 17, 616 b ἡ δὲ κρὲξ τὸ μὲν ἦθος μάχιμος, τὴν δὲ διάνοιαν εὐμήχανος πρὸς τὸν βίον, ἄλλως δὲ κακόποτμος ὄρνις. Arist. De Part. iv. 12, 695, mentioned among the long-legged birds with a short hind-toe.

κρέξ has been identified, on account of its pugnacity, with the Ruff, *Machetes pugnax*, L.; but the Ruffs fight *with one another* (cf. μέμνων), and, moreover, all the accounts of mutual hostilities between birds are unreliable, and in the main mythological. From the size, and the rudimentary hind-toe, the Black-winged Stilt, *Himantopus rufipes*, Bechst. was suggested first by Belon: its use by Herodotus as a standard of comparison with the Ibis is somewhat in favour of this bird, which is common in Egypt. The identification with the Corn-crake rests mainly on the assumption that the name is onomatopoeic. The facts that the Scholiasts knew little or nothing about the bird, and that the name is lost in Mod. Gk., suggest that the word was perhaps an exotic, and that its meaning was early lost.

ΚΡΙΓΗ'· ἡ γλαῦξ, Hesych.

ΚΡΙ'ΕΣ· ἡ χελιδών, Hesych. Doubtless corrupt: Meineke suggests κρί[δον]ες; or κρί[κ]ες, κρίξ.

ΚΥ'ΑΝΟΣ. Probably the **Wall-Creeper**, *Tichodroma muraria*, L.

Arist. H. A. ix. 21, 617 μάλιστα ἐν Νισύρῳ [ἐν Σκύρῳ, Ael.] ἐστί, ποιεῖται δ᾽ ἐπὶ τῶν πετρῶν τὰς διατριβάς· τὸ δὲ μέγεθος κοττύφου μὲν ἐλάττων,

ΚΥΑΝΟΣ (*continued*).

σπίζης δὲ μείζων μικρῷ· μεγαλόπους δέ, καὶ πρὸς τὰς πέτρας προσαναβαίνει. κυανοῖς ὅλος· τὸ δὲ ῥύγχος ἔχει λεπτὸν καὶ μακρόν, σκέλη δὲ βραχέα τῇ πίπῳ παρόμοια.

Ael. iv. 59 ὄρνις ἀπάνθρωπος τὸν τρόπον, μισῶν μὲν τὰς ἀστικὰς διατριβὰς καὶ τὰς κατ' οἰκίαν αὐλίσεις, ... οὔτε ἠπείροις φιληδεῖ, οὔτε νήσοις ἀγαθαῖς· Σκύρῳ δέ, καὶ εἴ τις τοιαύτη ἑτέρα ἄγαν λυπρὰ καὶ ἄγονος καὶ ἀνθρώπων χηρεύουσα, ὡς τὰ πολλά.

The description in Aristotle accords very perfectly with the Wall-Creeper (with which bird Gloger, Sundevall, and Heldreich identify it) as regards habitat, size, feet, and bill, as does Aelian's account of its solitary nature: but the bird is not κυανοῖς ὅλος, nor is Aelian's account of its habitat satisfactory. Aubert and Wimmer on the other hand, following Belon, Gesner, and other older commentators, identify κύανος with the Blue Thrush (Mod. Gk. πετροκόσσυφος, cf. infra, s. v. λαϊός), which agrees with the description in colour, but in little else, and is a very common bird, whereas κύανος is mentioned as scarce and local.

ΚΥΚΝΙΆΣ. An **Eagle**, white like a swan, at Sipylus near Lake Tantalus, Pausan. viii. 17, 3.

That Pausanias is here in error is rendered the more probable by the existence in Med. Gk. of the words τζυκνεᾶς, τζυκνέας, Mod. Gk. τσικνιᾶς, meaning a White Heron or Egret.

The White Eagle of Pythagoras (Iambl. Vit. Pythag. § 132, Ael. V. H. iv. 17) is supposed to be an allegory for the town of Croton, on whose coins an eagle is represented; cf. O. Keller, op. cit., pp. 238, 431.

ΚΥ΄ΚΝΟΣ. (Hesych. has also **κύδνος**.) Sk. *çak-uni*, a bird; Bopp, ii. p. 379, cf. Fick in Herzenberger's Beitr. z. I. Gr. Spr., vii. p. 94, 1883: cf. the Gk. use of ὄρνις for the constellation Cygnus (Arat. 275, 599, 628, &c.).

A **Swan**. Mod. Gk. κύκνος, νίαλμα (Heldr.), and in the Cyclades κοῦλος (Erh.). The Mute Swan, *Cygnus olor*, Gm., breeds in Greece; the Hooper or Whistling Swan, *C. musicus*, Bechst., is probably only a winter migrant; cf. Heldr., op. cit., p. 56.

Epithets.—ἀερσιπότης, Hes. Sc. H. 316; ἀχέτας (= ἠχέτης), Eur. El. 151; δολιχαύχην, Eur.(?) I. A. 794; δουλιχόδειρος, Il. ii. 460, xv. 692; ἱμερόφωνος, Christod. Ecphr. 384, λιγύθροος, id. 414, in Gk. Anth.; μαντιπόλος, Opp. Cyneg. ii. 547; μελῳδός, Eur. I. T. 1104; ποτάμιος, Id. Rh. 618; πολιόχρως, Id. Bacch. 1364: cf. Ar. Vesp. 1064; ὑμνήτηρ, Pallad. 40, in Gk. Anth. iii. 123; χιονόχρως, Eur. Hel. 216. A frequent emblem of whiteness: cf. Eur. Rh. 618 στίλβοντι δ' ὥστε ποταμίου κύκνου πτερόν. [Note the frequent allusions in Euripides;

ΚΥΚΝΟΣ (*continued*).

rare in Aeschylus; not in Sophocles, save for πτίλον κύκνειον in the dubious fr. 708, ap. Clem. Alex. Strom. 716.]

Description.—Arist. H. A. i. 1, 488, viii. 12, 597 b ὄρνις ἀγελαῖος: ib. viii. 3, 593 b, enumerated among τὰ βαρύτερα τῶν στεγανοπόδων: ib. ix. 12, 615 βιοτεύουσι περὶ λίμνας καὶ ἕλη, εὐβίοτοι δὲ καὶ εὐήθεις καὶ εὔτεκνοι καὶ εὔγηροι, καὶ τὸν ἀετόν, ἐὰν ἄρξηται, ἀμυνόμενοι νικῶσιν, αὐτοὶ δ' οὐκ ἄρχουσι μάχης. ᾠδικοὶ δέ, καὶ περὶ τὰς τελευτὰς μάλιστα ᾄδουσιν· ἀναπέτονται γὰρ καὶ εἰς τὸ πέλαγος, καί τινες ἤδη πλέοντες παρὰ τὴν Λιβύην περιέτυχον ἐν τῇ θαλάττῃ πολλοῖς ᾄδουσι φωνῇ γοώδει, καὶ τούτων ἑώρων ἀποθνῄσκοντας ἐνίους: cf. Ael. V. H. i. 14 λέγει Ἀριστοτέλης τὸν κύκνον καλλίπαιδα εἶναι καὶ πολύπαιδα, κ.τ.λ.: cf. also Athen. ix. 393 d; Eustath. ad Hom. Il. p. 193; Dion. De Avib. ii. 19. Arist. H. A. ii. 17, 509 ἔχει ἀποφυάδας ὀλίγας κάτωθεν κατὰ τὴν τοῦ ἐντέρου τελευτήν. Occur abundantly Ἀσίῳ ἐν λειμῶνι, Καϋστρίου ἀμφὶ ῥέεθρα, Il. ii. 461: cf. Virg. G. i. 383, Aen. vii. 699; on the river Hebrus, Ar. Av. 768; on Lake Aornos, in the spot called Pyriphlegethon, near Cumae, Arist. De Mirab. 102, 839. Its flight described, Plin. x. (23) 32. The swan as food, Athen. ix. 393, Plut. De Esu Carn. 2, &c.

Myth and Legend.—On the combat with the Eagle, vide s. v. ἀετός, and compare also the story of Leda; cf. also Ael. v. 34, xvii. 24; Dion. De Avib. ii. 19. Is hostile also to δράκων, Ael. v. 48, Phile 691. Is ἀλληλοφάγος μάλιστα τῶν ὀρνέων, Arist. H. A. ix. 1, 610 (cf. ἀλληλοφόνος, Picc., A. and W., ἀλληλοφίλος, Sund.), cf. Plin. x. (23) 32 mutua carne vescuntur inter se. Is killed by κώνειον, Ael. iii. 7; places the herb λυγαία in its nest as a charm, Boios ap. Athen. ix. 393 E. How the Indians do not favour the swan, from its want of filial affection, Ael. xiv. 13: yet the swan bewails its dead parent in Eur. El. 151, cf. Bacch. 1364 ὄρνις ὅπως κηφῆνα [ἀμφιβάλλει] πολιόχρως κύκνος. Associated with the ὀμφαλός at Delphi, Plut. De Orac. i. 409; vide s. v. ἀετός. A good omen to sailors, Virg. Aen. i. 393, Aemil. Macer in Ornithogr. Anthol. Vet. Lat. Epigr. et Poem. i. 116 (cf. Serv. in Aen. l. c.) Cygnus in auspiciis semper laetissimus ales, Hunc optant nautae, quia se non mergit in undas: see also Stat. Theb. iii. 524; cf. the Swan as a figure-head, Nicostr. iii. 282, &c.: cf. also the mythological (and astronomical) association of the Swan with Castor and Pollux (Hopf, Orakelthiere, p. 177): see also Drummond in Class. Journal, xvi. p. 94. The Swan-maidens, κόραι τρεῖς κυκνόμορφοι, Aesch. Pr. V. 797. According to Nicand. and Areus ap. Anton. Lib. c. xii, a certain Cycnus, and his mother Thuria, were metamorphosed into swans at Lake Conopa, καὶ πολλοὶ ἐν τῇ ὥρᾳ τοῦ ἀροτοῦ ἐνταῦθα φαίνονται κύκνοι.

On the Swan as the bird of Apollo, cf. Hymn. Hom. xxi, Callim. Hymn. Apoll. 5, id. Hymn. Del. 249, Ar. Av. 772, 870, Ael. xi. 1, Nonn. Dionys. xxxviii. 202 κύκνον ἄγων πτερόεντα, καὶ οὐ ταχὺν ἵππον Ἀπόλλων, &c.

ΚΥΚΝΟΣ (*continued*).

&c.; represented on coins of Clazomenae. With the Greek association of the Swan with Apollo, cf. the Hindoo connexion of the same bird with Brahma. Associated with Venus, in Latin only, Hor. C. iv. 1, 9, Sil. Ital. Punic. vii. 441, Stat. Silv. iii. 4, 22; cf. the Cilix of Aphrodite and the Swan in the British Museum: vide Kalkmann, Jahrb. d. k. d. Inst., 1886, i. 41, Collignon, Gk. Mythol. p. 132, fig. 56; see also Guignat, pl. C. 393, Creuzer, pl. liii. 2.

The Swan's Song.—Hesiod, Sc. H. 314 'Αμφὶ δ' ἴτην ῥέεν 'Ωκεανὸς πλήθοντι ἐοικώς | ... οἱ δὲ κατ' αὐτὸν | κύκνοι ἀερσιπόται μεγάλ' ἤπυον οἵ ῥά γε πολλοὶ | νῆχον ἐπ' ἄκρον ὕδωρ: cf. Virg. Aen. viii. 655. Hymn. Hom. xxi Φοῖβε, σὲ μὲν καὶ κύκνος ὑπὸ πτερύγων λίγ' ἀείδει, | ὄχθῃ ἐπιθρώσκων ποταμὸν πάρα δινήεντα, | Πηνειόν: cf. Meleager 110 in Gk. Anth. i. 31 ἀλκυόνες περὶ κῦμα, χελιδόνες ἀμφὶ μέλαθρα, | κύκνος ἐπ' ὄχθαισιν ποταμοῦ, καὶ ὑπ' ἄλσος ἀηδῶν [ᾄδουσι]: Eur. I. T. 1103 λίμναν θ' εἱλίσσουσαν ὕδωρ | κύκλον [s. κύκνειον], ἔνθα κύκνος μέλῳ | δὸς Μούσας θεραπεύει: Ar. Av. 769 τοιάδε κύκνοι | συμμιγῆ βοὴν ὁμοῦ | πτεροῖς κρέκοντες ἴακχον 'Απόλλω, | ὄχθῳ ἐφεζόμενοι παρ' Ἕβρον ποταμόν: Callim. Hymn. Del. 249 κύκνοι δὲ θεοῦ μέλποντες ἀοιδοὶ | Μῃόνιον Πάκτωλον ἐκυκλώσαντο λίποντες | Ἑβδομάκις περὶ Δῆλον, ἐπήεισαν δὲ λοχείῃ | Μουσάων ὄρνιθες, ἀοιδότατοι πετεηνῶν: Pratin. i. 7 (Bergk 457) οἷά τε κύκνον ἄγοντα ποικιλόπτερον μέλος: Dion. De Avib. ii. 19 ἀντηχοῦσιν αὐτοῖς ᾄδουσιν οἵ τε σκόπελοι καὶ αἱ φάραγγες, καὶ μουσικωτάτους πάντων τούτους ἴσμεν ὀρνίθων, καὶ ἱεροὺς καλοῖμεν 'Απόλλωνος. ᾄδουσι δ' οὐχὶ θρηνῶδες, ὥσπερ οἱ ἀλκυόνες, ἀλλ' ἡδύ τι καὶ μελιχρόν, καὶ οἷον αὐλοῖς ἢ κιθάραις χρώμενοι: Anon. 468 in Gk. Anth. iv. 218 εἰ κύκνῳ δύναται κόρυδος παραπλήσιον ᾄδειν: Antip. Sidon. 47, ib. ii. 19 λωΐτερος κίκνων ὁ μικρὸς θρόος ἠὲ κολοιῶν | κρωγμὸς ἐν εἰαρινοῖς κιδνάμενος νεφέλαις: Theocr. Id. v. 136 οὐ θεμιτόν ... ἔποπας κύκνοισιν ἐρίσδειν: cf. Ar. Ran. 207, Lucret. iii. 16, iv. 182, Virg. Ecl. viii. 36, 55, Mart. i. 54, Plut. El. ii. 387 μουσικῇ τε ἤδεται, καὶ κύκνων φωναῖς.

Especially of the dying Swan, Aesch. Ag. (1419), 1444 κύκνου δίκην, | τὸν ὕστατον μέλψασα θανάσιμον γόον | κεῖται φιλήτωρ τοῖδ': cf. Plato, Phaedo 85 B, Rep. 620 A; cf. Porphyr. De Abst. iii. p. 286 οὐ παίζων ὁμοδούλους αὐτοῦ ἔλεγεν τοὺς κύκνους [ὁ Σωκράτης]. Ael. ii. 32, v. 34 πεπίστευκε γὰρ ὅτι μηδενὸς ἀλγεινοῦ μηδὲ λιπαροῦ μέτεστι θανάτῳ, with which passage cf. Chrysipp. ap. Athen. xiv. 616 B φιλοσκώπτης, μέλλων ἀπὸ τοῦ δημίου σφάττεσθαι εἰπεῖν ἔφη θέλειν ὥσπερ τὸ κύκνειον ᾄσας ἀποθανεῖν: Plut. Mor. 161 C ἐξᾷσαι δὲ καὶ τὸν βίον τελευτῶν καὶ μὴ γενέσθαι κατὰ τοῦτο τῶν κύκνων ἀγεννέστερος: Phile, De An. Pr. x. 233 ἄνθρωπε φιλόψυχε, τὸν κίκνον βλέπων, | πρὸς τὴν τελευτήν, εἰ φρονεῖς, μὴ στυγνάσῃς: cf. Cic. De Orat. iii. 1, 1; see also Ael. x. 36, xi. 1; Fab. Aes. 215, 216, 416 b; Apoll. Rhod. iv. 1301; Polyb. xxx. 4, 7, xxxi. 20, 1; Opp. Cyneg. ii. 547 οὐκ ἄρα τοι μοίνοισιν ἐν ὀρνίθεσσιν ἔασι | κύκνοι μαντιπόλοι γόον ὕστατον ἀείδοντες: Dio Chrysost. Orat. Cor. p. 102

ΚΥΚΝΟΣ (*continued*).

(Reiske); cf. Hor. C. ii. 20, Ovid, Her. vii. 1, Met. xiv. 430, Mart. xiii. 77, Stat. Silv. ii. 4, 10, &c., &c. The singing swan a portent of death, Artemid. Oneirocr. ii. 20. Modern allusions are innumerable; cf. Chaucer, P. of Fowles, 342, Tennyson, 'The Dying Swan,' &c.; see also for numerous references, Douce's Illustr. of Shakspeare, i. 262, Lenz, Zool. d. Gr. u. R., pp. 384-400, &c.

The Swan's song was discredited by some, e.g. Alex. Mynd. ap. Athen. ix. 393 d; Lucian, De Electro seu Cycnis; Cic. Tusc. Quaest. i; Philostr. V. Apollon. iii. c. 23; Plin. x. (23) 32; cf. Greg. Nazianz. Ep. i. τότ' ᾄσονται κύκνοι, ὅταν κολοιοὶ σιωπήσωσιν. Cf. Scaliger, Ferrariae multos cygnos vidimus, sed cantores sane malos, neque melius ansere canere; cf. also Aldrov. Ornith. iii. 19, 5; Wormius in Mus. Worm. iii. c. 19; Mauduit ap. Plin. ed. Panckoucke, vii. 385; Voss. De Idol. ii. p. 1212; Pierius, De Cycnis, p. 254; Brown's Vulg. Errours, iii. p. 27; the curious conjectures of Bryant, Anc. Mythol. ii. 353-384; Pallas, Zoogr. ross.-asiat., ii. p. 212, and recent writers. Modern naturalists accept the story of the singing swans, asserting that though the Common Swan cannot sing, yet the Whooper or Whistling Swan does so. It is certain that the Whooper sings, for many ornithologists state the fact, but I do not think it can sing very well; at the very best, *dant sonitum rauci per stagna loquacia cygni*. This concrete explanation is quite inadequate; it is beyond a doubt that the Swan's Song (like the Halcyon's) veiled, and still hides, some mystical allusion.

Applied as an epithet to a poet, especially an old poet; Eur. H. F. 691 παιᾶνας δ' ἐπὶ σοῖς μελάθροις | κύκνος ὡς γέρων ἀοιδὸς | πολιᾶν ἐκ γενύων | κελαδήσω, Id. Bacch. 1361; Posidipp. xi in Gk. Anth. ii. 48 σιγάσθω Ζήνων ὁ σοφὸς κύκνος: Christod. Ecph. 384, ib. iii. 175 Θήβης δ' Ὠγυγίης Ἑλικώνιος ἵστατο κύκνος, Πίνδαρος ἱμερόφωνος: Anacreon is the 'Swan of Teos,' Antip. i. 26, cf. Hor. C. iv. 2, 25. Cf. Horap. ii. 39 γέροντα μουσικὸν βουλόμενοι σημῆναι κύκνον ζωγραφοῦσιν· οὗτος γὰρ ἡδύτατον μέλος ᾄδει γηράσκων.

The Swan of Leda.—Cf. Eur. I. T. 794, 1104, Hel. 19, &c., Herc. F. 690, Orest. 1388; also various passages in the Anthology, e.g. Pallad. 40, in Gk. Anth. iii. 123, Anon. ib. iv. 118, 128, &c.; cf. Lucian, De Deor. 20, 14 (I. 264). For mythographic references, see Hygin. Fab. 77, P. Astron. ii. 8, German. c. 24, Eratosth. c. 25, Theon. p. 136, &c. According to these latter authors, the mythology of the Swan is inseparable from the phenomena attending the constellation Cygnus. The stellar Swan lies in the Milky Way, 'the river of heaven'; it is adjacent to the constellation Lyra; it rose a little in advance of the Eagle, but, lying more to the north, it only set some time after the Eagle had gone down: that is to say, it was attacked by the Eagle, but in turn defeated it, cf. Arist. H. A. ix. 12, 615 b, Ael. xvii. 24, &c.;

ΚΥΚΝΟΣ (continued).

it stood in mid-heaven at the rising of the Pleiad ; at its own rising, the Virgin (Leda) was in mid-heaven, and the twins Castor and Pollux were just setting in the west. The stories of Cycnus, son of Mars (Hesiod, Anton. Lib. 12, Philochor. ap. Athen., Ovid, Met., &c.), of Cycnus, King of Liguria (Hygin. Fab. 144), Cycnus, brother of Phaethon (Lucian, De Electro, Virg. Aen. x. 189), and others, which are also similarly connected with astronomical myths, lie outside the scope of this book. Cf. (int. al.), Dupuis, Orig. de tous les cultes, iii. p. 813, vii. p. 367.

ΚΥ'ΜΒΗ. A very doubtful bird. πτεροβάμονες κύμβαι, Emped. 188. Supposed by L. and S. to be a Tumbler-pigeon ; but cf. κόμβα, supra. Hesych. has κύμβαι· ὄρνιθες : also κυμβ[ατ]ευτυί· ὀρνιθευταί.

ΚΥ'ΜΙΝΔΙΣ = χαλκίς = (?) **πτύγξ**, q. v. κύβινδις in some MSS., both of Hom. and Arist., cf. J. G. Schneider in Arist., vol. iv. p. 92. Hesych. has κυβήναις· γλαύξ[αις], query κύβηνδις : also κυδάναν· τὴν γλαῦκα, query κυβήνα. See also s. v. κικκάβη. An unknown or fabulous bird ; perhaps an Owl.

Il. xiv. 290 ὄρνιθι λιγυρῇ ἐναλίγκιος, ἥν τ' ἐν ὄρεσσιν | χαλκίδα κικλήσκουσι θεοί, ἄνδρες δὲ κύμινδιν.

Ar. Av. 1181 χωρεῖ δὲ πᾶς τις ὄνυχας ἠγκυλωμένος, | κερχνῄς, τριόρχης, γύψ, κύμινδις, αἰετός. Mentioned likewise among the rapacious birds, Ael. xii. 4.

Arist. H. A. ix. 12, 615 b ὀλιγάκις μὲν φαίνεται, οἰκεῖ γὰρ ὄρη, ἔστι δὲ μέλας, καὶ μέγεθος ὅσον ἱέραξ ὁ φασσοφόνος καλούμενος, καὶ τὴν ἰδέαν μακρὸς καὶ λεπτός. κύμινδιν δὲ καλοῦσιν Ἴωνες αὐτήν : the passage is very corrupt, and according to some texts (followed apparently by Pliny, x. 8, and by Eustath. in Hom.), the next clause concerning ὑβρίς or πτύγξ applies to the same bird, ἡ δ' ὑβρίς, φασὶ δέ τινες εἶναι τὸν αὐτὸν τοῦτον ὄρνιθα τῷ πτυγγί, οὗτος ἡμέρας μὲν οὐ φαίνεται διὰ τὸ μὴ βλέπειν ὀξύ, τὰς δὲ νύκτας θηρεύει ὥσπερ οἱ ἀετοί [οἱ ὦτοι, cj. Sundevall], καὶ μάχονται δὲ πρὸς τὸν ἀετὸν οὕτω σφόδρα ὥστ' ἄμφω λαμβάνεσθαι πολλάκις ζῶντας ὑπὸ τῶν νομέων. τίκτει μὲν οὖν δύο ᾠά, νεοττεύει δὲ καὶ οὗτος ἐν πέτραις καὶ σπηλαίοις.

Conjectured by Sundevall to be the Black or Glossy Ibis, from the suggestion of metallic colouring in χαλκίς, and from Mod. Gk. χαλκόκοτα, Erh. ; but this is certainly not a bird of the mountains, and the supposed derivation from χαλκός is imaginary. By Aub. and Wimmer, and others, ascribed to the Capercailzie, *Tetrao urogallus*, L. Usually taken to be a large Owl (cf. Suidas, χαλκίς, εἶδος ὀρνέου, ἡ γλαῦξ, cf. Schol. Ar. Av. 262), as by Belon, Gaza, and other older naturalists. Cuvier (Grandsaigne's Pliny, l. v. 11, pp. 374, 375) identifies it with the Hawk Owl, *Strix uralensis*, Pall., and Netolicka agrees.

ΚΥΜΙΝΔΙΣ (*continued*).

The bird being, in Homer, that in whose shape Ὕπνος appears, is an additional point in favour of identifying it with a nocturnal species: and this relation of ὕπνος to the bird χαλκίς suggests a connexion with the phrase χάλκεος ὕπνος. χαλκίς belongs to the language of the gods, that is to say, is probably a foreign word; it is not likely to be a simple derivative of χαλκός. Is there a possible alternative that χάλκεος ὕπνος is wrongly translated by *ferreus somnus*?

For an account of various Scholia relating to this bird, cf. J. G. Schneider, l. c. In some, if not all, of the names of this bird, we are undoubtedly confronted with foreign words.

ΚΥΠΑΡΙ'ΣΣΙΑ· εἶδος ἀλεκτρυόνων, Hesych. Query κυπαρίσσιοι.

ΚΥ'ΧΡΑΜΟΣ. MSS. have κίχραμος, κέχραμος, κεχράμος: Hesych. κυγχράνος, κιγχράμας: Schn. writes κέγχραμος (κέγχρος) as Belon translates *miliarius*.

An unknown bird: probably (as Sundevall takes it) identical with ὀρτυγομήτρα, the Corncrake, *Rallus crex*, L. One or both names doubtless apply also to the Water-rail, *Rallus aquaticus*, L., which is very abundant in Greece, and according to Von der Mühle abandons its usual haunts in Autumn and frequently associates with the quails (op. cit., p. 92).

Arist. H. A. viii. 12, 597 b. A bird which accompanies the quails, καὶ ἀνακαλεῖται αὐτοὺς νύκτωρ· καὶ ὅταν τούτου τὴν φωνὴν ἀκούσωσιν, οἱ θηρεύοντες ἴσασιν ὅτι οὐ καταμένουσιν [οἱ ὄρτυγες]: which expression Sundevall translates 'delay not their coming,' and A. and W. 'remain no longer.' Cf. Plin. x. (23) 33.

ΚΥ'ΨΕΛΟΣ, s. κυψέλλος. A bird of the Swallow kind; perhaps the *Sand-Martin*, *Hirundo riparia*, L. Hesych. κύψελος· ὄρνις ποιός, ὅμοιος χελιδόνι.

Arist. H. A. ix. 30, 680, mentioned as synonymous with ἄπους, q. v., ὅμοιοι ταῖς χελιδόσιν· οὐ γὰρ ῥᾴδιον διαγνῶναι πρὸς τὴν χελιδόνα, πλὴν τῷ τὴν κνήμην ἔχειν δασεῖαν: cf. Plin. x. (39) 55. In the description of the nest (loc. cit.), though κύψελις (a box, or beehive) would rather suggest the nest of the House-Martin (*H. urbica*, L.), yet the epithet μακρός would certainly not apply: moreover the House-Martin was certainly included in χελιδών. Accordingly the evidence leans to identifying κύψελος with the Sand-Martin, *H. riparia*, L.; this identification is followed by Sundevall, while A. and W., on the contrary, identify the bird with the House-Martin. There was doubtless a confusion of species. If the passage in Pliny suggests one more than another, it would seem to be the Swift; yet in the Aristotelian reference the

ΚΥΨΕΛΟΣ (*continued*).

hypothesis of the Sand-Martin, advocated by Sundevall, has strong claims.

ΚΩ'ΚΑΛΟΣ· κώκαλον· εἶδος ἀλεκτρυόνος, Hesych. Cf. s. v. **λόκαλος**.

ΚΩΝΩΠΟΘΗ'ΡΑΣ· ὄρνις ὁ κώνωπας θηρεύων, Hesych.

ΚΩΤΙΛΑ'Σ. The **Swallow**. A Boeotian word. Anacr. 99; Strattis, Φοιν. 3; cf. Simonid. 243.

ΛΑΓΟΘΗ'ΡΑΣ· Hesych., ἀετοῦ εἶδος. = **λαγωφόνος** = **μελανάετος** (q. v.). An epithet of the **Eagle**.

Arist. H. A. ix. 32, 618 b. The Eagle in combat with the hare is frequent on gems, and on coins of Agrigentum, Messana, Elis, &c.: cf. Imhoof-Blum. and Keller, passim; Keller, Th. d. cl. Alterth., p. 449. The wide occurrence of this subject (cf. Layard, Nineveh, ii. pl. 62) indicates a lost mythological significance, in which one is tempted to recognize a Solar or Stellar symbol; vide s. vv. **ἀετός**, **κόραξ**.

ΛΑΓΩΔΙ'ΑΣ. A synonym of **ὦτος**, Alex. Mynd. ap. Athen. ix. 390.

ΛΑΓΩΙ'ΝΗΣ· ὄρνις ποιός, Hesych.

ΛΑΓΩ'ΠΟΥΣ. A **Ptarmigan**.

Plin. x. (48) 68 praecipuo sapore lagopus: pedes leporino villo nomen ei hoc dedere, cetero candidae, columbarum magnitudine, &c. The *lagois*, s. *logois* of Hor. Sat. ii. 2, 22, is possibly akin. In Mart. vii. 87, an old reading was Si meus aurita gaudet *lagopode* Flaccus, altered by Scaliger to *glaucopide*.

ΛΑΓΩ'Σ. A bird-name, mentioned with the Swallow, in Artemid. Oneirocr. iv. 56. The name suggests a reference to δασύπους χελιδόνειος, Diph. s. Calliad. ap. Athen. ix. 401 a. According to Boios ap. Anton. Lib. c. xx a certain Oreius was metamorphosed into the bird λαγώς, ὄρνις ἐπ' οὐδενὶ φαινόμενος ἀγαθῷ.

ΛΑΕΔΟ'Σ (MSS. also λαιδός, λιβυός). A bird, in all probability identical with **λαϊός**, q. v.

Arist. H. A. ix. 1, 610 λαεδὸς καὶ κελεὸς φίλοι. ὁ δὲ λαεδὸς πέτρας καὶ ὄρη [οἰκεῖ], καὶ φιλοχωρεῖ οὗ ἂν οἰκῇ.

We may connect the reputed friendship of κελεός and λαεδός with the association of κελεός and λαϊός together, in the obscure story of the metamorphosis of those impious persons who entered the forbidden cave in Crete where Jupiter was born; Boios ap. Anton. Lib. c. xix.

ΛΑΙ"Ο'Σ. Probably the **Blue Thrush**, *Petrocichla cyanus*, L. The Stone-thrush, *P. saxatilis*, L., is less common in Greece, and

ΛΑΙΟΣ (continued).

is chiefly found in the northern and more mountainous parts. Both receive the Mod. Gk. name πετροκόσσυφος (Heldr.), and were probably confused under the ancient name also.

Arist. H. A. ix. 19, 617 ὅμοιος τῷ μέλανι κοττύφῳ ἐστὶν ὁ λαϊός, τὸ μέγεθος μικρῷ ἐλάττων· οὗτος ἐπὶ τῶν πετρῶν καὶ ἐπὶ τῶν κεράμων τὰς διατριβὰς ποιεῖται. A fabled metamorphosis, Boios ap. Anton. Lib. c. xix.

It seems all but certain that λαεδός and λαϊός refer to the same bird. The correct reading of the name, or names, is unknown. In Arist. H. A. ix. 19, edd. have also βαῖος and φώϊος (cf. Camus, i. 747, Schneider, ii. 120). The name λαϊός is taken from the passage in Anton. Lib., the supposed derivation from λᾶας helping to gain it acceptance. Schn. and Picc. read λαϊός also for λαεδός, q. v.

ΛΑ´ΛΑΓΕΣ· ὀρνέου εἶδος, Hesych. Possibly connected with Mod. Gk. λέλεκι, a Stork; vide s. v. πελαργός.

ΛΑ´ΡΟΣ, ὁ. A Sea-Gull. In Mod. (and doubtless also in Ancient) Gk. γλάρος includes both the Gulls and the Terns.

Od. v. 51, a perfect description. Arist. H. A. ii. 17, 509 ἔχει τὸν στόμαχον εὐρὺν καὶ πλατὺν ὅλον. Ib. v. 9, 542 b τίκτει τοῦ θέρους, ἐν ταῖς περὶ θάλατταν πέτραις, τὸ πλῆθος δύο ἢ τρία· οὐ φωλεύει; cf. Plin. x. 32. On its breeding habits, see also Dion. De Avib. ii. 4.

Varieties.—Arist. H. A. viii. 3, 593 b λάρος τὸ χρῶμα σποδοειδής, also λάρος ὁ λευκός. The former is, according to Aub. and Wimmer, one of the darker Terns, e.g. *Sterna nigra*, Briss.; but the epithet seems more descriptive of the ashy grey of the 'Black-backed' Gulls: cf. μαλακοκράνευς. Dion. De Avib. ii. 4 enumerates three sorts: οἱ μὲν λευκοὶ καὶ ὡς αἱ περιστεραὶ βραχεῖς· οἱ δὲ τούτων μέν εἰσι μείζονες καὶ ἰσχυρότεροι, πυκνοτάτοις δὲ πτεροῖς περισκέπονται· καί τινες ἔτι καὶ τούτων εὐμεγεθέστεροι· λευκὰ δ' ἐστὶ καὶ τούτοις πτερά, πλὴν ὅσον ἐπὶ ταῖς ἀκροτάταις πτέρυξι καὶ τοῖς τραχήλοις μελαίνονται. καὶ τούτοις ἅπαντες οἱ λοιποὶ λάροι νομῆς τε καὶ ἕδρας παραχωροῦσι καὶ ὡς βασιλεῦσιν ὑπείκουσι· καὶ γηράσκουσι δ' αὐτοῖς κυάνεα γίνεται πτερά. Here the first group are probably the Terns, the last the Black-backed Gulls.

A bye-word for greediness, Ar. Eq. 959, Nub. 591, Av. 567. Devour dolphins stranded on the beach, Ael. xv. 23. Open shell-fish by dropping them from a height, Ael. iii. 20.

Myth and Legend.—Hostile to βρένθος, ἅρπη, and ἐρωδιός, Arist. H. A. viii. 3, 593 b, Ael. iv. 5, Phile 682; friendly to κολοιός, Ael. v. 48. Killed by pomegranate-seed, Ael. vi. 46, Phile 657. Associated with Hercules, Ar. Av. 567. The Gulls are souls of disembodied fishermen, hence their gentle and peaceable disposition, Dion. l. c. A gull's feather was tied to a fishing-line as a kind of float, Ael. xv. 10.

Fable.—λάρος καὶ ἰκτῖνος, Aes. 239 (ed. Halm).

ΛΑ'ΡΟΣ, β. A kind of tame singing bird, Anth. Pal. vii. 199.

ΛΕΙ˜ΟΣ, vide s. v. ἐλειός.

ΛΕΥΚΕΡΩΔΙΟ'Σ (also λευκορώδιος). The Spoonbill, *Platalea leucorodius*, L. Mod. Gk. κουλιάρι (= Fr. *cueiller*).

Arist. H. A. viii. 3, 593 b τὸ μέγεθος ἐρωδιοῦ ἐλάττων, καὶ ἔχει τὸ ῥύγχος πλατὺ καὶ μακρόν.

The description of the bill easily identifies the bird in this passage (Belon, Sundevall, &c.), but the name would probably be likewise applied to the other White Herons or Egrets.

ΛΙΒΥΟ'Σ. (MSS. have λεβίος, κίβιος, κήβιος, cf. Schn. in Arist. iv. p. 7). An unknown bird: possibly to be compared with Λιβυκὸς ὄρνις, Ar. Av. 65.

Arist. H. A. ix. 1, 609 κελεὸς καὶ λιβυὸς πολέμιοι : cf. s. v. λαεδός.

ΛΟ'ΚΑΛΟΣ. An unknown bird.

Arist. H. A. ii. 17, 509, mentioned with ἀσκάλαφος as a bird having colic coeca. Omitted in Cod. Venetus and others. Gesner supposes the word to be Italian (?= *aluco*, an Owl), and to have come in as a marginal rendering of ἀσκάλαφος. Scaliger reads κώκαλος.

ΛΥ'ΚΟΣ. A sort of Jackdaw (Arist. H. A. ix. 24, 610 b); probably a nickname of the common Jackdaw, cf. βωμολόχος. (Schn. and Picc. read λύκιος, which form occurs in Hesych.: λύκιος, κολοιοῦ εἶδος). See also s. v. κίρκος.

ΜΑΚΕΣΙ'ΚΡΑΝΟΣ. A name for the Hoopoe.

Hesych. μακεσίκρανος. ἔποψ· διὰ τὸ ἔχειν ἐπὶ τῆς κεφαλῆς καθάπερ λόφον, καὶ κορυθαίολον αὐτὸν λέγουσι. πολυώνυμον δὲ λέγεται τὸ ζῷον· σίντην τε γὰρ αὐτὸν καὶ ἀλεκτρυόνα [ἄγριον, inser. Heinsius] καὶ γέλασον λέγουσι.

ΜΑΛΑΚΟΚΡΑΝΕΥ'Σ. An unknown bird.

Arist. H. A. ix. 22, 617 b ἀεὶ ἐπὶ τὸ αὐτὸ καθιζάνει, καὶ ἁλίσκεται ἐνταῦθα. τὸ δὲ εἶδος κεφαλὴ μὲν μεγάλη χονδρότυπος, τὸ δὲ μέγεθος ἐλάττων κίχλης μικρῷ. στόμα δ' εὔρωστον, μικρόν, στρογγύλον· τὸ δὲ χρῶμα σποδοειδὴς ὅλος. εὔπους δὲ καὶ κακόπτερος. ἁλίσκεται δὲ μάλιστα γλαυκί [? aucupium per noctuam].

Identified by Sundevall with the Lesser Grey Shrike, *Lanius minor*, L., in Mod. Gk. κεφαλᾶς and ἀετομάχος (Heldr.). Lindermayer (op. c. p. 114) states that this bird is extremely common in Greece, and sings all day long 'auf der äussersten Spitze eines Baumes oder Strauches sitzend.' This identification is more plausible than the many others that have been suggested, such as the Jay, the Bullfinch, and even the Snipe

ΜΑΛΑΚΟΚΡΑΝΕΥΣ (*continued*).

(Belon, Schneider, Brisson, &c.). It must, however, be remembered that the bird is mentioned once only, and in a portion of the Historia Animalium that is full of difficulties and incongruities: the epithets associated with it are numerous, but mean little or nothing ; χονδρότυπος does not occur elsewhere ; ἁλίσκεται γλαυκί is a phrase of doubtful meaning and questionable construction. The Aristotelian description seems at first sight copious and adequate, but in the words of Camus, ' autant qu'il semblerait devoir être facile de reconnoître le Crane-mol, autant est-il certain que jusqu'ici il ne l'a pas été.' The bird πάρδαλος, q. v., is next mentioned, and is in like manner impossible to identify.

ΜΑΡΑ´ΣΣΑΙ· ὄρνιθες, Hesych.

ΜΑΤΤΥ´ΗΣ· ἡ μὲν φωνὴ Μακεδονική, ὄρνις, Hesych. Cf. ματτύη, Artemid. ap. Athen. xiv. 663 D, &c.

ΜΕΘΥΘΡΙ´ΔΕΣ· εἶδος μικρῶν ὀρνίθων, Hesych.

ΜΕΛΑΓΚΟ´ΡΥΦΟΣ. Probably the **Marsh Tit**, *Parus palustris*, L.; in which identification Sundevall and Aub. and Wimm. agree. But there was a confusion between this bird and the **Blackcap Warbler**, *Motacilla atricapilla*, L., *Sylvia atricapilla*, auctt. The verb μελαγκορυφίζω, to warble like the μελαγκόρυφος, Hero Spir. p. 220, suggests the latter of these two. See also s.v. συκαλίς.
Mentioned in Ar. Av. 887.
Arist. H. A. ix. 15, 616 b ᾧᾂ πλεῖστα τίκτει μετὰ τὸν ἐν Λιβύῃ στρουθόν· ἑώραται μὲν γὰρ καὶ ἑπτακαίδεκα, τίκτει μέντοι καὶ πλείω ἢ εἴκοσιν. τίκτει δ᾽ ἀεὶ περιττά, ὥς φασίν. νεοττεύει δὲ καὶ οὗτος ἐν τοῖς δένδρεσι, καὶ βόσκεται τοὺς σκώληκας. ἴδιον δὲ τούτῳ καὶ ἀηδόνι παρὰ τοὺς ἄλλους ὄρνιθας τὸ μὴ ἔχειν τῆς γλώττης τὸ ὀξύ [vide s. v. ἔποψ]. ix. 49 B, 632 b μεταβάλλουσιν εἰς ἀλλήλους αἱ συκαλίδες καὶ οἱ μελαγκόρυφοι· γίνεται δ᾽ ἡ μὲν συκαλὶς περὶ τὴν ὀπώραν, ὁ δὲ μελαγκόρυφος εὐθέως μετὰ τὸ φθινόπωρον (cf. Geopon. xv. 1, 22 εὐθὺς μετὰ τὸ τρυγητόν). διαφέρουσι δὲ καὶ οὗτοι οὐδὲν ἀλλήλων πλὴν τῇ χρόᾳ καὶ τῇ φωνῇ. ὅτι δ᾽ ὁ αὐτός ἐστιν ὄρνις, ἤδη ὦπται περὶ τὴν μεταβολὴν ἑκάτερον τὸ γένος τοῦτο, οὔπω δὲ τελέως μεταβεβληκότα οὐδ᾽ ἐν θατέρῳ εἴδει ὄντα. Cf. Plin. x. 44, Alex. Mynd. ap. Athen. ii. 69, p. 65 b δύο δ᾽ εἶναι γένη αὐτοῦ συκαλίδα καὶ μελαγκόρυφον. Ael. vi. 46, Phile 601 τὸν μελαγκόρυφον ἄγνος ἐκτρίβει. A fabulous Arabian bird, Plin. xxxvii. 33.

ΜΕΛΑ´ΜΠΥΓΟΣ. A word applied to the Eagle in the Fable of the Fox and the Eagle, Archil. fr. 110 (86). Schol. Venet. Il. xxiv. 315 εἴωθε καὶ ὁ Ἀρχίλοχος μελάμπυγον τοῦτον καλεῖν: Schol. Lyc. 91 εἰσὶ γὰρ μελάμπυγοι, πύγαργοι, εἴδη ἀετῶν κατ᾽ Ἀρχίλοχον: cf. also Hesych., and Gaisford's note. Cf. also Schneidewin; Farnell, Gk. Lyr. Poets, p. 300, &c.

ΜΕΛΑΜΠΥΓΟΣ (*continued*).

A solar symbolism probably underlies this name and its correlative πύγαργος. Cf. the references to Ἡρακλῆς μελάμπυγος, ap. Diodor. Sic. iv. 31, &c.

ΜΕΛΑΝΑΈΤΟΣ = λαγωφόνος. An epithet of the Eagle.

Arist. H. A. ix. 32, 618 b μέλας τὴν χρόαν, καὶ μέγεθος ἐλάχιστος, κράτιστος τούτων [τῶν πυγάργων καὶ πλάγγων]. οὗτος οἰκεῖ ὄρη καὶ ὕλας· καλεῖται δὲ μελανάετος καὶ λαγωφόνος. ἐκτρέφει δὲ μόνος τὰ τέκνα οὗτος καὶ ἐξάγει. ἔστι δὲ ὠκυβόλος καὶ εὐθήμων καὶ ἄφθονος καὶ ἄφοβος καὶ μάχιμος καὶ εὔφημος· οὐ γὰρ μινυρίζει οὐδὲ λέληκεν: cf. Ib. vi. 6, 563 b οἱ δὲ μέλανες, κ. τ. λ. Plin. x. 3 Melanaetus a Graecis dicta, eademque Valeria [MSS. in Valeriâ], minimâ magnitudine, viribus praecipua, colore nigricans, &c.

Aubert and Wimmer suppose a small species of Eagle, e. g. *Aquila minuta*, Brehm, to be meant; Sundevall suggests the Peregrine Falcon. As is mentioned above, s. v. **λαγωφόνος**, I see no grounds for these or any other concrete interpretations: the passage is mystical and probably foreign. Aubert and Wimmer have already called attention to the want of meaning and irrational order of the six epithets ὠκυβόλος, εὐθήμων, &c.

On μέλας as an epithet of the Eagle, see s. vv. **ἀετός, μόρφνος**: cf. O. Keller, op. c., p. 237. Both **μελανάετος** and **λαγωφόνος** are applied to the constellation Aquila in the Comm. Alfrag. p. 106; and I am inclined to think that the 'Black Eagle' had originally a mystical and astronomical meaning. Cf. s. v. **μελάμπυγος**.

ΜΕΛΑΝΔΕΙΡΟΣ· ὀρνιθάριον ποιόν, Hesych. Perhaps connected with **δείρης** (q. v.), rather than with δειρή.

ΜΕΛΕΑΓΡΙΣ. Also μελέαγρος, ἡ κατοικίδιος ὄρνις, Hesych.; μελαγρίς, Salmas. ad Plin. p. 612.

A foreign word, connected with Sem. Melek; as in Melkart, Meleager, Melicertes, &c. (cf. Keller, Volksetym. p. 236, Lat. Etym. p. 180).

The Guinea-Fowl, *Numida sp.*

First mentioned by Soph. Meleag. fr. ap. Plin. xxxvii. (2) 11, the birds weeping tears of amber for the death of the hero. Mentioned in connexion with amber also by Mnaseas ap. Plin. l. c.

A full description in Clytus Miles. ap. Athen. xiv. 655 c-f ἄστοργον πρὸς τὰ ἔκγονα τὸ ὄρνεον· τὸ μὲν μέγεθος ὄρνιθος γενναίου, τὴν δὲ κεφαλὴν μικρὰν πρὸς τὸ σῶμα καὶ ταύτην ψιλήν, ἐπ' αὐτῆς δὲ λόφον σάρκινον, σκληρόν, στρογγύλον, ἐξέχοντα τῆς κεφαλῆς ὥσπερ πάτταλον, καὶ τὸ χρῶμα ξυλοειδή. τὸ δὲ σῶμα ἅπαν ποικίλον, μέλανος ὄντος τοῦ χρώματος ὅλου, πτίλοις λευκοῖς καὶ πυκνοῖς διειλημμένον· παραπλήσιαι δ' εἰσὶν αἱ θήλειαι τοῖς ἄρρεσιν, κ. τ. λ.

ΜΕΛΕΑΓΡΙΣ (*continued*).

Arist. H. A. vi. 2, 559 κατεστιγμένα τὰ ᾠὰ τῶν μελεαγρίδων : cf. Aristoph. H. A. Epit. i. 28 ᾠὰ ἀστερωτά.

See also the description given by Columella, viii. 8, 2 Africana est quam plerique Numidicam dicunt, meleagridi similis, nisi quod rutilam galeam (paleam, emend. Newton) et cristam capite gerit, quae utraque sunt in meleagride coerulea. This passage from Columella is very interesting as showing that the Greek μελεαγρίς and the Roman *Gallina africana* or *numidica* were different from one another, the latter having a *red* wattle, the former a *blue*. This would look as though the μελεαγρίς had sprung from what is now called *Numida ptilorhyncha*, an Abyssinian species, and had been brought to Athens by way of Egypt; while the *Afra avis* originated in the *Numida meleagris* of W. Africa. See Newton, Dict. of Birds, p. 399, footnote.

The μελεαγρίδες mentioned, however, by Scylax, Periplus, were seen beyond the Pillars of Hercules, in N. W. Africa, as were those mentioned by Mnaseas; and these were doubtless, therefore, of the redwattled species. Strabo and Diodorus report the birds as inhabiting an island in the Red Sea; Sophocles (l. c.), speaks of them poetically as Indian.

Mentioned as sacred birds, Clyt. Miles. l. c. περὶ δὲ τὸ ἱερὸν τῆς Παρθένου ἐν Λέρῳ εἰσὶν οἱ καλούμενοι ὄρνιθες μελεαγρίδες. Also in Aetolia, Menodot. ap. Athen. xiv. 655 a.

Ael. iv. 42: the metamorphosis of the sisters of Meleager; ὅσοι δὲ ἄρα αἰδοῦνται τὸ θεῖον καὶ μᾶλλον εἰ τὴν Ἄρτεμιν, οὐκ ἄν ποτε τῶνδε τῶν ὀρνίθων ἐπὶ τροφὴν προσάψαιντο, καὶ ἥτις ἡ αἰτία ἴσασί τε οἱ τὴν νῆσον οἰκοῦντες τὴν Λέρον καὶ ἔνεστι μαθεῖν ἀλλαχόθεν. Ib. v. 27 τὰς δ' ἐν Λέρῳ μελεαγρίδας ἀπὸ μηδενὸς ἀδικεῖσθαι τῶν γαμψωνύχων ὀρνέων λέγει Ἴστρος.

Sacrificed at the temple of Isis in Tithorea (Phocis), Pausan. x. 31 (x. 32, 9, ed. Teubn.).

Were kept also in the Acropolis: μελεαγρίδες· ὄρνεις αἳ ἐνέμοντο ἐν τῇ ἀκροπόλει, Hesych. ὄρνεα ἅπερ ἐνέμοντο ἐν τῇ ἀκροπόλει· λέγουσι δὲ οἱ μὲν ἀδελφὰς τοῦ Μελεαγροῦ μεταβαλεῖν εἰς τὰς μελεαγρίδας ὄρνιθας, οἱ δὲ τὰς συνήθεις Ἰοκαλλίδος τῆς ἐν Λέρνῃ παρθένου, ἣν τιμῶσι δαιμονίως, Suid., Phot.

On the story of the metamorphosis, cf. Nicand. ap. Anton. Lib. c. 1, Hygin. Fab. 174, Ovid, Met. viii. 534, Mart. iii. 58, 15, Lactant. viii. 4.

How the Meleagrides fought around the tomb of Meleager (cf. s. v. μέμνων) Plin. x. (26) 38, &c.

For other references, see Antig. Caryst. xi; Juv. xi. 142; Hor. Epod. ii. 53 Afrae aves; Mart. iii. 58, 15 Numidicae guttatae; xiii. 45 Libycae volucres; xiii. 75; Stat. Silv. i. 6, 78, ii. 4, 28; Suet. Calig. 22 (vide s. v. τετράων); Petron. 93; Varro, De R. R. iii. 9, 18, &c.

ΜΕ'ΜΝΩΝ, s. μεμνονίς, s. Μέμνονος ὄρνις. The **Ruff**, *Machetes pugnax*, L.

Mosch. iii. 42 οὐ τόσον ἀῴοισιν ἐν ἄγκεσι παῖδα τὸν Ἀοῦς | ἱπτάμενος περὶ σᾶμα κινύρατο Μέμνονος ὄρνις. Paus. x. 31, 6 μεμνονίδες ταῖς ὄρνισίν ἐστιν ὄνομα, κατὰ δὲ ἔτος οἱ Ἑλληπόντιοί φασιν αὐτὰς ἐν εἰρημέναις ἡμέραις ἰέναι τε ἐπὶ τοῦ Μέμνονος τὸν τάφον, καὶ ὁπόσον τοῦ μνήματος δένδρων ἐστὶν ἡ πόας ψιλόν, τοῦτο καὶ σαίρουσιν αἱ ὄρνιθες καὶ ὑγροῖς τοῖς πτεροῖς τοῦ Αἰσίπου τῷ ὕδατι ῥαίνουσι. Ael. v. 1 οὐκοῦν τοὺς ὄρνιθας τοὺς ἐπωνύμους τοῦ ἥρωος ἀφικνεῖσθαι κατὰ πᾶν ἔτος, καὶ διαιρεῖσθαί τε καὶ διασχίζεσθαι εἰς ἔχθραν καὶ διαφοράν, καὶ μάχεσθαι μάχην καρτεράν, κ.τ.λ.: cf. Anecd. Paris. Bekk. ii. p. 25. See also Dion. De Avib. i. 8; Quint. Smyrn. Posthomer. ii. 645, et seq.; Plin. x. (26) 37; Ovid, Met. xiii. 607, Amor. i. 13, 3; Solin. c. 40.

The identification, first suggested by Cuvier (Grandidier's Pliny, loc. cit.), is certain, the combats or 'hilling' of Ruffs being unmistakeably described: for modern descriptions, see Montagu, quoted in Yarrell, 4th ed. vol. iii. p. 428. At the same time, it is evident that the myth is a very ancient one, and its connexion with this particular species of bird and its peculiar annual combats may be a late version of an old and mysterious story: cf. Creuzer, Symb. ii. 181, &c. In other words, though Pausanias and Aelian undoubtedly alluded to the Ruff, I do not for a moment believe that Moschus did so. Vide s.v. ἀντίψυχοι.

ΜΕ'ΡΜΝΟΣ, s. μέρμνης, Hesych., also Cram. Anecd. Oxon. i. 64, 24. A kind of hawk, sacred to Cybele, Ael. xii. 4; according to Hesych., identical with τρίορχης.

ΜΕ'ΡΟΨ. The **Bee-eater**, *Merops apiaster*, L. Mod. Gk. μελισσοφάγος, μελισσουργός (Erh.), and on Parnassus βοργάρης (Heldr.).

In Arist. H. A. vi. 1, 559 ἀέροψ, s. εἴροψ (Bk.), ὃν δ' οἱ Βοιωτοὶ καλοῦσιν ἀέροπα: cf. Hesych. ἀέροπες, ὀρνεά τινα, also Schol. in Ar. Av. 1354; ἀερόπους, Suid. in verb. ἀντιπελαργεῖν: ἤροψ s. ἤροπος, Boios, ap. Anton. Liber. c. 18. A name similar to βοργάρης used by Scotus, aves quae dicuntur Graece Boarcia, ovant in foraminibus terrae, and by Albertus M., quam obarcham Graeci vocant: cf. Schneider in Arist. l. c. According to Bent (Cyclades, 1885, p. 325), μεροΐπας now means in Syra simply a bird, ὄρνις.

Arist. H. A. ix. 13, 615 b φασὶ δέ τινες καὶ τοὺς μέροπας ἀντεκτρέφεσθαι ὑπὸ τῶν ἐκγόνων οὐ μόνον γηράσκοντας ἀλλὰ καὶ εὐθύς, ὅταν οἷοί τ' ὦσιν· τὸν δὲ πατέρα καὶ τὴν μητέρα μένειν ἔνδον. ἡ δ' ἰδέα τοῦ ὄρνιθος τῶν πτερῶν ἐστὶ τὰ μὲν ὑποκάτω ὠχρόν, τὰ δὲ ἐπάνω ὥσπερ τῆς ἀλκυόνος κυάνεον, τὰ δ' ἐπ' ἄκρων τῶν πτερυγίων ἐρυθρά (cf. Plin. x. (33) 51). τίκτει δὲ περὶ ἓξ ἢ ἑπτὰ ὑπὸ τὴν ὀπώραν [it breeds in Greece about the middle of April, Lindermayer], ἐν τοῖς κρημνοῖς τοῖς μαλακοῖς· εἰσδύεται δ' εἴσω καὶ τέτταρας

ΜΕΡΟΨ (*continued*).

πήχεις. Ib. vi. 1, 559 ὃν δ' οἱ Βοιωτοὶ καλοῦσιν ἀέροπα, εἰς τὰς ὀπὰς ἐν τῇ γῇ καταδυόμενος νεοττεύει μόνος.

On the filial piety of μέροψ, δικαιότατος καὶ εὐσεβέστατος ὀρνίθων ἁπάντων, see Ael. xi. 30, Plin. x. (33) 51 ; cf. Boch. Hieroz. ii. p. 302.

Is destructive to bees, Arist. H. A. x. 40, 626, Ael. v. 11, vii. 6, Plut. Mor. 976 c, Geopon. xv. 2, Phile 650, Virg. Georg. iv. 14.

Is said to fly backwards, Ael. i. 49.

A fabled metamorphosis, Boios, l. c. Ἀπόλλων δὲ ὄρνιθα ἐποίησε τὸν παῖδα ἤροπον, ὃς ἔτι νῦν τίκτει μὲν ὑπὸ γῆς, ἀεὶ δὲ μελετᾷ πέτεσθαι.

ΜΗΔΙΚΟΙ ΟΡΝΕΙΣ. Μῆδοι ἀλεκτρυόνες, Hesych. Vide s. v. ἀλεκτρυών. Cf. also Plin. x. 21, Colum. viii. 2, Varr. R. R. iii. 9, and Festus. In Latin a common reading is *Melicae gallinae*; cf. Colum. l. c. The term 'Median bird' is applied also to the Peacock.

Suid. Μηδικὸς ὄρνις· ὁ ταώς. Id. ταὼς εὐπήληξ· ὁ Μηδικὸς καὶ χρυσόπτερος καὶ ἀλαζονικὸς ὄρνις. Cf. Schol. ad Ar. Ach. 63 ἥκοντες ἀπὸ Περσίδος ταῶν ἔχοντες ἐληλύθασιν : also Ar. Av. 707 ὁ δὲ Περσικὸν ὄρνιν, ubi Schol. τινὲς δὲ τὸν ἀλεκτρύονα, οἱ δὲ τὸν ταῶ : cf. also Clem. Alex. Paedag. ii. 1 ὄρνεις ἐπὶ τούτοις συνωνοῦνται τοῖς ἀπὸ φασίδος, ἀτταγᾶς Αἰγυπτίας, Μῆδον ταῶνα : ibid. iii. 4 ὄρνεις Ἰνδικούς, καὶ ταῶνας Μηδικοὺς ἐκτρέφουσι.

ΜΟΝΟΣΙΡΟΙ. A breed of fowls in Egypt.

ὄρνεις ἐν Ἀλεξανδρείᾳ τῇ πρὸς Αἴγυπτόν εἰσι, ἐξ ὧν οἱ μάχιμοι ἀλεκτρυόνες γεννῶνται, Geopon. xiv. 7, 30.

ΜΟΡΦΝΟΣ. An **Eagle** or **Vulture**. In Plin., the **Lämmergeier**. Supposed to be connected with the idea of dark or black ; cf. ὄρφνη, Russ. *mrachnoe*, Eng. *murky*. (μόρφνος = σκοτεινός, Suid., but = ξανθός, Hesych.).

Il. xxiv. 315 αὐτίκα δ' αἰετὸν ἧκε, τελειότατον πετεηνῶν, | μόρφνον θηρητῆρ', ὃν καὶ περκνὸν καλέουσιν (cf. Il. xx. 252 ; Porphyr. Schol.; also Heyne's note, in loc.). Hes. Scut. 134 μορφνοῖο φλεγύαο καλυπτόμενοι πτερύγεσσι. Lycophr. 838 τὸν χρυσόπατρον μόρφνον. According to Arist. H. A. ix. 32, 618 b, identical with πλάγγος and νηττοφόνος (here also written μόρφος, μορφός). Plin. x. 3 Phemonoë Apollinis dicta filia dentes ei esse prodidit, mutae alias, carentique lingua : eandem aquilarum nigerrimam, prominentiore cauda. Ingenium est ei testudines raptas frangere e sublimi iaciendo, &c. Cf. Suid., who definitely applies the name to a Vulture ; μόρφνος, εἶδος ἀετοῦ· μόνοι δὲ οὗτοι τῶν ἀετῶν οὐ κυνηγετοῦσιν, ἀλλὰ νεκροῖς σώμασι τρέφονται. Vide s. v. **μελανάετος**.

ΜΥΤΤΗΞ· ὄρνις ποιός, Hesych.

ΝΕΒΡΑΞ. νέβρακες· οἱ ἄρρενες νεοττοὶ τῶν ἀλεκτρυόνων, Hesych.

ΝΕΒΡΟΦΟΝΟΣ. Arist. H. A. ix. 32, 618 b = πύγαργος, q. v.

ΝΕ'ΡΤΟΣ. A Vulture.

Ar. Av. 303, mentioned together with γύψ and ἱέραξ. Hesych. νέρτος· ἱέραξ· οἱ δὲ εἶδος ὀρνέου (i.e. a species of vulture). This word, hitherto unexplained, I conjecture to be the Egyptian 𓄿𓂋𓏏𓅆 *nert*, Copt. ⲚⲞⲨⲢⲒ, a Vulture: cf. Chaeremon, fr. 9, and Lauth, in Horap. i. 3, Sitzungsber. Bayer. Akad., 1876, p. 73.

ΝΗ'ΤΤΑ, Boeot. νᾶσσα (Ar. Ach. 875). **A Duck.** Cf. Lat. *anat-is*, Lith. *antis*, A. S. *ened*, Ger. *Ente*. Dim. νηττάριον (a term of endearment), Ar. Pl. 1011, Menand. Inc. 422 (4, 316); νήττιον, Nicostr. Antyll. 3 (3, 280). See also βοσκάς, γλαύκιον, πηνέλοψ.

Description.—Arist. H. A. viii. 3, 593 b included among τὰ βαρύτερα τῶν στεγανοπόδων· περὶ ποταμοὺς καὶ λίμνας ἐστίν; ibid. ii. 17, 509 στόμαχον ἔχει εὐρὺν καὶ πλατὺν ὅλον, ἀποφυάδας ἔχει.

Alex. Mynd. ap. Athen. ix. 52. 395 c ὁ ἄρρην μείζων καὶ ποικιλώτερος.

An allusion to the particoloured plumage of the Common Drake, or else of some wild Duck, in Ar. Av. 1148.

Ael. v. 33 ἐξ ὠδίνων ἐστὶ νηκτική, καὶ μαθεῖν οὐ δεῖται, κ.τ.λ.

Use as Food.—Herod. ii. 77 Αἰγύπτιοι τὰς νήσσας ὠμοὺς σιτέονται, προταριχεύσαντες. Frequent in the Comic Poets. Its wholesomeness, Plut. V. Cat. Maj. xxiii (i. 359 D). On the Roman νησσοτροφεία, see Varro, De R. R. iii. 11, Colum. viii. 15. Mode of capture, Dion. De Avib. iii. 23.

Brought as tribute to Indian kings, Ael. xiii. 25.

Myth and Legend.—Sacred to Poseidon, Ar. Av. 566. According to Nicand. ap. Anton. Lib. c. ix, one of the Emathides, daughters of Pierus, was metamorphosed into the bird νῆσσα.

Its defence against the eagle, cf. Phile, De An. Pr. xiv.

Use the herb *sideritis* as a remedy, Plin. viii. 27.

A Weather-prophet.—Ael. vii. 7 πτερυγίζουσαι πνεῦμα δηλοῦσιν ἰσχυρόν: cf. Arist. fr. 241, 1522 b; Theophr. De Sign. fr. vi. 18, 28; Arat. 918, 970.

ΝΗΤΤΟΚΤΟ'ΝΟΣ, s. νηττοφόνος. A kind of **Eagle**, the *Anataria* of Plin. x. 3. Supposed, by Sundevall, to be the Spotted Eagle, *Aquila naevia*; vide s. v. ἁλιάετος. Compare, however, the notes on λαγωφόνος, πλάγγος, &c.

Κίρκος νηττοκτόνος, Phile, De An. Pr. xiv. 6. νηττοφόνος, Arist. H. A. ix. 32, 618 b = μόρφνος and πλάγγος, q.v. Cf. Ael. v. 33.

ΝΟΥΜΗ'ΝΙΟΣ. An unknown bird. ὄρνεον ὅμοιον ἀτταγᾷ· ὁ καὶ τρόχιλος, Hesych.

Proverb.—ξυνῆλθον ἀτταγᾶς τε καὶ νουμήνιος, Suid., &c. (for other

ΝΟΥΜΗΝΙΟΣ (*continued*).

references vide s. v. ἀτταγᾶς). In all probability, νουμήνιος was some bird associated with moon-worship; we have an obscure indication of a kindred symbolism in the case of ἀτταγᾶς, in the statement that that bird is hostile to the Cock (Ael. vi. 45). That ἀτταγᾶς had some mystical signification seems plain, though the precise allusion is obscure : the frequent reference to the bird as ποικίλος, and the statement of its friendship with the Stag, may in time furnish a clue to the mystery. For my part, I imagine I discern a stellar attribute in the one bird, and a lunar in the other. Tradition, of doubtful antiquity, associates the name Numenius with the Curlew, and it may well have this or some similar bird with a decurved or crescentic bill.

ΝΥΚΤΑΙ'ΕΤΟΣ· ὄρνις ἱερὸς Ἥρας, ὁ καὶ ἐρωδιός, Hesych. Cf. νυκτικόραξ.

ΝΥΚΤΙΚΟ'ΡΑΞ, *s.* νυκτοκόραξ, Hesych. Probably the **Horned** or **Long-eared Owl**, *Strix otus*, L.; but perhaps also applied to the **Night-Heron**.

Arist. H. A. viii. 12, 597 b ἔνιοι τὸν ὠτὸν νυκτικόρακα καλοῦσιν (loc. dub.). Ib. viii. 3, 592 b ἔτι τῶν νυκτερινῶν ἔνιοι γαμψώνυχές εἰσιν, οἷον νυκτικόραξ, γλαύξ, βρύας. Ib. ix. 34, 689 b γλαῦκες δὲ καὶ νυκτικόρακες, καὶ τὰ λοιπὰ ὅσα τῆς ἡμέρας ἀδυνατεῖ βλέπειν, τῆς νυκτὸς μὲν θηρεύοντα τὴν τροφὴν αὑτοῖς πορίζεται· θηρεύει δὲ μῖς καὶ σαύρας, κ.τ.λ. Cf. Athen. viii. 353 a, where in a similar passage, κόρακες = νυκτικόρακες.

Arist. H. A. ii. 17, 509 ἀποφυάδας ἔχει. [The caeca are rudimentary or absent altogether in the Herons; they are large and conspicuous in the Owls.] νυκτικόραξ is, therefore, in Arist. a nocturnal, rapacious bird, identical with, or confounded with, ὠτός. It can scarcely be other than the Long-Eared Owl.

It corresponds to Heb. כוס, an Owl, in Ps. 102. 6 (LXX).

A bird of evil omen. Horap. ii. 25 νυκτικόραξ θάνατον σημαίνει· ἄφνω γὰρ ἐπέρχεται τοῖς νεοσσοῖς τῶν κορωνῶν κατὰ τὰς νύκτας, ὡς ὁ θάνατος ἄφνω ἐπέρχεται. With this passage, cf. the legendary hostility of the Owl and the Crows, s. vv. **γλαῦξ, κορώνη** : there is, however, a very similar story of ἐρωδιός.

Anth. Pal. xi. 186 νυκτικόραξ ᾄδει θανατηφόρον, ἀλλ' ὅταν ᾄσῃ | Δημόφιλος, θνήσκει καὐτὸς ὁ νυκτικόραξ. Cf. the *carmen ferale* of the Owl, Virg. Aen. iv. 462 : vide also s. v. **βύας**. Cf. also Spenser's ' hoarse night-raven, trompe of doleful drere,' &c.

A fabled metamorphosis, Boios ap. Anton. Lib. c. xv ; cf. **χαραδριός**.

There is an old confusion between this bird and the Night-Heron, *Ardea nycticorax*, L. Gesner (ed. cit., p. 357), discussing the discrepant opinions regarding νυκτικόραξ, figures the Night-Heron, and adds, 'Wir haben hierbey die Figur des Vogels gesetzt, welcher zu Strasburg ein Nachtram anderswo ein Nachtrabe geheissen wird, welcher doch

ΝΥΚΤΙΚΟΡΑΞ (continued).

meines Bedenckens weder ein Caprimulgus noch Nycticorax ist.' And the confusion thus introduced seems to have been aided by Gaza having translated νυκτικόραξ by *cicuma* (Gr. κίκυμις, q. v.), afterwards misspelt *cicunia, ciconia* (vide Belon, ii. c. 36, Camus, ii. p. 250).

Nevertheless, although the above-cited passages all appear to apply to an *Owl*, yet *Ardea purpurea, nycticorax*, and other *Herons* are said to be now called νυκτικόραξ (Erh., Heldr.); further, it has been shown above that the attributes of ἐρωδιός are in part nocturnal. Lastly, it must be noted that there are evidences of Egyptian influence in the stories both of ἐρωδιός and νυκτικόραξ; vide s. v. ἀνοπαῖα.

ΟΙ'ΝΑ'ΝΘΗ. An unknown bird.

Arist. H. A. ix. 49 B, 633 (*loc. dub.*) ἀφονίζεται δὲ καὶ ἣν καλοῦσί τινες οἰνάνθην ἀνίσχοντος τοῦ σειρίου, δυομένου δὲ φαίνεται· φεύγει γὰρ ὁτὲ μὲν τὰ ψύχη, ὁτὲ δὲ τὴν ἀλέαν. Cf. Plin. x. (29) 45; perhaps identical with *parra*, ib. xviii. 69, or *vitiparra*, ib. x. (33) 50. Vide infra, s. v. οἰνάς.

Belon (Nat. des Oiseaux, vii. 12) first applied the name to the **Wheatear**, which (*Saxicola oenanthe*, L.) still retains it.

ΟΙ'ΝΑ'Σ. A kind of **Pigeon**: probably the wild **Rock-Pigeon**, *Columba livia*, L. Also οἰνίας, Poll. vi. 22 οἰνίας δὲ καὶ οἰνάς, ἡ ἀγρία περιστερά.

Arist. H. A. v. 13, 544 b ὄρνις περιστεροειδής, μικρῷ μείζων τῆς περιστερᾶς. Ib. viii. 3, 593 ἐλάττων δὲ φαβός. Ib. vi. 1, 558 b διτοκεῖ, i.e. lays two eggs; cf. De Gen. iv. 77, iii. 9, Plin. x. 79 (58). Arist. H. A. viii. 3. 593 τοῦ φθινοπώρου καὶ φαίνεται μάλιστα καὶ ἁλίσκεται· ἡ δ' ἅλωσις αὐτῆς γίνεται μάλιστα καππτούσης τὸ ὕδωρ· ἀφικνοῦνται δ' εἰς τοὺς τόπους τούτους ἔχουσαι νεοττούς.

Arist. ap. Athen. ix. 394 a μείζων ἐστὶ τῆς περιστερᾶς, χρῶμα δὲ ἔχει οἰνωπόν. φαίνεται φθινοπώρῳ μόνῳ. Athen. ib. 394 e λέγεται δ' ὅτι ἡ οἰνὰς ἐὰν φαγοῦσα τὸ τῆς ἰξίας σπέρμα ἐπί τινος ἀφοδεύσῃ δένδρου, ἰδίαν ἰξίαν φύεσθαι: cf. Plin. xvi. (44) 93, s. v. *palumbes*. Ael. iv. 58 τὴν οἰνάδα ὄρνεον εἰδέναι χρὴ οὖσαν, οὐ μὴν ὥς τινες ἄμπελον. λέγει δὲ Ἀριστοτέλης μεῖζον μὲν αὐτὸ εἶναι φάττης, περιστερᾶς γε μὴν ἧττον. Mentioned also, Lyc. 358.

οἰναδοθήρας, in Sparta, a dove-catcher, Ael. l. c.

The passage in Aelian, and the discrepancy between the accounts of the bird's size, indicate that οἰνάς was a little-known word. The later Greeks and early commentators derived it from οἶνος, with reference to the colour of the bird (Athen. l. c., Eustath. ad Odyss. p. 475, ed. Basil.) or to its appearance in the vintage-season (τοῦ φθινοπώρου); hence Gaza translates it *Vinago*; and most moderns have identified it with the Stock-dove, *C. oenas*, L., whose breast is purple-red. But the word is more probably identical with the Hebrew יונה, *jonah*, as has been suggested by Casaubon in Athen. p. 617, and Bochart, Hieroz. ii.

ΟΙΝΑΣ (*continued*).

2. Cf. **Ἰώνας**, Hesych., also Tzetz. Chiliad. vii. 126. [The same word is supposed by some to give its name to the island of S. *Columba*.] It was then probably either a sacred name, introduced with a foreign cult, or else a Phoenician sailor's name, especially for the wild Rock-pigeons of the coast; and on this latter interpretation the passage in Arist. viii. 3, 593 would refer naturally to an autumn flight inland from the sea-board breeding-places.

The Οἰνότροποι, who were turned into doves, Lyc. 570, cf. Simon. fr. 24 (39), ap. Schol. Hom. Od. iv. 164, Serv. Virg. Aen. iii. 8, Ovid, Met. xiii. 674, &c., may derive their name from the same root, and the story of their turning water into wine may then be due to a case of 'Volksetymologie.'

By this word, and its Semitic root, I would seek to explain the curious 'canting heraldry' which represents the constellation of the Pleiads as a bunch of grapes, and gives to it the name **βότρυς** (βότρυν γὰρ αὐτὰς λέγουσιν, Schol. Il. xviii. 486; Ideler, Sternnamen, p. 317). On coins of Mallos in Cilicia, we have Doves represented, whose bodies are formed by bunches of grapes, and in other cases the dove is lost and replaced simply by the grapes: on the relation of these figures and their other associated symbols to the constellation of the Pleiad, see M. J. Svoronos, Bull. de Corresp. Hellen., 1894, p. 107, &c. I imagine that an old confusion, intentional or unintentional, between οἰνάς and οἶνος may have been the cause of this strange and unwonted prefigurement of the constellation. The association of the dove with the bunch of grapes survives in early Christian symbolism; cf. Gorius, Diss. XIII. De Gemmis Astrif. Christian. (vol. iii. p. 249) 1750.

The symbolic meaning here assigned to οἰνάς tends to suggest a similar derivation and interpretation in the case of **οἰνάνθη**.

ΟΙ'ΝΙΑ'Ξ. According to Hesych. a kind of Raven, but probably = οἰνάς, which latter word Hesych. interprets γένος κόρακος· οἱ δὲ ἀγρίαν περιστεράν. Cf. **γοινέες**.

ΟΙ'ΣΤΡΟΣ. An unknown small bird.

Arist. H. A. viii. 3, 592 b, mentioned as a small insect-eating bird with τύραννος, ἐπιλαΐς, &c.

On the assumption that οἶστρος (the Gad-fly) must denote some very small bird, Sundevall follows the mediaeval naturalists in identifying it with the Willow-wren, *Sylvia trochilus*, L., our smallest bird next to the Gold-crests.

ὈΚΝΟΣ, *s.* ὀκνός. A bird of the Heron kind, with fabulous attributes; in Arist. H. A. ix. 1, 609 b, 18, 617, Ael. v. 36 = **ἀστερίας**, q. v.

Pausan. x. 29, 2 ὄκνον δ' οὖν καὶ μάντεων οἱ ὁρῶντες τοὺς οἰωνοὺς καλοῦσί

ΟΚΝΟΣ (*continued*).

τινα ὄρνιθα, καὶ ἔστιν οὗτος ὁ ὄκνος μέγιστος μὲν καὶ κάλλιστος ἐρωδιῶν, εἰ δὲ ἄλλος τις ὀρνίθων, σπάνιός ἐστι καὶ οὗτος.

According to Boios ap. Anton. Lib. c. vii, Autonous was metamorphosed into the bird ὄκνος, ὅτι ὤκνησε ἀπελάσαι τὰς ἵππους, his son being turned into an ἐρωδιός. On Ocnus as a mythological character, cf. Diodor. i. 97, p. 109, Pausan. l. c., &c.

Probably a foreign word, and perhaps Egyptian (cf. Ael., Diod. l. c.). Bearing in mind the close connexion of the Heron with Athene, I am almost tempted to see in ὄκνος a distorted reflection of Onkh, Ὄγγα, Ὄγκας (Hesych.), &c., a mystical name of the same goddess. Vide s. v. ἀνάγκης.

ΟΛΑΙΤΟΙ´, *s.* ὀλατοί· σπερμολόγοι, Hesych.

ΟΛΚΑ´Σ· ἀηδών, Hesych. (*loc. dub. et mutilus*).

ΟΝΟΚΡΟ´ΤΑΛΟΣ. A **Pelican**.

Plin. x. (47) 66, Mart. xi. 21, Hieron. in Lev. xi. 18, &c.; cf. Boch. Hieroz. ii. 276.

ΟΡΕΙΝΟ´Σ. A species of **αἰγίθαλος**, q. v.

Arist. H. A. viii. 3, 592 b ἕτερος δ' ὀρεινός, διὰ τὸ διατρίβειν ἐν τοῖς ὄρεσιν, οὐραῖον μακρὸν ἔχων.

Also a name or epithet, like ὀρείτης, of a Hawk or Eagle: cf. Plut. Amat. iv. 9.

ΟΡΕΙΠΕΛΑΡΓΟ´Σ, vide s. v. **περκνόπτερος**.

ΟΡΕΙ´ΤΗΣ. A kind of **Hawk**, mentioned with κεγχρηΐς, Ael. ii. 43.

ΟΡΘΟΚΟ´ΡΥΔΟΣ. A name or epithet for a **Lark** (verb. dub.); Alciphro iii. 48.

ΟΡΝΙΘΕΣ ΜΕΙ´ΖΟΝΕΣ ΒΟΩ͂Ν. Eudox. ap. Ael. xvii. 14 ὑπερβαλὼν τὰς Ἡρακλείους στήλας ἐν λίμναις ἑωρακέναι ὀρνιθάς τινας καὶ μείζους βοῶν.

ΟΡΟ´ΣΠΙΖΟΣ. The **Blue-throat**, *Cyanecula suecica*, L.

Arist. H. A. viii. 3, 592 b σπίζῃ ὅμοιος καὶ τὸ μέγεθος παραπλήσιος· ἔχει [τι περὶ] τὸν αὐχένα κυανοῦν, καὶ διατρίβει ἐν τοῖς ὄρεσιν. The bird is rare in Greece (Lindermayer, p. 104), nevertheless its identity is unmistakeable. The MSS. have several variants in the name.

ΟΡΤΑ´ΛΙΧΟΣ. Also ὀρταλίς, Nic. Alex. 295, &c. A Boeotian word (Stratt. Φοιν. 2, 781) for a **Chick**.

Theocr. xiii. 12 οὔθ' ὁπόκ' ὀρτάλιχοι μινυροὶ ποτὶ κοῖτον ὁρῷεν. Cf. Ar. Ach. 871 and Schol.; Aesch. Ag. 54. Applied to Swallow-chicks, Opp. Hal. v. 579.

ΌΡΤΥΓΟΜΗ'ΤΡΑ. The Corn-crake or Land-rail, *Rallus crex*, L., *Crex pratensis*, auctt.: cf. κρέξ, κύχραμος. In Mod. Gk. still called ὀρτυγομήτρα (Heldr. &c.), and in the Cyclades ῥεδιγονάλια (Erh.), It. Re di quaglie.

Arist. H. A. viii. 12, 597 b; a bird which accompanies the quails (vide s. v. κύχραμος). παραπλήσιος τὴν μορφὴν τοῖς λιμναίοις (i. e. to the wading birds): cf. Plin. x. 33; Frider. ii De Arte Venandi, i. 9 et modus rallorum terrestrium, quae dicuntur duces coturnicum. Alex. Mynd. ap. Athen. ix. 393 a ἐστὶ τὸ μέγεθος ἡλίκη τρυγών, σκέλη δὲ μακρά, δυσθαλὴς καὶ δείλη.

Cratin. (2. 158) ap. Athen. l. c. Ἰθακησία ὀρτυγομήτρα. Ar. Av. 870 associated with Latona, Λητοῖ Ὀρτυγομήτρᾳ, cf. Schol. in Argum. Pythiorum Pindari.

In Hesych. ὀρτυγομήτρα = ὄρτυξ ὑπερμεγέθης. The word is used also by the LXX, and by the Fathers, for ὄρτυξ (Ex. xvi. 13; Numb. xi. 31, 32; Ps. cv. 40): according to Bochart (Hieroz. ii. 94) qua tamen voce libentius usi sunt, quam simplici ὄρτυγες, ne crederetur Deus gregarias coturnices Israelitis immisisse, sed earum nobilissimas!

ΌΡΤΥΞ· Hesych. γόρτυξ, i. e. ϝόρτυξ. Sk. *vart-ika* (cf., int. al., Muir's Sk. Texts, i. 112. 8), cf. Lat. *vertere*, Lit. the *dancer* (?), or more probably and simply, the one who *returns*. The Quail, *Coturnix vulgaris*, auctt. Mod. Gk. ὄρτυκι, ὑρτύκιον. Dim. ὀρτύγιον, Eupolis and Antiph. ap. Athen. ix. 392 e. On the quantity of the υ, cf. Phot., p. 350, 10 ὄρτυγας· συστέλλοντες οἱ Ἀττικοὶ λέγουσι τὸ υ δηλοῖ ἐν Δαιταλεῦσιν Ἀριστοφάνης. Gen. ὄρτυκος, in Philem. ap. Chaerob. i. 82.

Description.—Arist. H. A. vi. 12, 597 b οὐ πτητικός: ib. ix. 9, 614 ἐπὶ δένδρου οὐ καθίζει, ἀλλ' ἐπὶ τῆς γῆς: ib. iv. 9, 536 μαχόμενος φθέγγεται· μᾶλλον ᾄδει ὁ ἄρρην, αἱ δὲ θήλειαι οὐκ ᾄδουσιν.

Alex. Mynd. ap. Athen. ix. 392 c ὁ θῆλυς ὄρτυξ λεπτοτράχηλός ἐστι, τοῦ ἄρρενος οὐκ ἔχων τὰ ὑπὸ τῷ γενείῳ μέλανα. Pratin. ib. ἀδίφωνον τὸν ὄρτυγα, πλὴν εἰ μή τι παρὰ τοῖς Φλιασίοις ἢ τοῖς Λάκωσι φωνήεντες, ὡς οἱ πέρδικες.

Anatomy.—Arist. H. A. ii. 15, 506 b πρὸς τοῖς ἐντέροις τὴν χόλην ἔχει. ib. 17, 509 ἔχει καὶ πρόλοβον καὶ πρὸ τῆς γαστρὸς τὸν στόμαχον εὐρὺν καὶ πλατὺν ἔχοντα· διέχει δ' ὁ πρόλοβος τοῦ πρὸ τῆς γαστρὸς στομάχου συχνὸν ὡς κατὰ μέγεθος. Alex. Mynd. l. c. ἀνατμηθεὶς δὲ πρόλοβον οὐχ ὁρᾶται μέγαν ἔχων, καρδίαν δ' ἔχει μεγάλην, καὶ ταύτην τρίλοβον, κ.τ.λ.

Nest and Breeding-habits.—A full description, together with πέρδιξ, Arist. H. A. ix. 8, 613 b, 614: cf. ib. vi. 1, 559. Cf. Xen. Memor. ii. 1, 4.

Migrations.—Arist. H. A. viii. 12, 597. Migrate in September, τοῦ Βοηδρομιῶνος. πιότεροι τοῦ φθινοπώρου μᾶλλον ἢ τοῦ ἔαρος. οἱ δ' ὄρτυγες

ΟΡΤΥΞ (*continued*).

ὅταν ἐμπέσωσιν, ἐὰν μὲν εὐδία ᾖ βόρειον ᾖ, συνδυάζονταί τε καὶ εὐημεροῦσιν. ἐὰν δὲ νότος, χαλεπῶς ἔχουσι διὰ τὸ μὴ εἶναι πτητικοί· ὑγρὸς γὰρ καὶ βαρὺς ὁ ἄνεμος· διὸ καὶ οἱ θηρεύοντες οὐκ ἐπιχειροῦσιν εὐδίας· τοῖς νοτίοις δ' οὐ πέτονται διὰ τὸ βάρος· πολὺ γὰρ τὸ σῶμα, διὸ καὶ βοῶντες πέτονται· πονοῦσι γάρ. ὅταν μὲν οὖν ἐκεῖθεν παραβάλλωσιν, οὐκ ἔχουσιν ἡγεμόνας. ὅταν δ' ἐντεῦθεν ἀπαίρωσιν, ἥ τε γλωττὶς συναπαίρει καὶ ἡ ὀρτυγομήτρα, κ.τ.λ. Cf. Dion. De Avib. i. 30; Plin. x. 33 (23); Varro, De Re Rust. iii. 5, 7. The connexion between the quails' flight and the wind is well known: cf. Numb. xi. 31; Joseph. Ant. iii. 1, 5.

Modes of capture.—With a mirror, Clearch. Sol. ap. Athen. ix. 393 οἱ ὄρτυγες περὶ τὸν τῆς ὀχείας καιρόν, ἐὰν κάτοπτρον ἐξ ἐναντίας τις αὐτῶν καὶ πρὸ τούτου βρόχον θῇ, τρέχοντες πρὸς τὸν ἐμφαινόμενον ἐν τῷ κατόπτρῳ ἐμπίπτουσιν εἰς τὸν βρόχον. With a sort of scare-crow, Dion. De Avib. iii. 9. With nets simply, on the coast of Egypt, Diodor. i. 60. A quail-catcher, ὀρτυγοθήρας, Plat. Euthyd. 290 D. Cf. Arist. H. A. ix. 8, 614 οὕτω δὲ σφόδρα καὶ οἱ πέρδικες καὶ οἱ ὄρτυγες ἐπτόηνται περὶ τὴν ὀχείαν, ὥστ' εἰς τοὺς θηρεύοντας ἐμπίπτουσι καὶ πολλάκις καθιζάνουσιν ἐπὶ τὰς κεφαλάς.

Abundance and cheapness: cf. Antiph. ap. Athen. ix. 397 πλείους δ' εἰσὶ νῦν [οἱ ταῶνες] τῶν ὀρτύγων. Juv. Sat. 12. 97.

In Egypt, according to Herod. ii. 77 τοὺς ὄρτυγας ὠμὰ σιτέονται, προταριχεύσαντες: cf. Diodor. l. c.: vide s. v. χέννιον. On potted Quails in the Morea, cf. G. St. Hilaire ap. Bory de St. Vincent, Morée, Oiseaux, p. 35.

Domesticated and pet Quails: Ar. Pax 789 ὄρτυγας οἰκογενεῖς: cf. Ar. Fr. 36; Arist. Probl. x. 12, 1; Plut. V. Alcib. i. 195 E, Mor. ii. 799 D; Varro, iii. 5, 2; M. Anton. i. 6. A lover's gift, Ar. Av. 707, Plat. Lys. 211 E: cf. Plaut. Capt. v. 4, 5; vide Jacobs ad Anthol. x. p. 13. Hence φιλόρτυξ, Plat. Lys. 212 D; φιλορτυγοτροφέω, Artemid. iii. 5, &c.

Quail-fights. Lucian, Anach. 37 (2, 918); Plat. Lys. 211 E; Plut. i. 930 E, cock and quail-fights between Antony and Caesar (cf. Ant. and Cl. ii. 4 'and his quails ever Beat mine, inhoop'd at odds'); ibid. ii. 207 B how in Egypt a procurator of Augustus killed and ate a victorious quail, and how retribution fell on him; Ovid, Amor. ii. 6, 27, &c. This sport, still common among the Chinese, Malays, &c., was practised in Italy in Aldrovandi's time (Ornith. ii. p. 74: cf. Voss., De Idol. c. 86, p. 596). For a Chinese picture of a quail-fight, showing the 'hoop' or τηλία (cf. supra, p. 22, s. v. ἀλεκτρυών), see Douce's Illustr. of Shakspeare, p. 367; cf. also Bell's Travels in China, i. p. 404 (8vo ed.). See also Becker's Charicles. The birds are said to have been stimulated to fight with bells, cf. Schol. in Ar. Lys. 485 (ἀκωδώνιστον); see also Aristarch. ap. Harpocrat. s. v. διεκωδώνισε.

Quail-striking, ὀρτυγοκοπία, Jul. Pollux, ix. 107. The player was ὀρτυγοκόπος, Plat. Com. Περίαλγ. 4, ap. Athen. xi. 506 D or στυφοκόπος.

ORTYX (*continued*).

Ar. Av. 1299 and Schol. Cf. Plut. ii. 34 D. See also Meursius, De Ludis Graecorum, in Gronov. Thes. Ant. Gr. vii. p. 979.

Immunity from poison.—Arist. De Plant. 5, 820 b ὑοσκύαμος καὶ ἐλλέβορος ἀνθρώποις μὲν δηλητήριοι, τροφὴ δὲ τοῖς ὄρτυξι. Cf. Plin. x. 33 (23), Geopon. xiv. 24, Galen. De Ther. ad Pison. i. 4, De Alim. Fac. ii. 6, De Temper. iii. 4, Basil. Hexaem. v. p. 59 (ed. Paris), Eustath. Hexaem. p. 9, Ambros. Hexaem. iii. 9, &c., Lucret. iv. 641. For similar oriental reff., see Bochart, ii. 97, 98.

Legend of Delos.—Phanodem. ap. Athen. ix. 392 d ὡς κατεῖδεν Ἐρυσίχθων Δῆλον τὴν νῆσον τὴν ὑπὸ τῶν ἀρχαίων καλουμένην Ὀρτυγίαν παρ' ὃ τὰς ἀγέλας τῶν ζῴων τοίτων φερομένας ἐκ τοῦ πελάγους ἱζάνειν εἰς τὴν νῆσον διὰ τὸ εὔορμον εἶναι ... Cf. Serv. ad Aen. iii. 73. On the metamorphosis of Artemis, Leto, and Asteria into Quails, see Apollod. i. 4, 1, Schol. Apoll. Rhod. i. 308, Hygin. Fab. 53, Tatian, Adv. Graec. c. xvi, &c. In yet another version it is Zeus himself who appears as a Quail : Argum. Pyth. Pindari, ed. Böckh, ii. p. 297.

Legend of Hercules.—Eudox. ap. Athen. ix. 392 d οἱ Φοίνικες θύουσι τῷ Ἡρακλεῖ ὄρτυγας διὰ τὸ τὸν Ἡρακλέα τὸν Ἀστερίας καὶ Διὸς πορευόμενον εἰς Λιβύην ἀναιρεθῆναι μὲν ὑπὸ Τυφῶνος, Ἰολάου δ' αὐτῷ προσενέγκαντος ὄρτυγα καὶ προσαγαγόντος ὀσφρανθέντα ἀναβιῶναι : cf. Arist. Probl. xxx. 1. Eustath. in Od. xi. 60, p. 1702. Prov. ὄρτυξ ἔσωσεν Ἡρακλῆ τὸν κάρτερον, Zenob. v. 56 ; Diog. vii. 10 ; Apostol. xiii. 1 ; Eutecnius in Cram. Anecd. Paris., i. p. 31 ; Paroemiogr. Gr. i. p. 143. In this passage various commentators read ὄρυγα for ὄρτυγα, the *Gazelle* being sacred to Typhon ; cf. Jablonski, Panth. 197, Dupuis, Orig. de tous les Cultes, ii. 350, Creuzer, Symb. ii. 100, Boch., l. c.; but the emendation is not justified, cf. Stark, op. infra cit. The Quail's brain was a specific for epilepsy, the morbus comitialis or herculeus, Galen, Parat. Facil. iii. 155, Plin. x. (23) 33. *Vartikâ*, the Quail, is said to be a solar emblem among the Hindoos : it is as the emblem of the returning Sun, that it figures in the legend of Delos, the birthplace of Phoebus, and in that of Hercules, the slayer of Typhon.

The principal allusions to the Island of Ortygia are collated and discussed by Hermann, De Apoll. et Diana, Opusc. vii. p. 310 (1839). See also, for a still more elaborate investigation, Stark, Die Wachtel, Sterneninsel und der Oelbaum im Bereiche phoinikischer und griechischer Mythen, Ber. K. Sächs. Ges. d. Wiss., 1856, pp. 32-120. It seems clear to me that in the superstitions regarding the Quail, and in the sacred reputation of Ortygia, the main point is with reference to the Solar Tropic ; cf. Od. xv. 403 νῆσός τις Συρίη κεκλήσκεται, εἴ που ἀκούεις, | Ὀρτυγίης καθύπερθεν, ὅθι τροπαὶ ἠελίοιο. The Quail derived its sanctity, and perhaps its name, from the circumstance that it returned with the returning Sun, and Ortygia was some spot where the τροπαὶ

ΟΡΤΥΞ (continued).

ἠελίοιο were observed and their festivals celebrated, as of old in Delos. Cf. (int. al.) Pind. Nem. i.
The word ΟΡΤΥΓΟΘΗΡΑ, on coins of Tarsus (Mionnet, Suppl. vii. p. 258, &c.) is supposed to refer to a similar symbolic festival (Stark, op. c., p. 44).
Hostile to πελεκάν, Ael. vi. 45, Phile, 684. A prey to hawks, Ael. vii. 9. Arist. H. A. ix. 11, 615 ὁ ἱέραξ τὴν τοῦ ὄρτυγος καρδίαν οὐ κατεσθίει.
How the Quails, migrating, carry each three stones, to hear by dropping them whether they be over the sea, Dion. De Avib. i. 30 : cf. Plin. x. 33 (sand for ballast) ; cf. s.v. γέρανος.
An obscure allusion in Lyc. 401 τύμβος δὲ γείτων ὄρτυγος πετρουμένης | τρέμων φυλάξει ῥόχθον Αἰγαίας ἁλός.

Proverbial References.—Philostr. V. Sophist., p. 253 (ed. Kayser) μὴ γὰρ δὴ ἐν τείχει ἐπιπτήξωμεν ὀρτύγων ἀναψάμενοι φύσιν. Antiph. ap. Athen. ix. p. 392 c ὡς δὴ σὺ τί ποιεῖν δυνάμενος ὀρτυγίου ψυχὴν ἔχων;

ὌΡΧΙΛΟΣ, s. ὀρχίλος. Probably the **Wren** ; cf. τρόχιλος. Hesych. ὀρνιθάριον τῶν εὐωνητῶν· λέγεται δὲ ὑπό τινων σαλπιγ[κ]τής : cf. Phot. 351. 12.
Ar. Av. 569 βασιλεύς ἐστ' ὀρχίλος ὄρνις : cf. *trochilus*, Plin. viii. 37, x. 95. Mentioned also Ar. Vesp. 1513.
Arist. H. A. ix. 1, 609 γλαῦξ καὶ ὄρχιλος πολέμια, τὰ γὰρ ᾠὰ κατεσθίει τῆς γλαυκός.
A sign of rain, Arat. 1025 ὄρχιλος ἢ καὶ ἐριθεὺς δύνων ἐς κοίλας ὀχεύς. Cf. Theophr. De Sign. vi. 3. 39, 4. 53. According to Nicand. ap. Anton. Lib. c. xiv, Alcander, son of Munychus, was metamorphosed into the bird ὄρχιλος.
An evil omen at weddings : Avienus in Arat. l. c. infestus floricomis hymenaeis orchilus. Cf. Euphor. ap. Tzetz. ad Lycophr. p. 83 (cit. Schn. in Arist. l.c.), ποικίλον οὐδὲ μέλαθρον ὀρχίλος ἔπτη Κύζικος. οὐδ' ᾔεισε κακὸν γάμον ἐχθόμενος κρέξ.

ὄρχιλος and τρόχιλος (qu. τ-ορχιλος) are probably identical words, and of foreign origin. κόρθιλος (q. v.) may be yet another corrupt form. Lauth (in Horap. i. 57, Sitzungsber. d. Bayer. Akad. 1876, p. 107), comparing Copt. ογρⳉ *avis*, and ογρο *rex*, affords a hint which may explain, by referring to an Egyptian source, the origin both of ὄρχιλος and of its synonym or epithet βασιλεύς.

ὈΣΤΟΚΑΤΑ΄ΚΤΗΣ, ὈΣΤΟΚΛΑ΄ΣΤΗΣ, ὈΣΤΟΚΟ΄ΡΑΞ. In Byz. Gk. for *ossifragus*.

ΟΥ῀ΡΑΞ. The Athenian name for τέτριξ (q.v.), Arist. H. A. vi. 1, 559.

ΟΥ'ΡΙ'Α.   A kind of water-bird.
Athen. ix. 395 e ἡ δὲ λεγομένη οὐρία οὐ πολὺ λείπεται νήττης, τῷ χρώματι δὲ ῥυπαροκέραμός ἐστι, τὸ δὲ ῥύγχος μακρόν τε καὶ στενὸν ἔχει.

'ΟΦΙ'ΟΥΡΟΣ· ὄρνις ποιὸς ἐν Αἰθιοπίᾳ, Hesych.

ΠΑ'ΠΠΟΣ.   An unknown bird (verb. dub.); ὀρνέου εἶδος, Hesych.
Mentioned Ael. iii. 30, in a somewhat doubtful passage, as a bird in whose nest the Cuckoo lays her egg. Sometimes supposed to be punned on in Ar. Av. 765 φυσάτω πάππους παρ' ἡμῖν, where however πάπποι are more probably young downy feathers (vide Kock, &c.). Coray cites, vaguely, Mod. Gk. πάππια, a duck.

ΠΑΡΑΟ'Σ· ἀετός, ὑπὸ Μακεδόνων, Hesych.

ΠΑ'ΡΔΑΛΟΣ, s. πάρδαλις, Hesych.   An undetermined bird.
Arist. H. A. ix. 23, 617 b ὄρνεόν ἐστιν ἀγελαῖον ὡς ἐπὶ τὸ πολύ, καὶ οὐκ ἔστι κατὰ ἕνα ἰδεῖν· τὸ δὲ χρῶμα σποδοειδὴς ὅλος, μέγεθος δὲ παραπλήσιος ἐκείνοις [? μαλακοκρανεύς, χλωρίων, τρυγών], εὔπους δὲ καὶ οὐ κακόπτερος, φωνὴ δὲ πολλὴ καὶ οὐ βαρεῖα· τὸ δὲ μέγεθος [τοῦ κολλυρίωνος] ταὐτόν.

A very doubtful passage, cf. Billerbeck, De loc. nonnull. Arist. H. A. difficilior., Hildesh. 1806. Sundevall, following Turner, Gesner, &c., identifies πάρδαλος with the Golden Plover, *Charadrius pluvialis*, L., which is frequent in flocks in Greece, and has a constant cry, and is about as large as τρυγών: in the name he sees a suggestion of the dappled plumage, in spite of σποδοειδὴς ὅλος. Billerbeck, following Aldrovandi, &c., identifies it with the Starling, for similar and equally good reasons. Vide supra, s. v. μαλακοκρανεύς.

ΠΕΛΑΡΓΟ'Σ.   (Said to be derived from πελός, ἀργός: lit. black-and-white; vide Suid. s. v. πελαργιδεῖς, ed. Bernhardy; Zonarus, p. 1528; Pott. Etym. Forsch. i. p. 131; cf. νῆες πελαργόχρωτες, Lycophr. 24; ὀρειπέλαργος, q. v.).   Dim. πελαργιδεύς, Ar. Av. 1356, Plut. ii. 992 B.   Cf. also γύγης.

The Stork, *Ciconia alba*, L.   Mod. Gk. λελέκι, λέλεκας, sometimes said to be a Turkish word; but Byzantios ingeniously compares λελέκι = πελαργός with Λέλεγες = Πελασγοί: cf. also λάλαγες.
Mentioned in Ar. Av. 1139, with a pun on τὸ Πελαργικόν; cf. ibid. 869.

Description.—Arist. H. A. viii. 3, 593 περὶ τὰς λίμνας καὶ τοὺς ποταμοὺς βιοτεύει.   Its clattering noise, Philostr. Ep. ad Epictet. τοὺς πελαργοὺς ἐπειδὰν παριόντας ἡμᾶς κροτῶσιν: cf. Ovid, Met. vi. 97 crepitante ciconia rostro.

Migrations.—Arist. H. A. viii. 16, 600, φωλεῖ. Cf. Plin. x. 23 (31) Ciconiae quonam e loco veniant aut quo se referant, incompertum adhuc est. Nemo videt agmen discedentium, cum discessurum appareat, nec

ΠΕΛΑΡΓΟΣ (continued).

venire sed venisse cernimus : utrumque nocturnis fit temporibus. Cf. Dionys. De Avib. i. 31. (Its departure is scarcely noticed ; Lindermayer, op. cit., p. 154). Ael. iii. 23 τῆς ὥρας δὲ τῆς κριμώδους διελθοίσης, ὅταν ὑποστρέψωσιν ἐς τὰ ἴδια, τὴν ἑαυτῶν ἕκαστος καλιὰν ἀναγνωρίζουσιν, ὡς τὴν οἰκίαν ἄνθρωποι. The precise regularity of their coming (cf. s. v. γέρανος): Lucullus to Pompey, ap. Plut. i. 518 D εἶτα, ἔφη, σοὶ δοκῶ ἐλάττονα τῶν γεράνων νοῦν ἔχειν καὶ τῶν πελαργῶν, ὥστε ταῖς ὥραις μὴ συμμεταβάλλειν τὰς διαίτας; Cf. ὁ πελαργὸς ἀλήτης, Call. Fr. 475. According to Strabo, 221, 397, connected with Πελασγοί, a nomad race; cf. Dion. Hal. i. 28.

Filial Piety.—Ar. Av. 1355 ἐπὴν ὁ πατὴρ ὁ πελαργὸς ἐκπετησίμους | πάντας ποιήσῃ τοὺς πελαργιδῆς τρέφων | δεῖ τοὺς νεοττοὺς τὸν πατέρα πάλιν τρέφειν. Cf. Plut. Alcib. i. 135 D, Arist. H. A. ix. 13, 615 b, Ael. iii. 23 τρέφειν μὲν τοὺς πατέρας πελαργοὶ γεγηρακότας καὶ ἐθέλουσι καὶ ἐμελέτησαν· κελεύει δὲ αὐτοὺς νόμος ἀνθρωπικὸς οὐδὲ εἷς τοῦτο, ἀλλὰ αἰτία τούτων φύσις· οἱ αὐτοὶ δὲ καὶ τὰ ἑαυτῶν ἔκγονα φιλοῦσι, κ.τ.λ. Origen, c. Celsum, iv εὐσεβεστέρους εἶναι τοὺς πελαργοὺς τῶν ἀνθρώπων. Cf. Fab. Aesop. γεωργὸς καὶ πελαργός, Fab. 100, 100 b (ed. Halm), Babr. xiii οὐκ εἰμὶ γέρανος, οὐ σπόρον καταφθείρω | πελαργός εἰμι (χὴ χρόη με σημαίνει) | πτηνῶν πελαργὸς εὐσεβέστατος ζῴων | τὸν ἐμὸν τιθηνῶ πατέρα καὶ νοσηλεύω. Cf. Soph. El. 1058. See also verb ἀντιπελαργεῖν, Suidas, Zenob. i. 94, &c., and Πελαργικοὶ νόμοι, Hesych., Suid., &c. The Stork as a primeval law-maker is alluded to in Ar. Av. 1353, perhaps also ibid. 1213. Hence the Stork was honoured by the Egyptians, as an emblem of piety : Ael. x. 16, Horap. ii. 55 φιλοπάτορα βουλόμενοι σημῆναι ἄνθρωπον, πελαργὸν ζωγραφοῦσιν. ἐν τοῖς σκήπτροις ἀνωτέρω μὲν πελαργὸν τυποῦσι, κατωτέρω δὲ ποτάμιον ἵππον. (Cf. Schol. in Ar. Av. l. c.) Cf. Phile, (vi.) 158 : Plin. x. (23) 33 ; Juv. Sat. i. 116 ; Porph. De Abst. iii. 11 ; Publius ap. Petron. Sat. 55 ciconia etiam grata, peregrina, hospita, Pietaticultrix, gracilipes, crotalistria.

How the Storks teach their children to fly, Plut. ii. 992 B καὶ τοῖς πελαργιδεῦσιν ὁρᾷς ἐπὶ τῶν τεγῶν ὡς οἱ τέλειοι παρόντες ἀναπειρωμένοις ὑφηγοῦνται τὴν πτῆσιν.

Destroys serpents, and hence honoured by the Thessalians. Arist. Mirab. 23, 832 περὶ Θετταλίαν μνημονεύουσιν ὄφεις ζῳογονηθῆναι τοσούτους ὥστε, εἰ μὴ ὑπὸ τῶν πελαργῶν ἀνῃροῦντο, ἐκχωρῆσαι ἂν αὐτούς. διὸ δὴ καὶ τιμῶσι τοὺς πελαργούς, καὶ κτείνειν οὐ νόμος· καὶ ἐάν τις κτείνῃ, ἔνοχος τοῖς αὐτοῖς γίνεται οἷσπερ καὶ ὁ ἀνδροφόνος : see also Plut. De Isid. c. 74, Symp. viii. 7, Plin. x. (23) 33, Solin. De Thessal. Cf. Juv. Sat. xiv. 74 serpente ciconia pullos, Nutrit et inventa per devia rura lacerta ; Virg. G. ii. 320.

The Stork as food, Hor. Sat. ii. 2, 50, and Scholia ; cf. Corn. Nepos, ap. Plin. x. (23) 30, Mart. Ep. xiii.

ΠΕΛΑΡΓΟΣ—ΠΕΛΕΙΑ 129

ΠΕΛΑΡΓΟΣ (*continued*).
Myth and Legend.—Hostile to αἴθυια, Ael. iv. 5, Phile, 680; to νυκτερίς, Ael. vi. 45. Uses ὀρίγανον as a remedy, Arist. H. A. ix. 6, 612, Ael. v. 46, Plin. viii. 27. How the bats (νυκτερίδες) render the Stork's eggs unfruitful, and how the Stork defeats them with a leaf of πλάτανος, Ael. i. 37, Geopon. xiii. 13, xv. 1, 18; according to Anatol. p. 298, a tortoise-bone is equally efficacious. A Stork's stomach is a specific for the murrain of sheep and goats, Geopon. xviii. 11; cf. Plin. xxix. 33.
A young Stork, a prophylactic against ophthalmia, Plin. xxix. 38.
A messenger of Athene (cf. ἐρωδιός), Porph. De Abst. iii. 5.
Story of Alcinoë, an unfaithful wife: Ael. viii. 20 τοῦτο συνιδὼν ὁ πελαργὸς ὁ οἰκέτης οὐχ ὑπέμεινεν, ἀλλὰ ἐτιμώρησε τῷ δεσπότῃ· προσπηδῶν γοῦν ἐπήρωσε τῆς ἀνθρώπου τὴν ὄψιν : cf. Apostol. xiv. 15, p. 609. Story of Heracleïs, to whom the Stork, healed of a broken leg, brought next year a magic pebble : ibid. viii. 22 τὴν δ' οὖν λίθον ἔνδον που κατέθετο, εἶτα νύκτωρ διυπνισθεῖσα ὁρᾷ αὐγήν τινα καὶ αἴγλην ἀφιεῖσαν, καὶ κατελάμπετο ὁ οἶκος ὡς ἐσκομισθείσης δᾳδός : cf. Dion. De Avib. i. 31. The stone was probably the stone λύχνις or λυχνίτης, cf. Plin. xxxvii. (17) 103, and Philostrat. V. Apoll. Tyan. ii. 14 πελαργοὶ καλιὰς οὐκ ἂν πήξαιντο, μὴ πρότερον αἰταῖς ἐναρμόσαντες τὸν λυχνίτην λίθον : cf. also Lucian, De Dea Syr. 32 ; Orph. Lith. 268.
Metempsychosis : Alex. Mynd. ap. Ael. iii. 23 ὅταν ἐς γῆρας ἀφίκωνται, παρελθόντας αὐτοὺς ἐς τὰς Ὠκεανίτιδας νήσους ἀμείβειν τὰ εἴδη ἐς ἀνθρώπου μορφήν, καὶ εὐσεβείας γε τῆς ἐς τοὺς γειναμένους ἆθλον τοῦτο ἴσχειν, ἄλλως τε, εἴ τι ἐγὼ νοῶ, καὶ ὑποθέσθαι τῶν θεῶν βουλομένων τοῦτο γοῦν τῶν ἀνθρώπων τῶν ἐκεῖθι τὸ γένος εὐσεβὲς καὶ ὅσιον, ἐπεὶ οὐχ οἷόν τε ἦν ἐν τῇ ἄλλῃ γῇ ἐφ' ἡλίῳ τοιοῦτον διαβιοῦν : cf. the story of the birds of Diomede (s. v. ἐρωδιός), and see for accounts of similar superstitions in recent times, Schwenk, Slav. Mythol. p. 129; cf. also August Marx, Griech. Märchen, pp. 50-55, Stuttgart, 1889.

ΠΕ'ΛΕΙΑ, s. πελειάς. Also πεληϊάς, Opp. Cyn. i. 351.

A **Pigeon** or **Dove**. The Epic word: used for περιστερά also by the Dorians (Sophron. ap. Athen. ix. 394 D), and by the Ionians (Hipp. 638. 8, 667. 3 : cf. Lat. *pal-umba*. Commonly said to be connected with πελός, πολιός, &c. ; cf. Hesych. πέλειαι· μέλαιναι περιστεραί, and Eustath. Hom. p. 1262 πέλεια δὲ οὐχ ἁπλῶς περιστερά, εἶδος δέ τι περιστερᾶς, ὡς ἡ λέξις ἐπιδηλοῖ· πελὸν γὰρ τὸ μελάνιζον, ἐξ οὗ καὶ ὁ πελαργός. Nevertheless, the derivation appears to me somewhat dubious; for all the wild pigeons, the Turtle-dove excepted, are very much of a colour, and I do not think the Greeks would have spoken of *black* pigeons until they had got

K

ΠΕΛΕΙΑ (*continued*).

white ones; cf. also Herod. ii. 55 μέλαιναι πελειάδες. Πέλεια seems lost as a current word in Mod. Gk.: it does not occur in Aristophanes, save in the Homeric parody in Ar. Av. 575.

In Hom. frequent; the only Homeric word for pigeon, save for the occurrence of φάσσα in the compound φασσοφόνος, Il. xv. 238. Usually with epithet τρήρων q.v., a word of equally doubtful etymology, the received derivation from τρέω appearing dubious in the light of such pigeon-names as τρυγών, turtur, תור, &c.; cf. πολυτρήρων (descriptive epithet of the towns Thisbe and Messe), Il. ii. 502, 582, and Lyc. 87, 423, where τρήρων=πέλεια: see also Eustath. Hom. Il. pp. 1262, 1712, Athen. xi. 490 D. A prey to ἴρηξ, Il. xxi. 493, to κίρκος, Il. xxii. 139; cf. Aesch. Pr. V. 858. Messengers of Zeus, when Rhea protected him from Cronos, Od. xii. 62 πέλειαι | τρήρωνες, ταί τ' ἀμβροσίην Διὶ πατρὶ φέρουσιν. As ornaments of Nestor's cup, Il. xi. 634 δοιαὶ δὲ πελειάδες ἀμφὶς ἕκαστον [οὔας] | χρύσειαι νεμέθοντο, cf. Athen. l. c. Captured in springes, Od. xxii. 468; cf. Dion. De Avib. iii. 12 (s. v. φάσσα). In Homer the pigeon is never spoken of as a domesticated bird, and is definitely a wild one in Il. xxi. 139, and Od. xxii. 468. Il. xxi. 495 suggests the Rock-dove, *C. livia*: ἢ ῥά θ' ὑφ' ἴρηκος κοίλην εἰσέπτατο πέτρην, | χηραμόν: cf. Q. Smyrn. xii. 12 ἴρηξ σεύε πέλειαν· ἐπειγομένη δ' ἄρα κείνη, | χηραμὸν ἐς πέτρης κατεδύσατο: cf. also Virg. Aen. v. 213.

In Aristotle distinguished from περιστερά: Η. Α. v. 13, 544 b ἕτερόν ἐστι περιστερὰ καὶ πελειάς· ἐλάττων μὲν οὖν ἡ πελειάς, τιθασσὸν δὲ γίνεται μᾶλλον ἡ περιστερά. ἡ δὲ πελειὰς καὶ μέλαν καὶ μικρὸν καὶ ἐρυθρόπουν καὶ τραχύπουν, διὸ καὶ οὐθεὶς τρέφει. [The contrary stated, Athen. ix. 394 C.] Ib. viii. 12, 597 b ἀπαίρουσι δὲ καὶ αἱ φάτται καὶ αἱ πελειάδες, καὶ οὐ χειμάζουσι, αἱ δὲ περιστεραὶ καταμένουσιν. According to Sundevall, πέλεια is here in Aristotle the Stock-dove, *C. oenas*, οἰνάς being the Rock-pigeon, *C. livia*, φάψ or φάττα, the Ring-dove, *C. palumbus*, and περιστερά, the Domestic Pigeon. Aubert and Wimmer, on the other hand, take οἰνάς as the Stock-dove, and leave πέλεια in doubt. For my part, I do not think the Stock-dove was recognized as a distinct species, but was included, as in Mod. Gk. (Erhard, Heldreich), under the name φάσσα with the Ring-dove. Excluding the Turtle-doves, there then only remain the wild Rock-pigeon (Mod. Gk. ἀγριοπεριστέρι) and the domestic variety; and I imagine that both οἰνάς (q.v.) and πέλεια refer, in Aristotle, to the wild Rock-pigeon, and περιστερά especially to the Tame Pigeon; cf. also Moeris (p. 405, ed. Koch, 1830) εἰωθάς, ἡ κατοικίδιος περιστερά, ἡ γὰρ ἀγρία, πελειάς. The account in Arist. H. A. v. 13 is corrupt and not to be too much depended on, especially in view of the discrepant quotation in Athenaeus. The chief difficulty in the whole interpretation is the passage H. A. viii. 12, where it is asserted that both φάτται and πελειάδες migrate and do not remain

ΠΕΛΕΙΑ (*continued*).

over the winter, whereas all the Pigeons occur more or less in Greece in winter-time, and it is in summer that the Ring-dove and Stock-dove, which breed elsewhere, are seldom found. The passage can hardly have been written in Attica; it would appear more consonant with the truth did we suppose it written, for instance, in Macedonia. Except in the doubtful case of Aristotle, πέλεια is in no sense a specific term: we have seen it applied in Homer to the Rock-pigeon, and on the other hand the πέλειαι in the Oak-woods of Dodona must have been either Ring-doves or Stock-doves (vide infra). In Opp. Cyn. i. 351, where pigeon-fanciers are said to cause the pigeons by a display of purple stuff to bring forth young of a like colour, πελῃάς and also τρήρων are used of tame pigeons.

On the Latin usage of columba, palumbes, &c., cf. W. W. Fowler, A Year with the Birds (3rd ed.), p. 218.

Various attributes.—Its timidity; Aesch. S. c. T. 292 πάντρομος [*al.* πάντροφος] πελειάς : Soph. Aj. 139 μέγαν ὄκνον ἔχω καὶ πεφόβημαι | πτηνῆς ὡς ὄμμα πελείας: Antip. Sid. xcii, Gk. Anth. ii. p. 33 δειλαί τοι δειλοῖσιν ἐφεδρήσουσι πέλειαι: cf. Varro, De R. R. iii. 7 nihil est timidius columba; Ovid, A. Amat. i. 117, ii. 363, &c., &c. Its swiftness: Soph. Oed. Col. 1081 ἀελλαία ταχυρρωστὸς πελειάς, cf. also Philoct. 289, 1146; Eur. Bacch. 1090 πελείας ὠκύτητ᾽ οὐχ ἥσσονες.

The Dove pursued by the Hawk or Eagle, a type of swiftness and of timidity: Il. xxi. 493, xxii. 139, Q. Smyrn. xii. 12; Aesch. Pr. V. 858 κίρκοι πελειῶν οὐ μακρὰν λελειμμένοι | ἥξουσι; Eurip. Andr. 1140 οἱ δ᾽ ὅπως πελειάδες | ἱέρακ᾽ ἰδοῦσαι πρὸς φυγὴν ἐνώτισαν: Ovid, Met. i. 507 sic aquilam penna fugiunt trepidante columbae; cf. ibid. v. 605, Trist. i. 1, 75; Virg. Ecl. ix. 11; Lucret. iii. 751; Phaedr. Fab. i. 31, 3, &c. Thus Medea comes to Jason, as a Dove seeking shelter from the Hawk, Val. Flacc. Argon. viii. 32.

The Dove in the clutches of the Eagle or Hawk, as an omen, Od. xx. 243, xv. 525, Sil. Ital. Pun. iv. 104; cf. Virg. Aen. xi. 721.

Hera and Athena, coming to the aid of the Argives, compared to Doves: Il. v. 778 αἱ δὲ βάτην, τρήρωσι πελειάσιν ἴθμαθ᾽ ὁμοῖαι. For various interpretations of this simile, see the Scholia, also Ameis and other commentators; but the allusion is probably neither to swiftness nor to dainty tread, but to the ancient and widespread prefigurement of the deity as a dove (cf. int. al., F. L. W. Schwartze, Urspr. d. Mythologie, p. 218); in the Homeric Delian Hymn, v. 114, Iris and Eileithyia βὰν δὲ ποσὶ τρήρωσι πελειάσιν ἴθμαθ᾽ ὁμοῖαι, with which cf. Ar. Av. 575 Ἶριν δέ γ᾽ Ὅμηρος ἔφασκ᾽ ἰκέλην εἶναι τρήρωνι πελείῃ, and Schol.

The story of the Dove bound by Achilles to the mast as a mark for the archers, Il. xxiii. 850 et seq.: it was shot by Meriones, ὕψι δ᾽ ἐπαὶ νεφέων εἶδε τρήρωνα πέλειαν, | τὴν ῥ᾽ ὅγε δινεύουσαν ὑπὸ πτέρυγος

ΠΕΛΕΙΑ (continued).

βάλε μέσσην: the same story transferred to Aeneas and Eurytion, Virg. Aen. v. 485-544.

On the pigeons that brought ambrosia to the infant Zeus, see Od. xii. 60; Moero Byz. ap. Athen. xi. 490 e; Ptolem. Hephaest. ap. Phot. i. p. 474.

The Dove that flew between the clashing rocks in the passage of the Hellespont: Apoll. Rh. ii. 328, ii. 557, &c., and Schol. οἰωνῷ δὴ πρόσθε πελειάδι πειρήσασθε | νηὸς ἀποπρὸ μεθέντες ἐφίεμεν· . . . ἄκρα δ' ἔκοψαν | οὐραῖα πτερὰ ταίγε πελειάδος· ἡ δ' ἀπόρουσεν | ἀσκηθής: see also Apollod. i. 9, 22, Hygin. Fab. xix, Propert. ii. 26, 39 cum rudis Argûs Dux erat ignoto missa columba mari, &c.; cf. the account of the Πλαγκταὶ πέτραι or Cyanean rocks, Od. xii. 62 τῇ μέν τ' οὐδὲ ποτητὰ παρέρχεται, οὐδὲ πέλειαι | τρήρωνες, ταί τ' ἀμβροσίην Διὶ πατρὶ φέρουσιν: cf. Plut. ii. 156 F. The Dove in the story of the Argonauts again, in connexion with the fire-breathing bulls, Apoll. Rh. iii. 541 τρήρων μὲν φεύγουσα βίην κίρκοιο πελειάς, | ὑψόθεν Αἰσονιδέῳ πεφοβημένη ἔμπεσε κόλποις.

In the above legends there are numerous traces of the mythical astronomy of the Pleiads. This view is a very ancient one; cf. Athen. xi. 490 E πρώτη δὲ Μοιρὼ ἡ Βυζαντία καλῶς ἐδέξατο τὸν νοῦν τῶν Ὁμήρου ποιημάτων, ἐν τῇ Μνημοσύνῃ ἐπιγραφομένῃ φάσκουσα τὴν ἀμβροσίαν τῷ Διὶ τὰς Πλειάδας κομίζειν. Κράτης δὲ ὁ κριτικὸς σφετερισάμενος αὐτῆς τὴν δόξαν, ὡς ἴδιον ἐκφέρει τὸν λόγον. Cf. Moero, ibi cit., in the story of the Infant Jove, ὡς δ' αὔτως τρήρωσι πελειάσιν ὤπασε τιμήν, | αἱ δή τοι θέρεος καὶ χείματος ἄγγελοί εἰσιν: also many references, ap. Athen. l. c., from Pindar, Simonides, Simmias, Lamprocles, &c., where the πλειάδες are called πελειάδες: e. g. Lampr. (p. 554 Bergk) αἵτε ποταναῖς ὁμώνυμοι πελειάσιν αἰθέρι κεῖσθε. The Pleiads are also supposed to be alluded to in Alcman, fr. 23 (Bergk) ταὶ πελειάδες γὰρ ἁμίν | Ὀρθίᾳ φᾶρος φεροίσαις, νύκτα δι' ἀμβροσίαν ἅτε σείριον | ἄστρον ἀνειρομέναι μάχονται.

The coincidences on which rests the foundation for an astronomical interpretation of the above myths are chiefly the following. As has been mentioned above, s. v. **ἀλκυών**, the sun rose together with the Pleiads in the sign of the Bull, at the vernal equinox, the ancient opening of the year. If the Cretan Jupiter was a Sun-god, he might be said to be nursed by the π[ε]λειάδες: the sign Taurus may have been the Cretan Bull; and a transit through that sign may have been the celestial Βόσπορος of the Argonautic voyage. The Dove as an attribute of Venus is similarly explained, the *domus Veneris* being in the sign Taurus, the sign of the Pleiad.

The Doves of Nestor's cup, Il. xvi. 634, are also supposed to have reference to the Pleiades, Athen. xi. 490-492.

On the Dove of Deucalion: cf. Plut. Mor. 968, 1185. On the dove in

ΠΕΛΕΙΑ (continued).

the Chaldaean deluge-myth, cf. Euseb. Chron. Armen. i. p. 50, &c., &c.; see also the representation on coins of Apamea, Eckhel, Doctr. Numm. iii. 132, Friedländer, Kgl. Münzkab. pl. ix, &c., &c.
A similar explanation is given of the Dove of the deluge-myth. The Pleiades (as doves?) fleeing before the hunter Orion, Hes. Op. et D. 619.
For references to the copious (and often unreliable) literature of Pleiad-symbolism. see int. al., Pluche, Hist. du ciel, Dupuis, Orig. de tous les cultes, Haliburton, New Materials for the Hist. of Man, 1863, von Bunsen, Plejaden und Thierkreis, 1879, Nitzsch in Od. v. 272, &c., &c.
How the soul of Ctesylla departed as a dove; Nicand. ap. Anton. Lib. i; cf. Ovid, Met. vii. 370.

The Pigeons of Dodona. Herod. ii. 55 τάδε δὲ Δωδωναίων φασὶ αἱ προμάντιες, δύο πελειάδας μελαίνας ἐκ Θηβέων τῶν Αἰγυπτιέων ἀναπταμένας, τὴν μὲν αὐτέων ἐς Λιβύην, τὴν δὲ παρὰ σφέας ἀπικέσθαι· ἱζομένην δέ μιν ἐπὶ φηγόν, αὐδάξασθαι φωνῇ ἀνθρωπηίῃ, ὡς χρεὼν εἴη μαντήϊον αὐτόθι Διὸς γενέσθαι. Ibid. 57 πελειάδες δέ μοι δοκέουσι κληθῆναι πρὸς Δωδωναίων ἐπὶ τοῦδε αἱ γυναῖκες, διότι βάρβαροι ἦσαν· ἐδόκεον δέ σφι ὁμοίως ὄρνισι φθέγγεσθαι... μέλαιναν δὲ λέγοντες εἶναι τὴν πελειάδα σημαίνουσι ὅτι Αἰγυπτίη ἡ γυνὴ ἦν. Cf. Pausan. vii. 21, x. 12. On Alexander and the doves at Ammon, cf. Curtius, iv. c. 7, Strabo, xvii. See also J. Arneth. Ueber das Taubenorakel von Dodona, Wien, 1841; Perthes, Die Peleiaden von Dodona, Progr. d. Progymn. zu Mörs, 1869; H. D. Müller, Philol. Anz. ii. p. 95, 1870; Lorenz, op. cit., p. 35; Creuzer. Symb. iii. pp. 183, 217.

According to Thrasybulus and Acestodorus, ap. Schol. Il. xvi. 233, a dove had founded the oracle in the time of Deucalion. On the pigeons of Dodona, see also Soph. Tr. 171 ὡς τὴν παλαιὰν φηγὸν αὐδῆσαί ποτε | Δωδῶνι δισσῶν ἐκ πελειάδων ἔφη : also ap. Schol. Pind. fr. Paean. 58 (30); Diod. i. 13, iii. 71; Sil. Ital. iii. 678; Serv. in Aen. iii. 466, Ecl. ix. 13. According to Strabo, ap. Eustath. in Od., p. 1760, and Geogr. vii. fr. 1a the priestesses were called πελειομάντεις, cf. κορακομάντεις. According to Philostr. Imagg. ii. 33 (387 k), a choir of priestesses danced round an oak, on which sat a golden dove. Dion. Halic. Ant. Rom. i. 14, 4f compares with the Dodonaean dove the πίκος or δρυοκολάπτης of the oracle of Mars. The whole story is intricate and confused. It seems clear that the priestesses were called πέλειαι (cf. Paley, Aesch. Suppl. ed. 2, p. xiv) or πελειομάντεις; and also that the oracle was not essentially an augury or bird-oracle, but one in which tree-worship, river-worship (cf. Macrob. v. 18), and thunder-worship (cf. Mommsen, Gr. Jahresz. p. 432, &c.) were alike involved. The doves of Dodona link on to the story of Deucalion, to the doves

ΠΕΛΕΙΑ (*continued*).

that fed the infant Zeus, to the dove in other Zeus-myths (cf. Athen. ix. 395 a, Ael. V. H. i. 15) and to the doves of Dione. If we seek to get further back, we enter the mist of Pleiad-symbolism.

It has been suggested by Landseer, Sabaean Researches, p. 186, from the study of an Assyrian symbolic monument, that the stars which Conon converted into the Coma Berenices (Hygin. P. A. ii. 24, cf. Ideler, Sternnamen, p. 295) and which lie in Leo opposite to the Pleiades in Taurus, were originally constellated as a Dove; and that this constellation, whose first stars rise with the latest of those of Argo, and whose last rise simultaneously with the hand of the Husbandman, links better than the Pleiad into the astronomical Deluge-myth. The case rests on very little evidence, and indeed is an illustration of the conflicting difficulties of such hypotheses: but it is deserving of investigation were it only for the reason that the Coma Berenices contains seven visible stars (Hygin.), and the Pleiad six, a faint hint at a possible explanation of the lost Pleiad.

πελειοθρέμμων, an epithet of Salamis (according to the Schol. and Hesych., but see Paley and other commentators), Aesch. Pers. 309; cf. πολυτρήρων (s. v. τρήρων); also the *Insula Columbaria*, Plin. iii. (6) 12.

Proverb.—ἠμένη πελειάς, a 'pigeon,' a simpleton: Eustath. Hom. p. 1333 παροιμία ἐπὶ τῶν ἁπλουστάτων τὸ ἠμένη πελειὰς διὰ τὸ εὔηθες τοῦ ζῴου: Suid., Hesych., Phot., &c.

In preparing this article on πέλεια, and the other cognate articles on the various Pigeon-names, I have drawn much from the learned pamphlet of Dr. Lorentz, Die Taube im Alterthume, Wurzen, 1886, as well as from the earlier compilation of Hehn, in his Culturpflanzen und Hausthiere.

ΠΕΛΕΙΑ'Σ ΧΛΩΡΟ'ΠΤΙΛΟΣ. An Indian Green **Fruit-Pigeon**, probably *Crocopus chlorogaster*, Blyth, cf. Val. Ball, Ind. Antiq., xiv. p. 303, 1885.

Ael. xvi. 2 φαίη τις ἂν πρῶτον θεασάμενος, καὶ οὐκ ἔχων ἐπιστήμην ὀρνιθογνώμονα σίττακον εἶναι καὶ οὐ πελειάδα. χείλη δὲ ἔχουσι καὶ σκέλη τοῖς "Ελλησι πέρδιξι τὴν χρόαν προσεοικότα.

ΠΕΛΕΚΑ'Ν. The **Pelican**, *Pelecanus crispus*, Bruch., and *P. onocrotalus*, L., which latter is rare in Greece (Von der Mühle). Mod. Gk. πελεκάνι (Von der M.), σακκάς (Turk. a water-carrier), τυμπανιᾶς. *Onocrotalus*, Plin. x. 47 (66). Vide s. vv. βαίβυκος, βαιήθ.

Arist. H. A. viii. 12, 597 οἱ πελεκᾶνες δ' ἐκτοπίζουσι, καὶ πέτονται ἀπὸ τοῦ Στρυμόνος ποταμοῦ ἐπὶ τὸν Ἴστρον, κἀκεῖ τεκνοποιοῦνται· ἀθρόοι δ' ἀπέρχονται, ἀναμένοντες οἱ πρότεροι τοὺς ὕστερον, διὰ τὸ ὅταν ὑπερπτῶνται τὸ

ΠΕΛΕΚΑΝ (continued).

ὄρος ἀδήλους γίνεσθαι τοὺς προτέρους τοῖς ὑστέροις. Ib. 597 b ὄρνις ἀγελαῖος, like the crane, the swan, and the little goose. Ib. ix. 10, 614 b οἱ δὲ πελεκᾶνες οἱ ἐν τοῖς ποταμοῖς γινόμενοι καταπίνουσι τὰς μεγάλας κόγχας καὶ λείας· ὅταν δ' ἐν τῷ πρὸ τῆς κοιλίας τόπῳ πέψωσιν, ἐξεμοῦσιν, ἵνα χασκουσῶν τὰ κρέα ἐξαιροῦντες ἐσθίωσιν. A similar account in Arist. De Mirab. 14, 831 b; Antig. Hist. Mirab. 41 (47); Ael. iii. 20, 23, v. 35; Apostol. Cent. 15; Phile, De An. (9), 215; Dion. De Avib. ii. 6 καί τις κόλπος αὐτοῖς ἐξήρτηται πρὸ τῶν στέρνων, εἰς ὃν ἅπασαν τὴν τροφὴν ἐπειγόμενοι τέως ἐμβάλλουσιν, οὔτε τῶν κτενῶν οὔτε τῶν σκληρῶν μυῶν ἀπεχόμενοι, κ. τ. λ.: cf. Plin. x. 47 (66) faucibus ipsis inest alterius uteri genus. That the Pelican can render up its food from its 'pouch' was much commented on by the ancients: hence the Hebr. name *kaath*, lit. 'to vomit.' But the Pelican feeds on fish, not (?) on shell-fish: and moreover *P. crispus* is common in Greece and is not limited to the north. Hence various writers have doubted the common interpretation, e. g. Gesner, Brandt (Descr. Animal. Rusticorum, 1836, p. 53), Van der Hoeven (Handb. d. Zool., ii. p. 396) and especially Aubert and Wimmer (op. cit., i. p. 104), who suppose a species of Heron to be meant. But the passage in Dionysius (s. v. πελεκῖνος) is only applicable to the Pelican, and the latter is distinguished from ἐρωδιός in Ael. v. 35, Phile, c. ix, &c.; the Heron and the Pelican seem however to be confounded by Plutarch, l. c.

Cicero (De Nat. D. ii. (49) 124) repeats the story under the name *Platalea*, and Plin. (x. (40) 56) under that of *Platea*, names which rather suggest the *Spoonbill*, to which the account may have been transferred, the Pelican not occurring in Italy (Gallia hos septentrionali proxima Oceano reddit, Plin. x. 47).

The Pelican and its 'piety,' Ael. iii. 23. Cf. Horap. i. 54 πελεκᾶνα δὲ γράφοντες, ἄνουν τε ἤδη καὶ ἄφρονα σημαίνουσιν· ἐπειδὴ δυνάμενος ἐν τοῖς ὑψηλοτέροις τόποις κατατίθεσθαι τὰ ἑαυτοῦ ᾠά, ὥσπερ καὶ τὰ λοιπὰ τῶν πετεηνῶν, τοῦτο οὐ ποιεῖ· ἀλλὰ γὰρ καὶ ἀνορύξας γῆν, ἐκεῖ κατατίθεται τὰ γεννώμενα· ὅπερ ἐπιγνόντες ἄνθρωποι, τῷ τόπῳ βοὸς ἀφόδευμα ξηρὸν περιτιθέασιν, ᾧ καὶ πῦρ ὑποβάλλουσι· θεασάμενος δὲ ὁ πελεκὰν τὸν καπνόν, τοῖς ἰδίοις πτεροῖς βουλόμενος ἀποσβέσαι τὸ πῦρ, ἐκ τῶν ἐναντίων κατὰ τὴν κίνησιν ἐξάπτει αὐτό. ὑφ' οὗ κατακαιόμενος τὰ ἑαυτοῦ πτερὰ εὐσυλληπτότερος τοῖς κυνηγοῖς γίνεται· δι' ἣν αἰτίαν οὐκ ἐνομίσθη ἐσθίειν τοὺς ἱερέας αὐτόν, ἐπειδὴ ἁπαξαπλῶς ὑπὲρ τέκνων ποιεῖται τὸν ἀγῶνα· Αἰγυπτίων δὲ οἱ λοιποὶ ἐσθίουσι, λέγοντες, ὅτι μὴ κατὰ νοῦν τὴν μάχην, ὥσπερ οἱ χηναλώπεκες, ἀλλὰ κατὰ ἄνοιαν ὁ πελεκὰν ποιεῖται. This statement follows an account of the parental affection of χηναλώπηξ; Lauth (Sitzungsb. Bayer. Akad., 1876, p. 105) shows that it is in part based on a confusion between two Egyptian words, *chemi*, 'a pelican,' and *chemi*, 'ignorant.' The parental affection of the Pelican is frequently referred to by the Fathers: cf.

ΠΕΛΕΚΑΝ (*continued*).

Epiphan. (ad Physiol. c. xx) Hexaem. c. viii ἔστι γὰρ ἡ πελεκὰν φιλότεκνον ὄρνεον παρὰ πάντα τὰ ὄρνεα· ἡ δὲ θήλεια καθέζεται ἐν τῇ νεοττίᾳ φυλάσσουσα τὰ τέκνα, καὶ περιθάλπει αὐτὰ ἀσπαζομένη, καὶ κολαφίζουσα ἐν φιλήματι ὁπὰς ταῖς πλευραῖς κατεργάζεται, καὶ τελευτῶσι· καὶ μεθ' ἡμέρας τρεῖς παραγενομένου τοῦ ἄρρενος πελεκάνος, καὶ εὑρίσκοντος αὐτὰ τεθνηκότα ὀλοφύρεται τὴν καρδίαν λίαν· πεπληγμένος δὲ τοῦ πόνου κολαφίζει τὴν ἰδίαν πλευράν, καὶ ὁπὰς αὐτῇ ἐμποιεῖ, καὶ καταρρεῖ αἷμα ἐπιστάζων ἐπὶ τὰς πληγὰς τῶν τεθνηκότων νεοσσῶν, καὶ οὕτως ζωοποιοῦνται: cf. also Ps.-Hieron. ad Praes. de Cer. Pasch. v. p. 149 (ed. 1693), Isid. Orig. xii. c. 7, Glycas, Annal. i. p. 44, S. August. in Ps. cii, &c., &c. A confusion with certain Woodpecker-myths (cf. πελεκᾶς) may be one of the various sources of these corrupt but popular stories.

ΠΕΛΕΚΑ͂Σ, *s.* πελεκάν. A **Woodpecker**. Mod. Gk. πελεκάνος, δενδροφάγος, τσικλιδάρα. Vide s. vv. **δρυοκολάπτης, κελεός, σπέλεκτος**.

Mentioned Ar. Av. 882, 1155 et seq. Cf. s. v. πελεκάν, Arist. H. A. ix. 10, 614 b οἱ δὲ πελεκᾶνες οἱ ἐν τοῖς ποταμοῖς, as indicating that the same word applied to the two different birds. Cf. Suid. (verb. q. del. Gaisford), ἔστι δὲ εἶδος ὀρνέου, τρυποῦν τὰ δένδρα, ἀφ' οὗ καὶ δενδροκολάπτης καλεῖται: also Hesych, s. v. πελεκάν.

In the version of the Itylus-myth, given by Boios ap. Anton. Lib. c. xi, Polytechnus, the husband of Aëdon, is metamorphosed into the bird πελεκάν, the brother of Aëdon being transmuted at the same time into ἔποψ. With the stories of the Woodpecker breaking open confined places, referred to above, s. vv. **δρυοκολάπτης** and **ἔποψ**, under the heading of the 'Samir-legend,' cf. the myth of Διόνυσος πέλεκυς (R. Brown, Dionysiac Myth, i. p. 332, ii. p. 81).

Hostile to ὄρτυξ, Ael. vi. 45, Phile, De An. 684: this statement is generally referred to the Pelican, but it more probably refers to the Woodpecker, that bird and the Quail being both alike associated with solar myths.

ΠΕΛΕΚΙ͂ΝΟΣ.

In Dion. De Avib. ii. 6, and probably therefore also in Ar. Av. 882, a **Pelican**.

ΠΕΛΗΑ'Ρ· περιστερᾶς καὶ περσικῆς τὸ ἥμισυ· Λάκωνες. Hesych. (verb. dub.: cf. Schmidt in Hesych.).

ΠΕ'ΛΛΟΣ. The **Heron**.

Arist. H. A. ix. 1, 609 b ὁ πέλλος χαλεπῶς εὐνάζεται καὶ ὀχεύει· κράζει τε γὰρ καὶ αἷμα, ὥς φασιν, ἀφίησιν ἐκ τῶν ὀφθαλμῶν ὀχείων, καὶ τίκτει φαύλως καὶ ὀδυνηρῶς. πολεμεῖ δὲ τοῖς βλάπτουσιν, ἀετῷ—ἁρπάζει γὰρ αὐτόν—καὶ ἀλώπεκι—φθείρει γὰρ αὐτὸν τῆς νυκτός—καὶ κορύδῳ—τὰ γὰρ ᾠὰ αὐτοῦ κλέπτει. Ibid. ix. 18, 616 b εὐμήχανος δὲ καὶ δειπνοφόρος καὶ ἔπαγρος,

ΠΕΛΕΚΑΝ—ΠΕΡΔΙΞ

ΠΕΛΛΟΣ (*continued*).

ἐργάζεται δὲ τὴν ἡμέραν. τὴν μέντοι χρόαν ἔχει φαύλην καὶ τὴν κοιλίαν ἀεὶ ὑγράν. Cf. Plin. x. (60) 79.

In Il. x. 275, there is an alternative reading πέλλον 'Αθηναίη, vide s. v. ἐρωδιός.

ΠΕΡΓΟΥ˜ΛΟΝ· ὀρνιθάριον 'Αργειλέγω [?'Αργεῖοι λέγουσι] Hesych. Cf. σπέργουλος. Vide s. vv. σποργίλος, στρουθός.

ΠΕΡΔΙΚΟΘΗ'ΡΑΣ. A specific appellation of a Hawk, sacred to Apollo; Ael. xii. 4.

ΠΕ'ΡΔΙΞ. (On the quantity of the ι, vide Athen. ix. 41, 388, and Soph. fr. 300, ibi cit.).

A **Partridge** (Etym. dub.) Mod. Gk. πέρδικα. Dim. περδικιδεύς. Eust. 753, 56; περδίκιον, Eubul. Inc. 14, Ephipp. Obeliaph. ap. Athen. ix. 359 b, &c. The species commonly referred to is *Perdix graeca* = *P. saxatilis*, auctt., the Common Partridge, *P. cinerea*, being distinguished from it chiefly by its note.

Arist. H. A. iv. 9, 536 B οἱ μὲν κακκαβίζουσιν, οἱ δὲ τρίζουσιν. *P. graeca* cries *cacabis*, *P. cinerea* on the other hand *girrah* or *ripipri*. The latter bird, our common Partridge, is now confined to the north of Greece. Cf. Athen. ix. 390 a, b : Theophr. ap. Athen. l. c. οἱ 'Αθήνησι ἐπὶ τάδε πέρδικες τοῦ Κοριδάλλου [a village on the road to Boeotia] πρὸς τὸ ἄστυ κακκαβίζουσιν, οἱ δ' ἐπέκεινα τιττυβίζουσιν; cf. Plin. x. (29) 41 Perdices non transvolant Boeotiae fines in Atticam ; Solin. vii. 23. Athen. ibid. τῶν δὲ περδίκων ἐστὶν ἕτερον γένος ἐν 'Ιταλίᾳ ἀμαυρὸν τῇ πτερώσει καὶ μικρότερον τῇ ἕξει, τὸ ῥύγχος οὐχὶ κινναβάρινον ἔχον: this seems to be again the common Partridge. The red legs of the Greek Partridge, Ael. xvi. 2 ; vide s.v. πελειὰς χλωρόπτιλος. Cf. Ael. iii. 35 ; Antig. H. Mirab., vi. See also s. vv. ἄμαλλος, κακκάβη, πῆριξ, σισίλαρος, συροπέρδιξ.

Description.—An epitomized account, mostly after Arist. (fr. 270), in Athen. ix. 389; χερσαῖος, σχιδανόπους, κονιστικός (H. A. ix. 498, 633 b), ζῇ δὲ ἔτη πεντεκαίδεκα (ib. ix. 7, 613 ; sixteen years, ib. vi. 4, 563), ἡ δὲ θήλεια καὶ πλείονα. ὅταν δὲ γνῷ ὅτι θηρεύεται, προελθὼν τῆς νεοττίας κυλινδεῖται παρὰ τὰ σκέλη τοῦ θηρεύοντος (H. A. ix. 8, 613 b, Ael. iii. 16, Plut. ii. 992 B, Antig. H. Mirab. 39 (45), Plin. x. (33) 51 ; cf. verb. ἐκπερδικίσαι, Ar. Av. 768, and Schol. ; also διαπερδικίζειν, Meineke, Com. Fr. iv. 634). In Ar. Av. 1292 πέρδιξ μὲν εἰς κάπηλος ὠνομάζετο | χωλός, the allusion is rather to its supposed habit of feigning lameness, than merely, in a general way, to the bird as a proverbial deceiver; cf. Prov. πέρδικος σκέλος, ap. Schol. κακοήθης καὶ πανοῦργος (H. A. ix. 8, 613, 614), πρωλοβος, στόμαχος, ἀποφυάδες, H. A. ii. 17, 508, 509. οὐ μόνον ᾄδει ἀλλὰ

ΠΕΡΔΙΞ *(continued).*

καὶ τριγμὸν ἀφίησι καὶ ἄλλας φωνάς, Η. Α. ix. 8, 614; cf. Plut. ii. 727 D. μεταβάλλει τὸ χρῶμα, De Color. 6. 798; albino variety, De Gen. v. 785 b. ὄσφρησιν δόκει ἔχειν ἐπίδηλον, H. A. vi. 2, 560 b, cf. De Gen. iii. 1, 751. κοχλίας ἐσθίει, H. A. ix. 37, 621, Athen. ix. 390 c (οἱ ἐν Σκιάθῳ), and how the snails (οἱ καλ. ἀρείονες) to elude them leave their shells behind, Ael. x. 5. ὁ ἡγεμὼν τῶν ἀγρίων, οἱ χῆροι, Athen. l. c., Arist. H. A. ix. 8, 614.

Nest and Breeding Habits.—Lays ten to sixteen eggs (Arist. H. A. ix. 8, 613 b, cf. Ael. x. 15) which are white (H. A. vi. 2, 559); ὑπηνέμια (Ib. 560). Nest: H. A. ix. 8, 613 b οὐ ποιοῦνται νεοττίαν. ἀλλ' ὅταν ποιήσωνται ἐν τῷ λείῳ κόνιστραν, ἐπηλυγασάμενοι ἄκανθάν τινα καὶ ὕλην τῆς περὶ τοὺς ἱέρακας ἕνεκα καὶ τοὺς ἀετοὺς ἀλεώρας, ἐνταῦθα τίκτουσι καὶ ἐπῳάζουσιν: cf. Ael. iii. 16, x. 15; Plin. x. (33) 51; Ovid, Met. viii. 258. Arist. H. A. vi. 8, 564 δύο ποιοῦνται τῶν ᾠῶν σηκούς, καὶ ἐφ' ᾧ μὲν ἡ θήλεια ἐπὶ δὲ θατέρῳ ὁ ἄρρην ἐπῳάζει, καὶ ἐκλέψας ἐκπέμπει ἑκάτερος ἑκάτερα: cf. Athen. l. c., Antig. H. Mirab. 101 (110). Hence, perhaps, the allusion in Ar. Av. 767 πέρδιξ γενέσθω, τοῦ πατρὸς νεοττίον: cf. also Phryn. ap. Athen. ix. 389 a τὸν Κλεόμβροτόν τε τοῦ | πέρδικος υἱόν. Dion. De Avib. i. 11 δολερὸν τὸ γένος ἐστίν, ὡς καὶ τοὺς νεοττοὺς γινώσκειν ὅπως ἄνδρα χρὴ προσιόντα ἐξαπατᾶν, φύλλοις ἢ βώλοις καλυψαμένους. Cf. Plut. De Solert. An. p. 971.

Its salacity. De Gen. ii. 746 b, iii. 749 b, Ael. iv. 1, vii. 19, &c., &c. διὸ καὶ τὰ ᾠὰ τῆς θηλείας συντρίβει ἵνα ἀπολαύῃ τῶν ἀφροδισίων: Arist. ap. Athen. l. c., Ael. iii. 5. (With this and similar fables, cf. Jerem. xvii. 11). μάχονται δὲ οἱ χῆροι αὐτῶν πρὸς ἀλλήλους καὶ ὁ ἡττηθεὶς ὀχεύεται ὑπὸ τοῦ νικήσαντος, Athen. l. c., Plin. l. c. ὀχεύουσι δὲ καὶ οἱ τιθασοὶ τοὺς ἀγρίους· γίνεται δὲ τοῦτο κατά τινα ὥραν τοῦ ἔτους, Alex. Mynd. ap. Athen. l. c. τοὺς νεοττοὺς ὀχεύουσι, H. A. vi. 8, 564. ἂν κατὰ ἄνεμον στῶσιν αἱ θήλειαι τῶν ἀρρένων, ἔγκυοι γίνονται· πολλάκις δὲ καὶ τῆς φωνῆς (ἀκούσασαι), ἐὰν ὀργῶσαι τύχωσι, καὶ ὑπερπετομένων ἐκ τοῦ καταπνεῖσαι τὸν ἄρρενα· χάσκει δὲ καὶ ἡ θήλεια καὶ ὁ ἄρρην, καὶ τὴν γλῶτταν ἔξω ἔχουσι περὶ τὴν τῆς ὀχείας ποίησιν, H. A. v. 5, 541; cf. De Gen. iii. 1, 751, Ael. xvii. 15, Antig. H. Mirab. 81 (87), Athen. l. c., Plin. l. c., &c.

Bastards, ἐκ πέρδικος καὶ ἀλεκτρυόνος, De Gen. ii. 738 b.

How the young chip the shell, ὥσπερ θυροκοποῦντες, and are independent from the first: Ael. iv. 12.

Capture and Domestication.—Decoy partridges, Arist. H. A. ix. 8, 614, vi. 2, 560 b, Ael. iv. 16, Xen. Mem. ii. 1. 4. Various modes of capture, Dion. De Avib. iii. 7; cf. Simm. Rh. iv, Gk. Anthol. i. p. 137 ἀγρότα πέρδιξ | οὐκέτι θηρεύσεις βαλίους συννομήλικας. Epitaph on a tame partridge, Agath. lxxxv, Gk. Anthol. iv. 35 τλῆμων σκοπέλων μετανάστρια πέρδιξ (also others by Democharis, &c.).

The sport of partridge-fighting (still practised in the Greek Islands), and how the females are kept at hand to stimulate the courage of the

ΠΕΡΔΙΞ (*continued*).

combatants, Ael. iv. 1. How the Cirrhaean (Phocian) Partridges, which can neither fight nor sing, deliberately starve themselves in order to be unfit for food also : but the singing and fighting birds deliver themselves up rather than be slain : Ael. iv. 13; cf. Athen. ix. 390. An Egyptian dwarf who imitated partridges in their cages, Philostorg. x. 11 (cf. J. E. B. Mayor in Juv. viii. 33).

The Partridge as food, Mart. Ep. iii. 58, 15, xiii. 65, 76, &c.

Myth and Legend.—(Besides the stories already told under the head of *Breeding-habits*, supra).

On πέρδικες in the wars of the Cranes and Pygmies ; Basilis and Menecles, ap. Athen. ix. 390 b.

An evil omen : Σάμιοι πλεύσαντες εἰς Σύβαριν καὶ κατασχόντες τὴν Σιρῖτιν χώραν, περδίκων ἀναπτάντων καὶ ποιησάντων ψόφον, ἐκπλαγέντες ἔφυγον, καὶ ἐμβάντες εἰς τὰς ναῦς ἀνέπλευσαν, Heges. ap. Athen. xiv. 656 c.

A fabled metamorphosis of Perdix, son of Daedalus, Hygin. Fab. 274, Ovid, Met. viii. 236-260. This subject is discussed in a curious essay by Gerland, Ueber die Perdixsage, Halle a. S., 1871. The writer identifies Perdix with the Lapwing.

Sacred to Zeus and Latona, Ael. x. 35.

δύο ἔχουσι καρδίας, Theophr. ap. Athen. l. c., Ael. x. 35 (in Paphlagonia ; cf. Plin. xi. 70).

Hostile to χελώνη, Ael. iv. 5, and to ἐχῖνος ὁ ποταμογείτων, Phile, 678. Friendly to ἔλαφος (hence a stag's head used as a decoy), Dion. De Avib. i. 11 ; to φάττα, Ael. v. 48.

Use κάλαμος as a remedy, Ael. i. 35, Phile, 723, Geopon. xv. 1 ; also ὀρίγανον, Ael. v. 46, or a leaf of laurel, Plin. viii. 27, or the herb variously known as perdicium, helxine, sideritis or parthenium, Plin. xxi. (16) 62; xxii. (17) 19.

Proverbial expressions. πέρδικος σκέλος, πέρδικος υἱός, &c. vide supra. Archil. 95, ap. Athen. ix. 388 f. πτώσσουσαν ὥστε πέρδικα : with which cf. Ar. Vesp. 1490, &c., s. v. ἀλεκτρυών. Pherecr. ap. Athen. l. c. ἡ τοῦ πεποιηκότος τὸν Χειρῶνα | ἔξεισιν ἄκων δεῦρο πέρδικος τρόπον.

ΠΕΡΙΣΤΕΡΑ'. Etym. dub. According to Benfey (ii. 106) from Sk. *prî*, 'to love'; a derivation not much more convincing than the old ὅτι περισσῶς ἐρᾷ (Schol. Apoll. Rh. iii. 549). Hehn (Wandering of Plants, &c., Eng. ed. p. 484), and others compare O. Slav. *pero*, 'a feather,' *prati, pariti*, 'to fly.'

Other forms are περιστερίς, Galen, vi. 708 (ed. Kühn) ; περιστερός, Pherecr. Γρα. 2 (2. 266), Alexid. Συντρεχ. 2 (3. 481) ap. Athen. ix. 395 a, b ; Eustath. Hom. p. 1712 ; a form censured by Lucian, Soloec. 7 ; cf. Lat. *columbus*, Varro, De L. L. ix. 38. Dim.

ΠΕΡΙΣΤΕΡΑ (continued).

περιστεριδεύς, Schol. Ar. Ach. 866, Eust. 753, Suid.; **περιστερίδιον**, LXX. Lev. i. 14, Athen. xiv. 654 a; **περιστέριον**, Pherecr. Πεταλ. 2 (2. 322), Phryn. Com. Τραγῳδ. 4 (2. 599) ap. Athen. ix. 395 c, xiv. 654 b, &c. (vide Meineke).

A **Pigeon**. See also s. vv. **οἰνάς, πέλεια, πυραλλίς, τρυγών, φάσσα, φάψ**.

First mentioned in Charon ap. Athen. ix. 394 c, and Herod. i. 138; in Attic, first in Sophocles, then in the Comic Poets and Plato.

Description.—ὄρνις ἀγελαῖος, Arist. H. A. i. 1, 488; τὸ σῶμα ὀγκῶδες, De Gen. iii. 1, 749 b; καρποφαγεῖ καὶ ποηφαγεῖ, H. A. viii. 3, 593. οὐκ ἀνακύπτει πίνουσα, H. A. ix. 7, 613. Blinks with both eyelids, De Part. An. ii. 12, 657, Plin. xi. (37) 57. καὶ κονίονται καὶ λοῦνται, Arist. H. A. ix. 49 B, 633 b; does not migrate, Ib. viii. 3, 593, 597 b. Lives to eight years old (when blinded as a decoy) Ib. ix. 7, 613, Plin. x. (35) 52. Is the prey of hawks, φασὶ τὰς περιστερὰς γινώσκειν ἕκαστον τῶν γενῶν [τῶν ἱεράκων], Arist. H. A. ix. 36, 620, Ael. v. 50, &c., &c. Its coo, J. Poll. v. 13 εἴποις ἂν περιστερὰς γογγύζειν.

How pigeons purge themselves with the herb *helxine*, Plin. viii. (27) 41, cf. Diosc. iv. 39, 86; feed greedily on περιστερεών or περιστέριον (verbena), Plin. xxv (10) 78, Diosc. iv. 60, Nic. Ther. 860 and Schol.; and on the white seeds of *Helioscopium*, Plin. xxvi. (8) 42.

Captured by nets (ἐπισπάστροις) or more easily by springes (βρόχοις), Dion. De Avib. iii. 12.

Anatomical particulars.—Arist. H. A. ii. 15, 506 μικρὸν ἔχει τὸν σπλῆνα, ὥστε λανθάνειν ὀλίγου τὴν αἴσθησιν. Ib. 506 b τὴν χολὴν ἔχει πρὸς τοῖς ἐντέροις, cf. Plin. xi. 37 (74). Said to lack gall, Horap. i. 57; see also Clem. Alex., Paedag. i. 15, Isidor. Orig. xii. 7, 61, and many mediaeval naturalists and poets, e. g. Walther v. d. Vogelw. xix. 13 rôs âne dorn, ein tûbe sunder gallen; cf. Hamlet, ii. 2. Galen, De Atra Bile 9, states correctly that the Pigeon possesses gall and merely lacks τὴν ἐπὶ τῷ ἥπατι κύστιν. Arist. H. A. ii. 17, 508 b πρόλοβον ἔχει πρὸ τῆς κοιλίας: cf. Plin. xi. 37 (79). θερμὴν τὴν κοιλίαν, De Gen. iii. 7, 670.

Her wings are covered with silver, and her feathers with yellow gold:—Arist. De Color. 3, 793 (6, 79, 96) οἱ τῶν περιστερῶν τράχηλοι φαίνονται χρυσοειδεῖς τοῦ φωτὸς ἀνακλωμένου. Philo, De Temulent. τὸν αὐχένα τῆς περιστερᾶς ἐν ἡλιακαῖς αὐγαῖς οὐ κατενόησας μυρίας χρωμάτων ἀλλάττοντα ἰδέας; ἢ οὐχὶ φοινικοῦν καὶ κυανοῦν πυροπόν τε καὶ ἀνθρακοειδές, ἔτι δὲ ὠχρὸν καὶ ἐρυθρὸν καὶ ἄλλα παντόδαπα ἴσχει χρώματα. See also Ael. Promot., 480 a, cit. Rhein. Mus. xxviii. p. 277, 1873. Cf. Lucret. ii. 801 Pluma columbarum quo pacto in sole videtur, Quae sita cervices circum collumque coronat; et seq. See also Cic. Acad. Pr. ii. 25 in columba plures videri colores, nec esse plus uno; Nero ap. Senec. Q.

ΠΕΡΙΣΤΕΡΑ (continued).

Nat., i. 5, 6 colla Cytheriacae splendent agitata columbae; Plin. x. (36) 52 nosse credas suos colores varietatemque dispositam; id. xxxvii. 5 (18); Auson. Epist. iii. 15. The young birds are plainer and darker in colour, Arist. De Gen. v. 6, 785 b.

Nesting and Breeding Habits.—Arist. H. A. vi. 2, 560 b κυνοῦσιν ἀλλήλας, ὅταν μέλλῃ ἀναβαίνειν ὁ ἄρρην, ἢ οὐκ ἂν ὀχεύσειεν ὅ γε πρεσβύτερος τὸ πρῶτον· ὕστερον μέντοι ἀναβαίνει καὶ μὴ κύσας· οἱ δὲ νεώτεροι ἀεὶ τοῦτο ποιήσαντες ὀχεύουσιν, καὶ ἔτι αἱ θήλειαι ἀλλήλαις ἀναβαίνουσιν, ὅταν ἄρρην μὴ παρῇ, κύσασαι ὥσπερ οἱ ἄρρενες· καὶ οὐθὲν προΐεμεναι εἰς ἀλλήλας τίκτουσιν ᾠὰ πλείω ἢ τὰ γόνῳ γινάμενα· ἐξ ὧν οὐ γίνεται νεοττὸς οὐθείς, ἀλλ' ὑπηνέμια πάντα τὰ τοιαῦτά εἰσιν. Cf. De Gen. iii. 6, 756 b, Athen. ix. 394 d, Ael. V. H. i. 15, Dion. De Avib. i. 25, Plin. x. 58 (79); Ovid, Am. ii. 6, 56 oscula dat cupido blanda columba mari.

Their prolific increase: τίκτει ἀπονεοττεύουσα πάλιν ἐν τριάκονθ' ἡμέραις, H. A. vi. 4, 563. τίκτουσι δ' αἱ περιστεραὶ πᾶσαν ὥραν καὶ ἐκτρέφουσιν, ἐὰν τόπον ἔχωσιν ἀλεεινὸν καὶ τὰ ἐπιτήδεια· εἰ δὲ μή, τοῦ θέρους μόνον. τὰ δ' ἔκγονα τοῦ ἔαρος βέλτιστα καὶ τοῦ φθινοπώρου. τὰ δὲ τοῦ θέρους καὶ ἐν ταῖς θερμημερίαις χείριστα, H. A. v. 13, 544 b. πολλὰ μὲν οὐ τίκτει, πολλάκις δέ, De Gen. iii. 1, 749 b. διτοκεῖ· τίκτει δεκάκις τοῦ ἐνιαυτοῦ, H. A. vi. 1, 558 b. ἤδη δέ τινες καὶ ἑνδεκάκις, αἱ δ' ἐν Αἰγύπτῳ καὶ δωδεκάκις, ibid. vi. 4, 562 b; Athen. ix. 394 c. ᾠὰ λευκά· ὑπηνέμια, H. A. vi. 2, 559, 561, &c. ὡς ἐπὶ τὸ πολὺ ἄρρεν καὶ θῆλυ, καὶ τούτων ὡς ἐπὶ τὸ πολὺ πρότερον τὸ ἄρρεν τίκτει (Athen. ix. 394, &c.: cf. Flourens, C. R., lxxiii. p. 740, 1864)· καὶ τεκοῦσα μίαν ἡμέραν διαλείπει, εἶτα πάλιν τίκτει θάτερον· ἐπῳάζει δὲ καὶ ὁ ἄρρην ἐν τῷ μέρει τῆς ἡμέρας, τὴν δὲ νύκτα ἡ θήλεια (cf. Ael. iii. 45, Athen. ix. 394 b). ἐκπέττεταί τε καὶ ἐκλέπεται ἐντὸς εἴκοσιν ἡμερῶν τὸ γενόμενον πρότερον τῶν ᾠῶν (cf. ibid. vi. 2)· τιτρώσκει δὲ τὸ ᾠὸν τῇ προτεραίᾳ ἢ ἐκλέπει, &c. ὀχεύει δὲ καὶ ὀχεύεται ἐντὸς ἐνιαυτοῦ· καὶ γὰρ ἔκμηνος, H. A. vi. 4, 562 b: cf. Arist. fr. 271, 1527.

Care and Nurture of the Young.—Arist. H. A. ix. 7, 613 γενομένων δὲ τῶν νεοττῶν τῆς ἁλμυριζούσης μάλιστα γῆς διαμασησάμενος εἰσπτίει τοῖς νεοττοῖς διοιγνὺς τὸ στόμα, προπαρασκευάζων πρὸς τὴν τροφήν. See also Ael. iii. 45, Athen. ix. 394 f, Plin. x (34) 52; hence the variant in Athen. 394 c, Ael. V. H. i. 15 ὁ ἄρρην ἐμπτύει αὐτοῖς, ἵνα μὴ βασκονθῶσι.

For other particulars regarding nesting, incubation, care of the young, &c., see Arist. H. A. vi. 1, 558, 2, 560, 8, 564, ix. 7, 612: De Gen. iii. 6, 756 b, iv. 6, 774; Athen. ix. 394; Geoponic. xiv. 1, 2, xvi. 1, 3; Plin. x (53) 75, (58) 79, (60) 80; Varro, De R. R. iii. 7, 9, &c.; Colum. R. R. viii. 8, 5; Eustath. p. 1712, &c., &c.

Conjugal Affection and Chastity.—Arist. H. A. ix. 7, 612 b οὔτε γὰρ συνδυάζεσθαι [Antig. H. M. 38 συνευνάζεσθαι] θέλουσι πλείοσιν, οὔτε προαπολείπουσι τὴν κοινωνίαν, πλὴν ἐὰν χῆρος ἢ χήρα γένηται. ἔτι δὲ περὶ τὴν ὠδῖνα δεινὴ ἡ τοῦ ἄρρενος θεραπεία καὶ συναγανάκτησις· ἐάν τ'

ΠΕΡΙΣΤΕΡΑ (*continued*).

ἀπομαλακίζηται πρὸς τὴν εἴσοδον τῆς νεοττιᾶς διὰ τὴν λοχείαν, τύπτει καὶ ἀναγκάζει εἰσιέναι. Ael. iii. 5 περιστερὰν δὲ ὀρνίθων σωφρονεστάτην, καὶ κεκολασμένην εἰς ἀφροδίτην μάλιστα ἀκούω λεγόντων· οὐ γάρ ποτε ἀλλήλων διασπῶνται, οὔτε ἡ θήλεια, ἐὰν μὴ ἀφαιρεθῇ τύχῃ τινὶ τοῦ συννόμου, οὔτε ὁ ἄρρην ἢν μὴ χῆρος γένηται : cf. also iii. 45, V. H. i. 15. See also Athen. ix. 394, Antig. H. M. 38 (44), Dion. De Avib. i. 25, Porphyr. De Abst. iii. 10, Plin. x. (34) 52, Propert. ii. 15, 27, &c., &c. Hence, in Egypt, a black dove a symbol of perpetual widowhood, Horap. ii. 30.

Its simplicity and harmlessness (ἀκεραιοσύνη) Matt. x. 16; cf. Cyrill. De Ador. Spir. xv πρὸς ἄκρον ἥκειν πρᾳότητος, &c., &c. With ep. placida, Ovid, Met. vii. 369, cf. Hor. Epist. i. 10, 4, &c., &c.

As **Epithets**, περιστερά and φάσσα are applied to a wife and mistress, Artemid. Oneir. ii. 20; similarly Lycophron calls Helen τρήρων (Cass. 87, ubi Schol. διὰ τὸ λαχνόν), πελειάς (ib. 131, Schol. πόρνη), and Cassandra (ib. 357) φάσσα. In Lat. *Columba* is very frequent as a term of endearment, Plaut. Cas. i. 50, Asin. iii. 3, 103, &c., &c., while *palumbes*, Id. Bacch. i. 1, 17 appears in the sense of lover, and *turtur*, Bacch. i. 1, 35 in that of mistress.

Varieties.—Aristotle enumerates the following names or varieties of pigeon : H. A. viii. 3, 593 φάψ [om. Aᵃ, Cᵃ], φάττα [om. Dᵃ], περιστερά, οἰνάς, τρυγών: ib. viii. 12, 597 b φάτται, πελειάδες, τρυγόνες, περιστεραί : ib. v. 13, 544 b περιστερά, πελειάς, φάττα, οἰνάς, τρυγών. Arist. ap. Athen. ix. 393 f περιστερά, οἰνάς, φάψ, φάσσα, τρυγών. Callim. περὶ ὀρνέων, ap. Athen. ix. 394 d, Ael. V. H. i. 15 φάσσα, πυραλλίς, περιστερά, τρυγών: for all which names, see under their proper headings.

περιστερά is usually the generic word : περιστερῶν μὲν εἶναι ἕν γένος εἴδη δὲ πέντε, Arist. fr. 271, 1527, &c. When used specifically, it refers to the Domestic Pigeon, *Columba livia*, var. *domestica*: Arist. H. A. i. 1, 488 b τὰ μὲν ἄγροικα ὥσπερ φάττα ... τὰ δὲ συνανθρωπίζει οἷον περιστερά: ib. v. 13, 544 b τιθασσὸν δὲ γίνεται μᾶλλον ἡ περιστερά : cf. Soph. fr. 745 (ap. Plut. Mor. 959 e) περιστερὰν ἐφέστιον οἰκέτιν τε : Plat. Theaet. 199 b λαβεῖν φάσσαν ἀντὶ περιστερᾶς, a wild pigeon for a tame one. Cf. **εἰωθάς**, ἡ κατοικίδιος περιστερά, ἡ γὰρ ἀγρία, πελειάς, Moeris (p. 405, ed. Koch, 1830); with which cf. Themist. Or. xxii. p. 273 C οὐ γὰρ δὴ τῶν περιστερῶν μὲν αἱ ἐθάδες πολλάκις τινὰς καὶ ξενὰς ἐπάγονται. In its generic use it appears, e. g., in the statement that in cities περιστεραί are tame, in country districts very wild, Ael. iii. 15 περιστεραὶ δὲ ἐν ταῖς πόλεσι τοῖς ἀνθρώποις συναγελάζονται, καί εἰσι πρᾳόταται καὶ εἱλοῦνται παρὰ τοῖς ποσίν, &c. The passage in Ar. Lys. 754 appears to refer to the extreme familiarity of the city-pigeons.

White pigeons : first seen in Greece near Athos, during the Persian War, Charon ap. Athen. ix. 394 d, Ael. V. H. i. 15; though white

ΠΕΡΙΣΤΕΡΑ (*continued*).

pigeons were not honoured in Persia, being deemed hostile to the Sun, Herod. i. 138; the white doves had probably been the property of Phoenician, Cilician, or Cypriote sailors (Hehn). On white pigeons, cf. also Alexid. 3, 481, ap. Athen. l. c. λευκός Ἀφροδίτης εἰμὶ γὰρ περιστερός: see also Varro, De R. R. iii. 7, Ovid, F. i. 452, Ep. xv. 37, Met. ii. 537, xiii. 674, xv. 715, Martial, &c. The white pigeons were apparently the sacred race of Babylon, which afterwards spread to Syria and to Europe: cf. Hehn, Culturpfl. p. 279, Engl. ed. p. 258; they are still numerous in Damascus (cf. Thomson, Land and Book, p. 271). Galen distinguishes between the κατοικίδιοι and the ἄγριαι, βοσκάδες, or νομάδες, De Comp. Medic. ii. 10 (xiii. p. 514, ed. Kühn), cf. De Simpl. Med. Temp. x. 25 (xii. p. 302); for the latter, dove-cotes were built in the fields near Pergamus. Varro, De R. R. iii. 7 gives a similar account: agrestes maxime sequuntur turres, in quas ex agro evolant, suapte sponte, et remeant. Alterum genus illud columbarum est clementius, quod cibo domestico contentum intra limina ianuae solet pasci. Hoc genus maxime est colore albo. There is also a mixed breed, genus miscellum, reared in the περιστεροτροφεῖον: cf. Ovid, Heroid. xv. 37 et variis albae iunguntur saepe columbae. See also on the care of domesticated and half-domesticated pigeons, Colum. De R. R. viii. 8, Pallad. i. 24, Geopon. xx.

Homing or Carrier-Pigeons.—Pherecr. fr., ap. Athen. ix. 395 b ἀπόπεμψον ἀγγέλλοντα τὸν περιστερόν. Anacreont. fr. 149, Bergk, iii. p. 305 (ed. 4) Ἀνακρέων μ' ἔπεμψεν | πρὸς παῖδα, πρὸς Βάθυλλον | . . . ἐγὼ δ' [ἐρασμίη πέλεια] Ἀνακρέοντι | διακονῶ τοσαῦτα· | καὶ νῦν, ὁρᾷς, ἐκείνου | ἐπιστολὰς κομίζω. A message sent from Pisa to Aegina, by Taurosthenes, a victor in the Olympian games, to his father, Ael. V. H. ix. 2. Cf. Varro, De R. R. iii. 7, 7 columbas redire solere ad locum licet animadvertere, quod multi in theatro e sinu missas faciunt. Pigeons sent into the Consuls' camp by Dec. Brutus at the siege of Mutina, Plin. x. (53) 37; cf. Frontin. Strategem. iii. 13, 8. See also Mart. Epigr. viii. 32, &c., &c.

On **Decoy Pigeons**, see (int. al.) Ar. Av. 1082 τὰς περιστεράς θ' ὁμοίως ξυλλαβὼν εἴρξας ἔχει, | κἀπαναγκάζει παλεύειν δεδεμένας ἐν δικτύῳ (cf. Schol. τοῦτο γλωσσηματικῶς παλεύειν ἔλεγον); they were blinded for the purpose, Arist. H. A. ix. 7, 613. Cf. Hesych. λέγονται γὰρ παλεύτριαι αὗται αἱ ἐξαπατῶσαι καὶ ὑπάγουσαι πρὸς ἑαυτὰ ἤγουν ἐνεδρεύουσαι.

A **Dove-cote**, περιστερεών, Plat. Theaet. 197 C, D, 198 B, 200 B, Galen, Aesop, &c.; also περιστεροτροφεῖον, Varro. On the dove-cotes in Herod's garden at Jerusalem, πύργοι πελειάδων ἡμέρων, Joseph. De Bell. Jud. v. 4, 4. Great dove-cotes are still conspicuous objects in many parts of the East; they are very numerous and large, for instance, in Tenos, the modern site of the Panhellenic shrine and festival (cf. Bent,

ΠΕΡΙΣΤΕΡΑ (*continued*).

Cyclades, 1885, p. 253). On the construction of dove-cotes, their internal niches (σηκοί, κυθρῖνοι, Geop. xiv. 6), and perches (σανίδες), on the duties of the περιστεροτρόφος, τιθασσοτρόφος (Opp. Cyn. i. 354) or pastor columbarius, on charms to keep the birds from straying, &c., &c., see Varro, Columella, Palladius, and Geoponica, loc. citt. For references to dove-cotes, see also Ovid, Met. iv. 48 albis in turribus; id. Tr. i. 4, 7 aspicis, ut veniant ad candida tecta columbae, Accipiat nullas sordida turris aves; Mart. xiii. 31 quaeque gerit similes candida turris aves.

According to Varro, a pair of full-grown pigeons was worth from 200–1000 sesterces; and L. Axius had purchased a pair of a dealer for 500 denarii.

The Sacred Doves of Venus or Astarte. Pigeons were sacred in the eyes of the Syrians, like the fishes of the river Chalos, Xen. Exp. Cyr. i. 4, 9; they were kept in great numbers at Ascalon, Ctes. ap. Diodor. ii. 4, Philo ap. Euseb. Prep. Evang. viii. 14, 64 (cf. the Dove on coins of Ascalon, Eckhel, Doctr. Numm. iii. p. 445); and at Hierapolis, Lucian, De Syr. Dea, c. 14, where the statue of Atargatis had a gold dove on her head, Lucian, ibid. c. 33. On Venus' doves, see also Virg. Aen. vi. 190, Ovid, Met. xiv. 597, Fulgent. Mythol. ii, &c., &c.

On the doves in Palestine, cf. Tibull. i. 7, 17 Quid referam, ut volitet crebras intacta per urbes Alba Palaestino sancta columba Syro? cf. Hygin. Fab. 197, Lucian, De Syr. p. 912, Joseph. loc. cit., Clem. Alex. πρὸς Ἕλλην ii, Philo ap. Euseb. P. E. viii. c. 14, p. 398, &c. See also the account given above of the introduction of white pigeons into Greece, and compare the sanctity of the bird in modern times at Mecca, Constantinople, Venice, Moscow, &c. On the cult of Doves in Syria, cf. Broeckhuis, ad Tibull. l. c.

The cult of the goddess, carried from Ascalon to Cyprus (Herod. i. 105, Pausan. i. 14, 7), brought thither the sacred doves; cf. Antiphon. ap. Athen. xiv. 635 B ἡ Κύπρος δ' ἔχει πελείας διαφόρους: the white Paphian doves, Martial, viii. 28, 13, cf. Nemes. fr. De Aucup. 22; see also Eustath. Hom. Il. p. 1035. See also Fr. Münter, Die himmlische Göttin zu Paphos, p. 25.

As evidences of the cult in islands of the Aegean, cf. the Dove on coins of Seriphos and Siphnos, and the ancient dove-cotes still standing on the latter island. On figures of Astarte with the Dove, see (int. al.) Lenormant, Gaz. Archéol. 1876, p. 133; de Longpérier, Mus. Napol. iii. pl. xxvi. 2, &c., &c.

At Eryx in Sicily; Athen. ix. 394 f τῆς δὲ Σικελίας ἐν Ἔρυκι καιρός τις ἐστίν, ὃν καλοῦσιν Ἀναγώγια, ἐν ᾧ φασι τὴν θεὸν εἰς Λιβύην ἀνάγεσθαι· τότ' οὖν αἱ περὶ τὸν τόπον περιστεραὶ ἀφανεῖς γίνονται ὡς δὴ τῇ θεῷ σιναποδημοῦσαι, κ.τ.λ. Cf. Ael. iv. 2, x. 50, V. H. i. 15. For the Dove on a silver coin of Eryx, see Du Mersan, Méd. inédites, Paris, 1832, p. 57.

ΠΕΡΙΣΤΕΡΑ (continued).

Sicilian doves mentioned, Alexis and Nicander, frr. ap. Athen. ix. 395 b, c, Philemon, ibid. xiv. 658 b.

The story of Semiramis, forsaken as an infant by her mother Derceto, and fed by Doves in the wilderness, Ctes. ap. Diodor. ii. 4, 4; Ctes. fr. ed. Bühr, p. 393. Cf. Lucian, De Syr. Dea, ii. p. 885, Athenag. Leg. pro Christ. p. 156 (ed. Otto), Ovid, Met. iv. 47. Cf. Phornutus, De Diis, cap. De Rheâ ἔοικε δὲ ἡ αὐτὴ ἡ παρὰ Σύροις Ἀρταγα εἶναι, ἣν διὰ τὸ περιστερᾶς καὶ ἰχθύος ἀπέχεσθαι τιμῶσι. See also Selden's De Diis Syriis. Cf. also Hesych. Σεμίραμις, περιστερὰ ὄρειος Ἑλληνιστί.

The Dove sacred also to Dione: Sil. Ital. iv. 106 Dilectas Veneri notasque ab honore Diones Turbabat violentus [accipiter] aves.

The Dove in connexion with the Cyprian Ἀδώνια, Diogen. ap. Gaisford, Paroem. i. Pref. p. 5. On the Dove in connexion with Aphrodite, see also Apollod. ap. Schol. Apollon. iii. 593.

How Doves hatched the egg from which Venus sprang, Hygin. Fab. 197; Theon, ad Arat. 131.

The Dove is not associated with Aphrodite in early Greek, unless, as is not likely, the obscure fragment of Sappho (Bergk 16 (8), Schol. Pind. Pyth. i. 10) indicate such an allusion. In later authors, the references are very frequent: cf. Alex. Com. ap. Athen. ix. 395 B λευκὸς Ἀφροδίτης περιστερός: Apoll. Rhod. iii. 548; Plut. De Is. 71 (Mor. i. 463), &c., &c. Cf. also Virg. Aen. vi. 192 tum maximus heros Maternas agnoscit aves; Sil. Ital. iii. 683 Cythereïus ales; cf. Nero ap. Senec. l. c. On Venus' car with its team of Doves, cf. Ovid, Met. xiv. 597; Apuleius, Met. vi. 6, 393; Claudian, Epithalam. 104.

Venus and her Dove are associated with the month of April on the cylindrical Zodiac of the Louvre, &c.: and the sign Taurus was the *domus Veneris*. This fact also has a direct reference to Pleiad-symbolism.

The Dove on the mystical monument of the 'Black Demeter' at Phigaleia, Paus. viii. 42, 3.

As an instance of the Syrian Dove adopted into Christian worship, cf. Hefele, Concil. ii. 771: how the clergy of Antioch, A.D. 518, complained that Servius had removed the gold and silver doves that hung over the altars and font [note the apparent confusion of ideas in κολυμβήθρα], on the ground that the symbolism was unfitting. On the περιστήριον, or receptacle in the form of a dove for the Blessed Sacrament, cf. Chardon, Hist. des Sacram. ii. 242. On the sacred symbolism of the dove, cf. also Euseb. H. E. vi. 29.

Various Legends.—How Zeus pursued the virgin Phthia in Aegium in the form of a Dove, Athen. ix. 395 a.

How Doves led the Chalcidians to Cumae, Philostr. Icon. ii. 8.

ΠΕΡΙΣΤΕΡΑ (*continued*).

How a Pigeon caused a war between Chaonians and Illyrians, Ael. xi. 27.

The Dove of Deucalion; Plut. Mor. ii. 968 F περιστερὰν ἐκ τῆς λάρνακος ἀφιεμένην, δήλωμα γενέσθαι χειμῶνος μὲν εἴσω πάλιν ἐνδυομένην, εὐδίας δὲ ἀποπτᾶσαν: cf. Lucian, Syr. Dea, c. 12, Apollod. i. 7, 2 (vide s. v. πέλεια).

The Pigeon in Medicine.—For references to the therapeutic value of Pigeons' dung, flesh, blood, feathers, and other parts in cases of poisoning, burns, ulcers, jaundice, and most other ailments, see Galen, De Simpl. Med. Temp. x, also Plin. iii. (6) 12, xxii. (25) 58, xxix. (6) 39, and xxx, passim.

Fables.—περιστερὰ καὶ κολοιός, Fab. Aes. (ed. Halm) 201 b. περιστερὰ καὶ κορώνη, ibid. 358. περιστερὰ καὶ μύρμηξ, ibid. 296. περιστερὰ διψῶσα, ibid. 357.

See also, in addition to articles cited s.v. πέλεια, T. Watters, Chinese Notions about Pigeons and Doves, N. China Br., R. As. Soc., iv. pp. 225-242, 1867. In this paper various resemblances are shown to exist between classical superstitions and Chinese popular notions, an important subject concerning which too little information is accessible. Among other points, the writer states that in Chinese legend the Dove is often confused with the Cuckoo, that the former as well as the latter bird is said to metamorphose into the Hawk, and that the Dove is said to lay in the Magpie's nest: these facts may have some bearing on the obscure Aristotelian statements referred to above (s.v. κόκκυξ) concerning the nesting of the Cuckoo in the nest of φάψ.

ΠΕΡΙΣΤΕΡΑ´ ΜΗΛΙ´ΝΗ. An Indian **Green Fruit-pigeon,** *Treron sp.*

Daemach. ap. Athen. 394 e; Ael. V. H. i. 15. Also περιστεραὶ ὠχραί, Ael. xv. 14, brought as presents to the Indian king; ἅσπερ λέγουσι μήτε ἡμεροῦσθαι μήτε ποτὲ πραΰνεσθαι. Cf. s.v. **πελειὰς χλωρόπτιλος.**

ΠΕΡΚΝΟ´ΠΤΕΡΟΣ = ὀρειπέλαργος = ὑπαίετος. A kind of **Vulture.**

Arist. H. A. ix. 32, 618 b λευκὴ κεφαλή, μεγέθει δὲ μέγιστος, πτερὰ δὲ βραχύτατα, καὶ οὐροπύγιον πρίμηκες, γυπὶ ὅμοιος. ὀρειπέλαργος καλεῖται καὶ ὑπαίετος, οἰκεῖ δ' ἄλση, τὰ μὲν κακὰ ταὐτὰ ἔχων τοῖς ἄλλοις, τῶν δ' ἀγαθῶν οὐδέν· ἁλίσκεται γὰρ καὶ διώκεται ὑπὸ κοράκων καὶ τῶν ἄλλων. βαρὺς γὰρ καὶ κακόβιος καὶ τὰ τεθνεῶτα φέρων, πεινῇ δ' ἀεὶ καὶ βοᾷ καὶ μινυρίζει: cf. Plin. x. (1) 3.

Of the three names, not one occurs elsewhere, save ὑπαίετος, Boios ap. Anton. Lib. c. 20 (loc. corr.). The description is insufficient, but agrees fairly, except as regards size, with the Egyptian Vulture; in which case the black and white plumage may explain περκνόπτερος, and, together perhaps with the stork-like nest, ὀρειπέλαργος.

Sundevall identifies περκνόπτερος with the Lämmergeier, *Gypaëtus barbatus*, L., with which the epithet λευκοκέφαλος agrees; but for this

ΠΕΡΚΝΟΠΤΕΡΟΣ (*continued*).

he has to suppose πτερὰ βραχύτατα (alis minimis, Plin. l. c.), to be an error for μακρότατα.

The Egyptian Vulture, *Neophron percnopterus*, L., Sav., though the black-and-white of its plumage might be associated with the name ὀρειπέλαργος, and though a comparison might also be drawn with the Stork in connexion with the Egyptian stories of its parental affection, is by no means μεγέθει μέγιστος, and is nearly all white, instead of merely on the head. In short, the bird is not to be clearly identified, and the passage, like much of its immediate context, is altogether obscure.

ΠΕΡΚΝΟ'Σ. A kind of **Eagle** = μόρφνος, νηττοφόνος, πλάγγος, q.v. (περκνός = μέλας, Suid.).

Il. xxiv. 316 αἰετὸν ... μόρφνον θηρητῆρ' ὃν καὶ περκνὸν καλέουσιν. Arist. De Mirab. 60, 835 ἐκ δὲ ἁλιαέτων φήνη γίνεται, ἐκ δὲ τούτων περκνοὶ καὶ γῦπες. Cf. Plin. x. (1) 3; Lyc. 260.

In regard to the obscure words **μόρφνος, περκνός, πέρκος**, it is hard to be content with the Scholiastic explanations which treat them as mere colour-epithets: such an interpretation may or may not be true, and various facts suggest that there is more to be learned regarding them. For instance, ἐπιπέρκνος (Xen. Cyn. v. 22) is said to be likewise a mere colour-epithet (J. Poll. v. 67), but the relations between περκνός, μόρφνος, μελανάετος and λαγωφόνος make it at least somewhat striking that ἐπιπέρκνος, in the only passage where it occurs, should be applied to the *Hare*.

ΠΕ'ΡΚΟΣ. A kind of **Hawk**.

Arist. H. A. ix. 36, 620 ἄλλοι δὲ πέρκοι καὶ σπιζίαι: fortasse nec Aristoteli ipsi cognita sunt, Scalig. p. 249. If πέρκος and σπιζίας are identical, the former, if it mean dark-coloured, agrees as an epithet with the traditional identification of the latter with the Sparrow-hawk.

ΠΕ'ΡΝΗΣ, v. ll. **πτέρνις, πτερνίς, πτέρνης**. A kind of **Hawk**.

Arist. H. A. ix. 36, 620 ὁ δ' ἀστερίας καὶ ὁ φασσοφόνος καὶ ὁ πέρνης ἀλλοῖοι. Hesych. πτερνίς, εἶδος ἱέρακος.

ΠΗΝΕ'ΛΟΨ. A kind of **Wild Duck** or **Goose**.

Ibyc. 8 (13) ποικίλαι πανέλοπες. Alcae. fr. 84 (Bergk) ὄρνιθές τινες οἶδ'; ὠκεάνω γᾶς τ' ἀπὺ περρύτων | ἦλθον πανέλοπες ποικιλόδειροι τανυσίπτεροι. Ion. ap. Hesych. s. v. φοινικόλεγνον· "Ἴων τὸν πηνέλοπα τὸ ὄρνεον, τὸν γὰρ τράχηλον ἐπίπαν φοινικοῦν, ἡ δὲ λέγνη παρέλκει.

Mentioned also, Arist. H. A. viii. 3, 593 b (with χηναλώπηξ, αἴξ, &c.); cf. Ar. Av. 298, 1302, and Schol. ὁ πηνέλοψ νήττῃ μέν ἐστιν ὅμοιον, περιστερᾶς δὲ μέγεθος· μέμνηται δὲ αὐτοῦ Στησίχορος καὶ Ἴβυκος.

From the superficial resemblance of the name to χηναλώπηξ, χηνάλαψ

ΠΗΝΕΛΟΨ *continued*).

Hesych., and from its occurrence in some MSS. for the latter in Plin. x. (22) 29, it seems probable that both names are identical, and possible that both are corruptions of a foreign (Egyptian?) word. The association of αἴξ and πηνέλοψ in an obscure and faulty Aristotelian passage, may be a mere confusion arising out of the story of Hermes visiting *Penelope* in the form of a goat (cf. Creuzer, Symb. iii. p. 502); in which case αἴξ should disappear from the list of bird-names.

ΠΗ´ΡΙΞ· πέρδιξ, Κρῆτες, Hesych.

ΠΙ´ΚΟΣ. A **Woodpecker**. Lat. *picus*; said to be an Oscan word.

Strabo, v. 2 πίκον γὰρ τὴν ὄρνιν τοῦτον ὀνομάζουσι, καὶ νομίζουσιν Ἄρεως ἱερόν. See also Dion. Halic. i. 14. Cf. Ovid, F. iii. 37, &c. Cf. also Grimm's D. Myth. p. 388, Creuzer's Symb. iii. 676, iv. 368.

ΠΙ´ΠΟΣ s. πίππος. A young chicken, Athen. ix. 368 f. (Casaub. for ἵππους).

ΠΙΠΩ´ (MSS. have also πίπα, πίπος, πίπρα. Some editors read ἵππῳ, cf. ἵππη). The **Greater** and **Lesser Spotted Woodpeckers**, *Picus major* and *minor*, L.

Arist. H. A. viii. 3, 593 ἄλλα δ' ἐστὶ σκνιποφάγα, ἃ τοὺς σκνῖπας θηρεύοντα ζῇ μάλιστα, οἷον πιπὼ ἥ τε μείζων καὶ ἡ ἐλάττων· καλοῦσι δέ τινες ἀμφότερα ταῦτα δρυοκολάπτας· ὅμοια δ' ἀλλήλοις καὶ φωνὴν ἔχουσιν ὁμοίαν, πλὴν μείζω τὸ μεῖζον. νέμεται δ' ἀμφότερα ταῦτα πρὸς τὰ ξύλα προσπετόμενα. Ibid. ix. 21, 617 τὰ σκέλη βραχέα [ἔχει ὁ κύανος] τῇ πίπῳ παρόμοια. Ibid. ix. 1, 609: hostile to ποικιλίς, κορυδών, χλωρεύς· τὰ γὰρ ᾠὰ κατεσθίουσιν ἀλλήλων, and to ἐρωδιός (cf. Hesych.): τὰ γὰρ ᾠὰ κατεσθίει καὶ τοὺς νεοττοὺς τοῦ ἐρωδιοῦ.

Nicand. ap. Anton. Lib. c. 14 ἡ δὲ μήτηρ αὐτῶν ἐγένετο κνιπολόγος πιπώ· πρὸς ταύτην ἀετῷ πόλεμός ἐστι καὶ ἐρωδιῷ· κατάγνυσι γὰρ αὐτῶν τὰ ᾠά, κόπτουσα τὴν δρῦν διὰ τοὺς κνῖπας (cf. σίττη, q. v.).

Lycoph. Cass. 476 ἀντὶ πιποῦς σκορπίον λαιμῷ σπάσῃς. Tzetz. in Lyc. (edit. Steph. p. 83) πιπὼ ὄρνεόν ἐστι θαλάσσιον εὐπρεπὲς καὶ εὐειδές.

The above identification, setting aside the statement of Tzetzes, depends solely on the existence of two species of Spotted Woodpecker, similar in appearance, but unequal in size.

ΠΙ´ΤΥΛΟΣ· ὀρνιθάριόν τι ἄγριον, Hesych. Also πίπυλος, Schol. Theocr. x. 50.

ΠΙ´ΦΥΓΞ (v. l. πίφιγξ, πίφηξ): πίφλιξ, Suid. An unknown bird = κορύδαλος = πίφαλλος, s. πιφαλλίς, Hesych.

Arist. H. A. ix. 1, 610 πίφιγξ καὶ ἅρπη καὶ ἰκτῖνος φίλοι. Mentioned also by Boios ap. Anton. Lib. c. xx, in a fabled metamorphosis, together with ἅρπη, ἅρπασος, &c. Cf. Etym. M. 673; Choerob. Cram. Anecd.

ΠΗΝΕΛΟΨ—ΠΟΡΦΥΡΙΣ

ΠΙΦΥΓΞ (*continued*).

Oxon. ii. p. 245; Lob. Proll. p. 96. I cannot help thinking that the word is akin to φῶυξ, and its allies.

ΠΛΑ'ΓΓΟΣ (v.l. πλάγχος, πλάνος, Niphus κλάγγος, q.v. supra) = νηττοφόνος = μόρφνος (Arist.).

A kind of **Eagle**.

Arist. H. A. ix. 32, 618 b ἕτερον δὲ γένος ἀετοῦ ἐστὶν ὃ πλάγγος καλεῖται, δεύτερος μεγέθει καὶ ῥώμῃ. οἰκεῖ δὲ βήσσας καὶ ἄγκη καὶ λίμνας. ἐπικαλεῖται δὲ νηττοφόνος καὶ μόρφνος· οὗ καὶ Ὅμηρος μέμνηται ἐν τῇ τοῦ Πριάμου ἐξόδῳ, Il. xxiv. 316.

Plin. x. 1 Tertii generis morphnus, quam Homerus et percnon vocat, aliqui et plancum et anatariam, secunda magnitudine et vi: huicque vita circa lacus, &c.

Commentators have given innumerable interpretations of this word. If it be really a concrete specific appellation, then the Spotted Eagle, *Aquila naevia*, fulfils the conditions best: it is large and powerful, but less so than the Golden Eagle; it frequents water, feeding partly on fish (especially on pieces of decomposing fish, cf. Shelley, Birds of Egypt, p. 206), and partly on waterfowl and sea-birds (cf. Buffon, Hist. des Ois. i. 127, Sundevall, p. 104): if μόρφνος, πέρκνος and (?) κλάγγος are to be taken as descriptive epithets (as they are by some), it is dusky, mottled, and noisy.

The passage quoted from Pliny is full of fables, and includes the story of the death of Aeschylus, which suggests rather the habits of the Lämmergeier (cf. s.v. ἀετός, Ael. vii. 16).

ΠΟΙΚΙΛΙ'Σ. An unknown bird: taken by mediaeval writers (Belon, Aldrovandi, &c.) for the **Goldfinch**, from the statement that it is identical with ἀκανθίς, q.v.

Arist. H. A. ix. 1, 609; hostile to κορυδών, πιπώ (πίπρα), and χλωρεύς. Schol. ad Theocr. vii. 171 (cit. Schn. in Arist. vol. ii. p. 5) ἀκανθὶς δὲ ὀρνεόν ἐστι ποικίλον καὶ λιγυρόν, καλεῖται δὲ καὶ ποικιλὶς διὰ τὴν χροίαν.

Ποικίλος ὄρνις was also an expression for the Peacock. Cf. Athen. ix. 397 c Ἀντιφῶντι δὲ τῷ ῥήτορι λόγος μὲν γέγραπται ἔχων ἐπίγραμμα Περὶ ταῶν· καὶ ἐν αὐτῷ τῷ λόγῳ οὐδεμία μνεία τοῦ ὀνόματος γίνεται, ὄρνεις δὲ ποικίλους πολλάκις ἐν αὐτῷ ὀνομάζει.

ΠΟΝΤΙΚΟ'Σ ΟΡΝΙΣ. The **Pheasant**.

Hesych. φασιανοί· ὄρνεις ποιοί, οἱ δὲ τοὺς Ποντικοὺς φασιν.

ΠΟΡΦΥΡΙ'Σ. An unknown bird = λαθιπορφυρίς.

Mentioned Ar. Av. 304. Ibyc. fr. 4, ap. Athen. ix. 388 τανύπτερος ὡς ὅκα πορφυρίς. Ibyc. fr. 8, l. c. αἰολόδειροι λαθιπορφυρίδες. According to Callimachus, ap. Athen. l. c., πορφυρίς differs from πορφυρίων.

ΠΟΡΦΥΡΙ'ΩΝ. The **Purple Gallinule**, *Porphyrio hyacinthus*, Temm. Mentioned Ar. Av. 707, 881, 1249. Arist. fr. 272, ap. Athen. ix. 388 c, d σχιδανόποδα αὐτὸν εἶναι, ἔχειν τε χρῶμα κυάνεον, σκέλη μακρά, ῥύγχος ἠργμένον ἐκ τῆς κεφαλῆς φοινικοῦν, μέγεθος ἀλεκτρυόνος. στόμαχον δ' ἔχει λεπτόν, διὸ τῶν λαμβανομένων εἰς τὸν πόδα ταμιεύεται μικρὰς τὰς ψωμίδας, κάπτων δὲ πίνει (H. A. viii. 6, 595 ; Plin. x. (46) 63 morsu bibit). πενταδάκτυλός τε (?) ὧν τὸν μέσον ἔχει μέγιστον. Dion. De Avib. i. 29, a similar description, ἐρυθρὸν αὐτῷ τὸ ῥάμφος ἐστί, καὶ κατὰ κεφαλῆς ὥσπερ τινὰ πῖλον ἔχει, ὁποίους οἱ τοξόται Πέρσαι φέρουσιν. Arist. H. A. ii. 17, 509 αὐχένα μακρὸν ἔχει· οὔτε τὸν πρόλοβον ἔχει οὔτε τὸν στόμαχον εὐρὺν ἀλλὰ σφόδρα μακρόν. Schol. Ar. Av. 1249 κυάνεοί εἰσι. Arist. De Inc. 10. 710. Callim. ap. Athen. l. c. τὴν τροφὴν λαμβάνειν τὸν πορφυρίωνα ἐν σκότῳ καταδυόμενον, ἵνα μή τις αὐτὸν θεάσηται· ἐχθραίνει γὰρ τοὺς προσιόντας αὐτοῦ τῇ τροφῇ. Ael. iii. 42 ὡραιότατός τε ἅμα καὶ φερωνυμώτατός ἐστι ζῴων, καὶ χαίρει κονιόμενος, &c. According to Alex. Mynd. ap. Athen. l. c., it inhabits Libya and is there held sacred. According to Plin. x. 63, it inhabits Commagene (Asia Min.) and a yet nobler sort (x. 69) the Balearic Islands.

A bird of lofty morals and great vigilance, Polemon ap. Athen. l. c., Ael. iii. 42, v. 28, vii. 25, viii. 20, xi. 15, Dion. De Avib. i. 29.

An easy mode of capture, Dion. De Avib. iii. 21.

The descriptions in Arist. fr. 272 and Dionysius clearly refer to the Purple Gallinule : that in Arist. H. A. ii. 17 is supposed by some (I think needlessly) to apply to the Flamingo, the Gallinule not having a very long neck. The bird occurs in Egypt and neighbouring countries: it is rare in Greece, but inhabits Lake Copaïs and Lake Dystos in Euboea (Erhard, l. c., also Naumannia, 1858, p. 21), though, according to other authorities (Von der Mühle, Heldreich, Krüper), nothing is known of its occurrence in Greece in recent times.

ΠΟΥ˜ΠΟΣ. A late word for the **Hoopoe** ; vide s. v. ἔποψ.

Anon. De Avibus et earum Virtutibus in Medicina (MS. cit. Du Cange, Gloss. s. v. κούκουφος), ἔποψ ὄρνεον ἐν ἀέρι ποτώμενον· οὗτος καλεῖται κούκουφος, καὶ ποῦπος.

ΠΡΕ'ΣΒΥΣ. A name for the **Wren** = τροχίλος, Hesych., Arist. H. A. ix. 11, 615. In this word one is much tempted to suspect a transposition of letters, and to suggest, as a conjectural emendation, σπέρβυς ; cf. also s.vv. σπέργυς, σποργίλος.

Arist. H. A. ix. 1, 609 πολέμιος δὲ καὶ ὁ πρέσβυς καλούμενος καὶ γαλῆ καὶ κορώνη [τῇ γλαυκί]· τὰ γὰρ ᾠὰ καὶ τοὺς νεοττοὺς κατεσθίουσιν αὐτῆς. In the preceding sentence ὄρχιλος and γλαῦξ are mentioned as hostile to one another. (Here Sundevall supposes the Jackdaw to be meant, on account of its egg-eating propensities, but the passage is mythological, not prosaic.)

ΠΡΕΣΒΥΣ (*continued*).

Cf. Plin. viii. 25 ; Munk. ad Anton. Lib. p. 100; Lob. Path. p. 132.

ΠΤΕ'ΡΝΙΣ. Vide s.v. πέρνης.

ΠΤΕΡΥΓΟΤΥ'ΡΑΝΝΟΣ· ὄρνις ποιὸς ἐν Ἰνδικῇ Ἀλεξάνδρῳ δοθείς, Hesych.

ΠΤΕ'ΡΩΝ· εἶδος ὀρνέου, Hesych.

Meineke, Com. Fr. iv. p. 647 (ap. Hesych.) ἀλλ' ἢ τρίορχος ἢ πτέρων ἢ στρουθίας. Cf. Etym. M. 226, 37, Theognost. 36. 19.

ΠΤΥ'ΓΞ. Arist. H. A. ix. 12, 615 b = ὕβρις, q. v. For πτυγγί, MSS. have πωγί, πτογγί, πτυγγιγί, for which Schn. reads πωνγγί; vide infra s. v. φῶυξ. Cf. Schn. in Arist. vol. ii. 97, 117 ; Anton. Lib. 5 ; Etym. M. 699, 10 ; Lob. Phryn. 72.

ΠΥ'ΓΑΡΓΟΣ, α. A sort of Eagle or Falcon ; εἶδος ἀετοῦ, Hesych.; vide infra.

Arist. H. A. ix. 32, 618 b γένος ἀετῶν· κατὰ τὰ πεδία καὶ τὰ ἄλση καὶ περὶ τὰς πόλεις γίνεται· ἔνιοι δὲ καλοῦσι νεβροφόνον αὐτόν· πέτεται δὲ καὶ εἰς τὰ ὄρη καὶ εἰς τὴν ὕλην διὰ τὸ θάρσος. Cf. Plin. x. (1) 3 secundi generis Pygargus, in oppidis mansitat et in campis, albicante cauda. Arist. H. A. vi. 6, 563b χαλεπὸς περὶ τὰ τέκνα.

Cf. Schol. Lyc. 91. Also Etym. M. 695, 50 πύγαργος· εἶδος ἀετοῦ· Σοφοκλῆς (fr. 932 a) ἐπὶ τοῦ δειλοῦ, ἀπὸ τῆς λευκῆς πυγῆς, ὥσπερ ἐναντίως μελαμπύγης ἀπὸ τῆς ἰσχυρᾶς.

Note.—Circus cyaneus, L. (♀ =*Falco pygargus*, L.), the Hen-harrier or Ring-tail, is now called πύγαργος in the Cyclades (Erhard, op. cit. p. 47). To it much of the description given is applicable, but certainly not the epithet νεβροφόνος. Sundevall imagines the Golden Eagle to be meant, Gloger and others the White-tailed Eagle or Erne, *Haliaetus albicilla* (L.), to which latter the description in Aesch. Ag. 115 ὁ ἐξόπιν ἀργίας, seems to apply: but these are surely excluded by the evidence as to size (cf. Pliny, l. c.), frequency, and affection for cities and plains. I incline to identify the bird with the Short-toed Eagle, *Circaëtus gallicus*, which in French, as perhaps also here, seems to share its popular name (Jean-le-Blanc) with *C. cyaneus*. But the name was originally mystical (cf. s.v. μελάμπυγος), however it may in later times have been specifically applied to a particular bird.

ΠΥ'ΓΑΡΓΟΣ, β. An undetermined bird.

Arist. H. A. viii. 3, 593 b. A water-bird, mentioned with σχοινίλος and κίγκλος, about the size of a thrush ; τὸ οὐραῖον κινεῖ: frequents rivers and streams.

The size agrees with Sundevall's suggestion of a Sandpiper. Aubert

ΠΥΓΑΡΓΟΣ (continued).

and Wimmer take the three birds to be different species of Wagtail (*Motacilla*). The name more strongly suggests to me the Dipper, *Cinclus aquaticus*, L., (Mod. Gk. νεροκόσσυφος, Heldr.): but all three birds are quite doubtful.

ΠΥΡΑΛΛΙ'Σ, *s.* πυρραλίς (Hesych.). An unknown bird: probably a kind of **Pigeon**.

Arist. H. A. ix. 1, 609, hostile to τρυγών, τόπος γὰρ τῆς νομῆς καὶ βίος ὁ αὐτός. Cf. Ael. iv. 48.

Callim. (fr. 100, c. 4) ap. Athen. ix. 394 d Καλλίμαχος ὡς διαφορὰς ἐκτίθεται φάσσαν, πυραλλίδα, περιστεράν, τρυγόνα. Cf. Ael. V. H. i. 15.

ΠΥΡΓΙ'ΤΗΣ· σπυργίτης, a **Sparrow**, Galen. Vide s. vv. σπογγίλος, στρουθός.

ΠΥ'ΡΡΑ. A bird, hostile to τρυγών. Ael. iv. 5, Phile, 685. Perhaps identical with πυραλλίς.

ΠΥΡΡΙ'ΑΣ, *s.* πιρίας = ἐλαιός, q.v.

ΠΥΡΡΟΚΟ'ΡΑΞ. The **Alpine Chough**, *Corvus pyrrhocorax*, L.

Plin. x. (48) 68 Alpium pyrrhocorax, luteo rostro, niger.

ΠΥΡΡΟΥ'ΛΑΣ (v. l. πυρροῦρας, &c. Lob. Prol. 132). Probably the **Bullfinch**, *Pyrrhula vulgaris*.

Arist. H. A. viii. 3, 592 b ὄρνις σκωληκοφάγος. Sundevall, op. c., p. 111, identifies πυρρούλας with the Robin, the Bullfinch being a seed-eater, and confined to the mountainous parts of Northern Greece: but Heldreich quotes the same word as the name for the Bullfinch in Mod. Gk.

ΠΩ'Υ''(Γ)Ξ· ποιὸς ὄρνις, Hesych. Cf. πτύγξ.

'ΡΑ'ΦΟΙ· ὄρνεις τινές, Hesych. (Verb. dub.)

'ΡΙΝΟ'ΚΕΡΩΣ· ποιὸς ὄρνις ἐν Αἰθιοπίᾳ, Hesych. Probably the **Hornbill**.

'ΡΟ'ΒΙΛΛΟΣ· βασιλίσκος ὄρνις, Hesych. (Possibly for ῥέγιλλος, L. *regulus*.). Vide s. v. βασιλεύς, &c.

'ΡΥΝΔΑ'ΚΗ. Supposed to be akin to Pers. رند (Rund) nomen avis, quae frequenter in oryzetis invenitur (J. Albertus in Hesych., &c.). An Indian bird, of the size of a pigeon, Ctes. Pers. 61; also Hesych. In Plut. Vit. Artax. 19, p. 1020, ῥυντάκης.

'ΡΩΔΙΟ'Σ = ἐρωδιός, q.v. Hippon. p. 63; also Hesych.

ΣΑ'ΛΠΙΓΞ. Also σαλπιγκτής, *s.* σαλπιστής.

A synonym of ὄρχιλος (q.v.), Hesych. Cf. Dind. Thes. vii. c. 45 B.

ΠΥΓΑΡΓΟΣ—ΣΕΛΕΥΚΙΣ 153

ΣΑΡΙ'Ν· ὀρνέου εἶδος, ὅμοιον ψάρῳ, Hesych. Also σαρκῶν, σπερμολόγος, Hesych.

In both cases it has been suggested to read σαρίον, *quasi* ψαρίον.

ΣΕΙΡΗ'Ν· ὀρνιθάριόν τι ποιόν, Hesych. Possibly, like the 'Sirens,' connected with the Heb. *sir*, to sing.

Cf. Hesych. s. v. σειρῆνες· οἱ μὲν ἔξω γυναῖκάς φασι μελῳδούσας, ὁ δὲ Ἀκύλας στρουθοκάμηλον.

ΣΕΙΣΟΠΥΓΙ'Σ, σείσουρα. Literally **Wagtail**, *Motacilla*. Identified with κίγκλος, Hesych.: and apparently with ἴυγξ, Schol. in Theophr. ii. 17. Cf. also Suid. ἴυγξ, τὸ ὄρνεον, τὸ λεγόμενον σεισοπυγίς. In Mod. Gk., σουσουράδα is the Wagtail. Vide s. v. κίγκλος.

ΣΕΙΣΟ'ΦΕΛΟΣ· τὸ τῶν τροχίλων εἶδος, Hesych.

Perhaps for σεισολόφος (J. Albertus in Hesych.), or σεισο[κέ]φαλος. *s.* σεισύκεβλος, Meineke, Philol. xii. 621.

ΣΕΛΕΥΚΙ'Σ, *s.* σελευκίας. The **Rose-coloured Pastor**, *Pastor roseus*. Temm.

Dion. De Avib. i. 22 πολυβορώτατον ὄρνεων ἡ σελευκίς, καὶ μετὰ πλείστης εὐχῆς ἀφικνούμενον τοῖς ἀγροίκοις, ἣν τοὺς καρποὺς ἀκρίδων ἔδηται πλῆθος. ὅτι τὰς μὲν φαγοῦσαι, τὰς δὲ καὶ ἀπὸ μόνης τῆς σκιᾶς ἀπαιροῦσαι, ἐκκρίνουσιν ἃς ἂν καταφάγωσι ῥαδίως αὐτίκα, καὶ πορθουμένοις ἀνδράσι ξενικὴν ἄν τις εἴποι συμμαχίαν ἐληλυθέναι. ἀλλ' εἰ τῆς χάριτός τις τοῖς ὄρνεις ἀποστερήσειε, διαφθείρουσιν αὗται τὸν σωθέντα καρπόν.

Zosimi Hist. i. 57. 6 (Schneid. Ecl. Phys. i. 51) ἐν Σελευκίᾳ τῇ κατὰ Κιλικίαν Ἀπόλλωνος ἱερὸν ἵδρυτο καλουμένου Σαρπηδονίου, καὶ ἐν τούτῳ χρηστήριον. Τὰ μὲν οὖν περὶ τοῦ θεοῦ τούτου λεγόμενα, καὶ ὡς ἅπασι τοῖς ὑπὸ λύμης ἀκρίδων ἐνοχλουμένοις σελευκιάδας παραδιδοὺς (ὄρνεα δὲ ταῦτα ἐνδιαιτώμενα τοῖς περὶ τὸ ἱερὸν τόποις) συνεξέπεμπε τοῖς αἰτοῦσι, αἱ δὲ ταῖς ἀκρίσι συμπεριπτάμεναι καὶ τοῖς στόμασι ταύτας δεχόμεναι παραχρῆμα πλῆθός τε ἄπειρον ἐν ἀκαριαίῳ διέφθειρον, καὶ τῆς ἐκ τούτων βλάβης τοὺς ἀνθρώπους ἀπήλλαττον, ταῦτα μὲν τῇ τηνικαῦτα τῶν ἀνθρώπων εὐδαιμονίᾳ παρίημι, τοῦ καθ' ἡμᾶς γένους ἀποσεισαμένου θείαν εὐεργεσίαν. Cf. Photius, Cod. ccxxiii. p. 681 (teste Bernhardy, ed. Suid.).

Plin. x. (27) 39 Seleucides aves vocantur quarum adventum ab Iove precibus impetrant Casii montis incolae, fruges eorum locustis vastantibus. Nec unde veniant, quove abeant, compertum, nunquam conspectis nisi cum praesidio indigetur.

Cf. Ael. xvii. 19; Galen, De Loc. Affect. vi. 3; Hesych., &c.

The bird, under the name *Samarmog* or *Samarmar* is in like manner reverenced to this day by the Arabs; cf. Niebuhr, Beschreib. v. Arabiens, p. 174. In Mod. Gk. it is called ἀγιοπούλι on its Spring migration, when it destroys the grasshoppers, and διαβολοπούλι in Autumn, when it devours the grapes (Heldr.).

ΣΕΜΙ'ΡΑΜΙΣ· περιστερὰ ὄρειος, Ἑλληνιστί, Hesych. Cf. Diodor. ii. 6. Vide s. v. **περιστερά**.

ΣΕ'ΡΚΟΣ· ἀλεκτρυών, καὶ ἀλεκτορίδες σέλκες, Hesych. Baethgen, De vi et signif. Galli, Diss. Inaug., Gotting. 1887, p. 10, collates ϝέλκος, a word inscribed together with the image of a Cock on a Cretan vase (Roulez, Choix de vases de Leide, p. 40, nr. 13), and this in turn with Γέλχανος, s. ϝέλχανος, ὁ Ζεὺς παρὰ Κρησίν, Hesych., inscribed also on a coin of Phaestus (Bull. Inst. Arch., 1841, p. 174); further he suggests a kindred reference to the ὄρνις Περσικός, in the corrupt Hesychian gloss, Σελχροί· Πέρσαι. A coin of Phaestus figured in the Brit. Mus. Cat. Coins (Crete, p. 63, pl. xv. 10), bears the same inscription and shows the god seated holding a Cock on his knee.

ΣΕ'ΡΤΗΣ· γέρανος, Πυλλυρρήνιοι, Hesych.

ΣΙΑΛΕΝΔΡΙ'Σ· ποιὸς ὄρνις παρὰ Καλλιμάχῳ, Hesych.
Schn. in Arist. H. A. viii. 3 (vol. ii. p. 596) suspects this bird to be identical with the corrupt **καλίδρις**, s. **σκανδρίς**, s. **σκαλίδρις**, of Arist., and suggests **σκαλυδρίς** as an emendation for both. Cf. also **σιαλίς**.

ΣΙΑΛΙ'Σ. A bird so-called from its cry. Didymus ap. Athen. ix. 392 f. Also Hesych.

ΣΙ'ΝΤΗΣ. Vide s. v. **μακεσίκρανος**.

ΣΙΣΙ'ΛΑΡΟΣ· πέρδιξ, Περγαῖοι, Hesych.

ΣΙΤΑΡΙ'Σ. An unknown bird. σίττη· ἡ νῦν οἶμαι λεγομένη σιταρίς, Suid.: cf. Zonar. 1645, Lob. Proll. p. 30.

ΣΙΤΤΑ'ΚΗ, Philostorg. II. E. iii. 11. σιττακός, Ael. xvi. 15, Arrian. Ind. i. 8, &c. Vide s. v. **ψιττακός**.

ΣΙ'ΤΤΑΣ = σιττακός. σίττας, ὄρνις ποιός· ἔνιοι δὲ τὸν ψιττακὸν λέγουσιν, Hesych.

ΣΙ'ΤΤΗ. (Some MSS. have σίππη in Arist. H. A. ix. 1.) With σίππη cf. ἴππη, q. v. Also ἴπτα· ὁ δρυοκόλαψ ἐθνικῶς, Hesych. We might conjecture a form ψίττη, akin to O. H. G. *spch, spehl, specht*, Lith. *spakas*, Sk. *pika*, &c.

A bird with fabulous attributes, allied to the Woodpecker; ὄρνις ποιός, οἱ δὲ δρυοκολάπτης, Hesych. Usually identified with the Nuthatch, *Sitta europaea* or *S. syriaca*, which latter very similar species is commoner in Greece (Von der Mühle, Lindermayer);

ΣΙΤΤΗ (continued).

Mod. Gk. σκαλοθάρης, σφυρικτής, and τσοπανοπούλι, i. e. the little shepherd (Heldr.).

Arist. H. A. ix. 1, 609 b ἀετῷ πολέμιον· καταγνύει γὰρ τὰ ᾠὰ τοῦ ἀετοῦ: ibid. 17, 616 b μάχιμος, τὴν δὲ διάνοιαν εὔθικτος καὶ εὐθήμων καὶ εὐβίωτος, καὶ λέγεται φαρμάκεια εἶναι διὰ τὸ πολυίδρις εἶναι· πολύγονος δὲ καὶ εὔτεκνος, καὶ ζῇ ὑλοκοποῦσα.

Callim. Fr. 173 (in Etym. M.) ὁ δ' ἠλεὸς οὐδ' ἐπὶ σίττην βλέψας.
A good omen to lovers, Schol. in Ar. Av. 705; fr. ap. Suid. ἐγὼ μὲν ὦ Λευκίππη δεξιὰ σίττη.

ΣΙ'ΤΤΟΣ· σίττον, οἱ μὲν γλαῦκα· ἢ κίσσαν· ἢ ἱέρακα, Hesych.

[σίττη, σίττας and σίττος are all doubtful and corrupt words. They are probably akin to the equally corrupt and obscure πιπώ, which bird, like σίττη, is allied to the woodpeckers and hostile to the eagle.]

ΣΚΑΛΙ'ΔΡΙΣ. (MSS. have καλίδρις, σκανδρίς, σκαλίδρες. Schneider suggests σκαλυδρίς. Possibly identical with σιαλενδρίς, q. v.)

An unknown bird; taken by Belon and later writers for a species of Sandpiper, e. g. *Totanus calidris*, auctt., the Redshank: but any one whom it pleases may interpret it as a Wagtail, whose gray plumage is enlivened with a 'ποικιλία' of yellow.

Arist. H. A. viii. 3, 593 b τὸ οὐραῖον κινεῖ, ποικιλίαν ἔχει, τὸ δ' ὅλον σποδοειδές (mentioned with σχοινίλος, κίγκλος, and πύγαργος).

ΣΚΙ'ΛΛΟΣ· ἰκτῖνος, Hesych. Cf. βάσκιλλος.

ΣΚΙ'Ψ. Vide s. v. σπαράσιον.

ΣΚΟΛΟ'ΠΑΞ. Generally supposed, and by all the older commentators, to be identical with ἀσκαλώπας, the **Woodcock**. Mod. Gk. ἀσκαλόπακας, ὀρνιθοσκαλίδα (Coray), ξυλόκοττα (Heldr.), ξυλόρνιθα (Bik.), μπεκάτσα (=Fr. *bécasse*). With σ-κολ-όπαξ, cf. Gk. σ-κώλ-οψ, σκάλοψ, σπάλαξ: rt. of L. *culter*, &c.

Arist. H. A. ix. 8, 614 ἐπὶ δένδρου οὐ καθίζει, ἀλλ' ἐπὶ τῆς γῆς. Nemesian. Aucup. fr. 21 (in Wernsdorf's Poet. Lat. Min.) praeda est facilis et amoena Scolopax.

[σπάλαξ or σκάλοψ in Theophr. De Sign. Temp. p. 439, ed. Heinsii, is sometimes taken to apply not to the mole but to this bird: cf. J. G. Schneider, in Arist., vol. iv. p. 131.]

ΣΚΩ'Ψ. Etym. doubtful. The derivation from σκέπτω is not more certain than the older one from σκώπτω (Athen. and Aelian). The σ may be a late prefix, from the false analogy with σκώπτειν. According to Alex. Myndius, ap. Athen. ix. 391 b, Homer wrote

ΣΚΩΨ (*continued*).

κώπας for σκώπας, and Aristotle likewise : so also Speusippus; cf. Ael. xv. 28, and Cobet's note [falso dixit hoc Alexander, Casaubon in Athen. ii. 358]. Doederlein, Hom. Gloss. § 2359, finds the stem in κυβήναις (γλαυξί), Hesych., L. *cucubare*, &c.; in which case κικκάβη (q. v.), and Mod. Gk. κουκουβαία, would seem to be cognate. Hesych. has also σκόπες. The name resembles the cry of the bird, and is in part at least onomatopoeic: cf. It. *jacopo*. In Switzerland it is called Todtenvogel, and cries Tod, Tod, Tod, Hopf. Orakelthiere, p. 102.

The **Little Horned Owl** or **Scops Owl**, *Ephialtes scops*, L. Mod. Gk. κλῶσσος, χιώνι (Erh.).

Od. v. 66 σκῶπές τ' ἴρηκές τε τανύγλωσσοί τε κορῶναι | εἰνάλιαι.
Theocr. Id. i. 134 κῇξ ὀρέων τοὶ σκῶπες ἀηδόσι γαρύσαιντο. Arist. H. A. viii. 3, 592 b ἐλάττων γλαυκός. Two varieties; H. A. ix. 28, 617 b σκῶπες δ' οἱ μὲν ἀεὶ πᾶσαν ὥραν εἰσί, καὶ καλοῦνται ἀεισκῶπες, καὶ οὐκ ἐσθίονται διὰ τὸ ἄβρωτοι εἶναι· ἕτεροι δὲ γίνονται ἐνίοτε τοῦ φθινοπώρου, φαίνονται δ' ἐφ' ἡμέραν μίαν ἢ δύο τὸ πλεῖστον, καὶ εἰσὶν ἐδώδιμοι καὶ σφόδρα εὐδοκιμοῦσιν· καὶ διαφέρουσι τῶν ἀεισκώπων καλουμένων οὗτοι ἄλλῳ μὲν ὡς εἰπεῖν οὐδενί, τῷ δὲ πάχει· καὶ οὗτοι μέν εἰσιν ἄφωνοι, ἐκεῖνοι δὲ φθέγγονται. περὶ δὲ γενέσεως αὐτῶν ἥτις ἐστίν, οὐθὲν ὦπται, πλὴν ὅτι τοῖς ζεφυρίοις φαίνονται. Cf. Callimachus ap. Athen. ix. 391 b; Ael. xv. 28 διαφέρουσι δὲ τῶν ἀεισκώπων τῷ πάχει, καί εἰσι παραπλήσιοι τρυγόνι καὶ φάττῃ (vide Jacobs, in loc.).

Alex. Mynd. ap. Athen. ix. 391 b μικρότερος ἐστὶ γλαυκός, καὶ ἐπὶ μολυβδοφανεῖ τῷ χρώματι ὑπόλευκα στίγματα ἔχει· δύο τε ἀπὸ τῶν ὀφρύων παρ' ἑκάτερον κρόταφον ἀναφέρει πτερά: cf. Ael. l. c.

The account given of the size of the bird and the descriptions in Athenaeus and Aelian agree perfectly with the Scops Owl; this is a noisy bird, repeating its cry with monotonous persistence. But it appears to spend the summer only in S. Europe, migrating to Africa in winter. The passage in Aristotle is perhaps faulty in this connexion, owing to misinterpretation of the name ἀείσκωψ as though from ἀεί. Sundevall supposes the other variety to be the Short-eared Owl, *Strix brachyotus*, a somewhat larger species, which appears merely to pass through Greece on its migrations: vide infra, s.v. **ὠτός**. The bird σκώψ was quite unknown to Pliny, x. (49) 70; as apparently also to Hesych., who has σκῶπες· εἶδος ὀρνέων, οἱ δὲ κολοιοῖς.

According to Metrodorus ap. Athen. l. c. ἀντορχουμένους ἁλίσκεσθαι τοὺς σκώπας. Hence σκώψ and σκωπεύμα as the name of a dance, Ael. xv. 28, Athen. ix. 391 a, xiv. 629 f, where there is a confusion between σκώψ and σκόπος, ὑπόσκοπος: cf. **γλαῦξ**. See also O. Jahn, Vasenbilder, p. 24; Rochett, J. des savans, 1837, pp. 514-517.

ΣΜΑ'ΡΔΙΚΟΝ· στρουθίον, Hesych. Cf. σπαράσιον.

ΣΜΗ'ΡΙΝΘΟΣ· ὄρνις ποιός, Hesych.

ΣΟΥ'ΣΦΑ, *s.* **σοῖσφα.** Indian birds which indicated to the mariner proximity to land, Cosmas, Indopl. ii. p. 182. Schneider, Lex.

ΣΠΑΡΑ'ΣΙΟΝ· ὄρνεον ἐμφερὲς στρουθῷ. ἔνιοι σκίψ, Hesych. Cf. ψάρ, σμάρδικον, &c.

ΣΠΕ'ΛΕΚΤΟΣ· πελεκάν, Hesych.

ΣΠΕ'ΡΓΟΥΛΟΣ· ὀρνιθάριον ἄγριον, Hesych. Vide s. v. **στρουθός.**

ΣΠΕ'ΡΓΥΣ· πρέσβυς, Hesych. This is apparently a bird-name allied to σπέργουλος; the gloss πρέσβυς may be itself corrupt. Cf. Ahr. Dial. ii. p. 111, &c. See also s.v. **πρέσβυς, σποργίλος.**

ΣΠΕΡΜΟΛΟ'ΓΟΣ (also **σπερμονόμος,** Hesych.).

Although commentators now take this word adjectivally (as it is in Athen. ix. 387 b) or generically, I have no doubt that it applies specifically to the **Rook,** *Corvus frugilegus,* L., in Ar. Av. 232 σπερμολόγων τε γένη | ταχὺ πετόμενα, μαλθακὴν ἱέντα γῆρυν: also ibid. 579; and accordingly also in Arist. H. A. viii. 3, 592 b. Cf. Hesych. σπερμολόγος· κολοιῶδες ζῷον; see also Suid.: cf. also Late Lat. *frugilega.* It is so interpreted by older writers, e. g. Caius, De Rarior. Anim. Hist. Libellus, p. 100. In Mod. Gk. the Rook is said to be called χαβαρῶνι. See also s.v. **ὀλαιτοί.**

ΣΠΙ'ΓΓΟΣ· σπίνος, Hesych.

ΣΠΙ'ΖΑ, ΣΠΙ'ΖΗ. (MSS. have also πίζαι). Dim. σπιζίον, Hesych. applied to all small birds;· cf. ἔπιζα· ὄρνεα, Κύπριοι, Hesych. Perhaps from rt. *ping,* to paint, connected with Germ. *fink, finch,* &c. Cf. Eng. *bunt-ing.*

The **Chaffinch,** *Fringilla coelebs,* L. Mod. Gk. σπῖνος, and, on Parnassus, τζόνι (Heldr.).

Soph. fr. 382 κάτω κρέμανται σπίζ' ὅπως ἐν ἕρκεσι. Timo ap. Diog. Laert. iv. 42 ἠΰτε γλαῦκα πέρι σπίζαι. Arist. H. A. viii. 3, 592 b ὄρνις σκωληκοφάγος: ib. ix. 7, 613 b διάγουσι τοῦ μὲν θέρους ἐν τοῖς ἀλεεινοῖς, τοῦ δὲ χειμῶνος ἐν τοῖς ψυχροῖς. Compared in size with ἴυγξ, κύανος, σπιζίτης, ὀροσπίζος, &c., ib. ii. 12, 504, viii. 3, 592 b, ix. 21, 617. σπίζα· ὀρνιθάριον, στρουθῷ ἐμφερές, Hesych.

Evidently some very common bird, from its use as a standard of comparison. I follow Sundevall (in spite of Aubert and Wimmer's scepticism) in identifying it with the Chaffinch, on the ground of

ΣΠΙΖΑ (continued).

tradition, and on the ground of the resemblance of the name to the various forms of the word σπῖνος, which is still the Mod. Gk. name of the bird: partly also because the other common birds which might be meant (Goldfinch, Greenfinch, and Linnet) are fairly well identified under other names.

ΣΠΙΖΙ'ΑΣ. (Cod. Med. στιγξίας).

Mentioned (by name only) in Arist. H. A. viii. 3, 592 b, ix. 36, 620. σπιζίας· ἱέρακος εἶδος, Hesych. Identified by tradition with the **Sparrow-hawk**, *Accipiter nisus*, L.; vide s.v. πέρκος.

ΣΠΙΖΙ'ΤΗΣ. The **Great Tit** or **Ox-eye**, *Parus major*, L. εἶδος αἰγιθαλοῦ ὀρνέου, Hesych.

Arist. H. A. viii. 3, 592 b. Vide s. v. αἰγίθαλος.

ΣΠΙ'ΝΟΣ. Also σπινός (Photius), σπίνα, σπίνη, σπίνθια, Hesych. Cf. also σπίγγος, σπύγγας, πίγγας, Hesych. Dim. σπινίδιον, Ar. fr. 344: σπινίον, Eubul. Incert. 14.

Probably identical with σπίγγος, σπίζα, the **Chaffinch**; still so-called (Heldr.).

Ar. Av. 1079 ὅτι συνείρων τοὺς σπίνους πωλεῖ καθ' ἑπτὰ τοὐβολοῦ. Pax, 1148, Fr. 443, Eubul. ap. Athen. ii. 65 c τίλλειν τε φάττας καὶ κίχλας ὁμοῦ | σπίνοις.

Ael. iv. 60 σπίνοι δὲ ἄρα σοφώτεροι καὶ ἀνθρώπων τὸ μέλλον προεγνωκέναι. ἴσασι γοῦν καὶ χειμῶνα μέλλοντα, καὶ χιόνα ἐσομένην προμηθέστατα ἐφυλάξαντο. καὶ τοῦ καταληφθῆναι δέει, ἀποδιδράσκουσιν ἐς τὰ ἀλσώδη χωρία, καὶ αὐτοῖς τὰ δάση κρησφύγετα ὡς ἂν εἴποις ἐστίν. Cf. Theophr. De Sign. vi. 1, 3; Arat. 1024.

Dion. De Avib. iii. 2, 4 ἅμα τοῖς ἄλλοις στρουθίοις τοῖς κατὰ τὸν βορρᾶν ἐπιδημοῦσι τοῦ ἔαρος ἰξῷ θηρῶνται, τοῖς καλάμοις ἐπικαθίσαντες, κ.τ.λ.— θεαμάτων δ' ἥδιστον στρουθοὺς ὁρᾶν ἰξῷ πεπεδημένους καὶ καταπίπτοντας (!).

ΣΠΟΡΓΙ'ΛΟΣ. In Ar. Av. 300, Σποργίλος probably means a **Sparrow**, and the usual reference to Sporgilos, a barber, if justified at all, makes the joke a double-barrelled one. The word is the same as σπέργουλος or σπέργυς, and as Mod. Gk. σπουργίτης, a Sparrow. πυργίτης, a word applied to a Sparrow by Galen, &c., is rendered in the dictionaries *turrilis*, as if from πύργος: it is obviously σ-πυργίτης; in like manner πέργουλος, Hesych. = σ-πέργουλος; and I have suggested above, somewhat less confidently, that πρέσβυς as a bird-name should perhaps read σπέρβυς = σπέργυς. These words form a parallel series, with π

ΣΠΟΡΓΙΛΟΣ (*continued*).

for τ, to στρουθός, &c.; they have a near ally in Eng. *Sparrow*, and a still nearer in *sprug*.

ΣΤΑΥΝΙ'Ξ· ἱέραξ, Hesych.

ΣΤΗΘΙ'ΑΣ· ὄρνις ποιός, Hesych. Perhaps a misreading for στρουθίας.

ΣΤΡΙ'Ξ. Also στρίγξ, στλίξ. Cf. Hesych., στρίγλος, οἱ δὲ νυκτικόρακι. Also στύξ, ὁ σκώψ τὸ ὄρνεον. An Owl, Lat. *strix*.

Boios ap. Anton. Lib. c. 21. Cf. Hygin. Fab. 28. Theognost. in Anecd. Oxon. ii. 41, 132.

A charm to scare them, στρίγγ' ἀπόπεμπον, νυκτιβόαν, τὰν στρίγγ' ἀπὸ λαοῦ | ὄρνιν ἀνώνυμον ὠκυπόρους ἐπὶ νῆας ἔλαυνε, Anon. fr. Bergk. 26, ap. Festus, p. 314. Cf. Plin. xi. (39) 95 quae sit avium constare non arbitror; Isidor. xii. 7, &c.

ΣΤΡΟΥΘΟΚΑ'ΜΗΛΟΣ, s. στρουθός.

στρουθὸς κατάγαιος (Herod.), στρ. ὁ μέγας s. ἡ μεγάλη (Ar., Xen., Ael.), στρ. ὁ ἐν Λιβύῃ or ὁ Λιβυκός (Arist.), στρ. ὁ τῶν ἀπτήνων (Paus.), στρ. ὁ χερσαῖος (Ael.), στρ. ὁ Ἀράβιος (Ath., Heraclid.), στρ. χαμαιπετής (Lucian), στρουθοκάμηλος (Diod. Sic., Strabo, Pliny), also simply στρουθός (Ar. Ach. 1106, Theophr. Hist. Pl.), στρ. μαυρούσιος (Herodian), στρ. ὁ ἄγριος (Hesych.).

The **Ostrich**, *Struthio Camelus*, L.

Herod. iv. 175 ἐς τὸν πόλεμον στρουθῶν καταγαίων δορὰς φορέουσι προβλήματα [οἱ Μάκαι (to the south of the Persian Gulf)]: ibid. 192 κατὰ τοὺς Νόμαδας (i. e. in the country of the Bedaween) εἰσὶ στρουθοὶ κατάγαιοι.

Xen. Anab. i. 5, 2 στρουθοὶ αἱ μεγάλαι, met with in 'Arabia,' near the Euphrates. στρουθὸν δὲ οὐδεὶς ἔλαβεν· οἱ δὲ διώξαντες τῶν ἱππέων ταχὺ ἐπαύοντο· πολὺ γὰρ ἀπεσπᾶτο φεύγουσα, τοῖς μὲν ποσὶ δρόμῳ, ταῖς δὲ πτέρυξιν ἄρασα, ὥσπερ ἱστίῳ χρωμένη (cf. Ael. ii. 27, iv. 37, viii. 10) εἰ δὲ ἁλίσκεσθαι μέλλοι, τοὺς παραπίπτοντας λίθους εἰς τοὐπίσω σφενδονᾷ τοῖς ποσίν: cf. Phile, De An. iv. 144; Claudian in Eutrop. ii.

Ar. Av. 875 καὶ στρουθῷ μεγάλῃ, μητρὶ θεῶν καὶ ἀνθρώπων.

Ar. Ach. (1106) 1118 καλόν γε καὶ λευκὸν τὸ τῆς στρουθοῦ πτερόν.

Arist. De Part. iv. 14, 697 τὰ μὲν γὰρ ὄρνιθος ἔχει, τὰ δὲ ζῴου τετράποδος. ὡς μὲν γὰρ οὐκ ὢν τετράπους πτερὰ ἔχει, ὡς δ' οὐκ ὢν ὄρνις οὔτε πέτεται μετεωριζόμενος, καὶ τὰ πτερὰ οὐ χρήσιμα πρὸς πτῆσιν ἀλλὰ τριχώδη. ἔτι δὲ ὡς μὲν τετράπους ὢν βλεφαρίδας ἔχει τὰς ἄνωθεν (ibid. ii. 14, 658) καὶ ψιλός ἐστι τὰ περὶ τὴν κεφαλὴν καὶ τὰ ἄνω τοῦ αὐχένος, ὥστε τριχωδεστέρας ἔχειν τὰς βλεφαρίδας, ὡς δ' ὄρνις ὢν τὰ κάτωθεν ἐπτέρωται, καὶ δίπους μέν ἐστιν ὡς ὄρνις, δίχαλος δὲ (ibid. iv. 12, 695) ὡς τετράπους; οὐ γὰρ δακτύλους

ΣΤΡΟΥΘΟΚΑΜΗΛΟΣ (*continued*).

ἔχει ἀλλὰ χηλάς. τούτου δ' αἴτιον ὅτι τὸ μέγεθος οὐκ ὄρνιθος ἔχει ἀλλὰ τετράποδος : cf. Plin. x. 1, x. (22) 29, xi. (37) 47, &c. Arist. H. A. ix. 15, 616 b, lays more eggs than any other bird (the fact being that several lay in one nest), cf. De Gen. iii. 1, 749 b, and Ael. iv. 37. On the number of eggs (ὑπὲρ τὰ ὀγδοήκοντα !), on the construction of the nest, and on its maternal affection, v. Ael. xiv. 7, Phile, l. c.

Heraclides ap. Athen. iv. 145 d στρουθοὶ οἱ Ἀράβιοι, at the banquets of the Persian King ; and of the 'Indian' King (στρ. οἱ χερσαῖοι), Ael. xiv. 13 ; also of Heliogabalus, Ael. Lampridius, De Heliog. 28.

On the capture of the Ostrich see also Diod. Sic. ii. 50, Ael. xiv. 7, Opp. De Ven. iii. 487. The interesting account in Strabo, xvi. 4, 11, doubtless refers to the Ostrich.

How the Ostrich swallows stones, which are a medicine for the eyes, and how its fat and sinews are a useful tonic, Ael. xiv. 7, Phile, l.c. The price of Ostrich-fat, Plin. xxix. 30.

Pausan. ix. 31, 1 τὴν δὲ Ἀρσινόην (a statue in Helicon) στρουθὸς φέρει χαλκῆ τῶν ἀπτήνων· πτερὰ μέν γε καὶ αὗται κατὰ ταὐτὰ ταῖς ἄλλαις φύουσιν, ὑπὸ δὲ βάρους καὶ διὰ μέγεθος οὐχ οἷά τέ ἐστιν ἀνέχειν σφᾶς ἐς τὸν ἀέρα τὰ πτερά. Cf. the *ales equos* of Cat. lxvi. 54, and Ellis's note thereon ; cf. also Flav. Vop. Firm. c. 6 sedentem ingentibus struthionibus vectum esse ut quasi volitasset.

Opp. De Ven. iii. 482 et seq. μέγα θαῦμα, μετὰ στρουθοῖο κάμηλον ... τῆς ἤτοι μέγεθος μὲν ὑπέρβιον, ὅσσον ὕπερθε | νώτοις εὐρυτάτοισι φέρειν νεοθηλέα κοῦρον· | οὐδὲ μὲν ὀρνίθεσσιν ὁμοῖος ἀμβαδὸν εὐνή, | Βάκτριον οἷα δὲ φῦλον ἔχουσιν ἀπόστροφα λέκτρα, &c.

Ostriches ἐν τῇ μὴ ὑομένῃ τῆς Λιβύης, Theophr. Hist. Pl. iv. 3, 5.

Callim. Rhod. ap. Athen. v. 200 f στρουθῶν συνωρίδες ὀκτώ, i. e. eight yoke of ostriches (drawing chariots?) in a procession of Ptolemy Philadelphus at Alexandria. Cf. Plautus, Pers. ii. 2, 17 Vola curriculo. Isthuc marinus passer per circum solet. Ostriches harnessed to the coach of the Emperor Firmus, Flav. Vopisc. Firm. c. 6.

Ostrich plumes mentioned, ibid. iv. 4, 5, ix. 12, 5.

How the eggs are eaten by the Garamantes (in the Libyan Desert), Lucian, Dipsad. 235, but are of inferior quality, Galen, De Ovis, xxii.

How the Ostrich hides its head in the sand, Oppian, Halieut. iv. 630 τοῖα δὲ καὶ Λιβύης πτερόεν βοτὸν ἀγκυλόδειρον | νήπια τεχνάζει, κ.τ.λ. Cf. Plin. x. 1.

The name στρουθοκάμηλος is modern, cf. Galen, De Alim. iii. 20 τὸ δὲ τῶν στρουθοκαμήλων [ὄνομα καὶ τοῖς παλαιοῖς] ἀηθές. ὀνομάζουσι γὰρ αὐτὰς μεγάλας στρουθούς : cf. ibid. De Prob. Succ. Alim. vi.

ΣΤΡΟΥΘΟ'Σ, ὁ and ἡ. Also στροῦς, Hesych. Dimin. στρουθίον, Arist., Anax., 3. 164, Ephipp. 3. 326; στρουθάριον Eubul. 3. 268 (14); στρουθίας, Com. Anon. 4. 647 (172); στρουθίς, Eust. Opusc. 312,

ΣΤΡΟΥΘΟΣ (*continued*).

cf. Alexid. 3. 449, and Meineke's note; στρουθίσκος, Theod. Prodr. Cf. σποργίλος, σπέργουλος, Goth. *spar-va*, O. H. G. *spar-o*, Eng. *sprug, sparrow,* &c.

A Sparrow, *Passer domesticus*, L., in Greece, as here, the commonest of birds (Von der Mühle, &c.): in Elis, called also δείρης, q. v. Mod. Gk. σπουργίτης (Erhard); on Parnassus τρυποφράκτης (Heldreich); and in Cyprus στροῦθος (Sakellarios).

Very often used generically, like Lat. *passer*, Heb. צפור, of any small birds (cf. Phavorinus, &c., στρουθία δ' οὐδετέρως πάντα τὰ μικρὰ τῶν ὀρνίθων); sometimes of larger birds, e. g. στρουθὸς κατοικάς, Nic. Alex. 60. 535; transferred to the Ostrich (vide s. v. στρουθοκάμηλος); applied to the Stymphalian birds, Epigr. Gr. 1802. 5.

Early and Poetic References.—The story of the serpent and the brood of sparrows, II. ii. 308-332: this is an instance where the name is used vaguely and not specifically (as is צפור in Deut. xxii. 6); the Homeric account of the nest is reflected in Ael. iv. 38, and the statement as to the number of eggs reappears in Arist. fr. 1527, ap. Athen. ix. 391 f.

Venus' team of sparrows, Sappho fr. 1. 9 κάλοι δέ σ' ἆγον | ὤκεες στρουθοὶ περὶ γᾶς μελαίνας | πύκνα δινεῦντες πτέρ' ἀπ' ὠράνω αἰθέρ|ος διὰ μέσσω. On the connexion between this image and the lascivious propensities of the sparrow, cf. Athen. l. c.

The story of Aristodicus and the sparrows' nests in the temple, Herod. i. 159.

Not mentioned in Attic Tragedy, save for Aesch. Ag. 145 κατάμομφά τε φάσματα στρουθῶν, on which line see the textual commentators. Frequent in Aristophanes: Vesp. 207, Lys. 723, Ach. 1106, &c.

Description.—Arist. H. A. viii. 3, 592 b ὄρνις σκωληκοφάγος. Ib. ii. 15, 505 b πρὸς τοῖς ἐντέροις τὴν χολὴν ἔχει. Ibid. 17, 509 οὐκ ἔχει οὔτε τὸν στόμαχον οὔτε τὸν πρόλοβον εὐρύν, ἀλλὰ τὴν κοιλίαν μακράν. ἀποφυάδας ἔχει· ἀλλὰ μικρὰ πάμπαν. Ib. ix. 49 B, 633 b καὶ κονίονται καὶ λοῦνται. Ibid. 7, 613 λέγουσι δέ τινες καὶ τῶν στρουθίων ἐνιαυτὸν μόνον ζῆν τοὺς ἄρρενας, ποιούμενοι σημεῖον ὅτι τοῦ ἔαρος οὐ φαίνονται ἔχοντες εὐθὺς τὰ περὶ τὸν πώγωνα μέλανα, ὕστερον δ' ἴσχουσιν, ὡς οὐδενὸς σωζομένου τῶν προτέρων· τὰς δὲ θηλείας μακροβιωτέρας εἶναι τῶν στρουθίων· ταύτας γὰρ ἀλίσκεσθαι ἐν τοῖς νέοις, καὶ διαδήλας εἶναι τῷ ἔχειν τὰ περὶ τὰ χείλη σκληρά. Arist. fr. 273. 1527 (ap. Athen. 392 a) μεταβάλλει. On albino varieties, cf. H. A. iii. 12, 519; De Gen. v. 6, 785 b.

Alex. Mynd. ap. Athen. ix. 391 b δύο γένη εἶναι τῶν στρουθῶν, τὸ μὲν ἥμερον, τὸ δ' ἄγριον· τὰς δὲ θηλείας αὐτῶν ἀσθενεστέρας τὰ τ' ἄλλα εἶναι, καὶ τὸ ῥύγχος κερατοειδὲς μᾶλλον τὴν χρόαν, τὸ δὲ πρόσωπον οὔτε λίαν λευκὸν ἐχούσας οὔτε μέλαν.

ΣΤΡΟΥΘΟΣ (*continued*).

Reproduction.—Arist. H. A. v. 2, 539 b ὀξέως συγγίνεται : De Gen. iv. 6, 774 b τίκτουσιν ἀτελῆ καὶ τυφλά· πολυτοκοῦσιν, cf. fr. 273. 1527 (ap. Athen. 391 b) τίκτει μέχρι ὀκτώ. Athen. ix. 391 c ὀχευτικοί εἰσιν. Hence used as an aphrodisiac, Terpsicles, ap. Athen. l. c. The erotic symbolism of the sparrow is alluded to by Festus, s. v. *struthcum*.

Whatever Lesbia's 'sparrow' may have been, I am pretty sure in my own mind, *pace* Professor Robinson Ellis, that it was not *Passer domesticus*, the most intractable and least amiable of cage-birds (*experto crede;* cf. also Bechstein's 'Cage-birds'; on the point at issue, see De Quincey, Selections, viii. p. 82). As to στρουθίον, or *passer*, used (non-specifically) of a cage-bird, cf. Job xl. 24 παίξῃ δὲ ἐν αὐτῷ ὥσπερ ὀρνέῳ; ἢ δήσεις αὐτὸν ὥσπερ στρουθίον παιδίῳ; cf. also Boch. Hieroz. ii. 152.

A Weather-prophet.—Theophr. Sign. vi. 3 στρουθὸς σπίζων ἕωθεν χειμέριον [σημαίνει]· στρουθὸς ἐὰν λευκὸς χειμῶνα μέγαν σημαίνει : cf. ibid. c. 2.

ΣΤΥΜΦΑΛΙ΄ΔΕΣ, *s.* **Στυμφηλίδες ὄρνιθες**. Fabulous and mystical birds.

They were met with by the Argonauts at the Island of Dia; they shot forth their feathers like arrows, and were put to flight by the beating of spears on shields, *ex more Curetum*, Apoll. Rhod. ii. 1054 and Schol., Q. Smyrn. vi. 227, Hygin. Fab. xx, Claud. Idyll. ii. They were shot by Hercules in his fifth labour, *in insula Martis*. Hygin. Fab. xxx, or at Lake Stymphalus, Paus. viii. 22, 4; or terrified by him with a brazen drum, Strab. viii. 371, 389: cf. Pisand. ap. Paus. l. c., &c. They inhabited Arabia, and had migrated thence; they were as large as cranes, and resembled the Ibis, but had stronger beaks; they pierced through iron and brass but were held by reed-mats, ἐσθῆτες φλόϊναι, as small birds by bird-lime, Paus. l. c. Represented, three in number, on the metopes of the temple of Zeus at Olympia (now in the Louvre) Paus. v. 10, 9; cf. Expéd. de la Morée, i. pl. 77, &c., &c. Also, together with female figures having birds' legs, on the temple of Artemis Stymphalia at Lake Stymphalus, Paus. l. c. Also on medals, cf. Méd. du Card. Alban. ii. p. 70, &c.; on an amphora in the Brit. Mus., J. de Witte, Gaz. Archéolog. 1876, pl. iii; on coins, as *crested* water-birds (B. C. 431-370), B. M. Cat. Coins, Peloponnese, p. 199.

According to Dupuis (Orig. de tous les cultes, ii. p. 260, 8vo, l'an iii), the Stymphalian birds are the constellations of Aquila, Cygnus and Vultur or Lyra, which rise together with, that is to say are *paranatellons* of, the sign Sagittarius (cf. Hygin., Columella, &c.). Starting from the Lion (with which the labours of Hercules began) the sign of the Archer is the fifth in order: it was moreover the domicile of Diana, to whom belonged the temple at Stymphalus. A similar explanation possibly underlies the story of the Birds of Diomede.

ΣΤΡΟΥΘΟΣ—ΣΧΟΙΝΙΛΟΣ

ΣΤΥ'Ξ. A bird-name, mentioned, in connexion with a fabled metamorphosis, by Boios ap. Anton. Lib. c. xxi. Vide s.v. στρίξ.

ΣΥΚΑΛΙ'Σ (MSS. have also καλίς, συκαλλίς, σικαλίς). On the form συκαλλίς, cf. Athen. ii. 65 c.

Probably the **Black-cap Warbler**, *Sylvia atricapilla*, auctt. Lat. *ficedula*. Vide s. v. μελαγκόρυφος; cf. also κουτίδες.
Epich. fr. 49 Ahr. ap. Athen. ii. 65 c ἀγλααὶ συκαλλίδες.
Arist. H. A. viii. 3, 592 b ὄρνις σκωληκοφάγος. Ib. ix. 49 B, 632 b οὗτοι (συκαλίδες καὶ μελαγκόρυφοι) μεταβάλλουσιν εἰς ἀλλήλους· γίνεται δ' ἡ μὲν συκαλὶς περὶ τὴν ὀπώραν, ὁ δὲ μελαγκόρυφος εὐθέως μετὰ τὸ φθινόπωρον. Cf. Plin. x. (29) 44, Geopon. xv. 1, 22, Festus.
Alex. Mynd. ap. Athen. ii. 65 b ἕτερος τῶν αἰγιθάλων ὑφ' ὧν μὲν ἔλαιον καλεῖται, ὑπὸ δέ τινων πυρρίας· συκαλὶς δ', ὅταν ἀκμάζῃ τὰ σῦκα. Athen. ibid. δύο δ' εἶναι γένη αὐτοῦ, συκαλίδα καὶ μελαγκόρυφον. ἁλίσκονται δ' αὗται τῷ τῶν σύκων καιρῷ. Mentioned also, Ael. xiii. 25.

Aubert and Wimmer suppose the Marsh Tit, *Parus palustris*, L., *P. atricapillus*, Gmel., to be meant. Sundevall supposes a confusion between that bird (μελαγκόρυφος) and the Black-headed or Pied Flycatcher, *Muscicapa atricapilla*, L., (συκαλίς), as accounting for the imaginary metamorphosis. But the Black-headed Flycatcher is probably chosen incorrectly, and should be the Black-cap Warbler or true *Beccafico*, *Sylvia atricapilla*. It is the latter and not the former bird which comes down into the plains in autumn and is caught in multitudes on the fig-trees (Krüper, p. 241, &c.). The former is a comparatively scarce bird in Greece (Krüper, Lindermayer). Coray, on the other hand, identifies συκαλίς with the Golden Oriole, in Mod. Gk. συκοφάγος. The Golden Oriole is also known now-a-days as κιτρινοποῦλι and σοχλαῖος, the latter of which names might possibly be a corruption of συκαλίς.

ΣΥΡΙΣΤΗ'Σ· γέρανος ἄρρην, Hesych.

ΣΥΡΟΠΕ'ΡΔΙΞ. A variety or species of **Partridge**.

Ael. xvi. 7 συροπέρδιξ γίνεται περὶ τὴν Ἀντιόχειαν τὴν Πισιδίας, καὶ σιτεῖται καὶ λίθους· μικρότερος δέ ἐστι τοῦ πέρδικος καὶ μέλας τὴν χρόαν, πυρρὸς δὲ τὸ ῥάμφος. οὐχ ἡμεροῦται δὲ κατὰ τὸν ἄλλον, οὐδὲ γίνεται τιθασός, ἀλλ' ἄγριος ἐς τὸ ἀεὶ διαμένει. ἔστι δὲ οὐ μέγας, βρωθῆναί τε ἡδίων τοῦ ἑτέρου, καὶ τὴν σάρκα πως δοκεῖ πυκνότερος. Cf. Phile, De Anim. 330. The species cannot be certainly identified from this account.

ΣΧΟΙΝΙ'ΛΟΣ. (Also σχοινίκλος, σχοινῖλος, &c. Hesych. σχοίνικος.) (From σχοῖνος, iuncus.)

Probably a **Wagtail**, *Motacilla* sp.

Arist. H. A. viii. 3, 593 b: mentioned with κίγκλος and πύγαργος

ΣΧΟΙΝΙΛΟΣ (continued).

as a small bird, smaller than a thrush, which moves its tail and frequents rivers and ponds.

The identification hangs by that of κίγκλος and πύγαργος, q.v. Of the three bird-names, not one is to be identified with any certainty; I am somewhat inclined to interpret πύγαργος, the largest of the three, as a Sandpiper, and to suppose the other two to be both Wagtails; at any rate, σχοινίλος, in its derivation, rather suggests a Wagtail than a Sandpiper. The same bird appears elsewhere under such names as κίλλουρος, σείσουρα, σεισοπυγίς; vide also s.v. σκαλίδρις. The identification with the Reed Bunting, *Emberiza schoeniclus*, adopted by Turner, Gaza, &c., &c., is based purely on the derivation of the word, and is contradicted by the fact that the Reed Bunting does not flick its tail as the others do.

ΣΧΟΙΝΙ'ΩΝ. An unknown bird; perhaps, as Gaza and others take it, identical with σχοινίλος.

Arist. H. A. ix. 1, 610 σχοινίων καὶ κόρυδος φίλοι.

ΣΩ͂ΔΕΣ, αἱ. An unknown small bird, caught with bird-lime: Dion. De Avib. iii. 2.

ΤΑΓΗ'Ν, ΤΑΓΗΝΑ'ΡΙΟΝ. Apparently names for ἀτταγάς (q.v.), Suid. ταγηνάρι is given by Tournefort (Voy. ii. p. 111), as Mod. Gk. for the Francolin.

ΤΑΝΥΣΙ'ΠΤΕΡΟΣ. A species of Hawk, sacred to Hera, Ael. xii. 4.

ΤΑΤΥ'ΡΑΣ. Vide s.v. τέταρος.

ΤΑΩ'Σ, s. ταῶς. According to Trypho, ap. Athen. ix. 397 e, in Attic, e.g. Ar. Av. 101, 269, ταῶς, i.e. ταϝῶς. The word is referred, with Hebr. *tukk-iyim*, Arab. *tāwus*, Pers. *tāūs*, to Tamil *tógai*, Sk. *çikhí* (v. Edl., &c.). Cf. Lat. *pavo*, A. S. *pawa*, Ger. *pfau*, &c. On the change of Semitic *t* into *p* see Hehn, Wanderings of Plants, &c., pp. 208, 266.

The **Peacock**. Mod. Gk. παγώνι (Heldr.), i.e. παϝώνι; also ὁ παών and τὸ παῶνιν, Πουλολόγος ap. Wagner's Carm. Gr. Med. Aevi.

History and Mythology.—Menodot. ap. Athen. xiv. 655 a οἱ ταοὶ ἱεροί εἰσι τῆς Ἥρας. καὶ μή ποτε πρώτιστοι καὶ ἐγένοντο καὶ ἐτράφησαν ἐν Σάμῳ, καὶ ἐντεῦθεν εἰς τοὺς ἔξω τόπους διεδόθησαν. Cf. Antiphanes, ibid., ἡ δ᾽ ἐν Σάμῳ | Ἥρα τὸ χρυσοῦν, φασίν, ὀρνίθων γένος [ἔχει], | τοὺς καλλιμόρφους καὶ περιβλέπτους ταῶς. The Peacock on coins of Samos, Athen. l.c., cf. Eckhel, Doctr. Numm. ii. p. 568; Imhoof-Blumer and Keller, pl. v. 49. Samos was, according to this evidence, the original home of the Peacock in Greece. The bird was sacred to Hera (as also at

ΤΑΩΣ (continued).

Tiryns, Paus. ii. 17, 6) as Queen of Heaven (cf. Eur. Hel. 1096) from its *starry* tail (Hehn): cf. Ovid, Met. xv. 385 Iunonis volucrem, quae caudâ sidera portat; ibid. i. 723; Juv. vii. 32; Stat. Silv. ii. 4, 26; Claudian, Eutrop. ii. 330. Cf. also Joh. Lydus, De Menss. p. 66 καὶ ταῶνα τὴν ὄρνιθα τοῖς ἱεροῖς τῆς Ἥρας οἱ φυσικοὶ διδόασιν, οἱονεὶ τὸν ἀστερωπὸν ἀέρα, ἤτοι οὐρανόν. Cf. also Lucian, De Domo, xi. p. 908; Hemsterh. ad Nigr. i. p. 247. The Peacock is associated with Hera on coins also of Cos, Halicarnassus, &c. On a Roman zodiac (Millin, Galér. Mythol. pl. xxix. fig. 86) a Peacock comes after Capricorn, coinciding with the Athenian month Gamelion, the month (Hesych.) of Hera; cf. Boetticher, Philologus xxii. p. 399, 1865, Pyl, Der Zwölfgötterkreis im Louvre, Greifswald, 1857, &c. [The association of Hera with the month Gamelion (Jan.-Feb.) is due to the fact that this was the month of the sign Aquarius; and the connexion in turn between Hera and Aquarius is connected with the fact that the Full Moon stood in that sign when the Sun was in Leo, in the month of Zeus, at the season of the Olympic festival.]

The story of Argus, Mosch. Id. ii. 58, Ovid, Met. i. 720, Dion. De Avib. i. 28 φρουρὸς οὗτος [ὁ ταώς] ἦν τῆς Ἰοῦς, ἡνίκα Ἥρα κατ' αὐτῆς ἐχαλέπαινεν· Ἑρμῆς δ' ἀνεῖλεν αὐτόν, καὶ τελευτήσαντος, ἀνῆκεν ὄρνιν ἡ γῆ τῶν ὀφθαλμῶν ἔχοντα τὰ σημεῖα τῶν πρόσθεν. Hence a Scholiast in Ar. Av. 102 suggests (sed hyeme gallica frigidior est haec coniectura, Bochart) Ταὼς ὁ Τηρεύς· παρὰ τὸ τηρεῖν τὴν Ἰώ.

On Peacocks in Athens, in the time of the Persian Wars, Antiphon ap. Athen. ix. 397 c τούτους τρέφειν Δῆμον τὸν Πυριλάμπους καὶ πολλοὺς παραγίνεσθαι κατὰ πόθον τῆς τῶν ὀρνίθων θέας ἔκ τε Λακεδαίμονος καὶ Θετταλίας καὶ σπουδὴν ποιεῖσθαι τῶν ᾠῶν μεταλαβεῖν . . . ἀλλὰ τὰς μὲν νουμηνίας ὁ βουλόμενος εἰσῄει, τὰς δ' ἄλλας ἡμέρας εἴ τις ἔλθοι βουλόμενος θεάσασθαι, οὐκ ἔστιν ὅστις ἔτυχε. καὶ ταῦτα οὐκ ἐχθὲς οὐδὲ πρῴην, ἀλλ' ἔτη πλέον ἢ τριάκοντά ἐστιν: cf. Ael. v. 21. Its rarity at the time is suggested in Ar. Av. 102, 270: but already a nickname in Ar. Ach. 63; cf. Strattis, Μακεδ. 7, ap. Athen. 654 F πολλῶν φλυάρων καὶ ταῶν ἀντάξια.

Its former rarity and subsequent abundance, Antiph. ap. Athen. ix. 397 a τῶν ταῶν μὲν ὡς ἅπαξ τις ζεῦγος ἤγαγεν μόνον | σπάνιον ὂν τὸ χρῆμα πλείους δ' εἰσὶ νῦν τῶν ὀρτύγων (at Rome), cf. Eubul. 3. 259; for other citations, see Athen. xiv. 654 e-655 a; ἐτιμῶντο δὲ τὸν ἄρρενα καὶ τὸν θῆλυν δραχμῶν μυρίων, Antiph. ap. Ael. v. 21; cf. also Plut. i. 160 d, Plin. x. (20) 22, Varro, R. R. iii. 6, Macrob. Sat. iii. 13, &c.

On the probably independent introduction of Peacocks into Rome, cf. Hehn, op. c.

The Peacock is an Indian bird, Aelian passim, Lucian, Navig., &c.; and was bred for the 'Indian' King, Ael. xiii. 18 ἐν τοῖς παραδείσοις

ΤΑΩΣ (continued).

τρέφονται ταώς ήμεροι. It was likewise kept in Babylon, Diod. Sic. ii; and the passage in Ar. Ach. 63 may imply that the Persian ambassador was bringing a present of peacocks to the City. How Alexander protected the Indian Peacocks on account of their beauty, under pain of a heavy penalty, Ael. v. 21. An Indian Peacock presented to the Egyptian King, Ael. xi. 33. The Indian Peacocks larger than elsewhere, ibid. xvi. 2. The Peacock throne at Babylon (as to this day, according to report, at Teheran), Philostr. 386 k.

The Peacock, like the Cock, was also called the Persian Bird. A Schol. on Ar. Av. 707 has τὰ πολυτελῆ πάντα, οἶς μόνος βασιλεὺς ἐχρῆτο, ἐκαλεῖτο Περσικά· καὶ νῦν οὐκ ἰδίως τις ὄρνις Περσικός. τινὲς δὲ τὸν ἀλεκτρυόνα, οἱ δὲ τὸν ταῶ. Cf. Suidas, Μηδικὸς ὄρνις, ὁ ταώς. Ταὼς εὐπήληξ, ὁ Μηδικὸς καὶ χρυσόπτερος καὶ ἀλαζονικὸς ὄρνις: cf. Philostr. loc. cit. Vide s. v. **Μηδικὸς ὄρνις**.

The Peacock as food, Ael. iii. 42; first so used by Hortensius, ibid. v. 21, Plin. x. (20) 23; cf. Hor. Sat. ii. 2. 28, Juv. Sat. ii. 143, vii. 32, Varro, De R. R. iii. 6, Columella, viii. 11, and innumerable other Lat. references.

Description.—Arist. H. A. vi. 9, 564 ὁ δὲ ταὼς ζῇ μὲν περὶ πέντε καὶ εἴκοσιν ἔτη (cf. Plin. x. (20) 22), γεννᾷ δὲ τριέτης μάλιστα, ἐν οἶς καὶ τὴν ποικιλίαν τῶν πτερῶν ἀπολαμβάνει· ἐκλέπει δ' ἐν τριάκονθ' ἡμέραις ἢ μικρῷ πλείοσιν. ἅπαξ δὲ τοῦ ἔτους μόνον τίκτει, τίκτει δ' ᾠὰ δώδεκα ἢ μικρῷ ἐλάττω. τίκτει δὲ διαλείπων δύο ἢ τρεῖς ἡμέρας καὶ οὐκ ἐφεξῆς (cf. Ael. v. 32, Plin. x. (59) 79, Colum. viii. 11, Pallad. i. 28, &c.). αἱ δὲ πρωτοτόκοι μάλιστα περὶ ὀκτὼ ᾠά. τίκτουσι δ' οἱ ταῷ καὶ ὑπηνέμια. ὀχεύονται δὲ περὶ τὸ ἔαρ· γίνεται δὲ καὶ ὁ τόκος εὐθέως μετὰ τὴν ὀχείαν. πτερορρυεῖ δὲ ἅμα τοῖς πρώτοις τῶν δένδρων καὶ ἄρχεται αὖθις ἀπολαμβάνειν τὴν πτέρωσιν ἅμα τῇ τούτων βλαστήσει. ἀλεκτορίδι δ' ὑποτιθέασιν αὐτῶν τὰ ᾠὰ ἐπῳάζειν οἱ τρέφοντες διὰ τὸ τὸν ἄρρενα τῆς θηλείας τοῦτο δρώσης ἐπιπετόμενον συντρίβειν: cf. Arist. fr. 274. 1527 b, ap. Athen. ix. 397 b.

Its plumage and its 'pride,' Mosch. Id. ii. 59 ὄρνις ἀγαλλόμενος πτερύγων πολυανθέϊ χροιῇ (cf. Ael. l. c. ἔοικεν ἀνθηρῷ λειμῶνι) | ταρσὰ δ' ἀναπλώσας, ὡσεί τέ τις ὠκύαλος νηῦς, | χρυσείου ταλάροιο περίσκεπε χείλεα τάρσοις. Ael. v. 21 ὁ ταὼς οἶδεν ὀρνίθων ὡραιότατος ὤν, καὶ ἔνθά οἱ τὸ κάλλος κάθηται καὶ τοῦτο οἶδε, καὶ ἐπ' αὐτῷ κομᾷ, καὶ σοβερός ἐστι, καὶ θαρρεῖ τοῖς πτεροῖς, ὡσπεροῦν αὐτῷ καὶ κόσμον παρατίθησι, καὶ πρὸς τοὺς ἔξωθεν φόβον ἀποστέλλει, κ.τ.λ. Ach. Tat. i ὁ δὲ τοῦ ταῶ λειμὼν εὐανθέστερος· πεφύτευται γὰρ αὐτῷ καὶ χρυσὸς ἐν τοῖς πτεροῖς, κύκλῳ δὲ τὸ ἀλοιργὲς τὸν χρυσὸν περιθέει τὸν ἴσον κύκλον. Arist. H. A. i. 1, 488 b ὄρνις φθονερὸς καὶ φιλόκαλος. Lucian. Dom. 11 (3. 196) ἐπιστρέφει γοῦν ἑαυτόν, καὶ περιάγει καὶ ἐμπομπεύει τῷ κάλλει. Dion. De Avib. i. 28 τὸ κάλλος δὲ ὁ ταὼς τὸ οἰκεῖον τεθαύμακε, καὶ εἰ καλόν τις αὐτὸν ὀνομάσειεν, εὐθὺς τῶν πτερῶν τὰ ἄνθη μεμιγμένα χρυσῷ, ὥσπερ τινὰ λειμῶνα, δείκνυσιν ἀναστήσας,

ΤΑΩΣ (*continued*).

περιάγων εἰς κύκλον αὐτὰ διατεταγμένοις ὄμμασιν· τὰ δὴ κατὰ τῆς οὐρᾶς λάμπουσιν ὥσπερ ἀστέρες αὐτῷ, κ.τ.λ. Chrysipp. ap. Plut. ii. 1044 C ὁ ταὼς ἕνεκα τῆς ὥρας γέγονε, διὰ τὸ κάλλος αὐτῆς. Cf. Opp. Cyneg. iii. 344 ὅσσον ἐν ἠερίοισι ταὼς καλὸς οἰωνοῖσι. Plin. x. (20) 22 Gemmantes laudatus expandit colores adverso maxime sole, quia sic fulgentius radiant : ... omnesque in acervum contrahit pennarum, quos spectari gaudet oculos. Colum. R. R. ix. 11 Semetipsum, veluti mirantem, caudae gemmantibus pennis protegit, idque cum facit, rotare dicitur. Ovid, Art. Amor. i. 627 Laudatas ostendit aves Iunonia pennas ; Si tacitus spectes, illa recondit opes : cf. id. De Medic. Fac. 33, Met. xiii. 802. Cf. also Hor. Sat. ii. 2, 24, Lucret. ii. 806, Stat. Silv. ii. 3, 26, Mart. xiii. 70, Propert. ii. 24, 11 ; Phaedr. iii. 57, &c., &c. It is, however, much ashamed of its ugly feet : Phile, 208 συστέλλεται δὲ καὶ κατασπᾷ τὸν τύφον | ὁρῶν δυσειδεῖς ἐκ ῥυτίδων τοὺς πόδας.

Its harsh cry, Anaxilaus ap. Ath. xiv. 655 a οἰμώζων ταώς : Eup. 2. 437 (4) μήποτε θρέψω παρὰ Περσεφόνῃ τοιόνδε ταῶν, ὃς τοὺς εὕδοντας ἐγείρει.

Various legends.

Uses as a charm λίνου ῥίζαν, which it carries under its wing, Ael. xi. 18. How the peacock swallows its excrement, lest we should use it in medicine, Plin. xxix. 38.

A peacock enamoured of a maid, Clearch. ap. Athen. xiii. 606 c.

Fable.—The Crane and the Peacock, Babr. lxv, cxlii (ed. Rutherford) " σὺ δ' ὡς ἀλέκτωρ ταῖσδε ταῖς καταχρύσοις | χαμαὶ πτερύσσῃ," φησίν, " οἶδ' ἄνω φαίνῃ." Cf. Suid., s. v. γέρανος.

ΤΕΛΕ´ΑΣ. A bird-name (?). Ar. Av. 168 and Schol.

ΤΕ´ΤΑΡΟΣ. A Pheasant. A Median word, whence Pers. *tedjrw*, adopted into Old Scl. *tetravi*, *tetria*, &c. ; also Lith. *teterva*, *teterwas*, *tettera*, whence Finn. *tetri* ; adopted further into Sw. *tjäder*, Dan. *tuir*, and possibly incorporated (Hehn) into Eng. *turkey*. Cf. Hind. *tittiri*, a Partridge or Francolin ; Lat. *tetrao*, Gk. τέτραξ, τετράων. Cf. Pott, Etym. Forsch. i. p. lxxx.

Ptolem. Euerg. ap. Athen. xiv. 654 c τά τε τῶν φασιανῶν οὓς τετάρους (*al.* τετράωνας) ὀνομάζουσιν. [οὓς] οὐ μόνον ἐκ Μηδείας μετεπέμπετο, ἀλλὰ καὶ νομάδας ὄρνιθας ὑποβαλὼν ἐποίησε πλῆθος, ὥστε καὶ σιτεῖσθαι. τὸ δὲ βρῶμα πολυτελὲς ἀποφαίνουσιν : cf. ibid. ix. 387 e.

Also τατύρας, Epaenetus, Artemid. and Pamph. ap. Athen. ix. 387 d ὁ φασιανὸς ὄρνις τατύρας καλεῖται : cf. Hesych., who gives also τιτύρας, τίτυρος, cf. Theophr. Char. vi. 2. Hesych. has further τετύργη· φασιανῶν εἶδος, where word and gloss are alike corrupt ; cj. τέταροι· φασιανῶν εἶδος. ταύτασος and τεγγύρος, Hesych., are probably also akin. See also s. vv. τέτραξ, τετράων.

ΤΕΤΡΆΔΩΝ ὄρνεόν τι, Ἀλκαῖος, Hesych. Cf. ibid. τετράδυσιν· ἀηδόνα. See Schmidt *in loc.*, and Bergk, P. Lyr. Gr. iii. p. 192, fr. 154 (116).

ΤΕΤΡΑΓΟΝ· ὀρνιθάριόν τι, Λάκωνες, Hesych. Cf. τετράδων.

ΤΈΤΡΑΞ. A doubtful word, applied to the Guinea-fowl.

Ar. Av. 885, Eust. 1205, 27.

A discussion concerning the identity of this bird in Athen. ix. (c. 58). 398, c–f. Alex. Mynd. ibid. τέτραξ τὸ μέγεθος ἴσος σπερμολόγῳ, τὸ χρῶμα κεραμεοῦς, ῥυπαραῖς στιγμαῖς καὶ μεγάλαις γραμμαῖς ποικίλος, καρποφάγος, ὅταν ᾠοτοκῇ δέ, τετράζει τῇ φωνῇ. [The disputants here seem to suppose that Alexander Myndius referred to some very little bird, τινὸς τῶν σμικροτάτων.] Epicharm., ibid. τέτραγας σπερματολόγους τε κἀγλαὰς συκαλίδας.... ἐρωδιοί... τέτραγές τε [καὶ] σπερματολόγοι. Athen. l. c. ἅμα δὲ ταῦτα λέγοντος αὐτοῦ, εἰσῆλθέ τις φέρων ἐν τῷ ταλάρῳ τὸν τέτρακα. ἦν δὲ τὸ μὲν μέγεθος ὑπὲρ ἀλεκτρυόνα τὸν μέγιστον, τὸ δὲ εἶδος πορφυρίωνι παραπλήσιος· καὶ ἀπὸ τῶν ὤτων ἑκατέρωθεν εἶχε κρεμάμενα ὥσπερ οἱ ἀλεκτρυόνες τὰ κάλλαια· βαρεῖα δ' ἦν ἡ φωνή. θαυμασάντων οὖν ἡμῶν τὸ εὐανθὲς τοῦ ὄρνιθος μετ' οὐ πολὺ καὶ ἐσκευασμένος παρηνέχθη, καὶ τὰ κρέα αὐτοῦ ἦν παραπλήσια [τοῖς τῆς μεγάλης] στρουθοῦ, ἣν καὶ αὐτὴν πολλάκις κατεδαισάμεθα.

According to Larensius (ap. Athen. l. c.), he had seen the bird and heard the name in Mysia and Paeonia: he probably alluded to some one of the Grouse family; cf. *tetraon* in Plin. x. (22) 29. The bird brought into the banquet was evidently a Guinea-fowl, the description given of the colour, wattles, &c. being characteristic. The account in Alex. Mynd. is not capable of identification: it also may possibly refer to the Guinea-fowl, which is not mentioned under the name μελεαγρίς by this author. Sundevall supposes that Alex. Mynd. alluded to some small bird, perhaps the Whinchat, *Pratincola rubetra*, L., and that the same was identical with **τέτριξ** and **οὔραξ**, J. G. Schneider (Anmerk. z. d. Ecl. Phys. p. 45) conjectures the Little Bustard, *Otis tetrax*, L., on whose cry at breeding-time, cf. Buffon, iv. p. 55.

The name occurs also in Nemesian, i. 128, Anthol. Lat. 883 (ed. Riese), in a passage, however, which adds nothing definite to our knowledge: Tetracem Romae quem nunc vocitare taracem Coeperunt, avium est multo stultissima; namque Cum pedicas necti sibi contemplaverit adstans, Immemor ipse sui tamen in dispendia currit... Hic prope Pentinum radicibus Apennini Nidificat, patulis quae se sol obiicit agris, Persimilis cineri dorsum, maculosaque terga Inficiunt pullae cacabantis imagine notae.

ΤΈΤΡΑΣ. A bird-name, Schol. in Ar. Av. 168. Probably = τέτραξ.

ΤΕΤΡΑ'ΩΝ, for τέταρος, Ptol. Euerg. ap. Athen. xiv. 654 c : Hesych., ὄρνις ποιός.

In Sueton. Calig. xxii tetraones numidicae were probably Guinea-fowl. In Plin. x. (22) 29 tetrao is the Black Grouse, *Tetrao tetrix*: decet tetraonas suus nitor, absolutaque nigritia, in superciliis cocci rubor. The larger variety mentioned next is the Capercaillie, *T. urogallus*: alterum eorum genus vulturum magnitudinem excedit, quorum et colorem reddit ; nec ulla ales, excepto Struthiocamelo, maius corpore implens pondus, &c.

ΤΕ'ΤΡΙΞ. An unidentified bird.

Arist. II. A. vi. 1, 559 a ἡ δὲ τέτριξ ἣν καλοῦσιν 'Αθηναῖοι οὔραγα, οὔτ' ἐπὶ τῆς γῆς νεοττεύει οὔτ' ἐπὶ τοῖς δένδρεσιν, ἀλλ' ἐπὶ τοῖς χαμαιζήλοις φυτοῖς. A few lines before it is mentioned with the lark as nesting on the ground.

Only these two conflicting references occur. Belon took τέτριξ for the Black Grouse, Camus and Buffon for the Capercaillie, neither of which occur in Attica. Sundevall identifies it with the Whinchat, vide s. v. τέτραξ.

ΤΙΤΙ'Σ. A small bird, Phot. (Cf. τιτίζω.)

ΤΟ'ΡΓΟΣ. A Vulture.

Hesych. τόργος· εἶδος γυπὸς αἱματορρόφου. ἔστι δὲ καὶ ὁ γὺψ παρὰ Σικελιώταις. Cf. ibid. Τόργιον· ὄρος ἐν Σικελίᾳ, ὅπου νεοττεύουσιν οἱ γῖπες. ἀφ' οὗ καὶ αὐτοὶ τόργοι.

Callim. fr. 204. Frequent in Lycophron. Cass. 1080 τόργοισιν αἰώρημα φοινίαις δέμας : ib. 86 λεύσσω θέοντα γρυνὸν ἐπτερωμένον | τρήρωνος εἰς ἅρπαγμα, Πεφναίας κυνὸς | ἣν τόργος ὑγρόφοιτος ἐκλοχεύεται | κελιφάνου στρόβιλον ὠστρακωμένην· ubi Schol. τόργος δὲ κυρίως ὁ γύψ, νῦν δὲ τὸν κύκνον λέγει, ὃν μιμησάμενος ὁ Ζεὺς συνεμίγη τῇ Λήδῃ : ibid. 357 τῆμος βιαίως φάσσα πρὸς τόργου λέχος | γαμψαῖσιν ἅρπαις οἰνὰς ἑλκυσθήσομαι, where the Scholiast is in doubt whether to translate οἰνάς by ἄμπελος, or (as is of course correct) by περιστερά.

The word τόργος comes to us through Alexandrine writers (late-brasque Lycophronis atri!). I take it (in spite of Hesychius) to be an Egyptian word, and to be connected with the root of ὄρχιλος (q. v.) and τρόχιλος ; see also s. v. τριόρχης. The name Τόργιον, cited by Hesychius, is at least more likely to be derived from τόργος, than the latter from it.

ΤΟΥ'ΤΙΣ· ὁ κόσσυφος, Hesych. A very doubtful word.

ΤΡΗ'ΡΩΝ. A **Pigeon** or **Dove**.

On the possibility of τρήρων being a true pigeon-name, and not merely an epithet derived from τρέω, vide supra, s. v. πέλεια.

ΤΡΗΡΩΝ (continued).

Moero, ap. Athen. xi. 491 B of the doves that fed the Infant Jupiter in the Cretan cave, τὸν μὲν ἄρα τρήρωνες ὑπὸ ζαθέῳ τρέφον ἄντρῳ | ἀμβροσίην φορέουσαι ἀπ' ὠκεανοῖο ῥοάων. Lyc. 87 (vide s. v. **τόργος**); ibid. 423 ὗτ' εἰς νόθων τρήρωνος ἠνάσθη λέχος. Opp. Cyn. i. 73 τρήρωνας ἕλον δονακῆες: ibid. i. 352 εὖτε γὰρ ἐς φιλότητα θοαὶ τρήρωνες ἴωσι | μιγνύμεναι στομάτεσσι βαρυφθόγγοις ἀλόχοισι: ibid. i. 385 εἴαρι καὶ τρήρωνες ἐπιθύουσι πελείαις.

Hence πολυτρήρων, an epithet of Laconian Messe, and Boeotian Thisbe, Il. ii. 502, 582; cf. Stat. Theb. vii. 261 Dionaeis avibus circumsona Thisbe. There is a curious apparent coincidence between the association with doves of the town Thisbe, and the connexion of Thisbe in the story of Pyramus and Thisbe (Ovid, Met. iv) with Babylon, urbs Semiramidis: on the dove-myth of Semiramis, vide s. v. **περιστερά**.

ΤΡΙ'ΚΚΟΣ· ὀρνιθάριον ὃ καὶ βασιλεὺς ὑπὸ Ἠλείων, Hesych. Cf. **δρίκκαι**, **δρικῆαι**, &c.; also possibly, **τριχάς**.

ΤΡΙΟ'ΡΧΗΣ. MSS. have also **τριορχίς**; **τριόρχις** in Ar. Av. 1206, Simon. Iambl. 8. **πυρίορχις** in Cram. An. Gr. Oxon. ii. 457. See also s. v. **βελλούνης**.

A Buzzard (?), *Buteo vulgaris*, auctt. Mod. Gk. βαρβακίνα.

Ar. Av. 1181, 1206; also in Ar. Vesp. 1532, where the Buzzards are called the children of Poseidon.

Arist. H. A. viii. 3, 592 b ἔστι δὲ ὁ τριόρχης τὸ μέγεθος ὅσον ἰκτῖνος. καὶ φαίνεται οὗτος διὰ παντός. Ib. ix. 36, 620 κράτιστος τῶν ἱεράκων. Ibid. 1, 609 τριόρχης καὶ φρῦνος καὶ ὄφις πολέμια· κατεσθίει γὰρ ὁ τριόρχης αὐτούς. Ael. xii. 4; sacred to Artemis. Mentioned also, Lyc. 147; Plin. x. (8) 9 Triorchem a numero testium. Buteonem hunc appellant Romani.

Tradition interprets τριόρχης as the Buzzard, with which the description given agrees save for the important epithet κράτιστος. Some writers, e.g. Thuanus, De Re Accip., 1612, pp. 22,100, repudiate the identification.

The mediaeval anatomists, Aldrovandi, Gesner, &c., sought and found (!) the abnormality from which the bird apparently derives its name: but the derivation is probably quite false, and the word corrupted by *Volksetymologie*. Is it possible that its origin lies hid under the name **τόργος**, (q. v.)?

According to Nicander, ap. Anton. Lib. c. xiv, Munychus was metamorphosed into the bird τριόρχης, and his son Alcander into ὄρχιλος, other two sons becoming ἰχνεύμων and κύων, both of which are here spoken of as birds. There is, to my mind, an Egyptian look about the whole story.

ΤΡΙΧΑ'Σ. The Song-Thrush, *Turdus musicus*, L. Mod. Gk. τζίγλα.
Arist. H. A. ix. 20, 617 κιχλῶν εἶδος· ὀξὺ φθέγγεται· τὸ δὲ μέγεθος ὅσον κόττυφος. Vide s. v. κίχλη.

This word (ἅπαξ λεγόμενον) was translated by Gaza *pilaris* (quasi a θρίξ), whence our modern name *Turdus pilaris*, L., the Fieldfare. The word survives in Mod. Gk. as τσίχλα, τζίγλα, τζήχλα, and is possibly the same as τρίκκος, q. v.; it is a parallel form to κίχλη, and is the same as our *thrush*. [Cf. Lith. *s-trazd-as* (Nessl. p. 506), Russ. *drosď*, Icel. *trast*, L. *turdus*, &c.]

ΤΡΟΧΙ'ΛΟΣ, s. τρόχιλος, a. (Most MSS. have τροχῖλος; for other forms, v. Lob. Par. 115.) Derived, in my opinion, from the root of ὄρχιλος (q. v.), and not connected with τρέχω.

The **Wren**, *Troglodytes europaeus*, L. Mod. Gk. κολύμβρι, τρυποκαρύδα (Erhard, Bikélas).

Arist. H. A. ix. 11, 615 λόχμας καὶ τρώγλας οἰκεῖ· δυσάλωτος δὲ καὶ δραπέτης καὶ τὸ ἦθος ἀσθενής, εὐβίοτος δὲ καὶ τεχνικός· καλεῖται δὲ καὶ πρέσβυς καὶ βασιλεύς (cf. Plin. viii. 37), διὸ καὶ τὸν ἀετὸν αὐτῷ φασὶ πολεμεῖν: cf. ibid. ix. 1, 609 b. Mentioned as an oracular bird, Plut. ii. 405 c ἀλλ' ἡμεῖς ἐρωδιοῖς οἰόμεθα καὶ τροχίλοις καὶ κόραξι χρῆσθαι φθεγγομένοις σημαίνοντα τὸν θεόν. On superstitions connected with the Wren, 'The king of all birds,' &c., Dyer, Brit. Pop. Customs, 1876, p. 497; id. Engl. Folk-lore, 1880, p. 67; Croker, Researches in S. Ireland, 1824, p. 233; N. and Q. (6), xi. p. 297, 1885, &c., &c.

ΤΡΟΧΙ'ΛΟΣ, β.

The **Egyptian Plover** or **Ziczac**, *Pluvianus aegyptius* = *Hyas aegyptiacus* = *Charadrius melanocephalus*. Also called κλαδαρόρυγχος. This identification, due in the first instance to Geoffroy St. Hilaire, is generally accepted: a recent writer, however, states that the true 'Crocodile-bird' is a somewhat larger species, the spur-winged Plover, *Hoplopterus spinosus* (Ibis, 1893, p. 277).

Herod. ii. 68 ὁ τροχῖλος ἐσδύνων ἐς τὸ στόμα [τοῦ κροκοδείλου] καταπίνει τὰς βδέλλας· ὁ δὲ ὠφελεύμενος ἥδεται, καὶ οὐδὲν σίνεται τὸν τροχίλον. Arist. H. A. ix. 6, 612 τῶν κροκοδείλων χασκόντων οἱ τροχίλοι καθαίρουσιν εἰσπετόμενοι τοὺς ὀδόντας καὶ αὐτοὶ μὲν τρόφην λαμβάνουσιν, κ. τ. λ. Cf. Arist. Mirab. 7, 831 a; Ammian. xxii. 15, 19; Antig. Car. c. 33; Ael. iii. 11, viii. 25, xii. 15; Plut. De Sol. Anim. ii. 980 d; Phile, De An. Pr. 97 (82). Mentioned among τοὺς ὄρνιθας τοὺς παρενδιαστὰς καλουμένους, Athen. x. 332 e. In Dion. De Avib. ii. 3, the name is apparently applied to various sandpipers. Mentioned also Ar. Av. 79 (ἔστι δὲ καὶ ὄρνεον τροχίλος, καὶ λέγεται εἶναι δριμύ, Schol., Suid.), Ach. 876, Pax, 1004, &c.

ΤΡΟΧΙΛΟΣ (*continued*).

Pliny confuses it with the foregoing: Parva avis quae trochilos ibi vocatur, rex avium in Italia, H. N. viii. (25) 37.

Cf. G. St. Hilaire, Descr. de l'Égypte, (2) xxiv. p. 440, Mém. du Mus. xv. p. 466; Curzon, Monast. of the Levant, c. xii; Brehm, Thierleben, Vögel, iii. p. 216 (2nd edit.); Newton, Dict. of Birds, pp. 442, 733, &c.

ΤΡΥΓΓΑΣ. In some MSS. and editions (Ald. Schn. &c.) for πύγαργος, Arist. H. A. viii. 3, 593 b.

ΤΡΥΓΩ'Ν. Cf. Heb. חור, L. *tur-tur*. On the derivation from τρύζειν, cf. Eust. Hom. Il. (xi. 311), p. 751, Od. pp. 229, 1951; Schol. ad Theocr. Id. vii. 140, &c.; cf. Isid. Orig. 12, 17 turtur de voce vocatur. I am inclined to think that τρυγών cannot be directly derived from τρύζειν, but that the verb was applied to the dove's note from mere coincidence of sound: and further that the root of τρυγών is probably foreign, like that of οἰνάς. See also s. v. τρήρων.

A **Turtle-dove**, *Columba turtur*, L. Mod. Gk. τριγῶνι (Heldr.), τριγόνι (Von der M.), τρυγώνιον (Erh.), δεκοκτοῦρα, Bikélas (from the cry). Mentioned Ar. Av. 302, 979, &c.

Description.—Arist. H. A. v. 13, 544 b τῶν περιστεροειδῶν ἐλαχίστη: cf. Athen. ix. 394 A. Compared in size with κελεός, H. A. viii. 3, 593, and with χλωρεύς, ib. ix. 22, 617. Arist. fr. 271, 1527, ap. Athen. l. c., τὸ χρῶμα τεφρόν, cf. Eust. Hom. Od. p. 1712. Arist. H. A. viii. 3, 593 καρποφαγεῖ καὶ ποηφαγεῖ· φαίνεται τοῦ θέρους, χειμῶνος ἀφανίζεται· φωλεῖ γάρ. Cf. ibid. 12, 597 b ἀγελάζονται δ᾽ αἴ τε φάτται καὶ αἱ τρυγόνες, ὅταν τε παραγίνωνται καὶ πάλιν ὅταν ὥρα ᾖ πρὸς τὴν ἀνακομιδήν. See also ibid. 16, 599 b φωλεῖ γὰρ . . . καὶ τρυγών· καὶ ἡ γε τρυγὼν ὁμολογούμενος μάλιστα πάντων. οὐθεὶς γὰρ ὥς εἰπεῖν λέγεται τρυγόνα ἰδεῖν οὐδαμοῦ χειμῶνος. ἄρχεται δὲ τῆς φωλείας σφόδρα πίειρα οὖσα, καὶ πτερορρυεῖ μὲν ἐν τῇ φωλείᾳ, παχεῖα μέντοι διατελεῖ οὖσα.

Cf. Plin. x. (24) 35 verius turtur occultatur, pennasque amittit. On its migration, see also Varro, De R. R. iii. 5, 7, &c. Arist. H. A. ix. 7, 613 οὐκ ἀνακύπτουσι πινοῦσαι, ἐὰν μὴ ἱκανὸν πίωσιν (cf. Alex. Mynd. ap. Athen. ix. 394 E, Plin. x. (34) 52); ζῶσι καὶ ὀκτὼ ἔτη (Plin. l. c.), αἱ τετυφλωμέναι ὑπὸ τῶν παλευτρίας τρεφόντων αὐτάς: on their capture by decoys, see also Dion. De Avib. iii. 4, 16.

The voice of the Turtle.—Theocr. Id. xv. 88 ὦ δύστανοι, ἀνάνυτα κωτίλλουσαι | τρυγόνες: cf. Virg. Ecl. i. 59. On the verb τρύζειν, vide supra; cf. also Pollux, v. 14 εἴποις δ᾽ ἂν τρυγόνας τρύζειν, περιστερὰς γογγύζειν: Suid. ἀσήμως φθέγγεται καὶ γογγυστικῶς: τρυγόζειν, A. B. 1452. Hence, of a talker, τρυγόνος λαλίστερος, Menand. Πλοκ. 13, ap. Ael. xii. 10, in which passage a 'double entendre' is expatiated on by Aelian, Suidas,

ΤΡΟΧΙΛΟΣ—ΤΡΥΓΩΝ   173

ΤΡΥΓΩΝ *(continued).*
&c.; see also Demetr. Sic., ap. Ael. l. c., Arist. H. A. ix. 49 B, 633 b, &c.; cf. also τρυλίζειν, of a quail, Poll. 5. 89.

Reproduction, Nesting, &c.—Arist. H. A. vi. I, 558 b διτοκεῖ (i. e. lays two eggs). Ibid. 4, 562 b τίκτουσι τρυγὼν καὶ φάττα ἐν τῷ ἔαρι, οὐ πλεονάκις ἢ δίς. τίκτει δὲ τὰ δεύτερα, ὅταν τὰ πρότερον γεννηθέντα διαφθαρῇ· πολλαὶ γὰρ διαφθείρουσιν αὐτὰ τῶν ὀρνίθων. τίκτει μὲν οὖν, ὥσπερ εἴρηται καὶ τρία ποτέ· ἀλλ' ἐξάγεται οὐδέποτε δυοῖν πλείω νεοττοῖν, ἐνίοτε δ' ἓν μόνον· τὸ δ' ὑπολειπόμενον τῶν ᾠῶν ἀεὶ οὔριόν ἐστιν (cf. Plin. x. 58 (79)), τὰς δὲ φάττας καὶ τὰς τρυγόνας ἔνιοί φασιν ὀχεύεσθαι καὶ γεννᾶν καὶ τρίμηνα ὄντα, σημεῖον ποιούμενοι τὴν πολυπλήθειαν αὐτῶν. ἔγκυα δὲ γίνεται δέκα καὶ τέτταρας ἡμέρας, καὶ ἐπῳάζει ἄλλας τοσαύτας· ἐν ἑτέραις δὲ δέκα καὶ τέτταρσι πτεροῦνται οὕτως ὥστε μὴ ῥᾳδίως καταλαμβάνεσθαι. Ib. ix. 7, 613 ἔχει δὲ τὸν ἄρρενα ἡ τρυγὼν τὸν αὐτὸν καὶ φάττα, καὶ ἄλλον οὐ προσίενται. (Concerning its chastity, see also Ael. iii. 44, x. 33; Dion. De Avib., Phile, De An. Pr. xxii, &c.) καὶ ἐπῳάζουσιν ἀμφότεροι καὶ ὁ ἄρρην καὶ ἡ θήλεια. διαγνῶναι δ' οὐ ῥᾴδιον τὴν θήλειαν καὶ τὸν ἄρρενα, ἀλλ' ἢ τοῖς ἐντός. νεοττεύουσι δὲ καὶ αἱ φάβες καὶ αἱ τρυγόνες ἐν τοῖς αὐτοῖς τόποις ἀεί.

The Cuckoo builds in its nest, Arist. De Mirab. 3, 830 b.

On White Turtle-doves, which are sacred not only to Aphrodite and to Demeter, but also to the Fates and the Furies, Ael. x. 33.

How Turtle-doves were brought as tribute to the Indian king, Ael. xiii. 25. How the Turtle-dove is slain by χλωρεύς, Arist. H. A. ix. I, 609, Phile, De An. Pr. 690; is hostile to πυραλλίς, Arist. l. c., and to πύρρα, Ael. iv. 5, Phile, l. c. 685; to κόραξ and to κίρκος, Ael. vi. 45; is friendly to κόττυφος, Arist. H. A. ix. 1,610 (cf. Plin. x. (76) 96; to περιστερά, Ael. v. 48, and to the Parrot, Plin. x. (76) 96, cf. Ovid, Heroid. xv. 38 et niger a viridi turtur amatur ave; id. Amor. ii. 6, 12 tu tamen ante alias, turtur amice, dole. Plena fuit vobis omni concordia vita, &c. These last references probably allude to the practice of keeping Turtle-doves together with Parrots in aviaries. On Turtle-doves in captivity, see Varro, iii. 8, Columella viii. 9, Geopon. xiv. 24, &c. Mentioned as a delicacy, Juven. vi. 39, Martial. xiii. 53, &c. Is killed by pomegranate seed, Ael. vi. 46, Phile, l. c. 657, and uses the fruit of the Iris as a charm, Ael. i. 35, Phile, l. c. 727. Possibly identical with the *trigon* or *trygon* that is said to issue tail first from the egg, Hylas ap. Plin. x. (16) 18.

They are captured by the aid of decoys, at their drinking-places, Dion. De Avib. iii. 12; or with bird-lime, ibid. 2. An incredible story of their being beguiled by dancing and music (sometimes referred to τρυγών = *pastinaca*) Ael. i. 39, Phile, De An. Pr. 22 (21), 464.

Proverbs.—τρυγόνος λαλίστερος, vide supra. τρυγόνα s. κατὰ τρυγόνα ψάλλειν: Suid. s. v. τρυγόνος· καὶ παροιμία τρυγόνα ψάλλειν ἐπὶ τῶν φαύλως πραττόντων: ibid. s. v. πονηρά· πονηρὰ κατὰ τρυγόνα ψάλλεις· ἐπὶ τῶν μοχθηρῶς καὶ ἐπιπόνως ζώντων, καὶ γὰρ ἡ τρυγὼν ἐπειδὰν πεινᾷ τότε μάλιστα ψάλλει. Cf. also Hesych.

ΤΡΩΓΛΙ'ΤΗΣ. A small bird, probably identical with **τρωγλοδύτης**.
Phile De An. Pr. 691 ἀετὸν δὲ τὸν μέγαν | αἰγυπιὸς δέδοικε· τὸν δέ, τρωγλίτης. Hdn. Epim. 136, 181; Eust. 228, 35.

ΤΡΩΓΛΟΔΥ'ΤΗΣ. The **Wren**, *Troglodytes europaeus*, L.
Philagr. Med. ap. Aët. xi. 11 (cit. Schn. in Arist. vol. iv. p. 85) στρουθίον ἐστὶ σμικρότατον σχεδὸν ἁπάντων τῶν ὀρνέων πλὴν τοῦ βασιλίσκου καλουμένου· παρέοικε δὲ τῷ βασιλίσκῳ κατὰ πολλά, ἄνευ τῶν χρυσιζόντων ἐν μετώπῳ πτερῶν· εὐμεγεθέστερον δ' ἐστὶ μικρῷ ὁ τρωγλοδύτης τοῦ βασιλίσκου καὶ μελάντερος, καὶ τὴν οὐρὰν ἐγηγερμένην ἔχει ἀεί, λευκῷ κατεστιγμένην ὄπισθεν χρώματι. Λαλίστερος δ' ἐστὶν οὗτος τοῦ βασιλίσκου, καί τις ὅτε ψαρώτερος ἐν ἄκρᾳ περιγραφῇ τῆς πτέρυγος. βραχείας δὲ τὰς πτερύσεις ποιεῖται, καὶ δύναμιν ἔχει φυσικὴν ἀξίαν θαυμασμοῦ. ἄφθονον οἶμαι τὸ γένος αὐτῶν πανταχοῦ κατὰ τὸν χειμῶνα φαινόμενον.

ΤΥ'ΓΓΑ· ὀρνιθάριόν τι, Hesych.
τ' ἴυγγα cj. Bourdelot, ad Heliod. p. 57, sed sine causa fortasse (M. Schmidt, ad Hesych.).

ΤΥ'ΛΑΣ, for ἴλλας, q. v. A kind of **Thrush**, Alex. Mynd. ap. Athen. ii. 65 a.

ΤΥ'ΠΑΝΟΣ. An unknown bird.
Arist. H. A. ix. 1, 609 ἀποκτείνει ἡ κορώνη τὸν καλούμενον τύπανον. The fact that the Crow is also said to be hostile to ὄρχιλος and to πρέσβυς, gives some ground for supposing that τύπανος is here a misreading for τύραννος.

ΤΥ'ΡΑΝΝΟΣ. The **Gold-crested Wren**, *Regulus cristatus* and *ignicapillus*. (Both species occur in Greece, Von der Mühle, p. 68, Lindermayer, p. 96.) Cf. Gk. βασιλίσκος, Lat. regulus, Fr. roitelet, Germ. Zaunkönig, &c.
Arist. H. A. viii. 3, 592 b τὸ μέγεθος μικρῷ μείζων ἀκρίδος, ἔστι δὲ φοινικοῦν λόφον ἔχων, καὶ ἄλλως εὔχαρι τὸ ὀρνίθιον καὶ εὔρυθμον.

ΤΥΤΩ'· ἡ γλαῦξ, Hesych.
Cf. Plaut. Menaechm. iv. 2, 90 Vim afferri noctuam, quae *tutu* usque dicat tibi? Cf. O. Keller, Lat. Etym., 1893, p. 111.

ΎΒΡΙ'Σ, s. ὕβρις. Probably the **Eagle-Owl**, *Strix bubo*; cf. βρύας (for βύας), of which word ὕβρίς is perhaps a corrupt form.
Arist. H. A. ix. 12, 615 b ἡ δ' ὕβρίς, φασὶ δέ τινες εἶναι τὸν αὐτὸν τοῦτον ὄρνιθα τῷ πτυγγί, οὗτος ἡμέρας μὲν οὐ φαίνεται διὰ τὸ μὴ βλέπειν ὀξύ, τὰς δὲ νύκτας θηρεύει ὥσπερ οἱ ἀετοί [cj. Sundevall, οἱ ὠτοί], καὶ μάχονται δὲ πρὸς τὸν ἀετὸν οὕτω σφόδρα ὥστ' ἄμφω λαμβάνεσθαι πολλάκις ζῶντας ὑπὸ τῶν νομέων. τίκτει μὲν οὖν δύο ᾠά, νεοττεύει δὲ καὶ οὗτος ἐν πέτραις καὶ σπηλαίοις. Hesych. ὑβρίς· ὄρνεον νυκτερινόν.

ὙΠΑΊΕΤΟΣ (*male* γυπαίετος); also ὑψιαίετος, (Boios ap. Anton. Lib.). An obscure name for an Eagle or Vulture.

Arist. H. A. ix. 32, 618 b περκνόπτερος· ὀρειπέλαργος καλεῖται καὶ ὑπαίετος. Boios ap. Anton. Lib. c. 20 καὶ ἐγένετο Κλεῖνις μὲν ὑψιαίετος· οὗτός ἐστι δεύτερος ὀρνίθων μετὰ τὸν αἰετόν, διαγνῶναι δ' οὐ χαλεπόν· ὁ μὲν γάρ ἐστι νεβροφόνος ἐρεμνός, μέγας τε καὶ ἄλκιμος, ὁ δ' ἀετὸς μελάντερος καὶ ἐλάσσων ἐκείνου. On this perplexing passage, see Schneider in Arist. l.c.

ὙΠΟΔΕΔΙΏΣ. A Libyan bird-name, Ar. Av. 65.

The word is commonly taken as a Comic derivative of ὑποδείδω (cf. Soph. Aj. 169). The five bird-names beginning with the syllable ὑπ- are all obscure, and what little is said about them is replete with signs of foreign influence. I am pretty certain that in none of these cases does ὑπο- mean *sub*, and for my own part I suspect it to be a corruption of a foreign, and probably Egyptian, word or prefix.

ὙΠΟΘΥΜΊΣ. An unknown bird. Ar. Av. 302.

ὙΠΟΛΑΪ́Σ. (MSS. have also ὑπολωΐς, ὑπολλίς, ὑπολίς· ὑπολῆΐς, Hesych.) An indeterminate small bird. Perhaps the **Wheatear**, *Saxicola* sp.

The Cuckoo lays her eggs in its nest, which is on the ground, Arist. H. A. viii. 7, 564. ix. 29, 618, Antig. H. Mir. 100 (109), Theophr. De Caus. Pl. ii. 17, 9. Also in some editions for ἐπιλαΐς, H. A. vi. 3, 592 b. Sundevall suggests the Wheatear, which makes its nest under a stone, from a supposed connection with λᾶας; and the conjecture is supported to some extent by the circumstance that the Cuckoo is known sometimes to use the Wheatear's nest in Greece (Krüper, p. 184); but the derivation is very doubtful. The Orphean Warbler is the bird in whose nest the Cuckoo in Greece usually lays its egg, and further the statements in Aristotle as to the birds in whose nest the Cuckoo lays are very untrustworthy.

ὙΠΟΤΡΙΌΡΧΗΣ. A kind of **Hawk**.

Arist. H. A. ix. 36, 620 οἱ δὲ πλατύτεροι [Schn. and others read πλατύπτεροι] ἱέρακες ὑποτριόρχαι καλοῦνται.

There is nothing by which to identify the name, which indeed seems to be to some extent generic. The name *subbuteo* is traditionally applied to the Hobby, which if πλατύπτερος means broad-winged, is, as Sundevall remarks, excluded by the epithet.

ΦΑΒΟΤΎΠΟΣ, *s*. φαβοκτόνος, Hesych. A kind of **Hawk**. Cf. φασσοφόνος, q. v.

Arist. H. A. viii. 3, 592 b ὅ τε φαβοτύπος καὶ ὁ σπιζίας· διαφέρουσι δ' οὗτοι τὸ μέγεθος πολὺ ἀλλήλων.

ΦΑΛΑΚΡΟΚΟ'ΡΑΞ. A bird, commonly identified, on the strength of its name (cf. φαλαρίς), with the Coot; according to others, the Cormorant. See also s. v. κόραξ, β.

Plin. x. (48) 68 Iam et in Gallia Hispaniaque capitur [attagen], et per Alpes etiam, ubi et phalacrocoraces, aves Balearium insularum peculiares. Cf. ib. xi. 47 quaedam animalium naturaliter calvent, sicut ... corvi aquatici, quibus apud Graecos nomen est inde.

ΦΑΛΑΡΙ'Σ, s. φαληρίς. (MSS. have also φαραλίς.)

(φάλος, the 'beak' of a helmet; φάλαρος, a white spot or 'blaze'; cf. Germ. *Blesshuhn*, from Bletz = *blaze*, Buttm. Lexil. s. v. φάλος: the Engl. *bald-coot* is analogous.)

The Coot (?), *Fulica atra*, L. Mod. Gk. φαλαρίδα (Heldr.).

Ar. Ach. 875, Av. 565 ἦν Ἀφροδίτῃ θύῃ, πυροὺς ὄρνιθι φαληρίδι θύειν (ubi Schol. ἡ δὲ φαληρὶς ὄρνεόν ἐστι λιμναῖον εὐπρεπές). Arist. H. A. viii. 3, 593 b ὄρνις στεγανόπους, βαρύτερος· περὶ ποταμοὺς καὶ λίμνας ἐστίν. (Mentioned with κύκνος, νῆττα, κολυμβίς.) Id. fr. 273, 1527 b ἀλλάττεσθαι ὡς τῶν κοσσύφων καὶ φαληρίδων ἀπολευκαινομένων κατὰ καιρούς.

Alex. Mynd. ap. Athen. ix. 395 e ἡ δὲ φαλαρὶς καὶ αὐτὴ στενὸν ἔχουσα τὸ ῥύγχος στρογγυλωτέρα τὴν ὄψιν οὖσα, ἔντεφρος τὴν γαστέρα, μικρῷ μελαντέρα τὸ νῶτον. Cleom. ap. Athen. ix. 393 c φαληρίδας ταριχηρὰς μυρίας. Its mode of capture, Dion. De Avib. iii. 23. Plin. x. (48) 57 Phalerides in Seleucia Parthorum et in Asia, aquaticarum laudatissimae; Colum. viii. 15, 1; Varro, R. R. iii. 11, 4.

The identification rests mainly on the modern name, of which Sundevall and Aubert and Wimmer seem to have been unaware, and is supported by the derivation of the word. Sundevall suggests *Mergus albellus*, and Aubert and Wimmer also suppose a species of *Mergus*. Gesner, Camus, and other older commentators agree in the identification of Coot. At best the identification is doubtful, and the various references perhaps refer to more birds than one. The allusion in Athenaeus to ten thousand salted φαληρίδας is especially puzzling. The connexion with Aphrodite in Ar. Av. 565, where we might rather have expected some such word as περιστερᾷ, is not explained.

ΦΑΣΙΑΝΟ'Σ, s. φασιανικός; sc. ὄρνις.

A Pheasant, *Phasianus colchicus*, L. Vide also s. v. τέταρος.

Mnesim. ap. Athen. ix. 387 b σπανιώτερον πάρεστιν ὀρνίθων γάλα | καὶ φασιανὸς ἀποτετιλμένος καλῶς.

Ar. Av. 69; Nub. 109 (sometimes supposed to refer, in the latter passage, to a Phasian horse, cf. Suidas, Lob. Phryn. 460, but not so according to Athen. ix. 387 a).

Agatharch. ap. Athen. ix. 387 c περὶ τοῦ Φάσιδος ποταμοῦ τὸν λόγον ποιούμενος γράφει καὶ ταῦτα· "πλῆθος δ' ὀρνίθων τῶν καλουμένων φασιανῶν

ΦΑΣΙΑΝΟΣ (*continued*).

φοιτᾷ τροφῆς χάριν πρὸς τὰς ἐκβολὰς τῶν στομάτων" : cf. Lucian, De Merc. Cond. 17, Navig. 23. Callix. Rhod. ap. Athen. l. c. (describing the procession of Ptolemy Philad. at Alexandria) εἶτα ἐφέροντο ἐν ἀγγείοις φασιανοί κ.τ.λ. Cf. Ptolem. ap. Athen. xiv. 654 c (cf. ix. 387 e) τά τε τῶν φασιανῶν, οὓς τετάρους [*s.* τετράωνας] ὀνομάζουσιν, [οὓς] οὐ μόνον ἐκ Μηδείας μετεπέμπετο, ἀλλὰ καὶ νομάδας ὄρνιθας ὑποβαλὼν ἐποίησε πλῆθος, ὥστε καὶ σιτεῖσθαι· τὸ γὰρ βρῶμα πολυτελὲς ἀποφαίνουσιν. αὕτη ἡ τοῦ λαμπροτάτου βασιλέως φωνή, ὃς οὐδὲ φασιανικοῦ ὀρνιθός ποτε γεύσασθαι ὡμολόγησεν, ἀλλ' ὥσπερ τι κειμήλιον ἀνακείμενον εἶχε τούσδε τοὺς ὄρνιθας. Arist. fr. 589, 1574 a (Theophr. fr. 179), ap. Athen. l. c. τῶν φασιανῶν οὐ κατὰ λόγον ἡ ὑπεροχὴ τῶν ἀρρένων, ἀλλὰ πολλῷ μείζων. Ulp. ap. Athen. l. c. εἰς τὴν ἀγορὰν πορευθεὶς ὠνήσομαι φασιανικόν, ὃν συγκατέδημαί σοι. Arist. H. A. ix. 49 B, 633 ὄρνις οὐ πτητικὸς ἀλλ' ἐπίγειος, κονιστικός (cf. Arist. fr., and Theophr. fr. ap. Athen. ix. 387 b). H. A. v. 31, 557 ἐὰν μὴ κονιῶνται, διαφθείρονται ὑπὸ τῶν φθειρῶν. Ib. vi. 2, 559 κατεστιγμένα τὰ ᾠὰ τῶν μελεαγρίδων καὶ φασιανῶν (this error is repeated by Buffon, Hist. Ois. iv. 78).

On Pheasants reared by the Indian kings, Ael. xiii. 18. On the breeding and rearing of Pheasants, see Pallad. R. R. i. 29, Colum. viii. 8, 10.

For Latin references to the Pheasant as a dainty, cf. Juv. xi. 139 Scythicae volucres ; Mart. xiii. 45, 72, &c. ; Stat. Silv. i. 6, 77, ii. 4, 27 ; Manil. Astron. v. 376 ; Suet. Cal. 22 ; Lampr. Alex. Sev. 37 Iovis epulo et Saturnalibus et huiusmodi festis diebus phasianus ; Capitol. Pert. 12 phasianum nunquam privato convivio comedit aut alicui misit ; Amm. xvi. 5, 3 phasianum et vulvam et sumen exigi vetuit (Iulianus) et inferri, munificis militis vili et fortuito cibo contentus; Ambr. Hexaem. vi. 5 exquisitum illud et accuratum opipare convivium, in quo phasiani aut turturis species apponitur.

ΦΑΣΚΑ'Σ. Alex. Mynd. ap. Athen. ix. 395 D. Vide s. v. βασκάς.

ΦΑ'ΣΣΑ, Att. φάττα.

A **Ringdove** or **Woodpigeon**, *Columba palumbus*, L. Mod. Gk. φάσα : L. *palumbus* s. *palumbes*. Identical with **φάψ**, q. v. Sometimes applied also to the Domestic Pigeon, v. infra. Dim. **φάττιον**, Ar. Pl. 1011, Ephipp. 3, 334 (Mein.). An artificial masc. form **φάττος** in Luc. Solœc. 7. Used as an illustration of the interchange of σσ and ττ, Luc. Jud. Voc. 8. [On the interchange of σ, π, φάσσα, φάψ, φάβος, cf. J. Schmidt, Philol. Anz. xxv. p. 139, 1881.]

In Homer, only in the compound φασσοφόνος : otherwise, first in Aristophanes.

ΦΑΣΣΑ (continued).

Description.—Arist. H. A. v. 13, 544 b μέγιστον [τῶν περιστεροειδῶν] ἡ φάττα ἐστι: cf. fr. 271, 1527 (ap. Athen. ix. 394 a) ἀλέκτορος τὸ μέγεθος ἔχει, χρῶμα δὲ σπόδιον. Alex. Mynd. ap. Schol. Theocr. Id. v. 96 ἡ μὲν φάσσα ὑποκυάνεον ἔχει τὴν κεφαλὴν καὶ μᾶλλόν γε ἐμπόρφυρον, τῶν δὲ ὀφθαλμῶν λευκῶν ὄντων τὸ ἐν αὐτοῖς μέλαν στρογγύλον ἔχει. Arist. H. A. ix. 7, 613 διαγνῶναι δ' οὐ ῥᾴδιον τὴν θήλειαν καὶ τὸν ἄρρενα, ἀλλ' ἢ τοῖς ἐντός. ζῶσι δ' αἱ φάτται πολὺν χρόνον· καὶ γὰρ εἴκοσιν ἔτη καὶ πέντε καὶ τριάκοντα ὠμμέναι εἰσίν, ἔνιαι δὲ καὶ τετταράκοντα ἔτη. πρεσβυτέρων δὲ γινομένων αὐτῶν οἱ ὄνυχες αὐξάνονται· ἀλλ' ἀποτέμνουσιν οἱ τρέφοντες (hence φάτται here are *tame* pigeons). ἄλλο δ' οὐδὲν βλάπτονται ἐπιδήλως γηράσκουσαι: with this somewhat incredible statement as to length of life, cf. ib. vi. 4, 563, Athen. ix. 394 b, Plin. x (32) 52. Arist. H. A. ii. 17, 508 b πρόλοβον πρὸ τῆς κοιλίας ἔχουσι. Ib. viii. 12, 597 b ἀπαίρουσι, καὶ οὐ χειμάζουσι [the contrary stated, viii. 3, 593]. ἀγελάζονται, ὅταν τε παραγίνωνται καὶ πάλιν ὅταν ὥρα ᾖ πρὸς τὴν ἀνακομιδήν. Ibid. 16, 600 τῶν δὲ φασσῶν ἔνιαι μὲν φωλοῦσιν, ἔνιαι δ' οὐ φωλοῦσιν, ἀπέρχονται δ' ἅμα ταῖς χελιδόσιν. Ib. ix. 49 B, 633 τοῦ μὲν χειμῶνος οὐ φθέγγεται, πλὴν ἤδη ποτὲ εὐδίας ἐκ χειμῶνος σφοδροῦ γενομένης ἐφθέγξατο καὶ ἐθαυμαστώθη ὑπὸ τῶν ἐμπείρων· ἀλλ' ὅταν ἔαρ γένηται, τότε ἄρχεται φωνεῖν: cf. Alex. Mynd. ap. Athen. 394 e. Arist. H. A. viii. 18, 601 οἱ αὐχμοὶ συμφέρουσι καὶ πρὸς τὴν ἄλλην ὑγίειαν καὶ πρὸς τοὺς τόκους, καὶ οὐχ ἥκιστα ταῖς φάτταις. Alex. Mynd. ap. Athen. l. c. οὐ πίνειν φησὶ τὴν φάσσαν ἀνακύπτουσαν ὡς τὴν τρυγόνα.

Reproduction, Nesting, &c.—Arist. H. A. vi. 4, 562 b ἔνιοί φασιν ὀχείεσθαι καὶ γεννᾶν καὶ τρίμηνα ὄντα, σημεῖον ποιούμενοι τὴν πολυπλήθειαν αὐτῶν. ἔγκυα δὲ γίνεται δέκα καὶ τέτταρας ἡμέρας, καὶ ἐπῳάζει ἄλλας τοσαύτας· ἐν ἑτέραις δὲ δέκα καὶ τέτταρσι πτεροῦνται οὕτως ὥστε μὴ ῥᾳδίως καταλαμβάνεσθαι... δύο τίκτουσι ἐπὶ τὸ πολύ, τὰ δὲ πλεῖστα τρία· ἐν τῷ ἔαρι τίκτει, οὐ πλεονάκις ἢ δίς: cf. vi. 1, 558 b, Plin. x. (58) 79, (53) 74. Arist. De Gen. iv. 6, 774 b τίκτουσιν ἀτελῆ καὶ τυφλά. H. A. iii. 1, 510 ὅταν ὀχείωσι, σφόδρα μεγάλους ἴσχουσιν (τοὺς ὄρχεις) ... ὥστ' ἔνιοι οἴονται οὐδ' ἔχειν τοῦ χειμῶνος ὄρχεις αὐτά. ix. 7, 613 ἔχει δὲ τὸν ἄρρενα ἡ τρυγὼν τὸν αὐτὸν καὶ φάττα, καὶ ἄλλον οὐ προσίενται· καὶ ἐπῳάζουσιν ἀμφότεροι καὶ ὁ ἄρρην καὶ ἡ θήλεια. Arist. fr. 271, ap. Athen. ix. 394 b οὐκ ἀπολείπουσι δ' ἕως θανάτου οὔτε οἱ ἄρρενες τὰς θηλείας, οὔτε αἱ θήλειαι τοὺς ἄρρενας, ἀλλὰ καὶ τελευτήσαντος χηρεύει ὁ ὑπολειπόμενος: cf. Porph. De Abst. iii. 11. How it places a branch of laurel, δάφνη, in its nest for a charm, Ael. i. 35, Phile, 722, Geopon. xv. 1, cf. Plin. viii. (27) 41. How the Cuckoo builds in its nest, and the young Cuckoo, assisted by their parents, casts out its foster-brothers, Arist. De Mirab. 3, 830 b, Ael. iii. 30.

In Plat. Theaet. 199 b λαβεῖν φάτταν ἀντὶ περιστερᾶς, is to take a wild pigeon for a tame one. Its flesh is mentioned as a dainty, Ar. Ach. 1105, 1107 καλόν γε καὶ ξανθὸν τὸ τῆς φάττης κρέας. Mentioned

ΦΑΣΣΑ (continued).

as coming from Boeotia, Ar. Pax 1104. In Anth. Pal. ix. 71 the oak is οἰκία φαττῶν. Its capture is difficult, but is effected by means of nets and by the aid of blinded decoy-birds, Dion. De Avib. iii. 12.

A lover's gift, Theocr. v. 133. The Dim. φάττιον, used as a term of endearment, Ar. Pl. 1011 νηττάριον ἂν καὶ φάττιον ὑπεκορίζετο: in Philip. Obel. fr. ap. Athen. viii. 359 b, a little pigeon, a skinny one.

Proverb.—Plut. ii. 1077 C φάττα φάττῃ, as like as two peas.
Cf. also φάψ, περιστερά, &c.

ΦΑΣΣΟΦΟ'ΝΟΣ, s. φασσοφόντης. Cf. φαβοτύπος.
A species of **Hawk**.

Il. xv. 238 ἴρηκι ἐοικὼς | ὠκέϊ φασσοφόνῳ. Arist. H. A. ix. 12, 615 b, 36, 620 ἡ δὲ κύμινδις μέγεθος ὅσον ἱέραξ ὁ φασσοφόνος καλούμενος. Ael. xii. 4 Ἑρμῇ τὸν φασσοφόντην ἄθυρμα εἶναι φασίν.

Commonly translated *Goshawk*, i. e. *Astur palumbarius*, L., which has moreover a reputation for extreme swiftness: but the Goshawk is rare in Greece (Lindermayer, Von der Mühle), and there is no definite tradition in regard to the name (Scaliger, in Arist. p. 249 certe periculosum sententiam suam dicere). The above references are all mystical; cf. s. v. πέλεια.

ΦΑ'Ψ. A **Wild Pigeon**; almost certainly identical with **φάσσα**, the Ringdove. Cf. φαβοτύπος, φασσοφόνος.

Apparently distinguished from φάσσα in Arist. H. A. viii. 3, 593 a, 15, where however, in the catalogue of pigeon-names, some MSS. (Aa, Ca) omit φάψ, and others (Da) φάττα. In the following line, φάττα μὲν οὖν καὶ περιστερὰ ἀεὶ φαίνονται, the MSS. PDa read φάψ, as in Arist. fr. 271, 1527, Athen. ix. 394 a. In Arist. ap. Athen. l. c. there is further confusion in the statements as to their size, φάσσα and φάψ being apparently cited as different, but the passage is corrupt.

Supposed to be connected with rt. φοβ. φέβομαι, but the derivation is as doubtful as its supposed parallel, τρήρων, τρέω. As *var. ll.* φλάβες, and φλάβων occur in Arist. *passim*; φαβῶν is specially cited in Aesch. Philoct. (fr. 232) ap. Athen. ix. 394 a.

First in Aesch. fr. Prot. (2) 194, ap. Athen. 394 a σιτουμένην δύστηνον ἀθλίαν φάβα, μέσακτα πλευρὰ πρὸς πτύοις πεπλεγμένην.

Description.—Arist. H. A. ix. 7, 613 οὐκ ἀνακύπτουσι πίνουσαι (vide s. v. **φάσσα**, Athen. ix. 394 c) νεοττεύουσι ἐν τοῖς αὐτοῖς τόποις ἀεί. Arist. H. A. vi. 8, 564 ἡ μὲν θήλεια ἀπὸ δείλης ἀρξαμένη τήν τε νύχθ' ὅλην ἐπῳάζει καὶ ἕως ἀκρατίσματος ὥρας, ὁ δ' ἄρρην τὸ λοιπὸν τοῦ χρόνου. Ibid. 7, 563 b,

ΦΑΨ (*continued*).

ix. 29, 618. The Cuckoo lays her eggs in its nest (cf. s. v. **φάσσα**, Arist. De Mirab. 3, 830 b).

Mentioned also Lyc. 580.

ΦΕΛΛΙ'ΝΑΣ. An unknown water-bird, mentioned, with epithet ταχύς, as being captured in nets, Dion. De Avib. iii. 23.

ΦΗ'ΝΗ. According to Doederlein, connected with φηνός (= λαμπρός), φάω, φαίνω, &c., i. e. having τὰ ὄμματα λαμπρά: or according to Von Edlinger and others, from root *bha-n* = φωνεῖν. I incline to think the word is an exotic, and probably Egyptian, connected with φοῖνιξ, Eg. *bennu*.

A kind of **Vulture**.

Od. iii. 371 Ἀθήνη | φήνῃ εἰδομένη. Od. xvi. 216 κλαῖον δὲ λιγέως, ἀδινώτερον ἤ τ' οἰωνοί, | φῆναι ἢ αἰγυπιοὶ γαμψώνυχες. Ar. Av. 304.

Arist. H. A. viii. 3, 592 b ἀετοῦ μείζων, τὸ χρῶμα σποδοειδές. Ib. ix. 32, 619 ἀετὸς ὁ γνήσιος μείζων τῆς φήνης. Ib. vi. 6, 563, ix. 34, 619 b ἐκβληθέντα τρέφει τὰ τοῦ ἀετοῦ τέκνα (cf. Ambros. Hexaem. v. 18). ἐπαργεμός τ' ἐστὶ καὶ πεπήρωται τοὺς ὀφθαλμούς (? a reference to the blood-red sclerotic of the eye). Its maternal affection referred to (cf. **αἰγυπιός**, &c.), Opp. Hal. i. 727 καὶ μ΄ν τις φήνης ἀδινὸν γόον ἔκλυεν ἀνὴρ | ὄρθριον ἀμφὶ τέκεσσιν.

Arist. De Mirab. 60, 835 a ἐξ ἀλιαιέτων φήνη γίνεται, ἐκ δὲ τούτων περκνοὶ καὶ γῖπες.

Ael. xii. 4 φήνην δὲ καὶ ἄρπην Ἀθήνᾳ προσνέμουσιν.

According to Boios ap. Anton. Lib. c. vi, Zeus metamorphoses the wife of Periphas into the bird φήνη, καὶ διδοῖ πρὸς ἅπασαν πρᾶξιν ἀνθρώποις αἰσίαν ἐπιφαίνεσθαι : cf. Ovid. Met. vii. 399.

Also **φίνις**, Diosc. ii. 58 φίνις τὸ ὄρνεον, ὃ Ῥωμαϊστὶ καλοῦσιν ὀσσίφραγον: cf. Plin. x. 3.

Identified by Aldrovandi, Gaza, and by most moderns, with the *Aquila barbata* of Pliny, N. H. x. 3, that is to say with our Lämmergeier, *Gypaëtus barbatus*, L., which is accurately described by Dion. De Avib. i. 4 under the name **ἅρπη**. The Lämmergeier is also identical with Lat. *ossifraga* (Plin. l. c.), a name accurately descriptive of its habits, and Lat. *sanqualis* (Festus, 316, 317). The brief description in Arist. H. A. viii, inclines Sundevall, Aubert, and Wimmer, to identify φήνη with *Vultur monachus*. The references are in the main poetical or mythical, and both the name and the stories of the bird's maternal affection seem to me to point to an Egyptian origin. With the stories of the Eagle's bastard brood, cf. the Mod. Gk. name μηλαδέλφι = ἑτεροθαλής (Coray, Ἄτακτα, v. 204), said by Heldreich to be applied to *Aquila Bonellii*.

ΦΛΕΓΥ'ΑΣ· ὁ ἀετός, Suid. ἀετὸς ξανθός, ὀξύς, Hesych.   Cf. Hes. Sc. 11. 134 (vide infra).

ΦΛΕ'ΞΙΣ.   An unknown bird.

Ar. Av. 882. Perhaps connected with **φλεγύας**, a name or ep. of **μόρφνος** in Hes. Sc. 11. 134, where it seems to mean the ' lightning bird,' from φλέγ-ω, *fulg-eo*, Sk. *bharg*, to shine. Cf. Steinthal, app. to Goldzieher, Myth. of the Hebrews, p. 384 (ed. London, 1877).

ΦΟΙΝΙΚΟ'ΠΤΕΡΟΣ.   The Flamingo, *Phoenicopterus antiquorum*, L.

Ar. Av. 271 'ΕΠ. οὗτος οὐ τῶν ἠθάδων τῶνδ' ὧν ὁρᾶθ' ὑμεῖς ἀεί, | ἀλλὰ λιμναῖος. ΠΕ. βαβαί, καλός γε καὶ φοινικιοῦς. 'ΕΠ. εἰκότως· καὶ γὰρ ὄνομ' αὐτῷ γ' ἐστὶ φοινικόπτερος. This is the only reference to the bird in classical Greek, and the identification here is at best doubtful. The succeeding reference to the Cock might lead one to suspect that under the name Phoenicopterus some bird less unlike the Cock than the Flamingo is, was here alluded to: such a bird, for example, as *Porphyrio hyacinthinus*, the Purple Water-hen (vide s.v. πορφυρίων). The question, however, is not capable of settlement. The Flamingo occurs in Greece only as a rare straggler, though abundant on the opposite coast of Asia Minor (Von der Mühle, p. 118; Lindermayer, p. 155, &c.). Cf. Gesner, H. Anim. lib. iii Mirum est huius tam pulchrae et eximiae avis nomen ab Aristoteli taceri, cum Aristophanes, qui vixit eadem aetate, meminerit; sed Graecis etiam raram esse hanc avem puto. Flamingos were seen, however, by Bory de St. Vincent, in the marshes of Osman Aga near Navarino.

Heliodorus, Aethiop. vi. 3 describes the bird as Νειλῷον φοινικόπτερον: and the Scholiast ad Juv. xi. 139 states in like manner, abundans est in Africa: it, apparently, is also mentioned as a dainty, by Philostr. Vit. Apoll. Tyan. viii. p. 387 (ed. Paris, 1605) as ὄρνις φοινίκεος.

In Crat. Nem. fr. 4, ap. Athen. ix. 373 d ὄρνις φοινικόπτερος, is probably the Cock.

It has been stated above, s. v. **γλωττίς**, that Belon (Hist. des Oyseaux, viii. 8) identified that bird with the Flamingo; so also did Aldrovandi (Ornithol. iii. 20, 4), with as little reason. To the opinion there ascribed to Linnaeus, the following words of Gesner should have been subjoined: ego vero iis quas Gallinulas aquaticas nostri vocant avibus Glottidem adnumero, quae omnes fissipedes sunt; cf. also Scaliger (in loc. Aristot.) Glottis autem quae sit nondum mihi constat; ridiculum quod quidam de Phoenicoptero ausus est pronuntiare.

In Latin, references to the Flamingo are frequent and free from doubt. Cf. Juv. xi. 139 et Scythiae volucres et phoenicopterus ingens; Martial, Ep. iii. 58, 14 nomenque debet quae rubentibus pennis; ib. xiii. 71 dat mihi penna rubens nomen; Suet. Cal. 22, &c., &c.

'That the Tongue of this Volatile was much commended, and in

ΦΟΙΝΙΚΟΠΤΕΡΟΣ (*continued*).

great Esteem, for its excellent Taste and most delicious Relish, will appear from the following Quotations' (Douglass, op. infra cit.) : Plin. x. (48) 68 Phoenicopteri linguam praecipui saporis esse, Apicius docuit ; Martial, xiii. 71 sed lingua gulosis Nostra sapit : quid si garrula lingua foret? cf. also Sueton. Vitell. xiii. The brain was also a tid-bit, and Heliogabalus (Lamprid. 20, p. 108) exhibuit Palatinis dapes extis et cerebellis Phoenicopterorum refertas. Receipts for the cookery of Flamingos are given (without mention of the tongue) by Apic. (?) De Re Coquin. vi. 7. I am inclined to believe that such costly indulgences of the palate were often determined by obscure superstitious motives (as are many Chinese luxuries) rather than by real or imaginary refinements of taste. Nevertheless the Flamingo's tongue is said to be still appreciated: cf. Von der Mühle, Ornithol. Griechenlands, p. 118 Ein französischer Schiffscapitain brachte mir einige von Smyrna, wo sie sehr häufig sind, und von den Jägern den Engländern zum Verkaufe angeboten werden, welche die dicke fleischige Zunge als Leckerbissen verzehren. Cf. (int. al.) the interesting paper by Dr. J. Douglass in Phil. Trans. v. p. 63, 1721.

ΦΟΙΝΙ΄ΚΟΥΡΟΣ. The **Redstart**, *Luscinia phoenicurus*, L., and *L. tithys* (Scop.). Mod. Gk. κοκκινόκωλος, γιαννακός, καλαντζῆς (Bikélas).

Arist. H. A. ix. 49 B, 632 b; Plin. x. (29) 44 ; vide s. v. ἐρίθακος. Cf. also Geop. xv. 1, 22.

ΦΟΙ˜ΝΙΞ *s.* φοίνιξ.· The **Phoenix**, an astronomical symbol of the Egyptians. Eg. *bennu*.

First in Hes. Fr. 50, 4.

Herod. ii. 73 ἔστι δὲ καὶ ἄλλος ὄρνις ἱρός, τῷ οὔνομα φοῖνιξ· ἐγὼ μέν μιν οὐκ εἶδον, εἰ μὴ ὅσον γραφῇ· καὶ γὰρ δὴ καὶ σπάνιος ἐπιφοιτᾷ σφι, διὰ ἐτέων (ὡς Ἡλιουπολῖται λέγουσι) πεντακοσίων. φοιτᾶν δὲ τότε φασί, ἐπεὰν οἱ ἀποθάνῃ ὁ πατήρ. ἔστι δέ, εἰ τῇ γραφῇ παρόμοιος, τοσόσδε καὶ τοιόσδε· τὰ μὲν αὐτοῦ χρυσόκομα τῶν πτερῶν, τὰ δὲ ἐρυθρά· ἐς τὰ μάλιστα αἰετῷ περιήγησιν ὁμοιότατος, καὶ τὸ μέγαθος. τοῦτον δὲ λέγουσι μηχανᾶσθαι τάδε, ἐμοὶ μὲν οὐ πιστὰ λέγοντες. ἐξ Ἀραβίης ὁρμεώμενον ἐς τὸ ἱρὸν τοῦ Ἡλίου κομίζειν τὸν πατέρα ἐν σμύρνῃ ἐμπλάσσοντα, καὶ θάπτειν ἐν τοῦ Ἡλίου τῷ ἱρῷ. κομίζειν δὲ οὕτω· πρῶτον, τῆς σμύρνης ᾠὸν πλάσσειν ὅσον τε δυνατός ἐστι φέρειν· μετὰ δὲ πειρᾶσθαι αὐτὸ φορέοντα· ἐπεὰν δὲ ἀποπειρηθῇ, οὕτω δὴ κοιλήναντα τὸ ᾠόν, τὸν πατέρα ἐς αὐτὸ ἐντιθέναι, σμύρνῃ δὲ ἄλλῃ ἐμπλάσσειν τοῦτο κατ᾽ ὅ τι τοῦ ᾠοῦ ἐκκοιλήνας ἐνέθηκε τὸν πατέρα· ἐσκειμένου δὲ τοῦ πατρὸς γίνεσθαι τὠυτὸ βάρος· ἐμπλάσαντα δὲ κομίζειν μιν ἐπ᾽ Αἰγύπτου ἐς τοῦ Ἡλίου τὸ ἱρόν. Cf. Ael. vi. 58, Philostr. Vit. Apollon. Tyan. iii. 49, p. 135 (Olear.), Antiph. Com. iii. 96 ἐν Ἡλίου μέν φασι γίγνεσθαι πύλει φοίνικας, ἐν Ἀθήναις δὲ γλαῦκας. Artemid., Suid., Ovid, Metam. xv. 392, &c.

ΦΟΙΝΙΚΟΠΤΕΡΟΣ—ΦΟΙΝΙΞ   183

ΦΟΙΝΙΞ (*continued*).

An Indian version, Dion. De Avib. i. 32 ἀκήκοα δέ, ὡς παρὰ τοῖς Ἰνδοῖς ὄρνις εἴη γονέων ἄτερ καὶ μίξεως χωρὶς ὑφιστάμενος, φοῖνιξ τοὔνομα, καὶ βιοῖν φασιν ἐπὶ πλεῖστον καὶ μετὰ πάσης ἀφοβίας αὐτόν, ὡς οὔτε τόξοις οὔτε λίθοις οὔτε καλάμοις ἢ πάγαις τῶν ἀνδρῶν τι κατ' αἰτῶν ποιεῖν πειρωμένων. Ὁ δὲ θάνατος αὐτῷ τὴν ἀρχὴν ποιεῖ τῆς ζωῆς· ἣν γάρ ποτε γηράσας πρὸς τὰς πτήσεις ἑαυτὸν ἴδῃ νωθέστερον, ἢ τὰς αὐγὰς τῶν ὀμμάτων ἐλασσουμένας, ἐφ' ὑψηλῆς πέτρας κάρφη συλλέξας πυράν τινα τῆς τελευτῆς, ἢ καλιὰν συντίθησι τῆς ζωῆς, ἣν ἐν μέσῳ καθημένου τοῦ φοίνικος ἡ τῶν ἡλιακῶν ἀκτίνων καταφλέγει θερμότης. οὕτω δὲ διαφθαρέντος αὐτοῦ νέος ἐκ τῆς τέφρας αὖθις ἕτερος γίνεται φοῖνιξ καὶ τοῖς πατρῴοις ἔθεσι χρῆται, ὥστε ὑπὸ τῆς ἡλιακῆς μόνον αὐγῆς, πατρός τε καὶ μητρὸς χωρίς, τὸν ὄρνιν γίνεσθαι τοῦτον. Cf. Physiol. Syr., c. xvi (who adds that the Phoenix builds its nest in the month Pamnuth, s. Faminoth, a Coptic word); Epiphan. in Physiol. c. xi, Eustath. Ant., p. 29 (ed. Lugd. 1677), Pseudo-Hieronym., p. 219 (ed. Venet. 1772).

Chaeremon, fr. 16 ἐνιαυτός· φοῖνιξ. Horap. i. 34 ἡλίου ἐστὶν ὁ φοῖνιξ σύμβολον . . . . ψυχὴν δὲ ἐνταῦθα πολὺν χρόνον διατρίβουσαν βουλόμενοι γράψαι, ἢ πλημμύραν, φοίνικα τὸ ὄρνεον ζωγραφοῦσιν : ibid. 35 καὶ τὸν χρονίως δὲ ἀπὸ ξένης ἐπιδημοῦντα δηλοῦντες, πάλιν φαίνικα τὸ ὄρνεον ζωγραφοῦσιν : ib. ii. 57 ἀποκατάστασιν δὲ πολυχρόνιον βουλόμενοι σημῆναι, φοίνικα τὸ ὄρνεον ζωγραφοῦσιν· ἐκεῖνος γὰρ ὅτε γεννᾶται, ἀποκατάστασις γίνεται πραγμάτων.

A symbol of long life, Prov. ἢν μὴ φοίνικος ἔτη βιώσῃ, Luc. Hermot. 53 (1, 793) ; cf. Job xxix. 18, where for *sand* read Phoenix.

Cf. also Nonnus Dion. xl. 394 καὶ ξύλα κηώεντα φέρων γαμψώνυχι τάρσῳ | χιλιέτης σαφὸς ὄρνις ἐπ' εὐόδμῳ σέο βωμῷ | φοῖνιξ, τέρμα βίοιο φέρων αὐτόσπορον ἀρχήν | τίκτεται, ἰσοτύποιο χρόνου πάλιν ἄγρετος εἰκών | λύσας δ' ἐν πυρὶ γῆρας, ἀμείβεται ἐκ πυρὸς ἥβην. See also the *Phoenix* of Claudian ; Auson. Id. xi ; Ovid, Met. xv. 402 ; Senec. Ep. xlii ; Pompon. Mela, iii. 9 ; Lactant. (?) Carm. Phoenice ; Lucian, iii. 27, 276, 350 ; Solin. Polyhistor. c. 36 ; Clem. Rom. Ep. i ad Corinth. c. 24, p. 120, &c.

Late apparitions of the Phoenix, Plin. x. 2 ; Tacit. vi. 28 ; Dio C. lvii ; Suidas ; Tzetz. Chiliad. v. 6. A new Phoenix-period is said to have commenced A.D. 139, in the reign of Antoninus Pius ; and a recrudescence of astronomical symbolism associated therewith is manifested on the coins of that Emperor.

Various remedies were to be obtained from its nest, Plin. xxix. 9 (Irridere est vitae remedia post millesimum annum reditura monstrare).

For further references, oriental and classical, see Bochart, Hieroz. ii. coll. 818, 849.

On the Phoenix as an astronomical symbol of a cyclic period, see (int. al.) Marsham, Canon. Chron. p. 9, 387 ; Creuzer's Symb. i. p. 438, ii. p. 163 ; Lewis, Astr. of Anc., p. 283 ; Kenrick's Egypt of Herod.,

ΦΟΙΝΙΞ (*continued*).

p. 100; Larcher's Herod. ii. p. 320; Encycl. Metrop., Art. Herodotus (8vo ed.), p. 249; Drummond in Class. Journal, xiv. 319; Ideler, Enchir. Chron. Math. i. p. 186. See the Bhagavad Gita, viii, for an account of the similar cyclical 'day and night of Brahma.' For a corresponding Chinese tradition, see Martini, Histor. Sinica, cit. Coray ad Heliod. p. 201; Creuzer, Symb. ii. 164; on the Persian account, cf. Dalberg, 'Simorg, der Persische Phönix,' in Von Hammer's Fundgruben des Orients, i. p. 199. See also Henrichsen, De Phoenicis fabula apud Graecos, Romanos, et populos orientales, Hafniae, 1825, 1827.

In Aristid. ii. p. 107 (Jebb) the Phoenix is called Ἰνδικὸς ὄρνις.

For representations of the Phoenix, see Jomard's Descr. de l'Ég. Antiq. i. c. 5.

The Phoenix has been taken by Cuvier, Lenz, and others, for the Golden Pheasant,—a coarse materialising of a mythic symbol (Hehn). On the study and interpretation of such sacred enigmas of the ancients, see Grote's Hist. i. c. 16.

The subject deserves to be studied under many heads; for example, the varying terms assigned to the Phoenix-period, and the various astronomical cycles thereby indicated; the relation of the Phoenix to the Palm-tree (Eg. *bennu* = φοῖνιξ τὸ ὄρνεον, *benne* = φοῖνιξ τὸ δένδρον, Lauth, Sitzungsber. Bayer. Akad., 1876, p. 94) in connexion with the whole symbolic imagery of the latter; the relation of the Phoenix to the Heron (Lauth, l. c.; cf. supra s.v. βαιήθ), involving also the depicting of the Soul as the Phoenix and the question of the term assigned to the Soul's wanderings. The whole subject is of great complexity, and lies beyond the scope of this book.

ΦΡΥΓΙΛΟΣ. An unknown bird, obscurely referred to in Ar. Av., with a play on the word 'Phrygian'; 763 φρυγίλος ὄρνις ἐνθάδ' ἔσται, τοῦ Φιλήμονος γένους: and 873 φρυγίλῳ Σαβαζίῳ. I conjecture it to be a form cognate to περγοῦλον, σπέργουλος, &c., and to mean a *Sparrow*; in which case φρυγίλῳ Σαβαζίῳ is an exact parallel to στρουθῷ μεγάλῃ μητρὶ θεῶν. Supposed also to be connected with Lat. *fringilla*.

ΦΡΥΝΟΛΟΓΟΣ, s. **φρυνολόχος** (φρύνη, a toad).

A kind of **Hawk**, probably a species of Harrier, *Circus* sp.

Arist. H. A. ix. 36, 620 οἱ δὲ λεῖοι καὶ οἱ φρυνολόγοι· οὗτοι εὐβίωτατοι καὶ χθαμαλοπτῆται. Vide s. v. ἐλειός.

Of the various hawks that feed on reptiles, the epithet 'low-flying' seems best applicable to the Harriers.

ΦΩΚΙΩΝ· ὄρνις ποιός, Hesych.

ΦΟΙΝΙΞ—ΧΑΡΑΔΡΙΟΣ

ΦΩ͂ΥΞ. (MSS. have φώυξ, θῶυξ, Ald. and Camus φώιξ, Schn. πώυξ. πώυγξ in Anton. Lib. c. 5; Et. M.)
A bird of the Heron kind ; supposed to be a name for the Bittern, but equally applicable to the Common Heron.
Arist. H. A. ix. 18, 617 οἱ μὲν οὖν ἐρωδιοὶ τοῦτον βιοῦσι τὸν τρόπον, ἡ δὲ καλουμένη φῶυξ ἴδιον ἔχει πρὸς τἆλλα· μάλιστα γάρ ἐστιν ὀφθαλμοβόρος τῶν ὀρνίθων. πολέμιος δὲ τῇ ἄρπῃ, καὶ γὰρ ἐκείνη ὁμοιοβίοτος.
Boios ap. Anton. Lib. l. c. ἡ δὲ Βουλὶς ἐγένετο πώϋγξ, καὶ αὐτῇ τροφὴν ἔδωκεν ὁ Ζεὺς μηδὲν ἐκ γῆς φυόμενον, ἀλλὰ ἐσθίειν ὀφθαλμοὺς ἰχθύος ἢ ὄρνιθος ἢ ὄφεως, ὅτι ἔμελλεν Αἰγυπτιοῦ τοῦ παιδὸς ἀφελέσθαι τὰς ὄψεις. Etym. M. Πώϋγγες, αἱ αἴθυιαι, αἱ κληθεῖσαι βοΐυγγες, παρὰ τὴν βοὴν καὶ ἰϋγήν.

ΧΑΛΚΙΔΙΚΟ͂Σ· εἶδος ἀλεκτρυόνος, Hesych. Vide s. v. ἀλεκτρυών, p. 24.

ΧΑΛΚΙ͂Σ. Vide supra, s. v. κύμινδις.

ΧΑΡΑΔΡΙΟ͂Σ. A bird conjectured to be the **Thick-knee** or **Norfolk Plover**, *Charadrius oedicnemus*, L., *Oedicnemus crepitans*, auctt.; so identified by Gesner, followed by Sundevall, Aubert and Wimmer, &c.. Mod. Gk. τουρλίδα (Erh.). Applied by the LXX. to Heb. אנפה. The derivation from χάραδρα is more than doubtful.
Ar. Av. 265 ἐς τὴν λόχμην | ἐμβὰς ἐπῷζε, χαραδριὸν μιμούμενος : ib. 1141 οἱ χαραδριοὶ καὶ τἆλλα ποτάμι' ὄρνεα.
Arist. H. A. viii. 3, 593 b, mentioned with λάρος, κέπφος, αἴθυια. Ib. ix. 11, 615 τὰς δ᾽ οἰκήσεις οἱ μὲν περὶ τὰς χαράδρας καὶ χηραμοὺς ποιοῦνται καὶ πέτρας, οἷον ὁ καλούμενος χαραδριός· ἔστι δ᾽ ὁ χαραδριὸς καὶ τὴν χρόαν καὶ τὴν φωνὴν φαῦλος, φαίνεται δὲ νύκτωρ, ἡμέρας δ᾽ ἀποδιδράσκει.
Proverb, χαραδριοῦ βίον ζῆν, of a glutton, Plat. Gorg. 494 B (ubi Schol. ὄρνις τις ὃς ἅμα τῷ ἐσθίειν ἐκκρίνει).
Is killed by ἄσφαλτος, Ael. vi. 46. πίπτει χαραδριὸς τιτάνου σπάσας, Phile, De An. Pr. 673.
According to Boios ap. Anton. Lib. c. xv, Agron is metamorphosed into the bird χαραδριός, the other characters in the story turning into various other nocturnal birds.
The sight of it is said to cure the jaundice, the bird catching it itself through the eyes ; hence ἀποστρέφεται τοὺς ἰκτεριῶντας, καὶ τὰ ὄμματα συγκλείσας ἔχει. [From which we may conjecture that the experiment has never been fairly tried. W. H. T.] Plut. Symp. ii. 681 c, Ael. xvii. 13. See also Suidas (and Schol. in Ar. Av. 267) Χαραδριός. ὄρνεον, εἰς ὃν ἀποβλέψαντες, ὡς λόγος, οἱ ἰκτεριῶντες ῥᾷον ἀπαλλάττονται· ὅθεν καὶ ἀποκρύπτουσιν αὐτοὺς οἱ πιπράσκοντες, ἵνα μὴ προῖκα ὠφελῶνται οἱ κάμνοντες. " Καὶ μὴν καλύπτει, μῶν χαραδριὸν περνᾷς ;" οὕτως Ἱππῶναξ. καὶ παροιμία ἐντεῦθεν, Χαραδριὸν μιμούμενος, ἐπὶ τῶν ἀποκρυπτομένων,

ΧΑΡΑΔΡΙΟΣ (*continued*).

οὕτως Εὐφρόνιος. ἐπεὶ γὰρ τοὺς ἰκτεριῶντας ὠφελεῖ ὁ χαραδριὸς ὀφθείς, καὶ τοῦτον οἱ περνῶντες κρύπτουσιν, ἵνα μὴ πρὸ τοῦ ὠνήσασθαί τις ἰαθῇ περιέργως. ἔστι δὲ εἶδος ὀρνέου μεταβαλλόμενον εἰς τὰ προκείμενα, κ.τ.λ. Cf. **ἴκτερος**.

In these mythical stories, with which compare Physiol. Syr. xv (volucris tota alba, nec ulla in ea nigredo est: reperitur in regum palatiis), Epiphan. in Physiol. xxiii, Eust. Hex. p. 32, Bochart, ii. p. 340, we have to do with eastern tales of the Stork, Heb. *chasad* (Lev. xi. 19, Deut. xiv. 18) arising from a confusion of names.

In Babr. lxxxii (lxxxviii, W. G. R.) Cod. Ath. has χαραδριός for κορυδαλλός: the word is here perhaps a corrupt connexion of κάλανδρος, It. *calandra*, which occurs in Dion. De Avib. iii. 15. Cf. W. H. Thompson's note on Plat. Gorg. l. c.

ΧΕΙΛΩ͂ΝΕΣ· τῶν ἀλεκτρυόνων τινές, Hesych. Cf. s. v. **κάλλων**.

ΧΕΛΙΔΩ͂Ν. Etymology very doubtful. Cf. Lat. *hirundo*, Sp. *golondrina*, &c. Supposed by some to be from Sk. rt. *har*, 'to catch or seize,' cf. Lat. *hir-udo*, a view somewhat akin to one much older, Isid. Orig. xii. 7 hirundo dicta est, quod cibos non sumat residens, sed in aëre rapiat escas et edat.

A **Swallow**. The Chimney Swallow, *Hirundo rustica*, and the House Martin, *H. urbica*. Mod. Gk. χελιδόνι. See also s. vv. **ἄπους, δρεπανίς, κύψελος, κωτιλάς**.

Dim. χελιδονιδεύς, Eust. 753. 56: χελιδόνιον, Galen. xiv. 386: χελιδονίς, Anth. Pal. vi. 160, vii. 210, &c. A Swallow-chick is called μόσχος χελιδόνος, Achae. ap. Ael. vii. 47, or ὀρτάλιχος (q. v.), Opp. Hal. v. 579.

In Homer, Od. xxi. 411 ἡ δ' ὑπὸ καλὸν ἄεισε, χελιδόνι εἰκέλη αὐδήν (of the bow of Ulysses). xxii. 240 ['Aθήνη] ἕζετ' ἀναΐξασα, χελιδόνι εἰκέλη ἄντην: cf. Plut. Is. and Osir. xvi, ii. 357 C, where Isis turns by night into a Swallow.

Epithets and Phrases. — αἰολόδειρος, Nonn. Dion. xii. 76. Ἀτθὶ Κόρα, μελίθρεπτε, λάλος λάλον ἁρπάξασα | τέττιγα (and other epithets), Even. xiii, Gk. Anth. i. 98. δίγαμος, Lucian, Traged. 49. ἡδυμελής, χαρίεσσα χελιδοῖ, Anacr. fr. 57 ap. Hephaest. vii. 39. 4, p. 22. χείλεσιν ἀμφιλάλοις | δεινὸν ἐπιβρέμεται | Θρηκία χελιδών, Ar. Ran. 679-681. λάλος, Arrian, Nonnus, Babr. ξουθή, Babr. Fab. cxviii (cf. Rutherford's note, and vide supra, s. v. **ἱππαλεκτρυών**). ὀρθρογόη, Hes. Op. et D. ii. 186. ὀρθρολάλος, Philip, xviii, Gk. Anth. ii. 200. Πανδιονίς, Hes. l. c.; Sappho, p. 88 (Bergk); freq. in Anthol. πέδοικος, Aesch. fr. 45 ap. Hesych.

ΧΕΛΙΔΩΝ (continued).

τανυσίπτερος, ποικίλος, Ar. Av. 1411 (cf. Alcaeus, fr. 84, ap. Schol.). φιλόπαις, φιλότεκνος, Anth. Φοιβόληπτος, I.yc. 1460.

Description.—Arist. H. A. vi. 5, 563, viii. 3, 592 b ὄρνις σαρκοφάγος. Ib. iii. 12, 519 μονόχροος. Ib. i. 1, 487 b, ix. 30, 68 ὅμοιος τῷ ἄποδι· εὔπτερος καὶ κακόπους. Ib. ix. 30, 618 τὴν κνήμην οὐκ ἔχει δασεῖαν. Ib. ii. 17, 509 οὔτε τὸν στόμαχον οὔτε τὸν πρόλοβον ἔχει εὐρύν, ἀλλὰ τὴν κοιλίαν μακρήν. Ib. ii. 15, 506 b πρὸς τοῖς ἐντέροις ἔχει τὴν χολήν. The Swallow is said, like the Nightingale, to have no tongue, Aes. Fab. 416, &c.

Nest and Reproduction.—Arist. H. A. ix. 7, 612 b συγκαταπλέκει γὰρ τοῖς κάρφεσι πηλόν· κἂν ἀπορῆται πηλοῦ, βρέχουσα αὐτὴν καλινδεῖται τοῖς πτεροῖς πρὸς τὴν κόνιν. ἔτι δὲ στιβαδοποιεῖται καθάπερ οἱ ἄνθρωποι, τὰ σκληρὰ πρῶτα ὑποτιθεῖσα καὶ τῷ μεγέθει σύμμετρον ποιοῦσα πρὸς αὐτήν. περί τε τὴν τροφὴν τῶν τέκνων ἐκπονεῖται ἀμφότερα· δίδωσι δ' ἑκατέρῳ διατηροῦσά τινι συνηθείᾳ τὸ προειληφός, ὅπως μὴ δὶς λάβῃ. καὶ τὴν κόπρον τὸ μὲν πρῶτον αὐταὶ ἐκβάλλουσιν, ὅταν δ' αὐξηθῶσι, μεταστρέφοντας ἔξω διδάσκουσι τοὺς νεοττοὺς προΐεναι. (This accurate account evidently refers in particular to the House Martin.) Cf. Ael. iii. 24, 25, Antig. Mirab. 37 (43), Plut. De Soll. An. ii. 966 d. Arist. H. A. vi. 5, 563 μόνον τῶν σαρκοφάγων δὶς νεοττεύει. The nests of the Swallow, House Martin and Sand Martin are adequately described by Plin. x. (33) 44.

Phile, De An. Pr. (20) 454 ἐναντίαν δέ φασι τῇ τῶν ὀρνέων, | τὴν μίξιν αὐτῶν εὑρεθῆναι καὶ ξένην.

For poetic references see (int. al.) Ar. Av. 1151 (which quotation is, however, by a recent emendation, no longer apt: cf. Rutherford, Class. Rev. 1891, p. 90); Antip. Sid. lxiii, Gk. Anth. ii. 23 χελιδών, μητέρα τέκνων | ἄρτι σε θάλπουσαν παῖδας ὑπὸ πτέρυγι : Agath. lvii, Gk. Anth. iv. 23 ἐπιτρύζει δὲ χελιδών, | κάρφεσι κολλητὸν πηξαμένη θάλαμον : Theaet. Schol. ii, Gk. Anth. iii. 214 καὶ φιλόπαις ὑπὸ γεῖσα δόμους τεύξασα χελιδών | ἔκγονα πηλοχύτοις ξεινοδοκεῖ θαλαμοῖς : Marc. Argent. xxiv, Gk. Anth. ii. 248 ἤδη καὶ φιλότεκνος ὑπὸ τραυλοῖσι χελιδών, | χείλεσι καρφίτην πηλοδομεῖ θάλαμον : Anth. Pal. x. 2 ἤδη δὲ πλάσσει μὲν ὑπώροφα γυρὰ χελιδών, | οἴκια. Nonn. Dion. ii. 132 καὶ ῥόδον ἀγγέλλουσα καὶ ἀνθεμόεσσαν ἐέρσην | ἔσσομαι εἰαρινοῖο φίλη Ζεφύροιο χελιδών, | φθεγγομένη, λάλος ὄρνις, ὑπωροφίης μέλος ἠχοῦς, | ὀρχηθμῷ πτερόεντι περισκαίρουσα καλιήν: cf. ibid. xlvii. 30. Opp. Hal. i. 729 ἠὲ καὶ εἰαρινῇσι χελιδόσιν ἐγγὺς ἔκυρσε | μυρομέναις ἑὰ τέκνα, τάτε σφίσι λῃσσαντο | ἐξ εὐνῆς ἢ φῶτες ἀπηνέες ἠὲ δράκοντες : cf. ibid. v. 579. See also the Fable of the Nightingale and the Swallow, Babr. xii (ed. Rutherford).

Migration.—Arist. H. A. viii. 16, 600 φωλοῖσι δὲ πολλοὶ καὶ τῶν ὀρνίθων, καὶ οὐχ ὥς τινες οἴονται, εἰς ἀλεεινοὺς τόπους ἀπέρχονται πάντες· ἀλλ' οἱ μὲν πλησίον ὄντες τοιούτων τόπων, ἐν οἷς ἀεὶ διαμένουσι, καὶ ἰκτῖνοι καὶ χελιδόνες ἀποχωροῦσιν ἐνταῦθα, οἱ δὲ πορρωτέρω ὄντες τῶν τοιούτων οὐκ ἐκτοπίζουσιν ἀλλὰ κρύπτουσιν ἑαυτούς. ἤδη γὰρ ὠμμέναι πολλαὶ χελιδόνες

ΧΕΛΙΔΩΝ (continued).

εἰσὶν ἐν ἀγγείοις ἐψιλωμέναι πάμπαν. Cf. Plin. x. (24) 34 in vicina abeunt apricos secutae montium recessus, inventaeque iam sunt ibi nudae atque deplumes ; Claudian, Eutrop. i. 118 Vel qualis gelidis pluma labente pruinis Arboris immoritur trunco brumalis hirundo. In reference to the migration, see also Aesch. fr. 48 πέδοικος (i. e. μέτοικος) χελιδών. Arch. xxvi, Gk. Anth. ii. 86 αἶαν ὅλην νήσους τε διπταμένη σὺ χελιδών. The Swallow as the bird of returning Spring : Hes. Op. et D. 568 (ii. 186) τὸν δὲ μετ' ὀρθρογόη Πανδιονὶς ὦρτο χελιδών | ἐς φάος ἀνθρώποις, ἔαρος νέον ἱσταμένοιο. Simon. 74 (121) ap. Schol. Ar. Av. 1410 ἄγγελε κλυτὰ ἔαρος ἀδυόδμου, | κυανέα χελιδοῖ. Stesich. fr. 45 (Bergk) ap. Eust. II. 10. 1 ὅταν ἦρος ὥρᾳ κελαδῇ χελιδών. Ar. Pax 800 ὕμνειν, ὅταν ἠρινὰ μὲν φωνῇ χελιδών | ἑζομένη κελαδῇ. Id. Eq. 419 σκέψασθε παῖδες· οὐχ ὁρᾶθ' ; ὥρα νία, χελιδών. Id. Av. 714, &c. Ael. i. 52. Babr. 131. Cf. Ovid, Fasti, ii. 853 Fallimur an veris praenuntia venit hirundo : Hor. Ep. i. 7, 13, &c. Cf. also a well-known vase (first figured in Mon. Inst. Corr. Archeol. ii. pl. xxiv) with the inscription 'Ἰδοὺ χελιδών. Νὴ τὸν Ἡρακλέα. Αἰτηΐ. Ἔαρ ἤδη.

How the Swallows come with the wind χελιδονίας or Favonius,Theophr. H. P. vii. 15, 1, Plin. ii. 47.

Artemid. p. 153 ὅταν δὲ τὸ ἔαρ παραβάλῃ πρώτη πρόσεισιν· ὡς ἂν εἴποι ἀποδεικνύουσα τῶν ἔργων ἕκαστα, καὶ ὅταν γε φαίνηται οὐδέποτε ἑσπέρας ᾄδει, ἀλλ' ἕωθεν ἡλίου ἀνίσχοντος οὓς ἂν ζῶντας καταλαμβάνοι ὑπομιμνήσκουσα τῶν ἔργων : cf. Nonn. Dionys. iii. 13 καὶ λιγυρή, μερόπεσσι συνέστιος, εἴαρι κῆρυξ, | ὄρθριον ὕπνον ἄμερσε λάλος τρίζουσα χελιδών | ἀντιφανής : Apul. Florid. ii. 13 cantum hirundinibus matutinum ; &c., &c.

Hence invoked at the Spring festival of the Thesmophoria : Ar. Thesm. 1 ὦ Ζεῦ, χελιδὼν ἀρά ποτε φανήσεται : cf. Ar. fr. 499 πυθοῦ χελιδὼν πηνίκ' ἄττα φαίνεται (Eratosth. ap. Schol. Plat. p. 371 ; vide also Suid. s. v. ἄττα).

How the Swallow is visible in Egypt all the year, Herod. ii. 22, Pausan. x. 4, 9 ; but never stays to nest in Daulis, the country of Tereus, Pausan. l. c. Neither does it visit Thebes, quoniam urbs illa saepius capta sit ; nor Bizya, in Thrace, propter scelera Terei, Plin. iv. (11) 18, x. (24) 34 ; it goes, however, to τὰς κάτω Θήβας, Babr. Fab. cxxxi.

On Swallows used as messengers, Plin. x. (24) 34.

Proverb.—μία χελιδὼν ἔαρ οὐ ποιεῖ, Arist. Eth. Nic. i. 6. 1098 (from Cratin., according to Cramer, An. Par. i. 182) ; cf. Ar. Av. 1417.

The Rhodian **Swallow Song**, χελιδόνισμα, sung in the month Boedromion (?), Athen. viii. 360 c ἦλθ', ἦλθε χελιδών, | καλὰς ὥρας ἄγουσα, | καλοὺς ἐνιαυτούς, | ἐπὶ γαστέρα λευκά, | ἐπὶ νῶτα μέλαινα | ... ἄνοιγ' ἄνοιγε | τὰν θύραν χελιδόνι· | οὐ γὰρ γέροντές | ἐσμεν, ἀλλὰ παιδία : emended by Ilgen, Opusc. Phil. i. p. 165, Bergk, P. Lyr. iii. p. 671. Cf. Eustath. 1914, 45.

ΧΕΛΙΔΩΝ (continued).

In Sappho, fr. (52) 88 τί με Πανδιονὶς ὠράνα χελιδών, we have perhaps a fragment of a 'Swallow-song.' This difficult line is variously read and interpreted: Hesychius gives ὦ 'ράννα χελιδών· ὀροφή, but the gloss is, in my opinion, fragmentary and meaningless: Bergk, after Is. Vossius, reads ὦ "ραννα; I venture to suggest ὦρα νέα, as in Ar. Eq. 419, which latter line is itself probably a fragment of a Swallow-song. Another fragment of a Swallow-song perhaps exists in Hom. Carm. Min. xv. 11 νεῦμαί τοι, νεῦμαι ἐνιαύσιος, ὥστε χελιδών | ἕστηκ' ἐν προθύροις ψιλὴ πόδας. In the Rhodian Swallow-song already referred to, two very curious features are the alternate balance or 'parallelism' of successive lines and the apparent influence of accent on rhythm: the text has been much emended by commentators, in order to obtain a more accurate scansion than the song ever, perhaps, possessed. It is easy to suggest yet other emendations: for instance in ll. 17, 18 ἂν δὴ φέρῃς τι, | μέγ' ἂν τι δὴ φέροιο seems better than the common reading μέγα δή τι. At the very best some of the lines (in their present state) seem to have little rhythm and not much sense.

A modern χελιδόνισμα, Fauriel, Chants de la Grèce mod., i. p. xxviii χελιδόνα ἔρχεται | ἀπ' τὴν ἄσπρην θάλασσαν· | κάθησε καὶ λάλησε. | Μάρτη, Μάρτη μου καλὲ | καὶ φλιβάρη φλιβερέ | κ' ἂν χιονίσῃς, κ' ἂν ποντίσῃς | πάλε ἄνοιξιν μυρίζεις.

According to Bent (Cyclades, 1885, p. 434) the Swallow-song is still sung in Kythnos (Thermia) and in Macedonia, on March 1. Cf. Grimm, D. Myth. p. 723; Swainson, Prov. Names of British Birds, p. 50, &c., &c. Cf. also the κορώνισμα, supra, s. v. κορώνη.

A Melancholy Bird.—The myth of Itylus. Agath. xii, Gk. Anth. iv. 8 ἀμφιπεριτρύζοισι χελιδόνες, ἐς δ' ἐμὲ δάκρυ | βάλλουσι. . . . ἀλλ' Ἴτυλον κλαίοιτε κατ' οὔρεα, καὶ γοάοιτε | εἰς ἔποπας κραναὴν αὖλιν ἐφεζόμεναι. Mnasalc. ix, Gk. Anth. i. 125 τρυυλὰ μινυρομένα, Πανδιονὶ παρθένε, φωνᾷ | Τηρέος οὐ θεμίτων ἁψαμένα λεχέων. | τίπτε παναμέριος γοάεις ἀνὰ δῶμα χελιδών: Anth. Pal. ix. 57 Πανδιονὶ κάμμορε κούρα, | μυρόμενα: Mosch. iii. 39 οὐδὲ τόσον θρήνησεν ἀν' ὤρεα μακρὰ χελιδών. Nonn. Dion. passim, &c., &c.

The Itylus-myth has been already discussed s. vv. ἀηδών and ἔποψ. In the association together of the Swallow and the Nightingale, a curious feature is the similarity of the poetical epithets applied to both. The epithet Πανδιονίς, and the inclusion of Pandion in the myth, whatever they may exactly mean, seem to me to have something to do with the festival of the Πανδία, which took place at Athens μετὰ τὰ Διονύσια (Photius); that is to say, at or near the Vernal Equinox, and not far from the time when the χελιδόνισμα is still sung. The statement of Photius that Πανδία is a name for the Moon, is also of great interest,

ΧΕΛΙΔΩΝ (*continued*).

especially in connexion with the Swallow's relation towards the undoubtedly solar ἔποψ.

Deprived of Sleep.—Hesiod ap. Ael. V. H. xii. 20 τὴν δὲ χελιδόνα οὐκ ἐς τὸ παντελὲς ἀγρυπνεῖν καὶ ταύτην, ἀποβεβληκέναι δὲ τοῦ ὕπνου τὸ ἥμισυ· τιμωρίαν δὲ ἄρα ταύτην ἐκτίνουσι διὰ τὸ πάθος τὸ ἐν Θρᾴκῃ κατατολμηθὲν τὸ ἐς τὸ δεῖπνον ἐκεῖνο τὸ ἄθεσμον. Cf. Himerius, Orat. iii. 3, p. 432 ἀφίημι δὲ καὶ ταῖς χελιδόσι ταῖς Ἀττικαῖς τὸν μῦθον ἐκεῖνον τὸν Θράκιον.

Other Myths and Legendary Allusions.—How the mother brings to her young, being blind at first, sight by means of a certain herb (χελιδόνιον), for which men have often sought in vain; Ael. ii. 3, iii. 24, Phil. 20. Cf. Arist. H. A. ii. 17, 508 b, vi. 5, 563 τῶν δὲ νεοττῶν ἄν τις ἔτι νέων ὄντων τῆς χελιδόνος τὰ ὄμματα ἐκκεντήσῃ, γίνονται ὑγιεῖς καὶ βλέπουσιν ὕστερον: also De Gen. iv. 6. 774 b; Antig. Mirab. 72 (78), 98 (106); Plin. viii. 27. On the χελιδονία or 'Swallow-stone,' a cure for blindness, epilepsy, &c., see Theoph. Nonn. 36, Diosc. ii de hirundine, Plin. xi. 79, xxxvii. 56; cf. Evangeline, I. ii. 133 'the wondrous stone which the Swallow Brings from the shore of the sea to restore the sight of its fledglings'; Baring-Gould, Myths of the M. Ages; Lebour, *Zoologist*, xxiv. p. 523, 1866, &c. Hence the ashes of Swallows are a remedy for cataract, Plin. xxix. 38; Galen, De Fac. Simpl. Med. Ch. Boiled swallow, a remedy for the bite of a mad dog, Plin. xxviii. (10) 43.

How the mother immolates herself over the bodies of her dead children: Opp. Hal. v. 579 ὡς δ' ὁπότ' ὀρταλίχοισι χελιδόσι νηπιάχοισι | νέρθεν ὑπὲξ ὀρόφοιο τυχὼν ὄφις ἄγχι πελάσσῃ | καὶ τοὺς μὲν κατέπεφνε ... μήτηρ δὲ πρῶτον μὲν ἀτυζομένη δεδόνηται | λοίγια τετριγυῖα φόνου γόον· ἀλλ' ὅτε παῖδας | ἀθρήσῃ φθιμένους, ἡ δ' οὐκέτι φύξιν ὀλέθρου | δίζεται, ἀλλ' αὐτῇσιν ὑπαὶ γενύεσσι δράκοντος | εἰλεῖται μέσφ' ὄρνιν ἕλῃ παιδοκτόνος ἄτη.

The twittering of Swallows likened to the speech of barbarous tongues, Aesch. Ag. 1050 χελιδόνος δίκην | ἀγνῶτα φωνὴν βάρβαρον κεκτημένη. Ar. Αv. 1681 εἰ μὴ βαβράζει (s. βαβάζει, βατίζει, βαύζει, τιτυβίζει, &c.) γ' ὥσπερ αἱ χελιδόνες. Hence ὁ χελιδών = ὁ βάρβαρος, cf. Ion. ap. Schol. Ar. Av. 1680; Ar. Ran. 680. Similarly, Eur. Alcmen. fr. 91 χελιδόνων μουσεῖα, explained by Hesych. ὡς βάρβαρα καὶ ἀσύνετα ποιούντων τῶν τραγικῶν: cf. Ar. Ran. 93 χελιδόνων μουσεῖα, λωβηταὶ τέχνης. See also Suidas. Cf. Nicostr. 3. 288 (Mein.) εἰ τὸ συνεχῶς καὶ πολλὰ καὶ ταχέως λαλεῖν | ἦν τοῦ φρονεῖν παράσημον, αἱ χελιδόνες | ἔλεγοντ' ἂν ἡμῶν σωφρονέστεραι πολύ.

The Pythagorean injunction χελιδόνα ἐν οἰκίᾳ μὴ δέχεσθαι, Pythag. ap. Iambl. Adhort., xxi, may be thus understood of foreigners: Arist. fr. 192, 1512 b, Hesych. τουτέστι λάλους ἀνθρώπους ὁμωροφίους μὴ ποιεῖσθαι. Other explanations in Plut. Symp. viii. 7 χελιδὼν τῇ φύσει μισάνθρωπος, παράδειγμα τοῦ ἀβεβαίου καὶ ἀχαρίστου: Diog. Laert. viii. 17,

ΧΕΛΙΔΩΝ (continued).

p. 578, Clem. Alex. Strom. v. p. 238, &c. Vide Class. Rev. 1891, pp. 1, 230.

On Swallows commonly building within the house, consult Darnel, Tour through Greece, p. 40, 1819, and recent travellers: on their entering ancient temples, cf. Clem. Alex. Protrept. iv. 52.

How the Swallows restrain the overflow of the Nile: Thrasyllus in Aegyptiac. ap. Plut. De Fluv. Nil. ii. 1159 γεννῶνται δὲ καὶ ἄλλοι λίθοι, κόλλωτες καλούμενοι· τούτους, κατὰ τὴν ἀσέβειαν τοῦ Νείλου, συλλέγουσαι χελιδόνες, κατασκευάζουσι τὸ προσαγορευόμενον χελιδόνιον τεῖχος, ὅπερ ἐπέχει τοῦ ὕδατος τὸν ῥοῖζον, καὶ οὐκ ἐᾷ κατακλυσμῷ φθείρεσθαι τὴν χώραν. Cf. Plin. x. (33) 49. Cf. also Ogilby's Fables of Aesop, 1651, p. 54, cit. N. and Q. (7) v. p. 346.

There is perhaps an allusion to this legend in the story of the building of the τεῖχος in Ar. Aves, in which account we may note the references not only to the Swallow but to Egypt and Egyptian birds. This conjecture is partly based on Rutherford's demonstration (supra cit.) that there is no distinct reference to mud-*nest*-building on the part of the Swallow in v. 1151.

White Swallows. Arist. H. A. iii. 12, 519 ὅταν ψυχὴ γίγνηται μᾶλλον, λευκὸς γίνεται. Cf. De Color. vi. 798, Theophr. De Sign. vi. 2, Alex. Mynd. ap. Ael. x. 34. A White Swallow in Samos (connected with the story of recovered sight), Arist. ap. Ael. xvii. 20, Antig. Mirab. 120 (132).

Is hostile to bees, Ael. i. 58 (cf. ibid. v. 11, Phile, 650) οἱ δὲ [μελιττουργοὶ] τὴν χελιδόνα αἰδοῖ τῆς μουσικῆς (cf. Ael. vi. 19) οὐκ ἀποκτείνουσι, καίτοι ῥᾳδίως ἂν αὐτὴν τοῦτο δράσαντες· ἀπόχρη δὲ αὐτοῖς κωλύειν τὴν χελιδόνα πλησίον τῶν σίμβλων καλιὰν ὑποπῆξαι. Cf. also Virg. G. iv. 15; Chaucer, P. of Fowles, 353, 'the swalow, mordrer of the beës small,' &c. Captures τέττιγες, Ael. viii. 6, Plut. ii. 976 C, Phile, 713; cf. Even. xiii, *supra cit.*, p. 186. Hostile to σίλφαι: Ael. i. 37 αἱ σίλφαι τὰ ᾠὰ ἀδικοῦσιν· οὐκοῦν αἱ μητέρες σέλινου κόμην προβάλλονται τῶν βρέφων, καὶ ἐκείναις τὸ ἐντεῦθεν ἄβατά ἐστιν: cf. Phile, 738, Geopon. xv. 1. Is fond of ivy (a Dionysiac plant) Eurip. Alcm. fr. 91 πολὺς δ' ἀνεῖρπε κισσός, εὐφυὴς κλάδος, | χελιδόνων μουσεῖον.

In Augury.—Ael. x. 342 τιμᾶται δὲ ἡ χελιδὼν θεοῖς μυχίοις καὶ Ἀφροδίτῃ. Swallows nesting in the general's tent were (very naturally) an evil omen, as in the cases of Alexander, son of Pyrrhus and Antiochus, Ael. l. c.: but by returning to the citadel foretold the safe home-coming of Dionysius (l. c.). See also Ar. Lys. 770 ἀλλ' ὁπόταν πτήξωσι χελιδόνες εἰς ἕνα χῶρον | τοὺς ἔποπας φεύγουσαι, ἀπόσχωνταί τε φαλήτων | παῦλα κακῶν ἔσται, τὰ δ' ὑπέρτερα νέρτερα θήσει | Ζεὺς ὑψιβρεμέτης | ... ἢν δὲ διαστῶσιν καὶ ἀναπτῶνται πτερύγεσσιν | ἐξ ἱεροῦ ναοῖο χελιδόνες, οὐκέτι δόξει | ὄρνεον οὐδ' ὁτιοῦν καταπυγωνέστερον εἶναι: the above passage is entirely mystical

ΧΕΛΙΔΩΝ (*continued*).

and obscure. How Swallows that had built in Cleopatra's galley were expelled by others before Actium, Plut. Anton. lx, i. 944 a ; cf. Ant. and Cl., 'Swallows in Cleopatra's sails Have built their nests.' The Swallow that fluttered round Alexander's head as an omen of treachery, Arr. Anab. i. 25 τὴν γὰρ χελιδόνα σύντροφόν τε εἶναι ὄρνιθα καὶ εὔνουν ἀνθρώποις καὶ λάλον μᾶλλον ἢ ἄλλην ὄρνιθα. See Class. Rev. 1891, p. 231.

A Sign of Rain.—Arat. Phen. 944 ἢ λίμνην πέρι δηθὰ χελιδόνες ἀίσσονται | γαστέρι τύπτουσαι αὔτως εἰλεύμενον ὕδωρ: cf. Theoph. Sign. vi. 1, Virg. G. i. 377.

Fables.—The Swallow and the Nightingale, vide s. v. **ἀηδών**. The Swallow and Eagle, Plut. ii. 223 F. The Wise Swallow and the Hen, Aes. 342 (ed. Halm). The Crow and the Swallow, τὸ μὲν σὸν κάλλος τὴν ἐαρινὴν ὥραν ἀνθεῖ, τὸ δὲ ἐμὸν σῶμα καὶ χειμῶνι παρατείνεται, Aes. 415. The Crow (or the Swans) and the Swallow, τί ἂν ἐποίησας, εἰ τὴν γλῶτταν εἶχες, ὅπου τμηθείσης τοσαῦτα λαλεῖς, Aes. 416, 416 b. The Swallow and other Birds, Aes. 417, 417 b. The Swallow building in the Law-court, οἴμοι τῇ ξένῃ, ὅτι ἔνθα πάντες δικαιοῦνται, μόνη ἔγωγε ἠδίκημαι, Aes. 418, 418 b: cf. Babr. 118. The Swallow out of due season, Babr. 131.

ΧΕΛΩΝΟΦΑ´ΓΟΣ. A kind of Eagle or Vulture, Hesych. The name suggests the **Lämmergeier**. In Sparta the name χελωνιάρης is said to be now applied to *Aquila imperialis*, but surely not to the exclusion of the Lämmergeier.

The Lämmergeier does indeed eat tortoises, as has been mentioned above ; and it may accordingly be held that the name χελωνοφάγος is manifestly so simple a descriptive term as to throw doubt on my astronomical interpretation of the Eagle that slew the Serpent or the Swan. But it is curious to note that the constellation of the Tortoise is placed in very much the same relation to that of the Eagle as is that of the Swan: moreover the Tortoise forms part of the constellation Lyra, another name for which is the Vulture, and to the latter 'bird' the Eagle is said also to be hostile. It is only natural that those astronomical 'hostilities' should be the most commented on, which are somewhat akin to zoological fact or possibility.

ΧΕ´ΝΝΙΟΝ, *s.* χεννίων.

A kind of **Quail**, eaten pickled by the Egyptians.

Athen. ix. 393 c μικρὸν δ᾽ ἐστὶν ὀρτύγιον: cf. Cleomen. and Hipparch. *ibi citt.*, &c. Pall. Alex. xxi, Gk. Anth. iii. 119 ἡμεῖς δ᾽ ἐσθίομεν κεκλημένοι ἁλμυρὰ πάντα | χέννια καὶ τύρους, χηνὸς ἁλιστὰ λίπη. According to Bent (Cyclades, 1885, p. 128) potted or pickled quails are still eaten in

XENNION (continued).

Santorini. Jablonsky, De Voc. Egypt., ap. Steph. Thes., suspects χέννιον to have been a locust, Eg. *sche*. See also Hercher in Jahn's Annal. 1856, Suppl. i. p. 285.

ΧΗ'Ν. A Goose.

Sk. *hansa, hamsa*, L. (*h*)*anser*. χην = χανς or χενς (cf. μην = μενς); Ger. *Gans*. Lat. *ganta* (the small wild northern species, Plin. x. (22) 27; also Venant. Fortunat., Miscell. vii. 4, 11, *teste* Keller) is a borrowed word; cf. O. H. G. *ganzo* (Keller), Engl. *gannet*. The connexion with χαίνω is doubtful (Curt.). An irreg. plur. in Gk. Anth. iv. 258 (A. P. vii. 546) ᾧ πτηνὺς ἠκροβόλιζε χένας. Dim. χηνάριον, Hdn. Epim. 150; χηνιδεύς, Ael. vii. 47, Eust. 753. 56; χηνίον, Menipp. ap. Athen. 664 e; χηνίσκος, Eubul. 3. 211.

In Hom. frequent; usually with the epithet ἀργός: cf. χαροπὸν χάνα, Antip. Sid. lxxxviii, Gk. Anth. ii. 31. The Geese in the Odyssey are tame birds, Od. xv. 161, 174, xix. 536, in the Iliad always wild, Il. ii. 460, xv. 690. Remains of the bird are not known from ancient Troy or Mycenae (Schliemann and Virchow, *teste* Keller, Th. d. cl. Alt., p. 288).

Description.—Arist. H. A. ii. 1, 499 ἔχουσί τι διὰ μέσον τῶν σχισμάτων πόδος. Ael. xi. 37 ὄρνις στεγανόπους καὶ πλατιώνυξ. Arist. H. A. ii. 17, 509 στόμαχος εὐρὺς καὶ πλατύς, ἀποφυάδες ὀλίγαι κάτωθεν κατὰ τὴν τοῦ ἐντέρου τελευτήν, αἰδοῖον φανερώτερον ὅταν ἡ ὀχεία πρόσφατος ᾖ. Ib. vi. 2, 560 b ὀχευθεῖσαι κατακολυμβῶσιν: ibid. 8, 564 αἱ θήλειαι ἐπωάζουσι μόναι, καὶ διαμένουσι διὰ παντὸς ἐφεδρεύουσαι, ὅτανπερ ἄρξωνται τοῦτο ποιεῖν: ibid. 6, 563 ἐπωάζει περὶ τριάκονθ' ἡμέρας: cf. Varro, De R. R. iii. 10, Colum. viii. 7, 1. Their splay feet alluded to, Ar. Av. 1145. The goose's cackle is expressed by χηνίζειν, Diphil. 4. 413, παππάζειν, J. Pollux, Lat. gingrire, Festus; its splashing movements in the water by πλατυγίζειν, Eubul. 3. 260.

Eggs.—Eriph. ap. Athen. ii. 58 b ᾠὰ λευκά γε | καὶ μεγάλα. B. χήνει' ἐστίν, ὥς γ' ἐμοὶ δοκεῖ· | οὗτος δέ φησι ταῦτα τὴν Λίδαν τεκεῖν. (Cf. Sappho, fr. 56 B, ap. Athen. l. c., Clem. Alex. Homil. v. 14.) Simon. fr. 11 B (l. c.) οἷόν τε χηνὸς ᾦεον Μαιανδρίον. Were not eaten by the Indians, Ael. xiv. 13. The Fable of the Golden Egg, Aesop, ed. Halm 343 b; cf. Keller, Gesch. d. Gr. Fab. p. 346 et seq.

Migrations.—Ael. v. 54 οἱ δὲ χῆνες διαμείβοντες τὸν Ταῦρον τὸ ὄρος δεδοίκασι τοὺς ἀετούς, καὶ ἕκαστός γε αὐτῶν λίθον ἐνδακόντες, ἵνα μὴ κλάζωσιν, ὥσπερ οὖν ἐμβαλόντες σφίσι στόμιον, διαπέτονται σιωπῶντες, καὶ τοὺς ἀετοὺς τὰ πολλὰ ταύτῃ διαλανθάνουσι. Cf. Dion. De Avib. ii. 18; Plut. De Soll. Anim. p. 967 B; Phile, De An. Pr. xv.

Sacred to Osiris and Isis, Pausan. x. 32, 16; cf. Juv. vi. 540; see also Philip. Thess. 10 (Gk. Anthol. ii. 197) πολιὸν χηνῶν ζεῖγος ἐνυδρο-

ΧΗΝ (*continued*).

βίων: whose priests used it as food, Herod. ii. 37; as did the Pharaohs, Diod. Sic. i. 70, and the sacred cats, ibid. i. 84.

The Geese of the Capitol, sacred to Juno, Diod. Sic. xiv. 116; Ael. xii. 32; cf. Liv. v. 47, Cicero pro Roscio, 20, Virg. Aen. viii. 655, Plin. x. 26, xxix. 14, Ovid, Fasti, i. 453. Cf. ref. to the bird's watchfulness, Arist. H. A. i. 1, 488 b ὄρνεον αἰσχυντηλὸν καὶ φυλακτικόν: also noted in the Vedas (Zimmer, Alt.-ind. Leben, p. 90, *cit*. Keller); cf. also Chaucer, 'the waker goose.' Its wisdom, Ael. v. 29, cf. Ovid, Met. viii. 684, xi. 599 canibus sagacior anser.

Sacred to Venus in Cyprus (Cesnola, Cyprus, pl. vi) and to Priapus, Petron. Sat. 136, 137.

The Goose was sacrificed to Isis and Osiris in Autumn (Paus. l. c.), as by the ancient Germans to Woden at Michaelmas (Keller, op. c. p. 301).

An erotic bird; a goose enamoured of a boy, Ael. v. 29; of a musician, ibid. i. 6; and of a philosopher, ibid. vii. 41. Cf. Ael. iv. 54; Athen. xiii. 606 c; Plut. Mor. 972 F. A lover's gift, Ar. Av. 707. Hence, in Mod. Gk., a term of endearment, χήνα μου, παππία μου (παππία meaning a duck, but cf. Ar. Vesp. 297, &c.). Portends, in dream-prophecy, the birth of a wanton maid, Artemid. Oneirocr. iv. 83. Goose-fat as an aphrodisiac, Plin. xxviii. (19) 80, &c. On sacrifices of the Goose vide Gust. Wolff, Porphyr. De Phil., Ex Orac. Haur. Libr. Reliq., Berlin, 1856; cf. Philologus xxviii. p. 189, 1869. On the erotic symbolism of the Goose, see (*int. al*.) Creuzer, Symb. iv. p. 423.

Tame Geese also mentioned, Soph. Fr. 745 τιθασὸν δὲ χῆνα καὶ περιστεράν, ἐφέστιον οἰκέτιν τε. Eubul. ap. Athen. xii. 519 καὶ γὰρ πόσῳ κάλλιον, ἱκετεύω, τρέφειν | ἄνθρωπον ἔστ' ἄνθρωπον ἂν ἔχῃ βίον, | ἢ χῆνα πλατυγίζοντα καὶ κεχηνότα: cf. Plut. Mor. 958 E. They were kept in the temples; Artemid. l. c. ἱεροὶ γὰρ οἱ χῆνες οἱ ἐν ναοῖς ἀνατρεφόμενοι. Brought as gifts to the Indian king, Ael. xiii. 25.

Fatted Geese, Epigen. ap. Athen. ix. 384 ὥσπερ χῆνα σιτευτὸν ἔτρεφέ με, &c. Eubul. Στεφ. ibid. εἰ μὴ σὺ χηνὸς ἧπαρ ἢ ψυχὴν ἔχεις: Pall. Alex. xxi, Gk. Anth. iii. 119 χηνὸς ἅλιστα λίπη: cf. Juv. v. 114, Colum. xiv. 8, &c. A favourite food of the younger Cyrus, Xen. Anab. i. 9, 26. Given by the Egyptians to Agesilaus, Athen. l. c. Brought from Boeotia to the Athenian market, Ar. Ach. 878, Pax 1004; kept likewise in Macedonia and in Thessaly, Plat. Gorg. 471 C, Polit. 264 C. Cf. Plut. ii. 210 c, Plin. x. (22) 27, &c.

They were kept, but not eaten, by the Celtic inhabitants of Britain, Caes. Bell. Gall. v. 12; very much as at the present day.

On goose-livers χήνεια ἥπατα, cf. (*int. al*.) Athen. ix. 384, Plut. ii. 965 a Geopon. xiv. 22, Plin. x. 52, Hor. Sat. ii. 8, 88, Juv. v. 114, Mart. xiii. 58, and many Comic fragments. A goose-herd, χηνοβοσκός, Cratin. ap. Athen, l. c., Diod. i. 74; a goose-farm or goose-pen, χηνοβοσκεῖον,

ΧΗΝ (*continued*).

Varro, R. R. iii. 10, 1, χηνοβόσκιον, Geopon. xiv. 12, 1, χηνοτροφεῖον, Colum. viii. 1, 3; cf. χηνοβωτία, Plat. Polit. 264 C.

On goose-fat, or goose-flesh, in medicine, Plin. xxix. 38, Nicand. Alex. 228, Celsus, ii. 18, &c.; the blood, in medicine, ibid. xxix. 33. cf. Diosc. Alexiph. c. 30, Galen, Comp. Medic. xi. 1. On the use and value of the feathers and down, Plin. x. 53; cf. Hesych, μνοῦς· τὸ λεπτότατον πτερόν, κυρίως δὲ τῶν χηνῶν.

Eubul. Πρόκρ. i. 5 (3. 247 M), γάλα χηνός, 'pigeons' milk,' of an unknown luxury.

Destructive to the crops, Babr. 13, Aesop, 76.

A weather prophet, Arat. 1021 καὶ χῆνες κλαγγηδὸν ἐπειγόμεναι βρωμοῖο | χειμῶνος μέγα σῆμα. Cf. Theophr. Sign. vi. 3; Geopon. i. 3, 9; Avien. Aratea, 432; Suid.

Capture by decoys, Dion. De Avib. iii. 23: see also Nemes. Cyn. 314.

Killed by laurel, δάφνη and ῥοδοδάφνη, Ael. v. 29, Phile, De An. xv. Use the herb *sideritis* as a remedy, Plin. viii. 27.

The Oath of Socrates, νὴ τὸν χῆνα, probably for νὴ τὸν Ζῆνα; cf. Ar. Av. 521; an oath prescribed by Rhadamanthus (Suid.). Cf. Philostr. vi, De Vita Apoll. c. 9; Cratin. 2. 155 (Mein.) οἷς ἦν μέγιστος ὅρκος | ἅπαντι λόγῳ κύων, ἔπειτα χήν.

Associated with Aquarius, in a representation of the month of February (doubtless with reference to Juno, cf. s. v. ταῶς), Graev. Thes. Ant. Rom. viii. 97; cf. Creuzer, Symb. iii. p. 626.

See for a further account of the Goose in classical art and mythology, O. Keller, Thiere d. Cl. Alterth., pp. 286-303.

ΧΗ´Ν· ὁ μικρός, ἀγελαῖος.

A wild species, unidentifiable, mentioned in Arist. H. A. viii. 3, 593 b, 12, 597 b.

ΧΗΝΑΛΩ´ΠΗΞ, *s*. χηνάλωψ, *s*. χηνέλωψ, Hesych. Dim. χηναλωπεκιδεύς, Ael. vii. 47.

The Egyptian Goose, *Chenalopex aegyptiaca*, Steph. This and πηνέλοψ are both probably renderings of an Egyptian word, corrupted by false etymology.

Arist. H. A. viii. 3, 593 b, mentioned among the heavier web-footed birds, after ὁ μικρὸς χὴν ὁ ἀγελαῖος. Ael. v. 30 ἔχει μὲν γὰρ τὸ εἶδος τὸ τοῦ χηνός, πανουργίαν δὲ δικαιότατα ἀντικρίνοιτο ἂν τῇ ἀλώπεκι. καὶ ἔστι μὲν χηνὸς βραχύτερος, ἀνδρειότερος δέ, καὶ χωρεῖν ὁμόσε δεινός. ἀμύνεται γοῦν καὶ ἀετὸν καὶ αἴλουρον καὶ τὰ λοιπά, ὅσα αὐτοῦ ἀντίπαλά ἐστιν. Reverenced in Egypt for parental affection, Ael. x. 16, xi. 38 φιλότεκνον δὲ ἄρα ζῷον ἦν καὶ ὁ χηναλώπηξ, καὶ ταῦτα τοῖς πέρδιξι δρᾷ. καὶ γὰρ οὗτος πρὸ τῶν νεοττῶν ἑαυτὸν κυλίει, καὶ ἐνδίδωσιν ἐλπίδα ὡς θηράσοντι αὐτὸν τῷ ἐπιόντι· οἱ δὲ ἀποδιδράσκουσιν ἐν τῷ τέως. As an hieroglyphic symbol, meaning

ΧΗΝΑΛΩΠΗΞ (continued).

'son,' Horap. i. 53 ; cf. Bailey in Class. Journ. xvi. p. 320, and especially Lauth, Sitzungsber. Bayer. Akad., 1876, p. 105, who cites from the Rosetta stone 🦆☉ *su-ra=υἱὸs* 'Ηλίου. Sacred to the Nile, Herod. ii. 72. With cognomen Θεογενής, Ar. Av. 1295. Its eggs second only to the peacock's, Athen. ii. 586. ὑπηνέμια τίκτει, Arist. H. A. vi. 2, 559 b. Mentioned also Plin. x. (22) 29.

ΧΗΝΕ'ΡΩΣ. A small kind of Goose, Plin. x. (22) 29 et quibus lautiores epulas non novit Britannia, chenerotes, fere ansere minores.

ΧΗΝΟΣΚΟ'ΠΟΣ. Name of an Eagle, Phile, De An. Pr. (15) 376. Cf. *νηττοφόνος*.

ΧΛΩΡΕΥ'Σ. An unknown bird, the statements regarding which are all fabulous.

Hesych. *ὀρνιθάριον χλωρόν*. Arist. H. A. ix. 1, 609 πολέμιοι τῶν ὀρνίθων ποικιλίδες καὶ κορυδῶνες καὶ πίπρα καὶ χλωρεύς, τρυγὼν καὶ χλωρεύς· ἀποκτείνει γὰρ τὴν τρυγόνα ὁ χλωρεύς. Hostile to τρυγών, also in Ael. v. 48 ; to τρυγών and κόραξ, Phile, De An. Pr. 690 ; to *corvus*, Plin. x. (74) 95 noctu invicem ova exquirentes. Supposed by Gesner and Sundevall to be identical with **χλωρίων**, and by Gaza with **χλωρίς**, q. v.

ΧΛΩΡΙ'Σ. The Greenfinch, *Fringilla chloris*, L. Mod. Gk. φλόρι, φιώρι (Erh. p. 44, Von der Mühle, p. 47), in Attica σπιγγάριος (Heldr.). Cf. It. *verdone*, &c.

Arist. H. A. viii. 3, 592 b ὄρνις σκωληκοφάγος. Ib. ix. 13, 615 b τὰ κάτω ἔχει ὠχρά· ἡλίκον ἐστὶ κόρυδος· τίκτει ᾠὰ τέτταρα ἢ πέντε· νεοττίαν ποιεῖται ἐκ τοῦ συμφύτου ἕλκουσα πρόρριζον, στρώματα δ' ὑποβάλλει τρίχας καὶ ἔρια. The cuckoo lays in its nest, which is placed in a tree, ibid. 29, 618.

Ael. iv. 47 Χλωρὶς ὄνομα ὄρνιθος, ἥπερ οὖν οὐκ ἂν ἀλλαχόθεν ποιήσαιτο τὴν καλιὰν ἢ ἐκ τοῦ λεγομένου συμφύτου· ἔστι δὲ ῥίζα τὸ σύμφυτον εὑρεθῆναί τε καὶ ὀρύξαι χαλεπή. στρωμνὴν δὲ ὑποβάλλεται τρίχας καὶ ἔρια. καὶ ὁ μὲν θῆλυς ὄρνις οὕτω κέκληται, ὁ δὲ ἄρρην, χλωρίωνα καλοῦσιν αὐτόν, καὶ ἔστι τὸν βίον μηχανικός, μαθεῖν τε πᾶν ὅ τι οὖν ἀγαθός, καὶ τλήμων ὑπομεῖναι τὴν ἐν τῷ μανθάνειν βάσανον, ὅταν ἁλῷ. καὶ διὰ μὲν τοῦ χειμῶνος ἄφετον καὶ ἐλεύθερον οὐκ ἂν ἴδοι τις αὐτόν, ἠρινοὶ δὲ ὅταν ὑπάρξωνται τροπαὶ τοῦ ἔτους, τηνικαῦτ' ἂν ἐπιφαίνοιτο. Ἀρκτοῦρός τε ἐπέτειλεν, ὁ δὲ ἀναχωρεῖ ἐς τὰ οἰκεῖα, ὁπόθεν καὶ δεῦρο ἐστάλη.

According to Nicand. ap. Anton. Lib. c. ix, one of the Emathides, daughters of Pierus, was metamorphosed into the bird χλωρίς.

On the plant σύμφυτον see also Diosc. iv. 10, Fraas, Fl. Cl., p. 163. Lindermayer, l.c., p. 62, says that the Greenfinch builds abundantly in the olive-groves of Attica, making its nest always of the same material,

ΧΛΩΡΙΣ (continued).

the roots of a species of *Symphytum* (?), lined with black goats' hair. In Ael. l. c. the bird is confused with the Golden Oriole, χλωρίων, which migrates in winter, while the Greenfinch does not.

ΧΛΩΡΙ'ΩΝ, s. χλωρεῖον, Suid.

Cf. Lat. *galbula* (galbus = gelb = yellow): *oriolus* qu. aureolus ; It. *rigogolo*, from auri-galbulus (Diez, p. 152).

The **Golden Oriole**, *Oriolus galbula*, L. Mod. Gk. συκοφάγος (Von der M.), κιτρυνοπούλι (Cyclades, Erh.), συχλαῖος (Krüper).

Arist. H. A. ix. 1, 609 b κρὲξ πολέμιος τῷ χλωρίωνι, ὃν ἔνιοι μυθολογοῦσι γενέσθαι ἐκ πυρκαϊᾶς. Ibid. 15, 616 b χλωρίων δὲ μαθεῖν μὲν ἀγαθὸς καὶ βιομήχανος, κακοπέτης δέ, καὶ χρόαν ἔχει μοχθηράν. Ibid. 22, 617 ὁ δὲ χλωρίων χλωρὸς ὅλος· οὗτος τὸν χειμῶνα οὐχ ὁρᾶται, περὶ δὲ τὰς τροπὰς τὰς θερινὰς φανερὸς μάλιστα γίνεται, ἀπαλλάττεται δὲ ὅταν Ἀρκτοῦρος ἐπιτέλλῃ, τὸ δὲ μέγεθός ἐστιν ὅσον τρυγών. Cf. Ael. iv. 47, supra s. v. **χλωρίς** : Plin. x. (29) 45.

The Oriole arrives in Greece in April, and appears in great numbers among the figs in August (Von der Mühle, &c.). Of the above accounts in Aristotle, the first is clearly mythical, and contains a suggestion of the Phoenix myth : the second is equally obscure, though Aubert and Wimmer see in βιομήχανος an allusion to the Oriole's surpassing skill in nest-building ; while the third, though undoubtedly referring to the Golden Oriole, is far from accurate : cf. Buffon, M. des Ois. v. 351 'Je me contenterai de dire ici que, selon toute apparence, Aristote n'a connu le loriot que par ouï-dire.'

ΧΡΥΣΑ'ΕΤΟΣ. The 'Golden Eagle,' a mystical name, already discussed s. v. **ἀετός**.

A fabulous account in Ael. ii. 39 χρυσάετος· ἄλλοι δὲ ἀστερίαν τὸν αὐτὸν καλοῦσιν. ὁρᾶται δὲ οὐ πολλάκις. λέγει δὲ Ἀριστοτέλης αὐτὸν θηρᾶν καὶ νεβροὺς καὶ λαγὼς καὶ γεράνους καὶ χῆνας ἐξ αὐλῆς. μέγιστος δὲ ἀετῶν εἶναι πεπίστευνται, καὶ λέγουσί γε καὶ εἰς τοὺς Κρῆτας καὶ τοῖς ταύροις ἐπιτίθεσθαι αὐτὸν κατὰ τὸ καρτερόν, κ.τ.λ.

ΧΡΥΣΟΜΗ'ΤΡΙΣ. v. ll. ῥυσομήτρις, χρυσομίτρης. Transl. *Aurivittis*, Gaza.

The **Goldfinch**, *Fringilla carduelis*, L.

Arist. H. A. viii. 3, 592 b, mentioned with ἀκανθίς, θραυπίς. ταῦτα γὰρ πάντα ἐπὶ τῶν ἀκανθῶν νέμεται, σκώληκα δ' οὐδὲν οὐδ' ἔμψυχον οὐδέν· ἐν ταὐτῷ δὲ καθεύδει καὶ νέμεται ταῦτα. It is remarkable that we have so little definite record of the Goldfinch, which in Greece is now, according to Lindermayer, next to the Sparrow the commonest of birds.

ΧΥ'ΡΡΑΒΟΣ· ὄρνις τις ποιός, Hesych.

ΨΑ'Ρ, s. ψάρ : also ψάρος, s. ψᾶρος.   Ion. ψήρ.   ψάριχος, Hesych.
A Starling, *Sturnus vulgaris*, L. Mod. Gk. ψαρόνι, μαυροπούλι.
The Etymology is confused and doubtful. Von Edlinger (op. c. p. 103) finds in Gk. ψάρ, O. H. G. *sprā*, Lith. *spakas*, a connexion with the root of πέρκ-νος, Lat. *spar-gere*, i. e. variegated, speckled. But there also seems to be a connexion of Gk. ψάρ or σπαρ- with the various names for *sparrow*, Goth. *sparwa*, O. Pr. *sperglo*, &c., as Engl. *starling*, *stare*. Ger. *Staar*, L. *sturnus*, form another series together with στρ-ουθός. The Hebr. *sippor* is perplexingly similar.

In Hom. always coupled with the Jackdaw, Il. xvi. 583 ὥρηκι ἐοικώς | ὠκεῖ, ὅστ' ἐφόβησε κολοιούς τε, ψῆράς τε. xvii. 755 ὥστε ψαρῶν νέφος, ἠὲ κολοιῶν. Arist. H. A. ix. 26, 617 b ὁ δὲ ψάρος ἐστὶ ποικίλος· μέγεθος δ' ἐστὶν ἡλίκον κόττυφος. Ib. viii. 16, 600 φωλεῖ. Antipat. Sid. cv ap. Suid. ὁ πρὶν ἐγὼ καὶ ψῆρα καὶ ἁρπάκτειραν ἐρύκων | σπέρματος ὑψιπετῆ Βιστονίαν γέρανον. Anth. Pal. ix. 373 ψᾶρας, ἀρουραίης ἅρπαγας εὐπορίης. Diosc. ii ψᾶρας ὀρύζῃ τρέφοντες. Is killed by σκόροδον, Ael. vi. 46, Phile, De An. Pr. 660. Used as food, Antiph. ap. Athen. ii. 65 c.

On talking starlings, Plut. ii. 972 F, Plin. x. 59 (43), Aul. Gell. xiii. 20. Stat. Silv. ii. 4, 18 auditasque memor penitus demittere voces, Sturnus, &c.

ΨΗ'ΛΗΚΕΣ· τῶν ἀλεκτρυόνων οἱ νοθογένναι, Hesych. Possibly akin to σέλκες, vide s. v. σέρκος (Schmidt, ad Hesych.).

ΨΙΤΤΑ'ΚΗ. Also ψιττακός (Paus., Ael., &c.), σιττακός (Arr.), σιττάκη (Philost.), βίττακος (Ctes.). A Parrot.

Arrian, Ind. i. 15, 8 σιττακοὺς δὲ Νέαρχος μὲν ὡς δή τι θῶμα ἀπηγέεται ὅτι γίνονται ἐν τῇ Ἰνδῶν γῇ, καὶ ὁκοῖος ὄρνις ἐστὶν ὁ σιττακός, καὶ ὅκως φωνὴν ἵει ἀνθρωπίνην. ἐγὼ δὲ ὅτι αὐτός τε πολλοὺς ὀπώπεα καὶ ἄλλους ἐπισταμένους ᾔδεα τὸν ὄρνιθα, οὐδὲν ὡς ὑπὲρ ἀτόπου δῆθεν ἀπηγήσομαι.

Arist. H. A. viii. 12, 597 b (spurious passage, A. and W.) ὅλως δὲ τὰ γαμψώνυχα πάντα βραχυτράχηλα καὶ πλατύγλωττα καὶ μιμητικά· καὶ γὰρ τὸ Ἰνδικὸν ὄρνεον ἡ ψιττάκη, τὸ λεγόμενον ἀνθρωπόγλωττον, τοιοῦτόν ἐστι· καὶ ἀκολαστότερον δὲ γίνεται ὅταν πίῃ οἶνον. (Cf. Plin. x. (42) 58.)

Pausan. ii. 28, (on animals of restricted geographical range), παρὰ δ' Ἰνδῶν μόνων ἄλλα τε κομίζεται, καὶ ὄρνιθες οἱ ψιττακοί. Diod. Sic. ii αἱ δὲ τῆς Συρίας ἐσχατιαὶ ψιττακοὺς καὶ πορφυρίωνας καὶ μελεαγρίδας [ἐκτρέφουσι]. Philostorg. 3 καὶ μὲν δὴ καὶ τὴν σιττάκην ἐκεῖθεν ἴσμεν κομιζομένην.

Ctes. ap. Phot. περὶ τοῦ ὀρνέου τοῦ βιττάκου, ὅτι γλῶσσαν ἀνθρωπίνην ἔχει καὶ φωνήν : cf. Plut. ii. 272 F ; Porph. De Abst. iii. 4 ; Stat. l. c. humanae solers imitator, Psittace, linguae.

Athen. ix. 387 d, parrots carried in Ptolemy's procession at Alexandria ; ibid. 391 b, mentioned as a mimic, with κίττα and σκώψ.

ΨΙΤΤΑΚΗ (*continued*).

Ael. vi. 19, xvi. 2, 15, its wisdom and vocal powers; xiii. 18, is reckoned sacred among the Brahmins; xvi. 2, is of three species.

Dion. De Avib. i. 19 τοῖς ψιττακοῖς δέ, οὓς οὐκ ἐν ξυλίνοις κλωβοῖς ἀλλ' ἐν σιδηροῖς φρουρεῖν ἀναγκαῖον, μέχρι καὶ τῆς ἡμετέρας γλώσσης ὡδήγησε τὰς μιμήσεις ἡ φύσις.

Is friendly to the wolf, Opp. Cyn. ii. 408, 409 ψιττακὸς αὖτε λύκος τε σὺν ἀλλήλοισι νέμονται· | αἰεὶ γὰρ ποθέουσι λύκοι ποεσίχροον ὄρνιν.

The Indian parrots above alluded to are the common parrots of Northern India, *Psittacus* (*Palaeornis*) *Alexandri*, L. (Cf. Val. Ball, Ind. Antiq. xiv. p. 304, 1885.) The parrots seen by Nero's army at Meroë (Plin. vi. (29) 35) must have been another species, *P. cubicularis*, Hass, and probably all the parrots described by Roman writers (Ovid, Amor. ii. 6, Statius, Silv. ii. 4, Apul. Florid. 12, Persius Prologue, and even Plin. x. (42) 58) came from Alexandria and belonged to that species. They are described as *green* by Stat., ille plagae viridis regnator Eoae; Ovid, Tu poteras virides pennis hebetare smaragdos, Tincta gerens rubro Punica rostra croco, &c. Cf. Sundevall, op. cit., pp. 126, 127.

ΨΙΦΑΙ͂ΟΝ· μικρὸν ὀρνιθάριον, Hesych.

ΏΚΥ΄ΠΤΕΡΟΣ. An epithet of a Hawk, used specifically in Ael. xii. 4. Cf. ll. xiii. 62, &c.

ΏΡΙ΄ΩΝ. s. ὠρίων. An unknown and mystical bird.

Clit. ap. Ael. xvii. 22: an Indian bird, like a Heron, red-legged, blue-eyed, musical, amative. Nonn. Dion. xxvi. 201 ὠρίων, γλυκὺς ὄρνις, ὁμοῖος ἔμφρονι κύκνῳ. Cf. Strab. xv. 718.

This bird, always associated with the equally mysterious κατρεύς, is evidently a poetic and allegorical creation, but what it signifies is unknown.

ΏΤΙ΄Σ. Also οὐτίς, Galen, Hesych.

The Bustard, *Otis tarda*, L.; including also the Houbara, *O. Houbara*. Mod. Gk. ἀγριόγαλλος, Erh.; ὀτίδα, Von der Mühle. Lat. *tarda*, whence *Bustard*, i.e. *avis Tarda*, Plin. x. (22) 29 Proximae eis (tetraonibus) sunt quae Hispania aves tardas appellat, Graecia otidas.

Description.—Arist. H. A. ii. 17, 509 τὸν στόμαχον ἔχει εὐρὺν καὶ πλατὺν ὅλον· ἀποφυάδας ἔχει. Ib. v. 2, 539 b συγκαθείσης τῆς θηλείας ἐπὶ τὴν γῆν ἐπιβαίνει τὸ ἄρρεν. Ib. vi. 6, 563 ἐπῳάζει περὶ τριάκονθ' ἡμέρας (like other *large* birds, e.g. goose and eagle). Arist. Fr. 275, 1527 b, ap. Athen. ix. 390 c ἐστὶ μὲν τῶν ἐκτοπιζόντων καὶ σχιδανοπόδων καὶ τριδακτίλων, μέγεθος ἀλεκτρυόνος μεγάλου, χρῶμα ὄρτυγος, κεφαλὴ προμήκης, ῥύγχος ὀξύ, τράχηλος λεπτός, ὀφθαλμοὶ μεγάλοι, γλῶσσα ὀστώδης, πρόλοβον δ' οὐκ ἔχει. (This

ΩΤΙΣ (continued).

last description is perhaps taken from the Little Bustard, *O. tetrax*, Mod. Gk. χαμοτίδα.) Paus. x. 34, 1 αἱ δὲ ὠτίδες καλούμεναι παρὰ τὸν Κηφισὸν (τὸν ἐν Φωκίδι) νέμοντ ι μάλιττα ὀρνίθων.

Capture by Coursing, with horse and dog. Xen. Anab. i. 5, 3 τὰς δὲ ὠτίδας ἄν τις ταχὺ ἀνιστῇ ἔστι λαμβάνειν· πέτονται τε γὰρ βραχὺ ὥσπερ οἱ πέρδικες καὶ ταχὺ ἀπαγορεύουσι· τὰ δὲ κρέα αὐτῶν ἡδέα ἐστιν (but cf. Plin. l.c.). Athen. ix. 393 d, quoting Xenophon, adds from Plutarch, ἀληθῆ λέγειν τὸν Ξενοφῶντα· φέρεσθαι γὰρ πάμπολλα τὰ ζῷα ταῦτα εἰς τὴν Ἀλεξάνδρειαν ἀπὸ τῆς παρακειμένης Λιβύης, τῆς θήρας αὐτῶν τοιαύτης γινομένης. Alex. Mynd. ap. Athen. l. c. προσαγορεύεσθαι αὐτὸν λαγωδίαν. Syncs. Ep. iv. p. 165 ἤδη δέ τις καὶ ὠτίδα ἔδωκεν, ὄρνεον ἐκτύπως ἡδύ.

Friendship for the horse. Ael. ii. 28 τὴν ὠτίδα τὸ ζῷον ὀρνίθων εἶναι φιλιππότατον ἀκούω... ἵππον δὲ ὅταν θεάσηται, ἥδιστα προσπέτεται. Alex. Mynd. l. c. φασὶ δ᾽ αὐτὸν καὶ τὴν τροφὴν ἀναμαρυκᾶσθαι ἥδεσθαί τε ἵππῳ, εἰ γοῦν τις δορὰν ἵππων περιθοῖτο, θηρεύσει ὅσους ἂν θέλῃ· προσίασι γάρ. Cf. Plut. Sol. Anim. xxxi. 7 (ii. 981 B); Opp. Cyn. ii. 406; Dion. De Avib. iii. 8.

Hostile to the dog, Ael. v. 24, and grossly deceived by the fox, ib. vi. 24.

Buffon and others have supposed from the name ὠτίς that the Houbara (which is very rare in Greece) is chiefly meant: but the etymology is doubtful; the 'ears' are not mentioned save by Oppian, Cyneg. ii. 407 ὠτίδες, αἷσι τέθηλεν ἀεὶ λασιώτατον οὖας: and besides the cheek-tufts of the Common Bustard might suggest *ears* as well as the crest of the Houbara. It is however the Houbara, as the common African species, which is alluded to in Plutarch ap. Athen. l.c.

ὯΤΟΣ, *s.* ὠτός.

A Horned Owl, especially the Short-eared Owl, *Strix brachyotus* or *Asio accipitrinus*.

Arist. H. A. viii. 12, 587 b, mentioned along with ὀρτυγομήτρα and κύχραμος as a migratory bird, in connexion with the migration of the quails. Further (loc. dub., A. and W.) ὁ δ᾽ ὠτὸς ὅμοιος ταῖς γλαυξὶ καὶ περὶ τὰ ὦτα πτερύγια ἔχων· ἔνιοι δ᾽ αὐτὸν νυκτικόρακα καλοῦσιν (cf. Hesych.). ἔστι δὲ κόβαλος καὶ μιμητής, καὶ ἀντορχούμενος ἁλίσκεται, περιελθόντος θατέρου τῶν θηρευτῶν, καθάπερ ἡ γλαύξ. Cf. Arist. ap. Athen. ix. 390 f ὁ ὠτός ἐστι μὲν παρόμοιος τῇ γλαυκί, οὐκ ἔστι δὲ νυκτερινός ... μέγεθος περιστερᾶς, κ.τ.λ.

In Athen. ix. 390 d, a ridiculous story of its capture by mimicry: οἱ δὲ στάντες αὐτῶν καταντικρὺ ὑπαλείφονται φαρμάκῳ τοὺς ὀφθαλμούς, παρασκευάσαντες ἄλλα φάρμακα κολλητικὰ ὀφθαλμῶν καὶ βλεφάρων, ἅπερ οὐ πόρρω ἑαυτῶν ἐν λεκανίσκαις βραχείαις τιθέασιν· οἱ οὖν ὦτοι θεωρούμενοι τοὺς ὑπαλειφομένους τὸ αὐτὸ καὶ αὐτοὶ ποιοῦσιν, ἐκ τῶν λεκανίδων λαμβά-

ΩΤΟΣ *continued*).

νοντες· καὶ ταχέως ἁλίσκονται. A less absurd version, ibid. 391 a; cf. Plut. Mor. ii. 961 E. Hence ὠτός, one easily taken in, a 'gull.'

Plin. x. (23) 33 Otus bubone minor est, noctuis maior, auribus plumeis eminentibus, unde et nomen illi; quidam Latine asionem vocant: imitatrix avis ac parasita, et quodam genere saltatrix, &c.

Casaubon and others, followed by Lidd. and Sc., state that Athenaeus confounds ὦτος with ὠτίς. There is indeed a confusion in the text, due to the interpolation in 360 d μιμητικὸν δέ ἐστι, κ.τ.λ., between two statements referring to ὠτίς; but the respective statements as to ὦτος and ὠτίς are correct.

The Short-eared Owl is indicated in the following statements: (1) as a migratory bird; (2) as associated with the quails, i.e. a bird of the open country; (3) as being diurnal and not nocturnal. The commentators have often fallen into error from ignorance of the habits of the Short-eared Owl: e.g. Gesner, *in gallinis, de otide,* ' nocturnam avem aut noctuae similem nullam migrare arbitror.' (Certain other species are, at least, partially migratory; cf. (*int. al.*) Giglioli, Avif. Ital., 1886, pp. 227, 228, &c.)

In Arist. H. A. viii. 12, and in Plin. l. c. there appears to be some confusion with the Long-eared or Common Horned Owl, *Strix otus*, L.

ADDITIONAL NOTES

ἈΕΤΟ´Σ.

Add the following references, concerning the Eagle in connexion with the sacred Olive : Nonn. Dion. xl. 523 ἐφέστιον ὄρνιν ἐλαίης, cf. ibid. 470; ibid. 493 ὁμόχρονον (s. ὁμόχροον) ὄρνιν ἐλαίης. The Eagle sacrificed to Neptune, ibid. 494. Add also the epithet χάρων, Lyc. 260.

ἈΗΔΩ´Ν.

Hesychius states that Ἀηδών was a surname or epithet of Athene among the Pamphylians. The connexion between Athene and the Nightingale or the Adonis-myth, lies perhaps in the fact that Athene or Minerva was associated, as for instance in the cylindrical zodiac of the Louvre, with the sign and month of the vernal equinox. Just as Adonis or Attis was, in like manner, a Spring-god and god of the opening flowers; Porph. ap. Euseb. P. E. iii. 11, p. 110 et seq.

While I am still convinced of a connexion between the attributes of ἀηδών and the veiled allusions to the mysteries of Adonis, I am inclined to admit that some of the minor arguments adduced by me in support of this hypothesis are overstrained : in particular the interpretation given (pp. 13, 14) of Thuc. ii. 29, and the suggested connexion between *Daulis*, δασύς, *Duzi*.

ἈΛΕΚΤΡΥΩ´Ν.

In preparing the article ἀλεκτρυών, I neglected to consult Baethgen, De Vi et Signific. Galli in Relig. et Art. Gr. et Romanorum, Diss. Inaug., Gotting. 1887, in which paper will be found (among other matters) a valuable account of monumental and numismatic representations of the Cock.

The Cock on coins of Himera (vide supra, p. 26) is traced by Baethgen (p. 35) to an association with Aesculapius ; cf. C. I. Gr. Nr. 5747 Ἀσκλαπιῷ καὶ Ἱμέρᾳ ποταμῷ ὁ δᾶμος . . . Σωτῆρσιν. See also Head, Hist. Numorum, p. 125.

ΓΕ´ΛΑΣΟΣ, a name for the Hoopoe ; vide s. v. μακεσίκρανος.

ΓΥ'Ψ.

The Βαρκαῖοι (vide supra, p. 49) are probably the Βαρκάνιοι (? Parsees) of Ctes. xi, Tzetz. Chil. i. 1, 82; cf. J. Macquart, Philologus, Supplement-bd. vi. p. 609, 1893.

ΔΡΥΟΚΟΛΑ'ΠΤΗΣ.

The eastern legend of the Woodpecker's imprisoned young is so suggestive of the walled-up nest of the Hornbill, that one is almost tempted to suspect a dim tradition, far-travelled from Africa or India, concerning the extraordinary nesting-habits of the latter bird.

BIBLIOGRAPHICAL REFERENCES

The following works, in addition to the Natural Histories of Pliny, Aelian, and Phile, are referred to merely under their authors' names :—

AUBERT UND WIMMER. Aristoteles' Thierkunde, 2 vols. Leipzig, 1868 (especially *Thierverzeichniss*, vol. I., pp. 77-113).

BIKÉLAS, O. La nomenclature de la Faune Grecque. Paris, 1879.

ERHARD, DR. Fauna der Cykladen. Leipzig, 1858.

KRÜPER, DR. Zeiten des Gehens und Kommens und des Brütens der Vögel in Griechenland und Ionien; in Mommsen's Griechische Jahreszeiten, 1875 (mit Citaten und Zusätzen von Dr. Hartlaub).

LINDERMAYER, DR. A. Die Vögel Griechenlands. Passau, 1860.

MÜHLE, H. VON DER. Beiträge zur Ornithologie Griechenlands. Leipzig, 1844.

SUNDEVALL, C. J. Thierarten des Aristoteles. Stockholm, 1863.

It is perhaps desirable that I should point out that I have several times in this book, quite with my eyes open, quoted authors whom scholars now look upon with distrust or even altogether reject. The student who is not ashamed to consult Creuzer, nor afraid to peep now and then even into Bryant, will not only find there a great useless mass of theories now deservedly repudiated, but will also find a great store of curious learning and will be guided to many obscure sources of useful knowledge.

ERRATA

Page 16, line 20, *for* εἰσι *read* ὄντας
" 20, " 24, *for* Scut. *read* Sent.
" 44, " 6, *for* πέτονται *read* πέτωνται
" 45, " 15, *for* ἀνεκράγη *read* ἀνακράγη
" 63, " 21, *for* πεπιστεύεται *read* πεπίστευται

For the detection of most of the above errors, and for infinite kindness in reading the final proofs of the whole book, I am indebted to my friend Mr. W. Wyse. I must record my debt also, for the like scholarly services, to Mr. P. Molyneux of the Clarendon Press. Lastly, I must pay a debt which should have been acknowledged more prominently than here, to Mrs. W. R. H. Valentine, of Dundee, for three beautiful wood-cuts, the work of her hands.

Oxford
PRINTED AT THE CLARENDON PRESS
BY HORACE HART, PRINTER TO THE UNIVERSITY

SELECT LIST
OF
𝕾tandard 𝕮heological 𝖂orks
PRINTED AT
THE CLARENDON PRESS, OXFORD.

THE HOLY SCRIPTURES, ETC.	page 1
FATHERS OF THE CHURCH, ETC.	,, 4
ECCLESIASTICAL HISTORY, ETC.	,, 5
ENGLISH THEOLOGY	,, 6
LITURGIOLOGY	,, 8

1. THE HOLY SCRIPTURES, ETC.

HEBREW, etc. *Notes on the Hebrew Text of the Book of Genesis.* By G. J. Spurrell, M.A. Crown 8vo. 10s. 6d.

—— *Notes on the Hebrew Text of the Books of Samuel.* By S. R. Driver, D.D. 8vo. 14s.

—— *Treatise on the use of the Tenses in Hebrew.* By S. R. Driver, D.D. Third Edition. Crown 8vo. 7s. 6d.

—— *The Psalms in Hebrew without points.* Stiff covers, 2s.

—— *A Commentary on the Book of Proverbs.* Attributed to Abraham Ibn Ezra. Edited from a MS. in the Bodleian Library by S. R. Driver, D.D. Crown 8vo. paper covers, 3s. 6d.

—— *The Book of Tobit.* A Chaldee Text, from a unique MS. in the Bodleian Library; with other Rabbinical Texts, English Translations, and the Itala. Edited by Ad. Neubauer, M.A. Crown 8vo. 6s.

—— *A Hebrew and English Lexicon of the Old Testament,* with an Appendix containing the Biblical Aramaic, based on the Thesaurus and Lexicon of Gesenius, by Francis Brown, D.D., S. R. Driver, D.D., and C. A. Briggs, D.D. Parts I and II. Small 4to. 2s. 6d. each. Part III. *In the Press.*

HEBREW, etc.—*Hebrew Accentuation of Psalms, Proverbs, and Job.* By William Wickes, D.D. 8vo. 5s.

—— *Hebrew Prose Accentuation.* By the same Author. 8vo. 10s. 6d.

—— *The Book of Hebrew Roots,* by Abu 'l-Walid Marwân ibn Janâh, otherwise called Rabbi Yônâh. Now first edited, with an appendix, by Ad. Neubauer. 4to. 2l. 7s. 6d.

ETHIOPIC. *The Book of Enoch.* Translated from Dillmann's Ethiopic Text emended and revised, and edited by R. H. Charles, M.A. 8vo. 16s.

GREEK. OLD TESTAMENT. *Vetus Testamentum ex Versione Septuaginta Interpretum secundum exemplar Vaticanum Romae editum.* Accedit potior varietas Codicis Alexandrini. Tomi III. 18mo. 18s.

Oxford: Clarendon Press. London: HENRY FROWDE, Amen Corner, E.C.

GREEK. *A Concordance to the Septuagint and the other Greek Versions of the Old Testament, including the Apocryphal Books.* By the late Edwin Hatch, M.A., and H. A. Redpath, M.A. Parts I and II. 4to. 21s. each. Part III, *Immediately.*

—— *Essays in Biblical Greek.* By Edwin Hatch, M.A., D.D. 8vo. 10s. 6d.

—— *Origenis Hexaplorum quae supersunt; sive, Veterum Interpretum Graecorum in totum Vetus Testamentum Fragmenta.* Edidit Fridericus Field, A.M. 2 vols. 4to. 5l. 5s.

—— NEW TESTAMENT. *Novum Testamentum Graece.* Antiquissimorum Codicum Textus in ordine parallelo dispositi. Accedit collatio Codicis Sinaitici. Edidit E. H. Hansell, S.T.B. Tomi III. 8vo. 24s.

—— *Novum Testamentum Graece.* Accedunt parallela S. Scripturae loca, etc. Edidit Carolus Lloyd, S.T.P.R. 18mo. 3s.
On writing paper, with wide margin, 7s. 6d.

—— *Appendices ad Novum Testamentum Stephanicum*, jam inde a Millii temporibus Oxoniensium manibus tritum; curante Gulmo. Sanday, A.M., S.T.P., LL.D. I. Collatio textus Westcottio-Hortiani (jure permisso) cum textu Stephanico anni MDL. II. Delectus lectionum notatu dignissimarum. III. Lectiones quaedam ex codicibus versionum Memphiticae Armeniacae Aethiopicae fusius illustratae. Extra fcap. 8vo, cloth. 3s. 6d.

—— *Novum Testamentum Graece juxta Exemplar Millianum.* 18mo. 2s. 6d. On writing paper, with wide margin, 7s. 6d.

GREEK. *The Greek Testament*, with the Readings adopted by the Revisers of the Authorised Version :—
(1) Pica type, with Marginal References. Demy 8vo. 10s. 6d.
(2) Long Primer type. Fcap. 8vo. 4s. 6d.
(3) The same, on writing paper, with wide margin, 15s.

—— *The Parallel New Testament, Greek and English;* being the Authorised Version, 1611; the Revised Version, 1881; and the Greek Text followed in the Revised Version. 8vo. 12s. 6d.

—— *Outlines of Textual Criticism applied to the New Testament.* By C. E. Hammond, M.A. *Fifth Edition.* Crown 8vo. 4s. 6d.

—— *A Greek Testament Primer.* An Easy Grammar and Reading Book for the use of Students beginning Greek. By E. Miller, M.A. Extra fcap. 8vo. 3s. 6d.

LATIN. *Libri Psalmorum Versio antiqua Latina, cum Paraphrasi Anglo-Saxonica.* Edidit B. Thorpe, F.A.S. 8vo. 10s. 6d.

—— *Old-Latin Biblical Texts:* No. I. The Gospel according to St. Matthew, from the St. Germain MS. (g_1). Edited with Introduction and Appendices by John Wordsworth, D.D. Small 4to, stiff covers, 6s.

—— *Old-Latin Biblical Texts:* No. II. Portions of the Gospels according to St. Mark and St. Matthew, from the Bobbio MS. (k), etc. Edited by John Wordsworth, D.D., W. Sanday, M.A., D.D., and H. J. White, M.A. Small 4to, stiff covers, 21s.

HOLY SCRIPTURES.

LATIN. *Old-Latin Biblical Texts*: No. III. The Four Gospels, from the Munich MS. (q), now numbered Lat. 6224 in the Royal Library at Munich. With a Fragment from St. John in the Hof-Bibliothek at Vienna (Cod. Lat. 502). Edited, with the aid of Tischendorf's transcript (under the direction of the Bishop of Salisbury), by H. J. White, M.A. Small 4to. stiff covers, 12s. 6d.

Nouum Testamentum Domini Nostri Iesu Christi Latine, secundum Editionem S. Hieronymi. Ad Codicum Manuscriptorum fidem recensuit Iohannes Wordsworth, S.T.P., Episcopus Sarisburiensis. In operis societatem adsumto Henrico Iuliano White, A.M. 4to.
Fasc. I. *Euangelium secundum Mattheum.* 12s. 6d.
Fasc. II. *Euangelium secundum Marcum.* 7s. 6d.
Fasc. III. *Euangelium secundum Lucam.* 12s. 6d.

OLD-FRENCH. *Libri Psalmorum Versio antiqua Gallica e Cod. ms. in Bibl. Bodleiana adservato, una cum Versione Metrica aliisque Monumentis pervetustis.* Nunc primum descripsit et edidit Franciscus Michel, Phil. Doc. 8vo. 10s. 6d.

ENGLISH. *The Holy Bible in the Earliest English Versions*, made from the Latin Vulgate by John Wycliffe and his followers: edited by Forshall and Madden. 4 vols. Royal 4to. 3l. 3s.

Also reprinted from the above, with Introduction and Glossary by W. W. Skeat, Litt. D.

The Books of Job, Psalms, Proverbs, Ecclesiastes, and the Song of Solomon. 3s. 6d.

The New Testament. 6s.

ENGLISH. *The Holy Bible, Revised Version**,

Cheap Editions for School Use.

Revised Bible. Pearl 16mo, cloth boards, 1s. 6d.

Revised New Testament. Nonpareil 32mo, 6d.; Brevier 16mo, 1s.; Long Primer 8vo, 1s. 6d.

* The Revised Version is the joint property of the Universities of Oxford and Cambridge.

—— *The Oxford Bible for Teachers*, containing the Holy Scriptures, together with a new, enlarged, and illustrated edition of the *Oxford Helps to the Study of the Bible*, comprising Introductions to the several Books, the History and Antiquities of the Jews, the results of Modern Discoveries, and the Natural History of Palestine, with copious Tables, Concordance and Indices, and a series of Maps. Prices in various sizes and bindings from 7s. 6d. to 2l. 2s.

—— *Helps to the Study of the Bible*, taken from the *Oxford Bible for Teachers*. Crown 8vo. 4s. 6d.

—— *The Psalter, or Psalms of David, and certain Canticles*, with a Translation and Exposition in English, by Richard Rolle of Hampole. Edited by H. R. Bramley, M.A. With an Introduction and Glossary. Demy 8vo. 1l. 1s.

—— *Studia Biblica et Ecclesiastica.* Essays in Biblical and Patristic Criticism, and kindred subjects. By Members of the University of Oxford.
Vol. I. 8vo. 10s. 6d.
Vol. II. 8vo. 12s. 6d.
Vol. III. 8vo. 16s.

London: HENRY FROWDE, Amen Corner, E.C.

ENGLISH. *The Book of Wisdom:* the Greek Text, the Latin Vulgate, and the Authorised English Version; with an Introduction, Critical Apparatus, and a Commentary. By W. J. Deane, M.A. 4to. 12s. 6d.

GOTHIC. *The Gospel of St. Mark in Gothic,* according to the translation made by Wulfila in the Fourth Century. Edited, with a Grammatical Introduction and Glossarial Index, by W. W. Skeat, Litt. D. Extra fcap. 8vo. 4s.

2. FATHERS OF THE CHURCH, ETC.

St. Athanasius: *Orations against the Arians.* With an account of his Life by William Bright, D.D. Crown 8vo. 9s.

—— *Historical Writings, according to the Benedictine Text.* With an Introduction by W. Bright, D.D. Crown 8vo. 10s. 6d.

St. Augustine: *Select Anti-Pelagian Treatises, and the Acts of the Second Council of Orange.* With an Introduction by William Bright, D.D. Crown 8vo. 9s.

St. Basil: *The Book of St. Basil on the Holy Spirit.* A Revised Text, with Notes and Introduction by C. F. H. Johnston, M.A. Crown 8vo. 7s. 6d.

Canons *of the First Four General Councils of Nicaea, Constantinople, Ephesus, and Chalcedon.* With Notes by W. Bright, D.D. Second Edition. Crown 8vo. 7s. 6d.

Catenae *Graecorum Patrum in Novum Testamentum.* Edidit J. A. Cramer, S.T.P. Tomi VIII. 8vo. 2l. 4s.

Clementis Alexandrini *Opera, ex recensione Guil. Dindorfii.* Tomi IV. 8vo. 3l.

Cyrilli *Archiepiscopi Alexandrini in XII Prophetas.* Edidit P. E. Pusey, A.M. Tomi II. 8vo. 2l. 2s.

—— *in D. Joannis Evangelium.* Accedunt Fragmenta Varia necnon Tractatus ad Tiberium Diaconum Duo. Edidit post Aubertum P. E. Pusey, A.M. Tomi III. 8vo. 2l. 5s.

—— *Commentarii in Lucae Evangelium quae supersunt Syriace.* E mss. apud Mus. Britan. edidit R. Payne Smith, A.M. 4to. 1l. 2s.

—— The same, translated by R. Payne Smith, M.A. 2 vols. 8vo. 14s.

Ephraemi Syri, *Rabulae Episcopi Edesseni, Balaei, aliorumque Opera Selecta.* E Codd. Syriacis mss. in Museo Britannico et Bibliotheca Bodleiana asservatis primus edidit J. J. Overbeck. 8vo. 1l. 1s.

Eusebii Pamphili *Evangelicae Praeparationis Libri XV.* Ad Codd. mss. recensuit T. Gaisford, S.T.P. Tomi IV. 8vo. 1l. 10s.

—— *Evangelicae Demonstrationis Libri X.* Recensuit T. Gaisford, S.T.P. Tomi II. 8vo. 15s.

—— *contra Hieroclem et Marcellum Libri.* Recensuit T. Gaisford, S.T.P. 8vo. 7s.

Eusebius' *Ecclesiastical History,* according to the text of Burton, with an Introduction by W. Bright, D.D. Crown 8vo. 8s. 6d.

Evagrii *Historia Ecclesiastica,* ex recensione H. Valesii. 8vo. 4s.

Irenaeus : *The Third Book of St. Irenaeus, Bishop of Lyons, against Heresies.* With short Notes and a Glossary by H. Deane, B.D. Crown 8vo. 5s. 6d.

Patrum Apostolicorum, *S. Clementis Romani, S. Ignatii, S. Polycarpi, quae supersunt.* Edidit Guil. Jacobson, S.T.P.R. Tomi II. *Fourth Edition.* 8vo. 1l. 1s.

Reliquiae Sacrae *secundi tertiique saeculi.* Recensuit M. J. Routh, S.T.P. Tomi V. *Second Edition.* 8vo. 1l. 5s.

Scriptorum *Ecclesiasticorum Opuscula.* Recensuit M. J. Routh, S.T.P. Tomi II. 8vo. 10s.

Socrates' *Ecclesiastical History,* according to the Text of Hussey, with an Introduction by William Bright, D.D. Crown 8vo. 7s. 6d.

Sozomeni *Historia Ecclesiastica.* Edidit R. Hussey, S.T.B. Tomi III. 8vo. 15s.

Tertulliani *Apologeticus adversus Gentes pro Christianis.* Edited, with Introduction and Notes, by T. Herbert Bindley, B.D. Crown 8vo. 6s.

────── *de Praescriptione Haereticorum ad Martyras: ad Scapulam.* Edited, with Introduction and Notes, by T. Herbert Bindley, B.D. *Immediately.*

Theodoreti *Ecclesiasticae Historiae Libri V.* Recensuit T. Gaisford, S.T.P. 8vo. 7s. 6d.

3. ECCLESIASTICAL HISTORY, ETC.

Baedae *Historia Ecclesiastica.* Edited, with English Notes, by G. H. Moberly, M.A. *New edition in the Press.*

Bigg. *The Christian Platonists of Alexandria;* being the Bampton Lectures for 1886. By Charles Bigg, D.D. 8vo. 10s. 6d.

Bingham's *Antiquities of the Christian Church, and other Works.* 10 vols. 8vo. 3l. 3s.

Bright. *Chapters of Early English Church History.* By W. Bright, D.D. *Second Edition.* 8vo. 12s.

Burnet's *History of the Reformation of the Church of England.* A new Edition. Carefully revised, and the Records collated with the originals, by N. Pocock, M.A. 7 vols. 8vo. 1l. 10s.

Cardwell's *Documentary Annals of the Reformed Church of England;* being a Collection of Injunctions, Declarations, Orders, Articles of Inquiry, etc. from 1546 to 1716. 2 vols. 8vo. 18s.

Councils *and Ecclesiastical Documents relating to Great Britain and Ireland.* Edited, after Spelman and Wilkins, by A. W. Haddan, B.D., and W. Stubbs, D.D. Vols. I and III. Medium 8vo, each 1l. 1s.

Vol. II, Part I. Medium 8vo, 10s. 6d.

Vol. II, Part II. *Church of Ireland; Memorials of St. Patrick.* Stiff covers, 3s. 6d.

Fuller's *Church History of Britain.* Edited by J. S. Brewer, M.A. 6 vols. 8vo. 1*l*. 19*s*.

Gibson's *Synodus Anglicana.* Edited by E. Cardwell, D.D. 8vo. 6*s*.

Hamilton's (*Archbishop John*) *Catechism*, 1552. Edited, with Introduction and Glossary, by Thomas Graves Law, Librarian of the Signet Library, Edinburgh. With a Preface by the Right Hon. W. E. Gladstone. Demy 8vo. 12*s*. 6*d*.

Hussey. *Rise of the Papal Power, traced in three Lectures.* By Robert Hussey, B.D. Second Edition. Fcap. 8vo. 4*s*. 6*d*.

John, *Bishop of Ephesus. The Third Part of his Ecclesiastical History.* [In Syriac.] Now first edited by William Cureton, M.A. 4to. 1*l*. 12*s*.

—— *The same*, translated by R. Payne Smith, M.A. 8vo. 10*s*.

Le Neve's *Fasti Ecclesiae Anglicanae.* Corrected and continued from 1715 to 1853 by T. Duffus Hardy. 3 vols. 8vo. 1*l*. 1*s*.

Noelli (A.) *Catechismus sive prima institutio disciplinaque Pietatis Christianae Latine explicata.* Editio nova cura Guil. Jacobson, A.M. 8vo. 5*s*. 6*d*.

Records of the Reformation. *The Divorce,* 1527–1533. Mostly now for the first time printed from MSS. in the British Museum and other Libraries. Collected and arranged by N. Pocock, M.A. 2 vols. 8vo. 1*l*. 16*s*.

Reformatio *Legum Ecclesiasticarum.* The Reformation of Ecclesiastical Laws, as attempted in the reigns of Henry VIII, Edward VI, and Elizabeth. Edited by E. Cardwell, D.D. 8vo. 6*s*. 6*d*.

Shirley. *Some Account of the Church in the Apostolic Age.* By W. W. Shirley, D.D. Second Edition. Fcap. 8vo. 3*s*. 6*d*.

Stillingfleet's *Origines Britannicae,* with Lloyd's Historical Account of Church Government. Edited by T. P. Pantin, M.A. 2 vols. 8vo. 10*s*.

Stubbs. *Registrum Sacrum Anglicanum.* An attempt to exhibit the course of Episcopal Succession in England. By W. Stubbs, D.D. Small 4to. 8*s*. 6*d*.

4. ENGLISH THEOLOGY.

Bradley. *Lectures on the Book of Job.* By George Granville Bradley, D.D., Dean of Westminster. Crown 8vo. 7*s*. 6*d*.

—— *Lectures on Ecclesiastes.* By G. G. Bradley, D.D., Dean of Westminster. Crown 8vo. 4*s*. 6*d*.

Bull's *Works, with Nelson's Life.* Edited by E. Burton, D.D. 8 vols. 8vo. 2*l*. 9*s*.

Burnet's *Exposition of the XXXIX Articles.* 8vo. 7*s*.

Butler's *Works.* 2 vols. 8vo. 11*s*.

Comber's *Companion to the Temple;* or a Help to Devotion in the use of the Common Prayer. 7 vols. 8vo. 1l. 11s. 6d.

Cranmer's *Works.* Collected and arranged by H. Jenkyns, M.A., Fellow of Oriel College. 4 vols. 8vo. 1l. 10s.

Enchiridion Theologicum *Anti-Romanum.*
- Vol. I. Jeremy Taylor's Dissuasive from Popery, and Treatise on the Real Presence. 8vo. 8s.
- Vol. II. Barrow on the Supremacy of the Pope, with his Discourse on the Unity of the Church. 8vo. 7s. 6d.
- Vol. III. Tracts selected from Wake, Patrick, Stillingfleet, Clagett, and others. 8vo. 11s.

Greswell's *Harmonia Evangelica.* Fifth Edition. 8vo. 9s. 6d.

Hall's *Works.* Edited by P. Wynter, D.D. 10 vols. 8vo. 3l. 3s.

Heurtley. *Harmonia Symbolica: Creeds of the Western Church.* By C. Heurtley, D.D. 8vo. 6s. 6d.

Homilies *appointed to be read in Churches.* Edited by J. Griffiths, M.A. 8vo. 7s. 6d.

Hooker's *Works,* with his Life by Walton, arranged by John Keble, M.A. *Seventh Edition.* Revised by R. W. Church, M.A., Dean of St. Paul's, and F. Paget, D.D. 3 vols. medium 8vo. 1l. 16s.

—— *the Text* as arranged by J. Keble, M.A. 2 vols. 8vo. 11s.

Jackson's (Dr. Thomas) *Works.* 12 vols. 8vo. 3l. 6s.

Jewel's *Works.* Edited by R. W. Jelf, D.D. 8 vols. 8vo. 1l. 10s.

Martineau. *A Study of Religion: its Sources and Contents.* By James Martineau, D.D. Second Edition. 2 vols. Crown 8vo. 15s.

Patrick's *Theological Works.* 9 vols. 8vo. 1l. 1s.

Pearson's *Exposition of the Creed.* Revised and corrected by E. Burton, D.D. Sixth Edition. 8vo. 10s. 6d.

—— *Minor Theological Works.* Edited with a Memoir, by Edward Churton, M.A. 2 vols. 8vo. 10s.

Sanderson's *Works.* Edited by W. Jacobson, D.D. 6 vols. 8vo. 1l. 10s.

Stillingfleet's *Origines Sacrae.* 2 vols. 8vo. 9s.

—— *Rational Account of the Grounds of Protestant Religion;* being a vindication of Archbishop Laud's Relation of a Conference, etc. 2 vols. 8vo. 10s.

Wall's *History of Infant Baptism.* Edited by H. Cotton, D.C.L. 2 vols. 8vo. 1l. 1s.

Waterland's *Works,* with Life, by Bp. Van Mildert. *A new Edition,* with copious Indexes. 6 vols. 8vo. 2l. 11s.

—— *Review of the Doctrine of the Eucharist,* with a Preface by the late Bishop of London. Crown 8vo. 6s. 6d.

Wheatly's *Illustration of the Book of Common Prayer.* 8vo. 5s.

Wyclif. *A Catalogue of the Original Works of John Wyclif.* By W. W. Shirley, D.D. 8vo. 3s. 6d.

Wyclif. *Select English Works.* By T. Arnold, M.A. 3 vols. 8vo. 1l. 1s.

—— *Trialogus.* With the Supplement now first edited. By Gotthard Lechler. 8vo. 7s.

5. LITURGIOLOGY.

Cardwell's *Two Books of Common Prayer*, set forth by authority in the Reign of King Edward VI, compared with each other. *Third Edition.* 8vo. 7s.

—— *History of Conferences on the Book of Common Prayer from 1551 to 1690.* Third Edition. 8vo. 7s. 6d.

Hammond. *Liturgies, Eastern and Western.* Edited, with Introduction, Notes, and a Liturgical Glossary, by C. E. Hammond, M.A. New edition, by F. E. Brightman, M.A., *In the Press.*

An Appendix to the above, crown 8vo, paper covers, 1s. 6d.

Helps to the Study of the Book of Common Prayer. Being a Companion to Church Worship. Crown 8vo. 3s. 6d.

Leofric Missal, *The,* as used in the Cathedral of Exeter during the Episcopate of its first Bishop, A.D. 1050-1072; together with some Account of the Red Book of Derby, the Missal of Robert of Jumièges, and a few other early MS. Service Books of the English Church. Edited, with Introduction and Notes, by F. E. Warren, B.D., F.S.A. 4to, half-morocco, 1l. 15s.

Maskell. *Ancient Liturgy of the Church of England,* according to the uses of Sarum, York, Hereford, and Bangor, and the Roman Liturgy arranged in parallel columns, with preface and notes. By W. Maskell, M.A. *Third Edition.* 8vo. 15s.

—— *Monumenta Ritualia Ecclesiae Anglicanae.* The occasional Offices of the Church of England according to the old use of Salisbury, the Prymer in English, and other prayers and forms, with dissertations and notes. *Second Edition.* 3 vols. 8vo. 2l. 10s.

Warren. *The Liturgy and Ritual of the Celtic Church.* By F. E. Warren, B.D. 8vo. 14s.

www.ingramcontent.com/pod-product-compliance
Lightning Source LLC
Chambersburg PA
CBHW020813230426
43666CB00007B/994